i

CONTENTS

INTRODUCTION

Only on a few occasions since the founding of our nation nearly 230 years ago have we confronted challenges to our national security like the threats we face today. We are a nation at war during an election year. This is a crucial time in our history.

The 2004 Dwight D. Eisenhower National Security Conference, the culminating event of the 2004 Eisenhower National Security Series, was held Sept. 14–15. The conference presentations and discussions worked to accomplish several objectives:

- provide a broad and unique forum to discuss and debate contemporary and future national security issues;
- examine and advance ways to more effectively focus the instruments of national power; and
- contribute to the ongoing national security dialogue while broadening the experience of mid-level and senior Army leaders through exposure to diverse issues, institutions and perspectives.

Five addresses challenged the participants with diverse viewpoints that provided for balanced and informative discussions. The five distinguished speakers were retired Army General Montgomery C. Meigs, Louis A. Bantle Chair in Business and Government Policy, Maxwell School, Syracuse University; Harry C. Stonecipher, president and chief executive officer, The Boeing Company; Paul Wolfowitz, deputy secretary of defense; Ambassador Michael Sheehan, deputy commissioner of counterterrorism, New York City Police Department; and Lee H. Hamilton, president and director of the Woodrow Wilson International Center for Scholars.

Four panel discussions, equally challenging and enlightening, were co-sponsored by The Atlantic Council of the United States, the International Institute for Strategic Studies, The Henry L. Stimson Center and the United States Military Academy's Combating Terrorism Center. This two-day conference was held in the Ronald Reagan Building and International Trade Center, Washington, D.C.

The first panel covered the topic of the evolution of American alliances and friendships. Introduced by Robin Dorff, executive director of the Institute of Political Leadership, this panel co-sponsored by The Atlantic Council was moderated by retired Army General Barry McCaffrey. It included the director of its International Security Program, John Sandrock, as well as Jonathan Pollack, chairman of the

Asia-Pacific Studies Group at the Naval War College, and Ambassador Robert Hunter, a senior adviser at the RAND Corporation.

The second panel, co-sponsored by the International Institute for Strategic Studies, provided insight from the diplomatic community into the difficult task of balancing nonproliferation tools, policies and strategies. Scott Sagan, co-director at Stanford's Center for International Security and Cooperation, introduced panel moderator Gary Samore, the director of studies and senior fellow for nonproliferation at the International Institute for Strategic Studies. Panelists included Robert Einhorn, a senior adviser at the Center for Strategic and International Studies; Philippe Errera, the deputy director of the policy planning staff for the French Foreign Ministry; His Excellency Nabil Fahmy, the Egyptian ambassador to the United States; and His Excellency Rakesh Sood, the Indian deputy chief of mission to the United States.

The third panel tackled the timely topic of integrating the U.S. government's interagency processes. Co-sponsored by The Henry L. Stimson Center, the panel was introduced by Janne Nolan, a professor at the Graduate School of Public and International Affairs at the University of Pittsburgh, and moderated by Ellen Laipson, the Stimson Center's president and CEO. The panel included Ambassador Chas. Freeman Jr., former ambassador to the Kingdom of Saudi Arabia and former assistant secretary of defense for international security affairs; Ambassador James Lilley, former CIA chief of station, former ambassador to the Republic of Korea and the People's Republic of China, as well as former assistant secretary of defense for international security affairs; and Marine Corps General Peter Pace, vice chairman of the Joint Chiefs of Staff.

The final panel, co-sponsored by the United States Military Academy's Combating Terrorism Center, was introduced by Brigadier General Robert Caslen Jr., the deputy director for the war on terrorism of the Joint Staff Strategic Plans and Policy Directorate. The panel discussed how to sharpen definitions, missions and roles to combat terrorism. The moderator was West Point's deputy head of the Department of Social Sciences, Colonel Michael Meese. It included Matthew Levitt, a senior fellow at the Washington Institute for Near East Policy; Colonel Michael Nagata, chief of the Combatant Command Support Branch in the Office of the Under Secretary of Defense for Intelligence; and Steven Nicgorski, a senior intelligence analyst.

Summary

National Security for the 21st Century

Day One—Determining Requirements and Achieving Balance

General Montgomery C. Meigs (Ret.) of the Maxwell School of Syracuse University opened the conference with a single edict, "Get the strategy right, then let the strategy define the operational objectives." After a discussion of the military operations in the war on terrorism, Meigs proposed five challenges that the Army must address immediately: jointness, adaptability, fiscal stability, leader development and quality of life.

Meigs criticized the pending strategy to reduce troop commitments to Europe, saying we will lose the essential contacts between U.S. Army units and European armies with a lily-pad system for forward deployment of U.S. troops. He also criticized the Army for being slow to take credit for its successes and its potential. The Army needs to "exploit" the fleeting opportunity to frame the national security debate.

The first panel looked at the evolution of American alliances and friendships. It provided an excellent, diverse series of views about the changing nature of our alliances, coalitions and partnerships. General Barry McCaffrey (Ret.) framed the discussion by asking questions concerning our alliances and rogue states, our alliances and the war on terrorism, changes in alliances in the Pacific, and the evolving role of the European Union. Ambassador Robert Hunter argued that we should approach alliance building not only as an exercise in finding common interests, but also sharing common values. Jonathan Pollack argued that the age of multiple, bilateral relationships in Asia is over. We must pursue regional partnerships if we intend to ensure stability and our interests in the region.

Boeing President and CEO Harry Stonecipher focused on leadership in the business world and what leaders from different sectors of society can learn from each other. He listed four important attributes of leaders at Boeing and elsewhere: Leaders must be willing to admit error, think globally, make education a priority and increase the "velocity" of decision making.

Gary Samore assembled an international panel to discuss nuclear nonproliferation. Each panelist approached the topic from a very different perspective. Robert Einhorn argued there are three proliferation challenges that face the United States: how to get North Korea to dismantle its arsenal, how to head off Iran's nuclear advance, and how to keep nuclear material out of the hands of terrorists. Philippe Errera stated France recognizes the Nuclear Nonproliferation Treaty (NPT) as the primary tool in the struggle to stop proliferation. As such, the NPT needs to be strengthened. His Excellency Nabil Fahmy, Egypt's ambassador to the United States, argued that the nonproliferation debate today operates on what he called an "incomplete premise." There is no evidence that non-nuclear members have greater access to peaceful nuclear technology. At the same time nuclear member countries have not made a "good faith" effort to pursue nuclear disarmament. His Excellency Rakesh Sood, India's deputy chief of mission to the United States, argued that the NPT "bargain" has changed for the worse. He sees "hedging" as the major structural NPT problem—that is, countries that hold nuclear technology in reserve, ready to go nuclear on a few weeks' notice.

The keynote address was delivered by Deputy Secretary of Defense Paul Wolfowitz. He invoked former President Ronald Reagan, stating, "History doesn't just happen, it is made." The secretary outlined four tenets that must guide our national strategy. He said the struggle will be long and no dramatic event will signal the end. We must deploy the whole of our national power arsenal—not just, or even primarily, military power. We must wage this campaign in many theaters, including the homeland. We must recognize the struggle as ideological as well as physical. The current struggle can be construed as our legacy to the future. In a crucial moment, America once again recognized that "something had to be done."

Day Two—Strengthening Essential Capabilities

The second day opened with an address by NYPD Deputy Commissioner for Counter-Terrorism Michael Sheehan, who told the audience, "The scourge of terrorism did not begin on 9/11, it began at least 10 years earlier, and it will continue for at least the next 10 years." The NYPD is committed to four main tasks in its counterterrorism strategy: detecting, deterring, investigating and arresting terrorists. The NYPD follows all leads, he continued, but the problem is that "credible reporting is not specific and specific reporting is not credible." There is no clear answer as to why there have been no al Qaeda attacks in New York City since Sept. 11, 2001. Perhaps the organization has been disrupted in its bases overseas, perhaps it has been disrupted at home, or perhaps its members are simply waiting.

The third panel discussed the topic of communication and integration between national security organizations. Not surprisingly, each panel member had a different view based on his experiences. Ambassador Chas. Freeman argued that the notion that security and military are synonymous is incorrect. New structures need to be considered and more foreign service officers need to be trained to help increase global security. Ambassador James Lilley stated that the clandestine services need to interact closely with academic communities. Essentially, he argued that clandestine infiltration into regional academic elite circles could be a catalyst for success in that region. Marine Corps General Peter Pace steered to more pragmatic recommendations such as increasing cross-disciplinary education and training in our national security organizations.

The final panel focused much of its discussion on defining the enemy, then establishing a strategy to address that enemy. Matthew Levitt said that defining terrorists by group is wrong; instead we should look to relationships, networks and connectivity. Colonel Michael Nagata said that the principal challenge to the intelligence community is not identifying the enemy, but finding the enemy. Among Steven Niegorski's key points, he emphasized that we need to work closely with partners in the war on terrorism. It is much easier to work with states like Pakistan and Saudi Arabia than it is to work without—or against—them.

Former Congressman Lee Hamilton gave a powerful closing speech to wrap up the conference and tie the discussions to the 2004 national elections. "...and the truth of the matter is that the dialogue of democracy does not always work. Many discussions produce a lot of heat. Not many of them produce light." He continued, "So the point, I guess, is that we should not approach terrorism and Iraq in a vacuum. If you know anything about American foreign policy you know that everything's connected with everything else." Near the end of his talk, Hamilton charged everyone in the room to take responsibility for our foreign policy, saying, "We just can't shift all of this off onto the candidates. You and I have a responsibility. We're Americans."

Conference Charter

National Security for the 21st Century—
Balancing Our Essential Requirements

The theme for this year's Eisenhower National Security Series and Conference is *National Security for the 21st Century—Balancing Our Essential Requirements.*

We live in an increasingly complex and globalized world—a world where national and international responsibilities and expectations are evolving. In such a world, how do we determine—and ultimately balance—our requirements as a nation? What requirements, if any, are essential? The metrics by which policy-makers balance requirements will always differ. Some view the world through a lens of morality, others through security. Some advocate unilateral actions, while others prefer a multinational approach. Who is correct? Should there be a balance between the various approaches? What course should our policy-makers chart when essential requirements stand in opposition to each other? This year's conference endeavors to contribute substantively to this important and ongoing national security dialogue.

The 2004 Eisenhower National Security Conference is the culminating event of the 2004 Dwight D. Eisenhower National Security Series, a yearlong progression of seminars, workshops and activities that address the crucial security issues of our time under a unifying annual theme. Participants and audiences at these events include a wide range of current and former national security policy-makers, senior military officials, congressional leaders, internationally recognized security specialists, corporate and industry leaders, and the media.

OPENING ADDRESS

STRATEGIES FOR AN UNCERTAIN FUTURE

General Montgomery C. Meigs (Ret.), Louis A. Bantle Chair in Business and
Government Policy, Maxwell School, Syracuse University

Introduction by: Susan Eisenhower, President and Chief Executive
Officer, The Eisenhower Institute

Summary

Susan Eisenhower, President and CEO, The Eisenhower Institute

Susan Eisenhower began her introductory remarks by drawing a historic
parallel between this year's theme, "Balancing Our Essential Requirements," and
the challenges faced by President Dwight D. Eisenhower 50 years ago. President
Eisenhower, she noted, faced not only the threat of thermonuclear war, but also
the rising tide of McCarthyism and the related threat to civil liberties. President
Eisenhower had to perform a delicate balancing act—a way to reconcile "national
security concerns with fiscal responsibilities," while at the same time "protecting
and securing our civil liberties." Even President Eisenhower's celebrated farewell
address, with its warning to future generations of a too-powerful "military-
industrial complex," should be read as part of a broader message urging balance
in the building of our national security infrastructure. Susan Eisenhower closed
by expressing hope that the exchange of ideas taking place during the Eisenhower
National Security Conference would help enable today's leaders to strike a balance
among our essential requirements.

General Montgomery C. Meigs (Ret.)

- Montgomery Meigs opened his talk with a simple recommendation: "Get
the strategy right, and let the strategy define the operational objectives."

- Echoing Secretary of Defense Donald Rumsfeld's prediction that the United
States is in for a "long, hard slog" against an unconventional opponent, Meigs
observed that the "center of gravity" of Islamic terrorism is its capacity to spin off
new terrorist cells or "nodes."

1. Meigs analyzed the nature of this opponent and of the new strategic environment by a reference to Klaus von Clausewitz, comparing the effects of the information revolution in the 20th and 21st centuries with those of the French Revolution in the 18th century.

2. Success in the fight against transnational terrorism is impossible without addressing some of its root causes. The highest priority is not the elimination of terrorists, terrorist cells or even terrorist groups like al Qaeda—it is instead altering the conditions from which terrorists are spawned.

• In the short and medium term, the United States must work with sovereign governments to root out terrorists within their borders, while engaging terrorists in failed and weak states. Success in the long term, however, will hinge on a more sophisticated U.S. approach to the socioeconomic problems that plague many parts of the Arab world.

• Waging an effective campaign against such networks requires that individual nations take action to suppress terrorist activities within their boundaries. We must insist that other countries do so and assist them in their efforts.

• Military force is necessary, but not sufficient to wage an effective campaign against terrorism. Our objective must be not merely to kill terrorists and destroy terrorist bases, but to reduce their ability to adapt and to recruit.

• In order to respond to the national security challenges of the 21st century, given the mounting deficit, the U.S. military must fully embrace jointness, become operationally adaptable, enhance leader development, improve the quality of life for uniformed personnel and their families, and build fiscal resiliency into planning for the future.

• On the subject of jointness, Meigs cited an example from his own career: getting the AH-64 Apache helicopter operational in the Balkan theater, and the institutional resistance that impeded him. The U.S. military has come a long way in this field, but clearly has further to go.

• Regarding adaptability, perpetual task-organizing may become the new reality for commanders in the 21st century, and officer training ought to reflect this possibility. The development of more light forces, including Stryker brigades, will boost the capability to respond rapidly to a variety of crises. The great demand on special forces may mean the need to render some conventional units more adaptable and able to take on less sophisticated elements of the U.S. Special Operations Command's work.

• Regarding fiscal stability and resilience, Meigs stated that a 3 percent structural deficit and large deficits of trade are untenable. Failure to balance the budget could have grievous consequences such as a decrease in the quality of public education and a "low-octane" war on terrorism. The era of massive supplemental funding for the Pentagon may also be coming to an end.

• In leader development, officer training must reflect changing battlefield realities: "You have to train to win in the way that you have to win."

• On the subject of improved quality of life, greater investment in this area is an absolute imperative for the military. Housing, in particular, stands out as a trouble area, both in Europe and the United States. The armed forces deserve world-class facilities. Improvement in this field will also make it easier to recruit competitively, drawing the best young people into the military.

• Although some adjustments in military culture are needed to effect these changes, it is important to note that the Army has scored some real successes in advancing these principles within the past 15 years. For example, operations in the Middle East and the Balkans have demonstrated that the military can work jointly in unfamiliar theaters, and can successfully improvise solutions to new problems.

• Despite its successes, the military has not taken enough credit—it has not "sold" its successes or its future potential. At a key moment in 2000, the Army failed to step up and exploit its opportunity to frame the national security debate in Washington.

• Meigs closed his address with the same advice that opened it: "Get the strategy right."

Question-and-Answer Period

• When asked about U.S. ability to work with the international forces, Meigs said U.S. forces are generally successful in this regard. However, he noted that these successes are often the result of strong interpersonal and improvisational skills on the part of U.S. commanders, rather than the strength of alliances. Above all, Meigs counseled clarity for the U.S. commander in a coalition: clarity as to the allies' rules of engagement, their training, their capabilities and the political mandates of the allies' home governments.

• On the issue of placing the terms "war" and "terrorism" together, Meigs agreed that it is correct to point out that the current struggle is asymmetric and lacks many characteristics of a war, including a readily identifiable opponent and a definite political endpoint. Nonetheless, the term "war" accurately describes the demands placed on U.S. political, diplomatic, military and economic resources.

• When addressing basing operations in forward areas and the changing interface with Europe, Meigs stated that the lily-pad concept of forward deployment, though currently popular, represents a less cost-effective solution to the problem of staging operations overseas.

• Regarding reduction of U.S. strength in Europe, Meigs cautioned any such move should follow a careful analysis of where U.S. combat forces for operations in Afghanistan and Iraq originated. A good criterion for choosing which U.S. units are returned to the homeland would be to select those that did not at some stage participate in or facilitate these operations. In this analysis, it seems that very few of the troops in Europe are in fact superfluous or should be repositioned in the homeland.

Analysis

General Meigs' astute opening assessment was that the nature of the transnational Islamic terrorist threat requires an adaptable strategy. The Islamic militant threat has matured over the course of two decades in terms of sophisticated lethality, both technological and methodological, and brutality. It is a revolutionary movement, which cannot be drawn into dialogue or negotiations. As with Hitler's Third Reich, Osama bin Laden's al Qaeda was born for conflict. Because it enjoyed nearly a decade of unfettered preparations, it has established global networks and financial underpinnings. It has since become a strategic threat both globally and temporally. The United States and its allies have no other option but to focus on the destruction of militant organizations and agents; however, the center of gravity of transnational Islamic terrorism is its ability to regenerate. This requires a focus on the socioeconomic, ideological and political factors that breed recruitment. Victory requires a two-front approach: the battlefront and the nation-building front through engagement.

Meigs outlined five criteria for change in the strategic environment:

• An even more pervasive joint ethic. The need to ingrain a joint ethic in the officer corps is essential. In order to effect a culture change in which commanders and staff officers transcend service parochialism, military units—down to at least the brigade level—must be truly joint. If the joint architecture is not integral to military units, then units of action are no different than regimental combat teams or brigade combat teams. Only through joint architecture can the U.S. military reduce the ad hoc nature of joint task forces, although a degree of ad hoc tailoring will occur due to the exigencies of crises. However, blaming the military culture or system because some division and corps commanders cannot think in a joint manner is surprising. Is it not possible that some generals are not appropriate for every command and situation? The task is to find the right person for the job rather than create a cookie-cutter approach for selecting joint commanders.

• Operational adaptability of mission-essential tasks. Encouraging commanders and staff officers to accelerate the decision-making process at all levels is absolutely essential for flexibility and speed. Napoleon once said, "It may be that in the future I may lose a battle, but I shall never lose a minute." As illustration, during operations on the Eastern Front during World War II, the *11th Panzer Division* commander, General Hermann Balck, formulated an operations order and issued it within 20 minutes to his subordinate commanders, resulting in the successful counterattack against a Russian penetration. Meigs is absolutely correct regarding this criterion for excellence. For training deployments, the Army has been afflicted with the mania of administrative and logistical coordination and training, as well as onerous in-processing and out-processing requirements at training centers. The Army can eliminate the tyranny of training bureaucracy, permitting the next higher command for the deploying unit to assume the burden of coordination. Alerting a commander to deploy within hours and begin an exercise quickly ensures operational adaptability at all levels.

Although Meigs mentioned this as a side issue, the Army must improve its institutional communication skills. The inability of the military to communicate with the civilian sector, as well as with itself, without falling into doctrinal jargon and run-on, complex sentences is atrocious. The Army needs to foster lucid, simple communication to address complex ideas.

• Fiscal resilience. Although this criterion is essential for the continued economic growth of the nation, Meigs' assessment that the 3 percent structural deficit is unsupportable is worthy of deeper debate. Other economists would reach different conclusions. Because economics is an inexact science, economists choose some variables, discard others and reach conclusions assuming all other factors remain the same. As an example, during World War II the United States devoted between 50 and 60 percent of its gross national product to military expenditures. By today's economic assessments, it should have imploded. That it did not is a confluence of numerous variables—public and market confidence in the economy being only one, albeit extremely important. Hence, although fiscal resilience is of strategic importance, the deficit may or may not lead to its demise.

• Enhanced leader development. Meigs' lament of the Army educational system's failure to produce adaptable leaders is another excellent issue worthy of sustained debate. Sufficient funding for graduate school may be the most effective way for the Army to sustain a force of adaptive and productive leaders. Because the military educational system tends toward the parochial, graduate school provides fresh and different perspectives worth experiencing. The danger for the officer corps is salient—a system that focuses ever inward will be unable to adapt to change. The history of the German general staff is sufficient admonition.

• Investment in more quality-of-life and human capital. Meigs' litany of examples regarding substandard Army living conditions and facilities is certainly true, has long been true, and has never been adequately resolved. The U.S. Air Force seems capable of providing modern, functioning facilities and housing. Will Soldiers vote with their feet? Probably not, but that is not an excuse for treating them so poorly.

Transcript

ANNOUNCER: Ladies and gentlemen, please welcome your master of ceremonies for the Eisenhower National Security Conference, the Army's deputy director for strategy, plans and policy, Brigadier General Kevin T. Ryan.

BRIGADIER GENERAL KEVIN T. RYAN: Thank you. Distinguished guests, ladies and gentlemen, on behalf of the chief of staff of the Army, General Peter J. Schoomaker, I want to welcome you to the 2004 Dwight D. Eisenhower National Security Conference. Along with the Army, four great organizations co-sponsored this major national security event, and without their participation this conference would not be possible. They are The Atlantic Council of the United States, the International Institute for Strategic Studies, The Henry L. Stimson Center and West Point's Combating Terrorism Center.

This is the third year of the Eisenhower Series, which began in 2002. Each year, through the Eisenhower program, the Army organizes and sponsors—with the help of key institutions like those just mentioned—a series of seminars, meetings and smaller conferences with the purpose of examining and improving the understanding of our nation's national security needs. This conference today culminates a series of meetings over the past year, bringing together some of the nation's top

Brig. Gen. Kevin T. Ryan

thinkers and makers of national security policy. The theme for this conference, *National Security in the 21st Century—Balancing Our Essential Requirements*, is described in your conference materials. We're excited about the panelists and you, the participants, who have assembled to tackle this important theme. We have purposely sought to bring together representatives of various communities from both inside and outside the United States. Among the 500 registered participants, 34 percent are military and the rest are from various groups, including academics, congressional staffs, corporations, departments and agencies of the government, nongovernmental organizations and several foreign governments.

Our success today and tomorrow depends on your participation. Our agenda of speakers and sessions is included in the conference material available in the lobby. We encourage questions and have microphones ready for your use during the question-and-answer periods. I ask that you identify yourself when asking questions. Before we begin, please take a moment and turn off any cell phones, pagers and other devices that you may have.

At this time, it is my honor to introduce the chief of staff of the Army, General Peter J. Schoomaker. General Schoomaker has served in a variety of command and staff assignments in both conventional and special operations forces. He is a veteran of numerous deployments, including DESERT ONE in Iran, URGENT FURY in Grenada, JUST CAUSE in Panama and DESERT SHIELD and DESERT STORM. He is a leader who has been actively engaged throughout his career in the struggle against the sources of terrorism.

General Peter J. Schoomaker

Ladies and gentlemen, the 35th chief of staff of the United States Army, General Peter J. Schoomaker.

GENERAL PETER J. SCHOO-MAKER: Thank you, General Ryan. Good morning everyone, and welcome.

There's a saying: "May you live in interesting times." Like it or not, these are some of the most interesting times that we've ever seen.

When we think about national security, its meaning and scope have evolved significantly over the past decade. The world as we knew it during the Cold War only exists today in the history books. We are rapidly forging new sets of rules and strategies to secure our nation in an era of interesting, but uncertain, times. Change is not new, and our country has navigated tumultuous change before. Our strength as a nation is a product of the democratic, economic, cultural and military accomplishments of past leaders who invested their time and energy into guiding our great nation through turbulent times.

President Eisenhower was one such leader. Our charter for this series is to perpetuate President Eisenhower's enduring legacy of leadership and to help promote a common knowledge and understanding of the critical issues of our time. Over the next two days, we will hear many distinguished speakers and guests, and I am sure the discussions will be thought-provoking. I challenge you to listen, to learn, to think and to contribute to the dialogue. We will all benefit from your participation. Our Army has a great association with the Dwight David Eisenhower National Security Series, and we are proud to be one of the co-sponsors of this capstone event. We are indebted to each of the partners for their continued dedication to broadening our national security dialogue and helping to refine our understanding of the challenges we face as a nation. We are especially grateful to the Eisenhower family for their continued involvement and gracious support.

It is now my great pleasure and honor to introduce Ms. Susan Eisenhower, a well-recognized and widely consulted scholar of United States-Russian relations. She is a best-selling author and a much sought-after speaker for insights across many disciplines. Her expertise is well respected and we are privileged that she could join us here today. Ladies and gentlemen, please join me in a warm welcome for Ms. Susan Eisenhower.

SUSAN EISENHOWER: General Schoomaker, thank you so much for that warm and generous introduction. I'd like to thank the general for hosting this very distinguished event, and I must say that after those wonderful remarks, I can't emphasize enough how much this conference has come to mean to my family. This is the third annual conference. It started in 2002, and I think it's very significant that this conference has been convened at such an extremely important period in our modern history. I think the theme this year is particularly appropriate. Once again this conference brings together an extraordinary array of Soldiers, statesmen, businessmen, academics, legislators and policy-makers. In fact, it's this opportunity to exchange ideas across multiple disciplines that makes

Susan Eisenhower

this conference so important. Certainly in the last three years, since the establishment of this conference, this process has become well known and has developed a very fine and important reputation. It is truly a great honor to the Eisenhower family that my grandfather's name be associated with this process.

I think it's also particularly meaningful—at least for me—that Dwight Eisenhower's name is associated with the theme this year, because if there's anything quintessentially "Eisenhower," it was his search for balance. You may remember that his presidency started just a little over 50 years ago, and this was also another very, very dangerous time in the United States. It was little more than 50 years ago that the Soviet Union broke the U.S. monopoly on the hydrogen bomb. The fear and terror that this created in the body politic and among ordinary citizens all over the world cannot be overestimated. This Soviet capability also fueled the power of one senator, Joseph McCarthy, who, 50 years ago this year, began what would be the beginning of the end of his power in American politics—the Army-McCarthy Hearings. We can look back on that as a particularly dangerous time, not only in terms of national security, but also what it meant for civil liberties in our country. These were huge challenges, and Eisenhower fought constantly throughout his two-term presidency about the myriad roles that the United States would have to reconcile between our national security and fiscal responsibility, and mesh these with the importance of protecting and securing our civil liberties.

By the end of his two-term career, he gave a very famous farewell address. Being a student of history, perhaps I think he was extremely impressed by George

Washington's farewell address and wished to leave some parting thoughts for America. He had tried very hard to reconcile national security issues with fiscal responsibility and, being a fiscal conservative myself, I'm proud to say that in an eight-year period as president, he balanced the federal budget three times. He did this during a period when it was extremely important to ramp up to meet this very dangerous Soviet challenge. At the end of his presidency in January 1961, he gave his farewell address. While certain parts of this address are remembered for identifying, for instance, the military industrial complex, he also talked about the scientific, technological elite and a number of other relationships that developed as a result of trying to establish a necessary, permanent infrastructure for meeting the challenges of the Cold War. He went on to say that it would be important to find a balance in and among these national programs. I believe the legacy of this address was when he said, "Each proposal must be weighed in light of broader considerations: the need to maintain balance in and among national programs, balance between the private and public economy, balance between costs and hope for advantages, balance between the clearly necessary and the comfortably desirable, balance between our essential requirements as a nation and the duties imposed by the nation upon the individual, balance between the actions of the moment and the national welfare of the future. Good judgment seeks balance and progress and lack of it eventually finds imbalance and frustration."

He understood that the Cold War would be a long-haul effort. He developed, during his administration, a multilayered strategy for meeting that challenge, and he never stopped thinking about the future. At the end of his farewell address, he said, "As we peer into society's future, we—you and I and our government—must avoid the impulse to live only for today, plundering, for our own ease and convenience, the precious resources of tomorrow. We cannot mortgage the material assets of our grandchildren without risking the loss also of their political and spiritual heritage. We want democracy to survive for all generations to come, not to become the insolvent phantom of tomorrow."

And now it's my great honor to introduce General Montgomery C. Meigs. General Meigs is the Louis A. Bantle Chair in Business and Government Policy at the Maxwell School of Syracuse University. General Meigs served on active duty for more than 35 years, most recently as commander of U.S. Army forces in Europe from 1998 to 2002 and as commander of the North Atlantic Treaty Organization Peacekeeping Force in Bosnia from 1998 to 1999. He was a multinational division commander in Bosnia, a brigade commander in DESERT STORM and a senior planner with the Joint Chiefs of Staff in Washington, D.C. General Meigs earned his bachelor's degree from the United States Military Academy and his master's degree and doctorate in history from the University of Wisconsin at Madison. He has published a variety of articles on military policy and leadership as well as a book entitled, Slide Rules and Submarines. Since 2003, General Meigs has been the Distinguished Visiting Tom Slick Professor of World Peace at the Lyndon B. Johnson School of Public Affairs, University of Texas at Austin. From 1997 to 1998 he was commander of the

U.S. Army Command and General Staff College at Fort Leavenworth [Kan.], and, before that, assistant professor of history at the United States Military Academy. He's had a distinguished career lecturing at many military institutions around the world. It is a great honor and pleasure for me to introduce General Meigs.

GENERAL MONTGOMERY C. MEIGS (Ret.). Thank you very much. Susan Eisenhower, for that kind introduction. Unfortunately, there are a lot of people in the audience who wouldn't call my Army activity distinguished, but that's OK. We can go on from there. I'm only going to make two points today because there are too many armor officers in the crowd and they would forget the third one anyway.

General Montgomery C. Meigs

First, we have to ensure, in this current strategic environment, that we have the strategy right, and that the objectives we derive from that strategy have us do the right things in our defense establishment and for the interests of the community here and for the Army. I'm going to suggest to you that there are five areas to which the strategic environment is forcing us to pay attention.

One area is an even greater understanding of the need for joint synergy as an Army strength. The others are operational adaptability, which is a mission-essential task; fiscal resilience; enhanced leader development; and investments in quality of life. It's no surprise to anyone that transnational Islamic terrorism has changed the strategic landscape. In Kenya, Tanzania and on 9/11, we saw the opening shots. Those were only the opening shots. Remember Khobar Towers? Remember Lebanon? We missed those. We didn't understand the importance. Madrid, Spain, and Beslan, Russia, added a new dimension to this problem. Imagine terrorists telling little children close to terminal thirst to drink their own urine.

In his appearance at the National Press Club last week, the secretary of defense put the problem very squarely. No one can make his own deal with these people. We're all in this together. Watching the French foreign minister last week unsuccessfully pull strings to try to free two hostages adds a very important exclamation point to the secretary's statement. Secretary Rumsfeld was right when he wrote last year, however belatedly, that we're in for "a long, hard slog." Defense establishments have seen these challenges before, however. Note the French Revolution. I go back to Clausewitz, who went through 20 years of transformational strategic change and wrote about it in a very telling way. If we bring Clausewitz's framework up to date, we can see things haven't changed very much.

The strategic realities are clear. Now we have to get the strategy right. Yes, we have to have a preemptive defense. Yes, we have to take out terrorists' operational cells as they become visible. But unless we stop the ability of transnational terrorism to adapt new forms and methods—to spin off new command-and-control cells that embed themselves in weak and failed states and to recruit and train cohorts of other operational cells that migrate worldwide to attack us—we are in for a very tough time that will test our resources and our people in immeasurable ways.

Remember, Madrid was carried out by locals, and it looks as if Beslan was as well, with only indirect assistance from al Qaeda central. A similar pattern seems to be at work in the attack on the Australian Embassy in Indonesia. Think of transnational terrorism as a hydra. I know you have studied mythology, so you know the hydra was a beast that had a head with snakes coming out of it, all of which were poisonous. But its most powerful weapon was its ability to turn victims who looked into its eyes into stone. The way the hydra was defeated was not by attacking the snakes, but by cutting off the larger head.

The center of gravity of transnational Islamic terrorism does not lie in Iraq—an area of concentration in which al Qaeda can afford to lose and now we cannot. That center of gravity, in fact, is not geographically based at all. It lies in the ability of al Qaeda and its surrogates to continually spin off or sponsor new cells that go on mission to perfect the venture capitalism of newer, more innovative and horrific attacks. Yes, we must destroy operational teams and nodes as they become visible, but unless we permanently disrupt the process that creates generations of new terrorists as quickly as we destroy the old ones, winning is going to be very, very tough. Only individual nations are going to be able to control the nascent terrorist organizations within their own boundaries. We can become very active in failed states, in weak states. And make no mistake about it that working in places like the Philippines, Pakistan and Saudi Arabia, to name a few, means engagement. Now, I understand that "engagement" is not a politically correct term, but we are engaged. Troops in the field are engaged. Let me give you an example of engagement.

Recently, SETAF [Southern European Task Force] and the 173rd [Airborne Brigade] came back from Exercise TORGAU 2004, an exercise that occurred in Russia. There was a U.S. brigade headquarters, a Russian brigade headquarters—a combined joint task force commanded by a Russian flag officer—and it was a six-day exercise. Now, remember last year, SETAF was the JTF [joint task force] that handled the mission off Nigeria. Last year, the 173rd was in the northern sector of Iraq for a year. It is going back this spring. If these kinds of exercises—if these kinds of engagement activities—are part of the annual cycle of deployment to harm's way for a year, back home for a year, deployment to harm's way for a year, we need to recognize that, if that's a reality for cadre and Soldiers.

Now, why is getting a center of gravity right? Osama bin Laden thinks he has found our center of gravity: our will—our ability to persist. He and Ayman al Zawahiri, his deputy, believe they have us in a strategically untenable place. Now, that's a pretty clear, simple, elegant statement of strategy that came up last week. That's what that is. With a revised center of gravity, as we understand it, our objectives become clear.

We must help Muslim countries and their moderate leaders deal with the problems that emerge in their societies. We must continue to forge alliances: true friends, the willing, the publicly unwilling (but willing to cooperate under the table). But, as Anthony Cordesman [security analyst, Center for Strategic and International Studies] argues, unless we attack the social and economic problems—unless we engage—we're in for trouble.

Another note about strategy: fiscal realities. I commend to you the recent Congressional Budget Office [CBO] report. For those of you who are interested in the long-term effects of strategy, right here you see a chart, and I apologize for the numerology on there. Actually, on the bottom, the scale goes from 1988 to 2009. If you read the front part of this CBO report, the figures that come out, in terms of a structural deficit—that is, a permanent deficit, like the credit card bill you cannot pay off—is fairly moderate. If you go back in the report to this figure, you'll see that the CBO, when it cranks in the political likelihood of generating the revenues and cutting the costs to fix the deficit, comes out with about a 3 percent deficit annually to GDP [gross domestic product]. That's called a structural deficit. The bottom of that dark blue area is where they assess we will likely be in 2009, given political will. Ladies and gentlemen, you can't stand a 3 percent structural deficit. If you read the Financial Times last week, you would have seen an article predicting that the U.S. current account deficit—that's the deficit in terms of what we sell and buy abroad—is 5 percent now and will be 8 percent of GDP in the out years.

I'm not an economist, so I can't assess likelihood and give you a very detailed picture of what this means, but go to your local banker and ask him what those two numbers mean if they come true. It seems there's a possibility they will come true—for home loans, car loans, student loans, interest rates. Go to your local school board or the president of your local university and ask what impact that has on federal and state discretionary income and what that will mean for the operating budgets of, say, Fairfax County [Va.] schools; Syracuse, N.Y., schools; Concord, N.H., schools. Last year, the president of the University of Texas [UT] walked through the numbers for an audience and predicted that in about 10 years, 58 percent of the income of every median family in the state of Texas is going to be required for a UT degree—in a state in which university education has been basically free. That's politically untenable. That's not going to happen, but that's where the economics are forcing our state universities.

If you really want to get your hair on fire, go talk to a bond broker and ask him what a 3 percent structural deficit, in terms of normal deficit, and an 8 percent current account deficit are going to do to the value of the dollar downrange. Ask him the likelihood that foreign countries are going to continue to buy our debt at the rates they do today. You will find they will tell you these patterns could lead to unsustainable pressure on the federal budget to get smaller. Given the proportion of that budget that is for defense, it's very likely, even with Republican appropriation committees and a Republican president, that the days of huge supplemental funding for operations are numbered. How do we account for that?

In summary, strategic objectives flow from a watershed international political environment. Military power against al Qaeda is a necessary, but not a sufficient, condition. The sufficient condition has to be closing down the ability of the terrorist system to punch out new command cells—new terrorist cells. If you look at the problem that way, where does it lead? I think it leads us back to those five areas that I talked about at the beginning: real jointness, embedded in the Army culture; operational adaptability as a hallmark of every unit in the Army—in the gut of every unit of the Army; an Army program for change engineered for resiliency; enhanced leader development; and better quality of life.

General Schoomaker has done the Army a great service by making it clear that war fighters wear purple, not green. If you noticed, when he first took over, a little memo came out inadvertently that said, "What's good for the nation is good for the Army; what's good for the Army isn't necessarily good for the nation." Have you noticed that the mantra "the Army wins the nation's wars" has faded into the background? The Army never did win the nation's wars. The national command authorities and the combatant commanders won the nation's wars. General Dwight D. Eisenhower, when he entered the continent of Europe, was a combined joint-force commander. He just happened to be wearing an Army uniform. That is the part of culture that we have to change in our warrior psyche in the Army.

Culture is very important to change, as Louis Gerstner [IBM chairman and CEO] found out in turning around IBM. Here you had a corporation that was headed for the dustbin, and the people in it didn't want to change, as a function of culture. Now, I'm not suggesting that the Army is in that kind of shape. It's not, but it's something we have to be very aware of. Granted, OSD [Office of the Secretary of Defense] and the combatant commanders have to do better, as well, and I'll give you a couple of examples. During one of my tours in USAREUR [U.S. Army Europe], we were trying to develop the capability—this is fairly recently—to have AH-64s [Blackhawk helicopters] fly off of Navy flat decks. We were going through the process and making that happen. My four-star Navy counterpart was in favor of the initiative and supported it. We had challenges in the Balkans that required that capability and it really didn't exist; it was in anticipation of long boats coming into theater the following summer. I was getting a lot of resistance from some of my counterparts' subordinates. So I went to one of my joint bosses and said, "Look, I'm about to buy the dunking gear that's going to allow me to qualify these pilots to do the final qualification drills on the flat decks. I'm getting some resistance. I'm going to need your support to blow through this, to give you a capability you don't have right now." The answer was, "I would rather not do it. I'm going to get too much flak from the Marine Corps." That is not jointness.

In Millennium Challenge [operation sponsored by U.S. Joint Forces Command combining live field exercises and computer simulation], the JTF was trained to do the kind of work that needed to be done for Jay Garner [retired Army lieutenant general, first post-conflict administrator for Iraq] in Iraq. I am JTF trained and certified, but I know some of you know more about this than I do. When it came time to provide a JTF to Jay Garner, downrange, working national equities in harm's way, did they send a trained and certified JTF? No. They went to 58 locations around the defense establishment and pulled people out from all over the place and sent in an untrained, uncertified JTF to do the nation's business. That is not jointness.

Now, the Army is not clean on this. If you go into a BCTP [battle command training program], you're not going to see the full weight of a joint campaign bearing down on that division commander. You're not going to see the entire constellation of simulations being run with people at the switches that know the problems that result. You've got to ask yourself, if that's what Buff Blount [commanding general, 3rd Infantry Division during Operation IRAQI FREEDOM] and Scott Wallace [V Corps commander during Operation Iraqi Freedom] had to put up with down range, why isn't that an absolute basic part of how we do our basic training for division and core commanders? Battle cry is generally from the exercise directors, so that really gets in the way of us doing ground force business. That is ground force business. If you don't understand how to maximize the effect of the ATO [air tasking order] as part of your ground campaign, you don't understand your business. You may have to give up some of your truck assets to I MEF [1st Marine Expeditionary Force] at the last minute—that is ground business. You need to understand that. It's got to be part of how we do our thing.

You have to train to win in the way that you have to win.

Now, the other interesting thing about what's been going on during the last decade is that the variety of our operational tasks is absolutely startling. Every time I see a new article that's written about the Cold War Army by someone who lives here in Washington and doesn't get out much, I sit there and scratch my head and say, "Now, where has this person been?" Under what rock does he or she live? Let's talk about European-based Soldiers, because they are the ones I'm most familiar with. They're in DESERT STORM, fighting in a place we never thought we would go, in a structure and an environment that was totally different and unprecedented, facing down paramilitaries in Bosnia-Herzegovina, often at gunpoint. Also, something we don't talk about much, conventional units helping in the assistance of PIFWC [Persons Indicted for War Crimes Operations]. Very dicey business fighting insurgents on the Macedonian border. Not many of you know that in the summer of 2001, our troops were routinely engaged in firefights with Albanian Kosovar insurgents in the Dinaric Alps. Routinely. And they won every one of them.

Let's look at combat and peace enforcement and counterinsurgency in Afghanistan and Iraq. Now, every one of these operations was done in a place no one ever thought they were going to go. No one was necessarily trained for this, in a task organization that was totally different, and in a command arrangement that was totally unprecedented. That's Cold War? The critical point here is that's the reality. That's the reality. Why am I banging away on that? Because that's the way we have to train, if that's where we're going to send our troops and how we're going to send them.

Granted, it's our conventional long-haul capability on the ground that we have to preserve because, among other things, that's what forces our enemies to seek asymmetrical advantages. If we ever lose the air-land battle, deep-strike-on-the-ground capability, we have missed the boat. We've got to continue to enhance the capability of Stryker units. We've got to continue to enhance the reliability and capabilities of our light forces. The interesting thing is, with 30 to 40 percent of the Army brigades deployed all the time, you're never going to be able to have enough of X or Y to do a specific mission. We're always going to be task organizing on the fly. This is not new, as you have seen from my previous discussion. Plus, Army special operations forces are very committed, more heavily committed than they have been. The conventional side is going to have to pick up some of the less dicey, less politically sensitive, less surgical tasks and be able to do them as a matter of routine. That shouldn't cost a lot of money. It will take some training and some personnel selection, but it's doable.

This all goes to operational adaptability as a mental task. How do you get to that? Well, picture yourself as a BCTP student, a division commander. Fifteen to 20 days before your BCTP, someone walks in from Fort Leavenworth and says, "OK, general, here is your mission, here is your map area and here is the general scenario. Your orders process starts today." It doesn't start six months ago. It doesn't start before the rehearsal exercise you have to get you ready for the BCTP. It starts like it started for the division commanders downrange when they got their peacekeeping sectors while they were fighting, two days before they had to go execute. How about the brigade commander who is sitting in his headquarters at Fort Hood and two weeks before he's due to move to some combat training center, he finds out, "OK, buddy, you're going to Gowen Field [Air National Guard base, Boise, Idaho]. Here is your task organization list. You now have liaison authority to contact all these units." He meets them in the dust bowl. He doesn't practice with them at home station for six months. He meets them in the dust bowl, like you do in the real world. For example, during DESERT STORM, I was without—well, our brigade was without—engineers. In our final assembly area, the 54th Engineers rolled in and said, "We're your direct support engineer battalion." They were terrific. But I didn't know those characters from beans. Hardly knew they existed. The lesson learned: The Army can do all this and still not get credit for it. You can be wonderful, terrific, winning, doing multiple tours in Bosnia, Kosovo, never losing Soldiers to accidents, which shows a level of NCO [noncommissioned officer] competence that is unprecedented in armies, let alone ours. If you're not selling it, it's not happening.

I remember some congressional testimony just before I left active duty. It was closed testimony affecting Crusader [now-canceled, Army 155mm self-propelled

Howitzer], but it was sort of after-the-fact. There were two people there from the Army staff—general officers, good men I know. A very concerned congressman, a friend of the Army, broke in, used his time and said, "Look, I need your help here. I want to understand this idea, Objective Force, because I want to help you." Following his comment, I watched as these two people gave the standard line. I watched everybody's eyes glaze over and even I couldn't understand them. In this case, "doctrine speak" and jargon completely made a mess of what they were trying to say. If intense, CTC [combat training center]-based collective training, leader development, fiscal resiliency, rapid improvement of C4ISR [command, control, communications, computers, information, surveillance, reconnaissance], and task-organization-on-the-fly are Army strengths that have to be preserved, Army officers have to sell it.

Now, the current Army leadership is doing a wonderful job of improving Soldier gear, refurbishing our aviation fleet and changing the focus of Future Combat Systems [FCS] from platforms to an emphasis on the ubiquity of real-time information. This is a huge step in the right direction. If we do see 3 percent deficits against GDP and structural deficits on our national budget, accelerating inflation, higher interest rates and a dormant economy in the out years, we're going to be sustaining the war on terrorism on low-octane fuel. We have to design resiliency into our programs for change, or we're going to have some big speed bumps and they're going to be very painful. We have to sell those hard points. In 2000 it was obvious to all of us in the Army leadership that we were going to have a very difficult time in the next year. It didn't matter which administration was coming in. You were going to get all the questions; all the pins were going to be pulled on the strategy. We knew we were going to get a lot of new faces. We had time to try to frame the debate. We didn't do it, and we paid for it.

Remember, folks, next year, regardless of administration, you're going to get new faces in OSD, OMB [Office of Management and Budget] and on the NSC [National Security Council] staff. Some of them will be uninformed newcomers who want to know, want to understand and want to help. Some of them will be pundits with newly given authority who think they know everything they need to know. The debate will take place and decisions will be made, whether the Army takes a voice or not. So as we build more adaptable units and get ready to continue to do things on the fly, we have to make sure we're creating the men and women who can handle the change for our Soldiers. By the way, I wonder if we paid enough attention to the Army schoolhouse, which I ran for about a year. It has taken huge cuts. It has taken huge cuts in the quality of the faculty.

At Leavenworth, if you have an instructor who is not current on operations, who doesn't have mud on his boots, who does not plan on going back into the active Army—is that the way to train an adaptable officer corps?

I worry that cutting back on graduate education is going to continue to make us an even more insular officer corps. Now, be careful on how you interpret how I said that. We have a very strong, professional culture, but it tends to be inward looking.

not outward looking. Armies tend to be like that and ours is no different than anyone else's. Services, in general, tend to be like that. If you want to learn state-of-the-art communications theory, information management, logistics management, business practice or civil-military relations, you're not going to get that at Leavenworth, which is world-class in teaching the art of operations and leadership. You ought to go to a first-rate graduate program at a research university.

"Adaptable" means that we must address the leader-to-led ratio in the Army structure. If units, just back from Iraq and Afghanistan, are going to be tasked with joint exercises and if headquarters, slimmed and flattened, working 24 hours a day, are going to send key people to be in joint task forces, which happens all the time, we need to resource that in the chain of staff and command. If units in the annual cycle of redeployment, retraining and certification are going to participate in engagement activities, we need to resource that in the chain of staff and command.

We have to look at the historical demands on headquarters caused by operations and engagement and put in the personnel needed to run the store; otherwise, joint requirements and the drain of this cycle of deployment in harm's way could become very damaging.

Finally, the Army has got to invest more money in quality of life and human capital. I may hurt some feelings here, but I never understood why Congress passed the law that requires us to pay a certain TDY [temporary duty] rate to Soldiers who log more than 400 days of deployment in two years, when the services couldn't afford that. That money would have come out of training had we had to pay it, and that would have ensured higher casualties when we went in harm's way. Training is where your discretionary money is in the year of execution.

Army commanders weren't mandating those days. Most of that was coming from the joint world. Services weren't doing that. Why pay a Soldier that kind of a TDY bill when captains at Fort Stewart, Ga., elect to live off post and on their salary can rent a house better than the battalion and brigade commanders who have to live in designated housing? Why do that when students at Leavenworth, in a survey done a couple of years ago, said they're embarrassed to invite their parents to visit them because their houses are so ramshackle? Why invest that money in TDY when families and Soldiers in Europe live in stairwell apartments where the electrical system is unsafe and in the barracks where human waste seeps into the insulation spaces of the walls? Every year there is a survey done about the 100 best companies to work for by one of the major business magazines. One of the top criteria is "my company has world-class facilities." Why can't a Soldier returning from Iraq—whose family supported him in Grenada, Bosnia, Kosovo, and who has five tours in harm's way—have world-class facilities at home? Why can't we do that for our troops?

There you have it. We have got to get the strategy right and pull out of that strategy what the operational objectives are. And I would argue that means a more pervasive joint ethic in the United States Army culture. Operational adaptability is the hallmark of our training, with the leader density required to manage that, resourced and sold; fiscal resilience; enhanced leader development; and a bigger investment in the quality of life.

I think I have broken enough china. At least I hope so.

Maybe there is a question out there. Got one right down here on the right, and I'll come back to the left on the next question. Go ahead.

AUDIENCE: Sir, Colonel Tim Coffin. You talked about how culture is an obstacle. Structure is also an obstacle. You have talked about how we have withdrawn resources and allocation from education and other areas and perhaps we're not invested heavily enough in OSD and the Joint Staff, because of our culture of where we want to put the war fighter. How do you suggest, then, that we balance all of this, given the realities we have fiscally and with force structure?

MEIGS: First of all, I have to give the current Army leadership credit for, at this point, doing a pretty good job at that. I'm trying to look out a little further.

We have made progress in how we see ourselves, and I suggest that we've got to go further. If the Army doesn't have capabilities that the combatant commanders want, it is irrelevant and the Army is going to go away. I had a hard time selling this to my subordinate flag officers when I was still on active duty. We have to be absolutely sure that as we go through and look at how we want our force structure to be, we have got to make sure those capabilities are operationally relevant in the force structure that's going to be here in four years, not today. The reason I made the comment I did about the Future Combat Systems is, if you look at the C4ISR modernization properly, you are going to have to upgrade things every nine months, not every five to seven years like they do in the POM. PPBES [Planning, Programming, Budgeting, Executing System] is completely out of sync with the way the civilian world does C4ISR modernization, and that's a huge problem. We've got try to get OSD to fix that. Rapid prototyping is one way to do that, but it's not instilled in the way we do C4ISR. That's how we got Blue Force Tracker [BFT]. That was an instance of rapid prototyping done with CONOPS [concept of operations] funding, not in normal research and development.

When I say that culture is an obstacle of change, this is not peculiar to the United States Army. Read Clayton Christenson's book, The Innovator's Dilemma. It's been the problem in every business that's failed to adapt to the future in our business history. I think that takes continual education. It also takes officers who understand that they have to try to gravitate to joint assignments. I have a good friend, one of my counterparts in the Army, who prided himself on never serving in Washington. I'd tell him, "You're an incomplete professional. You don't know how the war plans are done, you don't know how the Army is resourced, and you don't understand the fistfights we have to go through in the interservice rivalries and in dealing with civilians in OSD."

Another question over here somewhere. Come on. I couldn't have put that many people to sleep.

AUDIENCE: Hello, my name is Suzanne Kurstein. I come from Denmark, and I know the Danish forces are part of the coalition forces in Iraq. How do you foresee your ability to work with the international forces? I think that that is needed if we are going to fight this threat.

MEIGS: I don't think working with allies is a problem. I did a lot of it in Europe for a long time, not just the four years I was CG USAREUR [commanding general U.S. Army Europe], and I had two tours in Bosnia. I have done PIFWC operations with special operation forces of four different countries. There's nothing that gets much more dicey than that, and defense ministers are watching everything you do. The important part of this is not technological. It has to do with the command relationships and understanding the operational sensitivities of the other country. The Danish forces, especially the special operations forces, are very capable. The issue is more in the troop-leading process and in understanding the rules of engagement that affect that particular contingent. In Bosnia, when I was commander, SFOR [stabilization force] we had contingents that could not use lethal force without checking with their nation's capital. I couldn't put them in a mission that might put their Soldiers at risk in a way that demanded the use of lethal force. I just had to know that and I had to work around that.

You have to admit it seems fairly odd that you're going to put Soldiers in harm's way and put that kind of restriction on them, but that was the political restriction. So I don't see that as a problem as long as the forces are relatively capable, which is that nation's responsibility to ensure. That's training. That's not technology. You can work through a lot of technological issues, but if a country doesn't have the C4ISR constellation, you need to work with it. You can put that capability in a liaison mode and put it next to that commander, if necessary—which, by the way, is something that we ought to resource in our own force structure.

Another question? Right here, down on the right.

AUDIENCE: I'm Tom Hodge, from Canada. I am wondering about the term "war on terrorism." I don't have a military background, but traditionally you would associate the term "war" as having a clearly identified enemy, and you usually know when you win, lose or agree to draw in a war. Terrorism—you talk about it in terms almost like an ideology such as communism or fascism, but I'm not sure if terrorism is an ideology. Therefore, when you talk about the need for cultural change within the Army or the approach to that, how do you do that when you're using such traditional terms such as "war" and "terrorism," which is really a historical view of an enemy versus what you have to face today?

MEIGS: That is a great point. To some extent it's a result of the paucity of the English language or at least the way Americans speak it, and it is a function of political reality. We are engaged in an activity—a contest, if you will—that is going to require the same kind of national commitment and sacrifices, perhaps not in the numbers of fallen troops, but certainly in national treasure and the effort and patience that a war requires. The threats to our way of life and the endemic institutions that we hold dear are as great as they were in World War II or World War I. So, we are rather stuck with the word "war," when, in fact, you're exactly right. You have a set of economic, social and political conditions, which are being manipulated by a very small nucleus of hard-core professional terrorists to generate a huge problem. The scary thing about the operation in Beslan is that, from what I can read, it seems like they were strictly Chechens acting on nationalist and not religious motives. Could it be that what we're starting to see is the acceptance of terrorism for that kind of grievance? That's a whole new dimension to this problem. It's huge, because it may have very little to do with the Islamic aspects we now face. But the Islamists will sponsor it because it goes to the objective that they're interested in. Yes, it's a very varied and difficult problem, which is why I put Anthony Cordesman's quotation up there. You can nip off the cells and be very good at that. The folks in the field have done some absolutely superb things that they don't get credit for because you can't talk about it. But if you don't solve the problem you're addressing—this social and economic alienation that's going on—if we don't help weak nations or nations that have tremendous pressures on them to deal with this problem internally before it gets outside, this is going to go on and on and on. Now, the cultural point I was making isn't specifically about the Army and terrorism. The Army is pretty good about adapting to a threat when the threat becomes visible. It works very, very quickly on that basis, I can assure you.

The problem is looking around the bend to see something that's four to five years out. It was extremely difficult for us in the late 1990s when we were doing this—we're going to march out into the future 25 years and look back. You know, I always look at that stuff and scratch my head and say, "That doesn't make a lot of sense to me." What did come out of it is tremendous confidence in C4ISR, which was dynamite; we've spun off of that tremendously in the last two or three years. But the culture thing is this sort of understanding when you're in a situation like that, not to default inside, which is what we did. We didn't keep our tentacles out as well as we should have or keep in touch with the wider universe of defense people out there who were going to have an effect on the Army's future. For about three years there, it was really hard—in part, I think, as a result of that.

Another question, perhaps?

AUDIENCE: Yes, sir. I'm Colonel Friedling, French military attaché. I would like to answer what you mentioned at the beginning of your lecture, about the French so-called failure of liberation of our hostages in Iraq. I think, of course, our hostages are not free right now, but you cannot say that it is tentative of France to deal with terrorists on its own. I think we saw in the last couple of weeks the international community with France, and especially the Muslim world mobilizing itself along with my nation to try to get these hostages free. I think it is important to realize that there is a reason for that. The reason for this extraordinary mobilization of the

Muslim world, along with my country, is because of the difference in approach. It is not a question of dealing with terrorists, but a question of understanding that, as you said, terrorism is a very different context than the Cold War. It is a very different struggle. It is not really a war. We have to make progress in a lot of areas, especially intelligence. Intelligence is a huge problem. It requires good intelligence to find the terrorists. You cannot imagine that they are where they are not, because, if you do, when you try to kill terrorists where they are not, you'll kill innocent people and create new terrorists. We are watching the problem grow and are not solving it.

MEIGS: *Mon ami, ce n'est pas pour moi pour battre les français.* What I told him is it's not for me to beat up on the French. Look, Charles de Gaulle [former president of France] told Lyndon Johnson that you cannot solve a political, social or economic problem with military force. He did that about four times and he was right. The French point of view on the war on terrorism is a very valuable one. In fact, I personally, in my operational life as commander, SFOR, profited from my cooperation with the French and with French intelligence. The problem with the way the United States and France and Germany handle their disagreements over Iraq was it became too personal, too vituperative. Let me give you an example. When de Villepin [French Foreign Minister Dominique de Villepin] invited [Secretary of State] Colin Powell to the United Nations to a talk that he knew was going to be an ambush for Colin Powell on Martin Luther King Jr. Day, that was an abrogation of diplomatic competence. It's inexcusable, and I have been told that by French officials. That was not helpful. Now, there's a French officer taking over in Kosovo again. There are French troops in Afghanistan, there is tremendous cooperation going on under the table in the intelligence world. So my comment about the difficulty in freeing those two French hostages just happened to be a good data point on what happens if you think you can get around this thing in dealing with people like [Abu Musab al] Zarqawi. We can't. No one can. It just so happened that was the example on the screen last week that was most useful. So I accept most of your comments. But France has a couple of things to answer for here. One, why did the disagreement with the United States have to be so personal? Two, there are things that weren't done in the PIFWC business in Bosnia that should have been done and someday we'll get the answer to that, but right now we don't have it.

Yes. Down here in the light gray jacket.

AUDIENCE: Bill Jones from Executive Intelligence Review. General, if I could ask you a question that I get from some of the European officers whom I run into with regard to the transfer or the taking down of the large chunk of the European/ U.S. operations.

One of the issues is, of course, culture. In many respects the close cooperation that has been had by having U.S. Soldiers in Europe has created kind of a rapport, which otherwise might not have been there and made the alliance as effective as it has been. With the new situation, it seems there won't be the same continual interfacing between European and U.S. forces. Thus, the understanding of the other's culture, which is an important aspect in working together on the battlefield, will not be the same as it has been over the last 50 years. I was wondering if you see this as a problem and how we should address it, given the fiscal constraints in terms of moving people one place to another.

MEIGS: I was afraid this would come up.

This is a hard one to answer briefly, but I'll give it a try. In fact, I'm trying to get an editorial published on this very issue. The lily-pad strategy makes no sense. I say that because you should base your forward operating profile on some very hard issues. First, is it worth the cost? Second, what do I need to have there to do the kinds of operations I think I'm going to have to do? Recently, when senior defense officials were asked about the cost differential between forces in the United States and forces in Europe and Korea, the answer was the difference it takes to PCS [permanent change of station] a Soldier out of the United States versus in the United States. That was the only cost differential they cited. I suspect that wasn't entirely accurate, having dealt with this to some extent. If that's the only cost that's bothering them, other than the operational tempo required by those transfers, that doesn't even get on the radar screen. That's background noise.

The issue then is, what is the strategic requirement for forward-deployed forces? I am not an expert on Korea. I do know a fair amount about Europe and southwest Asia, supported by Europe. Let's dissect U.S. Army Europe and see what parts of it were not used in the campaign in southwest Asia and agree those Soldiers and units should come home right away. V Corps and a significant part of the V Corps slice commanded the Army forces and provided logistics in Iraq. A portion of the V Corps logistics slice went to support I MEF because it didn't have those logistic capabilities organic to its expeditionary structure. The 173rd Airborne jumped into northern Iraq. The 1st Infantry Division would have prepared the joint logistics area in Turkey, had the 4th Infantry Division been allowed to go through Turkey. It was all there. It was all set up. It was a huge effort. First Armored Division, as I understand it, was part of the actual combat force and was kept back later and then wound up going in right at the end. It stayed in country for 15 months—not 12, but 15 months. The flag officer commanding the party to return home initially had arrived in Germany and was told, "Get back on the plane. Go back. We're staying another three months."

I have just taken you through all the component parts of the United States Army in Europe except the training base, and the four-star headquarters that had to push all that stuff out. So, tell me what part of the United States Army Europe would not be needed to support a major campaign in SWA [Southwest Asia]. I'm not suggesting you keep it all. I mean, I submitted a number of plans to the Army Staff. We really do need to reduce our forces in Europe. The question is, how much? OSD has left us sufficiently opaque, so it's not really clear what the design is. I don't know what the design is, but the cost of keeping two brigades that far forward is about as much as keeping four brigades too far forward if you assume certain cuts in the global armed forces. It's very expensive. The point about lily pads is Operation TORGAU. Think what it takes to sponsor Operation TORGAU from Italy versus Fort Bragg [N.C.]. I mean, let's go tell the FORSCOM [Forces Command] commander there were something like 45,000 mandates of contact by U.S. Army troops. U.S. Army European troops, in Europe and southwest Asia. We're going to give that burden to FORSCOM. You get some troops back, but you've got to pay for all that coming and going. And, oh, by the way, you've got to take all that coming and going out of your normal training schedule. And remember, three years ago 10th Mountain Division, which had six infantry battalions, had five of them in five different countries.

So the point I'm trying to make here is, you will not get the contact between U.S. Army units in cadre with the lily-pad system that you are getting today. And if we agree that our ability to work with allies is fundamental to winning the war on terror and doing all this armed peace enforcement we have around the world, why are we doing that to the extent that it looks like that we're doing with a 70,000-person realignment? The thing that would worry me—I don't have to think about it too much now because I'm just a college professor—is that if realignment takes place in 2006 and 2007 and the budget has really started to bind us, how much of realignment might become reduction? Not that it might not, anyway. So it's not so much an issue of culture for me. Because you can't stand in front of the secretary of defense and make a cultural argument, nor should we.

What's the strategic requirement? How much contact do you want with European armies? Oh, by the way, some of the armies are on the Mediterranean Littoral, because USAREUR does that as well. How many exercises do you want to do with Egypt, where you would want to call on 1st Infantry Division to come and help out like they did in 2001? How much flexibility do you want? What is the differential in cost that makes me willing to come to you and say, "You really need to spend this amount of money to keep the strategic capability?" That's the issue for Washington. Not culture. However, if you don't have a certain amount of contact and working together, you're right. You aren't going to have that kind of easy familiarity with other armies. One of the reasons it was so easy to work with the Germans with all those years in the GDP, quite frankly, was the tremendous amount of trust that was there. So, I mean, that's worth keeping. But you cannot make the argument other than in strategic and operational terms of value and cost. It just won't fly.

Yes. Over here, on the left.

AUDIENCE: I'm Paolo Serra from Italy. I'm the Army attaché. I would like to know something about how you envision this nation building, which I think will be a great problem for the future. We have been in Bosnia, the Balkans and Kosovo for 15 years now. What kinds of lessons learned can we use from these in the future in Afghanistan and Iraq? Thank you.

MEIGS. I don't think it's going to go away. Look, I used to write a document called the Joint Strategic Capabilities Plan until April of 1990. We never dreamed of putting U.S. forces in a place like Bosnia or Afghanistan. It just wasn't even on the screen. Now, that's ancient history; I understand, but fast forward to 1993. We're going to put troops on the Macedonian border? I don't think peacekeeping and peace enforcement are going to go away. If that's the reality, once you get stuck in a place, you're in there for a while. I was recommending a couple of years ago it was time for the United States to try to get NATO to push Bosnia over to the E.U. [European Union]. It wasn't really armed peacekeeping anymore. Kosovo was a different problem. I think it's a reality in the future. It's going to be a drain on resources. It's going to require combined operations, and thank God for the Caribinieri [Italy's national police force]. We have to resource it, but who at this point can say how much of that is going to continue or not? I mean, who would have thought in 2002 that we were going to be sending an Air Force task force to Mozambique to help them with their humanitarian problem? Believe me, Mozambique is a long way from Ramstein [Germany]. That's the reality of our future. How do we build a force structure within the United States—I've given you some of my hints—and in NATO, because NATO is the most capable military alliance or body anywhere to do that kind of stuff. I regret having to answer a question with a question, but that's the challenge that faces us now. NATO has to do a better job of articulating that, because in my humble view the European Union, the European Defense Initiative or structure is never going to be as capable as what we have got with NATO. This is true to some extent because the United States and Canada aren't going to play—not at the ground floor. They'll only be an add-on. One of the things Americans tend to overlook when it comes to this is that the European Union will have a larger population and a larger GDP than the United States. It will have a charter that's very restrictive on the ability of member states to go out from under a foreign-policy decision. The United States will not have a seat at the table like it does in NATO. It has an ambassador who may be invited in after the decision is made. That's something you need to think about when you think about Europe.

Kevin?

RYAN: Sir, on behalf of everyone here, I would like to thank you very much for your thought-provoking kick-off to our conference. Thank you very much, sir.

And thank you all very much for your participation during this first agenda item.

The next agenda item is our first panel sponsored by The Atlantic Council of the United States, moderated by General Barry McCaffrey. The subject is *Changing Power Centers: The Evolution of American Alliances and Friendships.*

PANEL 1

CHANGING POWER CENTERS: THE EVOLUTION OF AMERICAN ALLIANCES AND FRIENDSHIPS

Co-sponsor: The Atlantic Council of the United States

Introduction by: Robert H. "Robin" Dorff, Ph.D., Executive Director, Institute of Political Leadership

Moderator: General Barry R. McCaffrey (Ret.), Bradley Distinguished Professor of International Security Studies, United States Military Academy

Ambassador Robert E. Hunter, Ph.D., Senior Advisor, RAND Corporation, former U.S. Ambassador to NATO

Jonathan D. Pollack, Ph.D., Chairman, Asia-Pacific Studies Group, Naval War College

John H. Sandrock, Director, International Security Program, The Atlantic Council of the United States

Panel Charter

Although our founding fathers warned us against "entangling alliances," the United States has entered into many international treaty alliances and has relied on friends and allies to assist and advise throughout our history. Certainly, going it alone is not the preferred mode of operation in the current, complex and uncertain international security environment. Even though the United States may choose to act unilaterally in certain circumstances, at some point it will be desirable to bring in other countries to help stabilize the situation, share the burden and add legitimacy to the effort. Given this basic need to join with others, the challenge is to lay the necessary groundwork before a specific crisis arises. This can be managed through institutional arrangements, such as alliances and partnerships that provide mechanisms for regular high-level security consultations, as well as through systematic military planning and joint exercises. Without the political will that is generated and sustained by reliable alliances and friendships and sustained efforts

Left to right: *Barry R. McCaffrey, Robert E. Hunter, Johanthan D. Pollack, and John H. Sandrock.*

to forge a broad consensus, the collective military power that may be brought to bear on a security problem will be far less than the sum of its parts.

"The Evolution of American Alliances and Friendships," the theme for the first panel of the 2004 Eisenhower National Security Conference, is a major topic of interest not only to the United States, but also to the rest of the world. The fundamental changes in the international strategic landscape over the past dozen or so years, the war on terrorism and the conflict in Iraq have introduced a new global dynamic that has raised questions about the future relevance of U.S. alliances that have been basic to U.S. post-World War II security strategy and structure.

It is well understood that a political consensus is required prior to any collective action, whether it be by well-established military alliances such as the North Atlantic Treaty Organization or a "coalition of the willing." Such a consensus is predicated on several factors, including a common threat assessment and understanding of the specific nature of the problem, the interests at stake, the strategic objectives and analysis of appropriate options, the likelihood of success, and, ultimately, an understanding of whom will pay what share of the various costs.

To examine the new global dynamic and to address its impact on U.S. alliances and friendships, The Atlantic Council has convened a distinguished panel of experts to address the future of U.S. interrelationships with key nations.

Discussion Points

• To what extent can existing alliances deal with post-Sept. 11 situations?

• How can our alliances deal with rogue states?

• How can our alliances deal with the problems posed by Saudi Arabia and Pakistan?

• How can we get the United Nations to perform a useful role in peacekeeping, given its inability to produce or pay for forces without heavy U.S. support?

• Given NATO's engagement in Afghanistan, are we facing another Srebrenica in the making?

• How can we make the NATO mission effective?

• How can we steer the co-evolution of the European Union and NATO?

• How can we secure the Organization of American States' help in Haiti, on Cuba and on interdicting the drug trade?

• How can alliances help ease the tensions between and among China, Taiwan, the Korean Peninsula and Japan?

• What must be done to establish lasting peace between Israel and the Arab world?

Summary

Ambassador Robert E. Hunter, Ph.D.

• Ambassador Robert Hunter examined the future of U.S. alliances and friendships in Europe, starting with the enormous progress of the 20th century. The "20th Century Agenda" included winning World War I, World War II and the Cold War—and then building a Europe "whole and free." This meant not only the abolition of war in Western Europe, but also the extension of peace and security to those central and eastern European states that had languished under the tender mercies of the Soviet Union from 1945 to 1991.

• NATO changed markedly at the end of the 20th century in order to adapt to the needs and opportunities of the post-Cold War world. Through the Euro-Atlantic Partnership Council, the NATO-Ukraine Council, the NATO-Russia Council and the expansion of the alliance to 26 members in 2004, NATO has worked to extend the sphere of mutually assured defense. NATO reformed its command structures to ensure that all countries wishing to work together on security matters could do so, and it accepted the fact that going "out-of-area" would be necessary to keep the alliance relevant and safe. NATO completed successful missions in Bosnia and Kosovo, knowing that failure would have gravely compromised its international standing and ability to deter potential adversaries.

• Though NATO's missions in the Balkans helped to usher out the 20th century, the "war on terrorism" is the principal challenge on the "21st Century Agenda." Sept. 11 fundamentally transformed both the United States—representing the first attack on the lower 48 states since August 1814—and the world. As the attack on Pearl Harbor ended U.S. isolation, so Sept. 11 ended its international insulation. Moreover, the first-ever invocation of NATO's Article 5, which states an attack on one is an attack on all, confirmed that fighting the causes and implications of international terrorism will require—and must include—full efforts of the United States and its allies working in concert. In the post-Sept. 11 world, the trans-Atlantic alliance, personified by NATO, would have to be more than just a Euro-centric caretaker in order to prove its worth.

• The United States' key allies in Europe and elsewhere have stood with it to fight terrorism not just because they, too, are vulnerable, nor because the United States has come to their aid in the past. The United States' allies recognize that they must stand with America now, in its hour of need, so that they may count on America to stand with them in the future. In the first phase of the international struggle against terrorism—the war in Afghanistan—the United States was reasonable not to ask more of its allies. The U.S. military simply had to get the job done—a job nobody thought it would have to do. But the impetus for longer-term U.S. and allied cooperation in fighting terrorism is clear. The struggle is likely to last a generation or more, and only a small part of it will require the impressive military power of the United States.

• Many of the current difficulties in relations between the United States and some of its European allies stem from the Iraq question. However, given the pressing need to replace the shattered former security systems of the Middle East, the allies must stop rehearsing the origins of the Iraq war and get on with the difficult tasks ahead in this troubled region. Similarly, the United States must present its doctrine of "pre-emption" carefully, so as not to threaten its friends around the world. It must realize planned troop redeployment in ways that preserve and/or build valuable bilateral relationships. The European allies must spend more and spend more wisely so that they can cooperate effectively with the United States when military means are necessary, as in Afghanistan. Indeed, the first priority of the alliance must be to get Afghanistan right—lest it become NATO's first failure.

• NATO is transforming itself to deal successfully with the tasks of the future; however, NATO, collectively and as individual member militaries, must be more than just ready and able to assure alliance security. It must also be willing to do so. Shared decision making and deductive consensus building are the prices that must be paid for the realization of an equitable sharing of risks and burdens. The United States has gained little and lost much by trying to do more than it has to by itself. Besides, the heart of the alliance is not narrow common interests, but, rather, the common values, perspectives and human understanding that have emerged from decades of shared history.

Jonathan D. Pollack, Ph.D.

• The United States' strategic destinies have been intertwined in the Asia-Pacific region for more than a century. However, its strategy in the region is changing. The

United States' preoccupations with Islamic radicalism, and the wars in Afghanistan and Iraq, have shifted its attention away from its long-standing focus on East and Northeast Asia.

• The strategic gravity across East Asia also is shifting, with particular reference to China. China's policies of reform and opening to the outside world are now a quarter-century old, and it has manifested itself internally through profound societal and institutional transformations. Over the past decade China has emerged as one of the world's leading trading states. It has materialized a more confident nationalism among both the elites and the politically attentive public. It has become increasingly enmeshed in global and regional institutions and has begun to develop a more capable military force that is relevant beyond the mainland of Asia.

• Early in 2000, the Bush administration characterized China as a "strategic competitor" and a presumptive challenge to U.S. predominance. In the aftermath of Sept. 11, however, both leaderships have sought to collaborate. As a sign of China's ever-growing political and economic weight, there are no plans for a containment strategy by any states in the region. Even those most wary of China's growing power seek normal relations with Beijing. All recognize that China must be part of any regional security order, as it is the only regional power with security-related involvement in all four of Asia's subregions. The United Sates must cultivate a stable, amicable relationship with China for the simple reason that there is no realistic alternative.

• The United States has never had a multilateral alliance structure in the Asia-Pacific region; all of its alliances have been bilateral, configured to specific security circumstances and highly asymmetrical. However, this has changed irrevocably as a result of pivotal developments internal to the region and by the three Ds— development, democratization and demilitarization. In the Republic of Korea (ROK), for example, there is a noticeable shift in the views of the older and younger generations, with the latter focusing on the asymmetric nature of Korea's alliance with the United States. While there is general support in Asian nations for maintaining bilateral alliances, younger generations often harbor strong grievances against the United States. The Korean case is indicative of a regional trend. Ultimately, the United States' partners are expressing interests and ideas that will require a recrafting of the existing alliances, and potentially a reduced U.S. footprint in Asia.

• At the same time, U.S. strategy is being redefined across East Asia in terms of our regional military presence, security goals and expectations of security partners. The United States is adopting a military strategy focused on flexibility and agility. In the ROK, for example, the Department of Defense is moving away from static deployments in the area. It argues that North Korea can be deterred by U.S. capability to bring overwhelming lethal force to bear in the form of long-range air and naval power, Marine Corps brigades and, presumably, some ballistic missile assets. The major augmentation of U.S. long-range air power and increased submarine deployments planned for Guam are occurring simultaneous with the ROK withdrawals, underscoring a shift away from a predominant strategic orientation in Northeast Asia. Emerging trends seem to suggest that the United States is moving more fully to a regional maritime strategy focused heavily on Japan.

• There are certain questions that need to be considered, and these issues are sorely lacking in the U.S. strategy dialogue:

1. Is there a place for regional partnerships—independent of specific roles and missions—advocated by the United States, and how do Russia and China fit into these concepts, if at all? For example, the Proliferation Security Initiative's only three Asia-Pacific member states are Australia, Japan and Singapore—the states most closely identified with the United States in the region.

2. Will our military posture be ever more contingency-driven, and is there even a common concept of threats and interests? Indeed, how does Taiwan fit into these strategies?

3. Should our plans be made on the assumption that North Korean missiles and even nuclear weapons are now a given in the strategic landscape?

John H. Sandrock

• Few events in our history have had such a profound effect on United States security and foreign policy as the attacks of Sept. 11. Aside from within the United States itself, nowhere has the impact of that day been of greater significance than in Central and South Asia.

• Although representing ancient cultures, the nations of the region are relatively young and have only a short tradition of national sovereignty and independent political development. Afghanistan, the initial focus of post-Sept. 11 action and still the major theater for NATO in its new, out-of-area operational mode, achieved total independence in 1919. Pakistan, which plays a crucial role in the war on terrorism, gained its independence in 1947 along with its neighbor and chief antagonist, India. The nations of Central Asia—Kazakhstan, Kyrgyzstan, Tajikistan, Turkmenistan, and Uzbekistan—have enjoyed their independence only since the demise of the Soviet Union in 1991.

• While India may justifiably claim to be the largest democracy in the world, the other nations in the region have not yet achieved the same stability or political maturity.

• In Afghanistan, NATO has taken responsibility for the International Security Assistance Force and is a full and active partner in promoting peace and stability. The United States has reinvigorated its relationship with Pakistan and has established close ties with several nations of Central Asia, especially with Uzbekistan, Kyrgyzstan and Tajikistan. We also have received important assistance and cooperation from several others in the region including India, Georgia, and Azerbaijan.

• Beyond the immediate prosecution of the war on terrorism, the United States needs to forge more lasting ties with all of the countries in the region.

• Healthy U.S. relations with India will become increasingly important as India plays an ever more prominent role in the region and in the world. With more than

1.3 million men under arms, a demonstrated nuclear weapons capability, and both short- and intermediate-range ballistic missiles already in or soon to be incorporated into its arsenal, India is one of the most capable military powers in a tier second only to that of the United States. India can and should play a very constructive and positive role in resolving international tensions and conflict.

• The confrontation between India and Pakistan is a major problem for the region that must be resolved by peaceful means. A major success of U.S. foreign policy has been the maintenance of very good relations with both India and Pakistan. The challenge for the United States will be to continue and strengthen its friendship with both while it also assists Pakistan in coping with its many internal and external problems.

• Pakistan will continue to have a key role in the war on terrorism. President Pervez Musharraf and his government have proved that Pakistan is a reliable and willing ally in dealing with some of the most difficult challenges encountered since the U.S. decision to eliminate the Taliban regime in Afghanistan. Pakistan's efforts to root out and defeat the remaining support of al Qaeda and the Taliban in its frontier regions have been undertaken with considerable political risk and certainly not without casualties.

• Pakistan's government faces substantial internal dissent and much of the population appears to be opposed to its support for U.S. operations, not only in Afghanistan but also in Iraq. The United States must do all it can to support the Musharraf government and recognize the principled and very supportive stand it has taken. The longer-term relationship between the United States and Pakistan will depend greatly on U.S. actions and our ability to assist Afghanistan in building a stable government and society.

Question-and-Answer Period

• When asked what the United States must do to confront China's status as an arrived regional power, Pollack suggested that to presume an aggressive China is misguided. We must recognize and respect China for what it is, including the limitations of its political system. The rebuilding of the Chinese military is essentially an overdue process and not really a pointed threat in any direction. We must take China seriously—but that does not mean exaggerating its military power, or speaking in terms of conflict before one exists.

1. The future of China in the next 20 to 25 years is a key problem for the United States according to Hunter. China appears to profit more than the United States from the current geopolitical configuration, since the United States is, in effect, ensuring the continued security of China's oil supply.

2. McCaffrey responded by stating, the key questions about China today are: Who is in charge, and who will be in charge in 10 years? China's government continues to be both opaque and unpredictable, presenting policy-makers with a difficult challenge.

• When asked how the United States should react to the European Union's formulation of a common security framework, in which the United States will have no say, Hunter answered with the United States and NATO. He said in any security discussion, the United States and NATO are—and will remain—two, 800-pound gorillas. Even in the context of a future E.U. security and defense policy, the United States and NATO will not only still be relevant—they will dominate. Still, NATO should welcome a common E.U. defense policy if it leads to greater European defense spending.

• When asked if the ongoing division of the Korean Peninsula serves U.S. interests, Pollack responded that future unification of Korea will depend more on what South Korea and China want than on U.S. interests. We must ask ourselves: What will a unified Korea look like? The North Korean regime has long defied expectations that it would collapse, and it is difficult to envision unification without some kind of post-Stalinist regime in the North.

• Pollack also said high-intensity warfare is unlikely. At present, both sides are effectively deterred. Their rhetoric notwithstanding, North Korean forces have avoided clashing with U.S. forces along the Demilitarized Zone, suggesting that North Korea has deliberately avoided provoking the United States.

• McCaffrey said it may be premature to speak of unification, given the mystery that shrouds North Korean politics and the miscalculations that could be made by that regime. The possibility of a high-intensity war erupting still exists.

• When asked how we can ensure that the upcoming Afghan election succeeds, Sandrock responded that concerns over security have been addressed to a large extent. Voter registration seems to be a success, with a far greater turnout than had been expected. There will be problems during the election, and we should not expect a perfect one. It is worth remembering that one election does not equal a democratic government. Still, we can be guardedly optimistic.

• According to McCaffrey, two serious security problems remain in Afghanistan: the warlords' militias and the drug trade. Nonetheless, Afghanistan has been a positive experience for the United States and for NATO. In the coming 10 years we will probably see new alliances organized around law enforcement, counterterror, drug interdiction and other capacities. The day of the heavy alliances centered on tanks and fighter planes may be over.

Analysis

Moderator Barry McCaffrey opened Panel I with a series of thought-provoking—if not controversial—questions. In light of the subsequent panel discussions, two were of particular interest: To what extent do existing alliances deal with post-Sept. 11 circumstances? How can U.S. alliances contribute in a positive and consequential way to a strategic environment populated by a range of security challenges that are often principally nonmilitary in character? Three regionalists—Robert Hunter, Jonathan Pollack and John Sandrock—tackled McCaffrey's charge.

Hunter asserted the continuing primary relevance and utility of the traditional U.S.-European relationships with regard to wider international security. Pollack reminded the assembled security professionals that the strategic center of gravity in Asia had shifted to China. He cautioned against those prone to see confrontation with China as inevitable and warned of the prospect of fissures in the U.S.-Republic of Korea relationship. Sandrock observed that Sept. 11 and subsequent events were transformational with regard to U.S. relationships in South and Central Asia and urged U.S. policy-makers to establish more enduring relationships with key regional powers.

Common to all was the sense that traditional and nascent strategic partnerships required substantial adaptation to a decidedly more complex environment. This, in turn, suggested that the United States should redouble its efforts to build partnerships worldwide and assure that its partnerships endure through adversity. Hunter, for example, suggested that NATO is capable of greater burden sharing, but is not necessarily willing. Pollack believed our current relationship with the ROK now transcends Korea-specific issues and should be expanded in scope to encompass broader Asian security interests. Finally, Sandrock saw our relationship both with India and Pakistan as crucial and, thus, called for nimble management of a delicate balance to achieve U.S. ends. All agreed that the scale and diversity of American interests demand a robust, multilateral approach to global security issues that allows the United States to call upon the strength and capacity of partners who are both capable and willing to assume greater responsibility.

Transcript

ANNOUNCER: Ladies and gentlemen, please welcome the executive director of the Institute of Political Leadership, Dr. Robert Dorff.

ROBERT H. "ROBIN" DORFF, Ph.D.: Thank you. Good morning. I'm Robin Dorff, the executive director of the Institute of Political Leadership in Raleigh, N.C.; senior advisor on democracy and governance for Creative Associates International; and a former member of the faculty at the U.S. Army War College. It has been my privilege to have a close working relationship with the Eisenhower National Security Series for several years, and I hope everyone here recognizes what a marvelous job is done by those great people working behind the scenes to make this and other Eisenhower Series events happen.

I'm sure you'll agree that this third Eisenhower National Security Conference has gotten off to a great start, and I'm sure you'll also agree with this observation—you didn't come here to listen to me. So let me do two things quickly. One is acknowledge and thank The Atlantic Council of the United States. It is the co-sponsor of this fine panel. Two, let me present to you the moderator for this panel, General Barry McCaffrey [U.S. Army retired]. General McCaffrey is well-known to everyone here. You have his bio, I won't read it to you. Let me simply say that General McCaffrey's careers—and I choose the plural carefully—are linked by one overarching theme: exceptional service. This distinguished military officer has commanded at the highest levels, and he has been recognized for outstanding performance, leadership and courage. While serving as director of the White House Office of National Drug Control Policy, he graciously gave his time on several occasions to come and speak to our students at the U.S. Army War College, for which I remain, to this day, very grateful. He has also served as a teacher at West Point while on active duty and serves again today as the Bradley Distinguished Professor of International Security Studies.

Robert H. "Robin" Dorff

Ladies and gentlemen, distinguished guests, it is indeed my honor to present to you an individual who has served his country, its citizens and, indeed, international security and peace so well, General Barry McCaffrey.

GENERAL BARRY R. McCAFFREY (Ret.): Robin, thanks for that great windup and to all the attendees. Every time I get a nice, gracious introduction like that my standard response is, it's the second best intro I ever had. For the last several years I have been going out every year to give a lecture on combat leadership at Fort Leavenworth. Eleven hundred of these shiny majors all arrayed. The first year I did it, my son was plucked out of the audience, having been told in advance that he would be introducing me. He complained about it. He called me, and I told him to shut up and do what he was told. The peer-group pressure is terrific to introduce the guy you're an aide to, or your XO or whatever. So he gets there on stage and he reads, laboriously, this long, honorific introduction. He finished by saying, "However, I have known this great man for more than 21 years, primarily in the areas of lawn and automotive maintenance."

Robin, thanks for that intro. Let me also thank Army Chief Pete Schoomaker for his leadership, for his example, for his strength during the period of such enormous challenge to the armed forces. To Susan Eisenhower, let me say what a wonderful legacy that wonderful man, our former president, left to all of us. To Chris Makins [president of The Atlantic Council], who I'm sorry isn't here, and John Sandrock, for their leadership over at The Atlantic Council. I'm very proud to be involved in their study on NATO and terrorism. I co-chaired that study over the winter and led one of our delegations to Moscow, Warsaw and Brussels. I think The Atlantic Council does some spectacular work, and I'm honored to be a part of it. Let me begin, if I may, by asking the panel members to come out and grab a seat and array yourselves so we can spot your faces and I'll introduce you.

Let me begin with Ambassador Bob Hunter, an old friend and public servant, who needs little introduction in terms of his career. He's currently a senior adviser at the RAND Corporation. He is also president of the Atlantic Treaty Association, chairman of the Community of Democracy, senior consultant at Lockheed Martin, an associate to Harvard University's Belfer

General Barry R. McCaffrey

Center, and is a member of the senior advisory group for the U.S./European Command. Most of us know him from his distinguished service as the U.S. ambassador to NATO, and he really was, in many ways, a principal architect in the new NATO. He did a lot of work for Partnership for Peace, worked the Bosnia issue and IFOR/SFOR [implementation force/stabilization force]. He's been very highly decorated. He twice received the Pentagon's highest civilian award. As many of you probably remember, during the Carter administration he was director of Western European and Middle East Affairs at the National Security Council. He served on the White House staff during the Johnson administration, so he has a long and distinguished record. Please join me in welcoming Ambassador Bob Hunter.

Dr. Jonathan Pollack, a professor of Asian and Pacific studies and chairman of the Asian and Pacific Studies Group at the Naval War College, is also joining us. He has a long, distinguished membership with the RAND Corporation. He has taught at Brandeis University, UCLA, RAND Graduate School of Policy Studies and the Naval War College. He's widely published; many of you have read his papers and articles on China's political and strategic roles, U.S. policy in Northeast Asia, and Pacific and Chinese technological and military development. He has his master's and doctoral degrees from the University of Michigan and did postdoctoral research at Harvard University. Welcome to Dr. Pollack.

Our cleanup speaker, John Sandrock, is now the director of the international security program at The Atlantic Council. I was really honored to work with him on the last project. More than 30 years' experience in international security affairs.

He has lots of time in Europe, the Middle East, and Central and South Asia. He was the project and program manager with SAIC [Science Applications International Corporation] in direct support for the Coalition Provisional Authority in Iraq. He just logged five months in beautiful Baghdad. Before that, he'd been an international civil servant with OSCE [Organization for Security and Co-operation in Europe] in Vienna, where he was deputy director for missions support, chief of operations. He also had a long military career and served as U.S. Air Force attaché in both India and Afghanistan. His military career included tours with the office of the Joint Chiefs of Staff, the Air Staff and NATO. He was a command combat pilot and flew in Vietnam. He had three years of service in India, 15 months in Tajikistan and another three years in Afghanistan. He has written policy papers on India, Pakistan, as well as central Asia and South Caucuses. Please welcome John, our final panel member.

As is my wont, when I get a hefty intellectual challenge like joining this group and trying to moderate their efforts, I go to my department at West Point. I teach some of these brilliant young majors with their brand-new doctorates from the country's leading schools. I said to them, "Look, give me the right questions to ask. We're going to talk about 50 years of alliances, about changing power centers, the evolution of American alliances and friendships—what are the questions we ought to be asking?"

Question number one, obviously, is, to what extent do existing alliances relate to post-9/11 threat factors facing United States and our allies? How do they deal with 37 foreign terrorist organizations, at least 12 of which are principally funded by drug-related crime? We're talking about terrorist organizations that now have access to literally hundreds of millions of dollars. It's a terrorist organization that may have front organizations like international public relations or legal firms, or can affect block-voting behavior in national legislatures. How do alliances deal with rogue states? The secretary of state is required to catalog those nation states that we allege are in violation of international law. The normal suspects: Cuba, Libya, North Korea, Sudan, Syria, formerly Iraq and Afghanistan. How do alliances deal with this post-9/11 threat situation we find ourselves in? I think one of our national treasures, and I say this unabashedly, is General John Abizaid—he's now running Central Command. I used to kid him when he was younger, saying, "I don't even know how you ended up as an Army officer." He's introspective, thoughtful, kind, also a Ranger battalion commander, Stanford fellow, Uimstead scholar; he has a Harvard master's degree and is fluent in Arabic, Italian and German. If you ask him what he's concerned about, it's not the front-line warfare states of Iraq and Afghanistan, it's what are we going to do about Saudi Arabia and Pakistan? I won't presume to answer the question, but to what extent can we have—can we create—alliances that deal with Pakistan and Saudi Arabia?

The United Nations can be of enormous assistance to U.S. foreign policy, if we choose to support them intelligently. How can we get the United Nations to do peacekeeping, voter registration, economic development, political development, counterdrug operations and alternative economic development? How do we get the

United Nations to act usefully in these areas, when at the same time—and I don't mean to be in any way hostile to the U.N.—the U.N. can't produce peacekeeping forces that can fight? They can't be trusted without careful oversight with sizable U.S. funding sources. The United Nations is there to be thought about as a potential extender of U.S. foreign policy concerns.

The big alliance, the one that's been central to U.S. security for 50 years, is NATO—my dad, my son and I are, you know, creatures of NATO. I just spent a very interesting day with ISAF [International Security Assistance Force] in Afghanistan. Is ISAF a Srebeniza in the making? Right now it's just a snapshot of 5,500 NATO forces deployed in Afghanistan. The forces are inadequate; they are the wrong forces, the wrong ROE [rules of engagement]. These are forces that, in many cases, are neither trained nor willing to fight. In addition, there is the political challenge of NATO forces in Afghanistan who hear instructions from their NATO field tactical leadership that they don't like. They go back through national channels, into Brussels, and get new directions issued out of the operating elements. What are we going to do about it? How do we get NATO to work usefully in and out of area operations?

Next question, how do we get the E.U. and NATO to involve compatible, capable missions and capabilities? Depending on whether you want to feel good about the issue or talk rationally about it, you can say that never has the question been more in doubt. How can the OAS [Organization of American States] help with the challenges of the Americas? Eight hundred million people. Our economic, political and social futures are tied up in this hemisphere. And how do you get the OAS or its extensions to deal with the coming end of Cuba? I have it under good information—good authority—that Fidel [Castro] is going to die. Now, people have been saying that for years. He's going to die. We're right on the front end of a major crisis in Cuba that could happen any day and will happen in the next five years. How do we get the OAS to help build Haiti, this poor cesspool of despair and injustice? How do we deal with cocaine and heroin in Latin America and failing expectations of democracy and humanitarian crises?

Next question, how can alliances broker conflicting tensions among China, Japan, the Korean Peninsula and Taiwan? This is an era of enormous importance to us and is fraught with risk. How can alliances be constructed—they don't exist now—to build a blueprint for peace between Israel and the Arabs? Finally, how do alliances work in the next 25 years when the principal tools to establish world stability, peace and justice are no longer military, but are instead other institutions—the FBI; the CIA; customs, dealing with money laundering; [B]ATF [Bureau of Alcohol, Tobacco and Firearms], dealing with gun running; DEA [Drug Enforcement Agency], dealing with drugs, cooperative border patrol, human smuggling, public health and bio warfare. Tommy Thompson [secretary of Health and Human Services] has a bio warfare command center over in HHS [Health and Human Services] of incredible sophistication. And the Coast Guard, the most useful agency in the U.S. government, I sometimes think—thank God for the United

States Coast Guard, its 35,000 people,
its law-enforcement function and its
humanitarian operations. We're in a
different era.

On that note, again, welcome to
the panel. I look forward to hearing
your remarks. Each member will make
remarks one after the other, 15 or 20
minutes, then we'll open it to a dialogue.
Thanks very much to all of you.

AMBASSADOR ROBERT E.
HUNTER, Ph.D.: Mr. Chairman, I
accept your nomination. I have always
wanted to say that. I think it's the closest
I'll ever get.

I very much appreciate your
generous introduction. It reminds me of
something that the late, great secretary
general of NATO, Manfred Worner,
would have said on such an occasion

Robert E. Hunter

about such an introduction: "My father would have been pleased and my mother
would have believed it." It's an honor to be here today with all of these distinguished
people in the audience and with this distinguished panel at this difficult time for
the nation and difficult time for the world. As an American citizen, I just want to
say to all of you out there, thank you. Particularly, given that he's on the panel,
thanks to Barry McCaffrey. Those of us who have followed his career recognize that
he was one of the people who came out of Vietnam where the American military
took a very hard shot from American society for failures that weren't its failures at
all in a difficult time in American history. Barry was one of these people who said,
"Never again would the American military be used that way. Let us reform ourselves.
Let us reform the attitude toward the military. Let us reform the way in which we
use military power." I think what we have seen, particularly in Iraq, twice now in
Afghanistan, and elsewhere, Barry, what you and your generation did. Maybe you
aren't the greatest generation, but by God you're the second greatest generation,
and I want to say thank you to you and everyone like you.

So, ladies and gentlemen, this is the Eisenhower forum and it is a great honor
for me to have a chance to speak at such a forum. Eisenhower was the first supreme
allied commander Europe. Because we weren't going to send that many troops to
Europe, we sent somebody who was a substitute for a lot of troops at that time.
He was a person who represented the very best of America in every way that it
means to be the best of America. He was not just somebody who had led a great
coalition in combat—for freedom, for democracy, for liberation—but somebody

who, in his core of being, brought back to Europe the very finest there is in our country. One likes to believe that we can, in our generation, emulate what Dwight Eisenhower did in Europe and elsewhere. I'm pleased, of course, that it follows on in his own genetic tradition. Susan Eisenhower is out here somewhere. Susan's leadership in this generation follows on as another great American and another great Eisenhower. I hope she won't denounce me afterwards. Which reminds me: I spoke a few years ago in a meeting of graduates from the École Nationale d'Administration—you know, the people who run France. It was in the French Senate, and I thought I would be a little cute by showing what we were doing to get France back into NATO. I quoted some lines from a French president about what had to happen at NATO and what the new French president, Mr. [Jacques] Chirac, was doing to bring this to fulfillment. I said, of course the president I was quoting who set the challenge was General [Charles] de Gaulle [French general during World War II, later French president], and it's been fulfilled. This one tall Frenchman got up afterward and started, in French, denouncing everything that President Chirac was doing. It was incredible. It was blistering. It made today's election campaign in the United States look like a love fest. I was just stunned by this attack on the French president by this individual in the senate for things he had done regarding NATO. I said to my neighbor, "Who is that?" Oh, he said, that's the admiral. I said, "Admiral who?" He said, Admiral [Philippe] de Gaulle, de Gaulle's son. So you have to be a little careful.

Eisenhower gave us leitmotif [dominant theme] for what we have today. One of the things he said, I think, has a lot of truth in it. Plans are nothing. Planning is everything. Of course, he also put that in a somewhat more pithy way for some of us who are in the urban environment. He also said, "Farming looks mighty easy when your plow is a pencil and you're a thousand miles from the cornfield." Only a son of Kansas, perhaps, could have said that. But then he said another admonition that I have to be a little careful with and so, perhaps, does my colleague Jonathan, formerly at RAND. (Formerly at RAND. I have to tell you that there are three institutions that once you have been in you can never get out. One is the Jesuits, the second is the CIA, and the third is the RAND Corporation. So he'll be with us forever.) Eisenhower also said, "An intellectual is a man who takes more words than necessary to tell you more than he knows." So that's my job this morning.

Incidentally, Barry, you said that Castro will, indeed, die sometime. Back when I served in the Carter administration and even earlier than that, it was always about Tito [Josip Broz, Yugoslavia's leader 1945-1980]. Tito, we knew at some point, was going to die, but he didn't. Every single administration—every one from about [Franklin Delano] Roosevelt, when Tito took power, until the time Tito died under Carter—wrote a contingency plan, because Yugoslavia is kind of a difficult thing. I wrote the contingency plan for the early years of the Carter administration, updating it from previous administrations. Then, when I was doing some other work, Tito died, and we couldn't find the contingency plan. We managed, anyway. So there you are. Plans are nothing. Planning is everything.

Europe is still the central alliance for the United States, and thank goodness it did not go out of existence in 1991. There are a lot of people sitting here who understood Voltaire on God—if NATO had not existed, it would have been necessary to invent it. NATO, which carried through after the Cold War, with the United States in the lead, to do what we had done before. With a new vision set forth by [former President] George H.W. Bush in very few words: to create a Europe whole and free. Very simple words, but most of history is about fulfilling the promise that is required by a few simple words. What does it mean? It means to try to abolish history in Europe and to bring a common perspective about security in that part of the world, which alone in just the 20th century accounted for probably half of the people who died in all the wars of human experience. To get to the point of abolishing war as it had been done, with American participation and a lot of leadership in Western Europe, where war has become unthinkable among France, Germany and others. This is a dramatic, remarkable human achievement, and the United States—the American people and the American military—deserves a lot of credit for that. To try to do that across Europe, we stayed engaged, recognizing it was the fourth great task of the 20th century after the First and Second World Wars and the Cold War. During the 1990s, NATO set about the full engagement of America and all the allies, completing what I would call the 20th century agenda: to keep America engaged as a European power to preserve Allied Command Europe, which was and remains the greatest military coalition that has ever existed. Where the 16 countries, now 26, decided that they would see their military affairs and their security in common, and not separately. I think all of them, including our French friends ... whatever we say about them and they about us, they are always there with everybody else when the chips are down. That's one thing we can rely upon. You know the problem with the French—our dealing with the French—is we have never forgiven them for saving our revolution at Yorktown, and they have never forgiven us for D-Day. Maybe someday we will get over that and recognize what we have done together over 200 years and what we'll do in the future.

NATO enlargement took in more countries, but it was part of a much broader element, to try to extend the Europe whole and free. It was to try to create, with remarkable success, a way of engaging countries in the east that had been under the tender mercies of Soviet power and communism. Partnership for Peace; your American Partnership Council; the NATO-Ukraine Council; the Permanent Joint Council with Russia, which is now the NATO-Russia Council; the reform of the NATO command to combine joint task forces; and on and on—these were a package that meant every country in Europe and in North America that decided to work together and build security could move in that particular direction. It was a stunning success. People recognized that in order to be successful, it was necessary to go beyond what had been done in the past, in effect, outside of area. Dick Luger [Republican senator from Indiana] said, "NATO out of area or out of business." I just mentioned Dick Lugar, a Republican senator. One of the great things about NATO is that it has always had bipartisan support. In fact, I would argue that as we go through this campaign season we have to think about the future—that the world does not look at us as Republicans and Democrats. They look at us as Americans. Wherever we come out in this election, once again, we have to have a bipartisan foreign policy. Our military people demand it, and require it and deserve it, and frankly, the nation and the world do as well. We've always had that in NATO.

We recognize that NATO would not be taken seriously unless it went into Bosnia and brought the war to a halt in a 20-day air campaign—and it did just that. Again, three years later in a 78-day campaign, it did just that in Kosovo, which laid the basis for bringing to an end the 20th century. The thing about this particular alliance is that it was not just enough to be a caretaker and to take over and deal with Europe. We had a shock here in this town and in New York and in the western world and, yes, in the world in general on 9/11. We just passed the three-year mark, a three-year understanding that it has had as fundamental and transforming effect upon the world, and certainly our psychology, as did Pearl Harbor. Pearl Harbor ended our sense of isolation in the world; 9/11 has ended our sense of insulation to the world. We are permanently engaged and permanently responsible, not just for homeland security after the first major attack on the lower-48 since August of 1814, but a new responsibility with friends and allies abroad. We must deal with those things at this great moment of history, similar to the great moments in the past.

Dwight Eisenhower himself would have responded today as he did 50 years ago. It would have been done with a lot of people working together. We need the very best. I can't resist, even though I think we're mostly Army here today, something said by Admiral Ernest King, who was brought back to the commander in chief, U.S. (Fleet), after Pearl Harbor. He said, well, you know it's when they get in trouble that they send for us sons of bitches. Well, that's what we need today. We need an all-talents government, all-talents administration. Everyone pulling together just the way we did in the two last great moments of American redefinition, pulling together after Pearl Harbor and at the beginning of the Cold War. We need everybody. We need everybody together and, God willing, we're going to have it once again because we are Americans.

The 21st century agenda began in places like Bosnia and Kosovo; it has now gone to the war on terrorism. We have had extraordinary support from allies just as we have supported them. The day after 9/11, there was the famous Le Monde headline in Paris Nous sommes tous Américains—we are all Americans. In the war on terrorism that sentiment continues, not just because the French recognize that they, too, are vulnerable. It continues not just because they recognize what the United States has done for them in the past, but also this is something we have in common. Unless they would stand with America in our hour of need, could they again rely upon us to stand with them in their hour of need?

NATO declared the first-ever Article 5 invocation on Sept. 12, 2001. We did not take it up—and, frankly, I think that was probably right and proper on our part. We had to get the job done and get it done in a hurry. The American military recreated itself in a moment, was able to do a job nobody thought they were going to have to do and did it in brilliant fashion; and our allies have been with us.

The difficulty, as we know, is not so much with regard to that; it has had to do with the Iraq question. It has had to do with some questions in Europe about whether we will continue the outward-looking perspective that we have had. This question has been raised for some years now. There is some concern about the way in which we presented a doctrine of preemption. Now any country is going to preempt when it has to. My only regret is that talking about it tends not to confound your enemies but frighten your friends. It's like the occasion when a new draft of rather inferior soldiers were sent to the Peninsula War, and Wellington [Arthur Wellesley, Duke of Wellington] wrote back to King George III, "Sire, I'm not so sure whether these troops will scare the enemy, but, by God, they sure scare me." It's the kind of thing we need to set a new pattern because we will preempt or have a preemptive war if we have to, just as anybody else will. The question is getting it right in terms of relations with allies. I do not think there's any point in rehearsing how we got to where we are in Iraq. A lot of brave Americans and others are now fighting and dying to try to preserve what's going on out there, as they are in Afghanistan. The fact is, we are now engaged in the Middle East for the foreseeable future—a generation and more. The old system of security is shattered, and we in our common interest—not just the United States, but also the allies—have to put something in its place. I think we need a new security system for the entire Middle East, so we don't have to be there forever. We don't have to try to be responsible for all that goes on in that area forever. I think we need a new security system and new burst of creativity, the way we had at the founding of NATO. It's going to take a lot of effort, and we cannot do it by ourselves. We can do an awful lot by ourselves in the world. We're the most potent force in every dimension of power in living memory and maybe, as some people say, since the collapse of the Roman Empire. Right now, if you add in the Iraq money, we are now spending on military affairs more than 50 percent of all that's being spent in the world. But, we, the American people; we, the American military; we, the western alliance, understand that if you're going to do it right, you do it with others because we're in it together. And if you want the support of the American people you do need to reach out to others. You need to put it on a bipartisan basis. You do need to get others to be engaged because only part of the task is military, certainly in terrorism and also elsewhere in the Middle East. Somebody said a few years ago that the terrorism task is only about 10 percent military, and it's 90 percent other things, and he is the secretary of defense. We need to reach out. They, the Europeans, need to reach out, and we need to do it together.

Now, what is the good news? The good news is that NATO has gone through another transformation, under allied command transformation, under the Supreme Allied Commander Europe, where we continue to have among the finest of the American military who are not actually in combat and serving in NATO. There is another transformation of NATO, as during the 1990s, to be able to do the tasks of the future. If you haven't seen it, go to NATO, watch what's happening, and watch the esprit within that institution. There's no mud-slinging there. There's no name-calling. It's getting on with the common job, just as in the past. Now I would say NATO is ready and able, but not yet necessarily willing, and that's the task of our political leadership. There's also no longer a debate about being outside of area. NATO, as Barry has already said, is in charge in Afghanistan, not just the U.S.-led fighting piece, which includes the French and others on the pointy end of the stick, but also the ISAF, a NATO-run force. Let me underscore one thing. The number one responsibility of NATO and the alliance is to get that right. NATO has never failed, and Afghanistan must not be the first place. We all have to work together on that.

We also have good news that the European community, the European Union, has now adopted a paper done by its secretary general, Mr. Solana, who will be the foreign minister, who used to be NATO secretary general. What are the priorities they've set down? Number one, terrorism. Number two, rogue states. Number three, weapons of mass destruction. Number four, crime. Et cetera. This is the same agenda we would probably have. Maybe we still have some differences about how it's to be done, but we're in there together and we're going to be in the Middle East to stay.

Now what's problematic is capabilities on the part of the Europeans. They don't spend enough money. They don't spend enough money, and they don't spend it on the right things. They are going to have to spend it on the right things. The right things are not to try to do everything across the board; it is being able to interoperate with good C4ISR [command, control, communications, computers, information, surveillance, reconnaissance]. We're left with sustainability, with good command and control and with a good understanding of our central purposes. An awful lot has to be done.

We're working now on repositioning the U.S. forces. We need to do that right. We must understand the need to have a lot of American forces deployed abroad in order to build the kind of relationships you need so that, if you have to deploy forces from the United States, you're going to have a welcome reception. That's one of the great secrets of NATO throughout its history and will continue to be in the future.

One thing we also have to recognize is, we ask the Europeans to recognize that they have to be in this with us. If we're going to ask others to share risk and responsibility, we have to be willing to share influence and decisions. We're going to have to take those decisions together in our common interest to a common purpose, preferably within the NATO framework, and also from time to time on a bilateral framework. We can't just write the strategy here and ask others to write the checks. I think we'll be surprised that there is a tremendous degree of common understanding about the threats, challenges and opportunities, and also what we need to do and when, if we will reach back to where we were 40 years ago and come together as we were.

We also have to understand something else. The heart of the alliance is not just about common interests, but common values, common perspectives and common human understanding. We have to understand that there are growing pains in every alliance, as there are in NATO today. Let us recognize that the experiment in trying to do more by ourselves than we needed to is leading us to a lesson that, once again, doing it with others and getting them to respond is the nature of the future.

Three things Dwight Eisenhower said, I think, illustrate this. First, "Whatever America hopes to bring to pass in the world must first come to pass in the heart of America." Second, what we are and what we stand for and what we project continues to be the "be all and end all" of getting others to do it with us. Third, "Peace and justice are two sides of the same coin." What we do with the Europeans and with others in a new strategic partnership to build relations with our allies in the Middle East and elsewhere is going to be the key to the future and to validating and supporting what we do militarily. Finally Eisenhower said then, and, I believe, would say again today, "History does not long entrust the care of freedom to the weak or the timid." Well, I see in front of me the strong and the brave. This is what America is all about, and this is why this century is going to be as successful as we made the end of the last century.

Thank you.

JONATHAN D. POLLACK, Ph.D.: Well, thank you, very much, General McCaffrey, for your kind words of introduction, and let me convey my appreciation, as well, to the Eisenhower National Security Conference for the opportunity to speak to this distinguished gathering. Let me emphasize that my remarks today are my personal opinions, not those of the Naval War College or the U.S. government.

America's strategic destinies have been intertwined with the Asia-Pacific region for more than a century. The character of America's connections with East Asia is changing profoundly with our traditional allies, with regional friends, with major powers and with our adversaries. The past patterns of American political-military predominance and the singularity of American power are now changing, in some ways naturally and quite congenially, and in other ways in a less favorable fashion. The issues we face are to rebalance our central requirements, as the title there shows; to recalibrate our relations with regional states; and to see whether there is a practicable coalition strategy to supplant previous policies. Then, we must assess what the implications might be for American interests if a reconstituted strategy does not prove feasible, or if it fails to anticipate potential crises or challenges that might confront us in the region. These emerging challenges occur against the backdrop of extraordinary changes in U.S. national security strategy to which Bob Hunter has already alluded. Without question, America's preoccupations with Islamic radicalism and the ongoing struggles in Iraq and Afghanistan have shifted our attention away from our long-standing focus on East Asia and Northeast Asia in particular, notwithstanding the resumption of North Korea's nuclear weapons activities, to which I will return later.

Jonathan D. Pollack

Let me lay out three areas that I'll try to talk about today. First, I want to characterize what I see as the shifting center of strategic gravity that is evident across East Asia, with particular reference to China. Second, I'm going to examine some of the internal political factors that are redefining our principal bilateral alliances and review some of the changes that are underway in the U.S.-Korean alliance, as it is an especially relevant example. Third, I want to talk a bit about how American strategy itself is being redefined across East Asia, in the aftermath of 9/11, and what these shifts seem to portend for our future regional military presence, our regional security goals and our expectations of security partners.

Let me begin with the big strategic transition and China's role in it. It has become a truism that to understand what is happening in East Asia, we need to begin with what is happening in China. I don't disagree with that proposition. Let's look at some basic facts. China's policy of reform and opening to the outside world, as it is called, is now a quarter-century old. It is not new. It is not transitory. It is manifesting itself in a profound societal and institutional transformation within China, especially in the more developed coastal regions. Over the past decade, China has emerged as one of the world's leading trading states. A more confident nationalism has emerged among the elites and the politically attentive public of China. The country is ever-more enmeshed with global and regional institutions. Last and by no means least, the indications of a modernized military are increasingly evident with China beginning to develop a more capable military force that is relevant beyond the mainland of Asia.

In a word, China is now an arrived regional power. This is a change of strategic consequence. Though this transition process within China and between China and its neighbors is fraught with uncertainties and potential risks, the primacy of China's development goals and Beijing's incentives for accommodation with neighboring states are self-evident. This also redefines American strategic options. During the 2000 presidential campaign and in the earliest months of the Bush administration, senior U.S. officials, including the president himself, characterized China as a "strategic competitor and a presumptive challenger to U.S. predominance." These judgments have since subsided as leaders on both sides sought to collaborate in the aftermath of 9/11. I would not want to characterize U.S.-China relations as smooth sailing; far from it. But the Sino-American accommodation in recent years is beyond dispute. For those who might still be tempted to somehow shoehorn China into an older template, as a latter-day, more economically robust Soviet Union, let me emphasize there are no takers for a containment strategy in East Asia—not in Korea, not in Australia, not in South East Asia, not in India, not in Japan and not even in Taiwan. All recognize China's ever-growing economic and political weight. All recognize that there is no way to stigmatize or singularize China. All, even those most wary of China's growing power, seek normal relations with Beijing. All also recognize that if China is outside the emergent regional security order, then such an order will not be viable.

China is the only regional power with meaningful security involvement in all four of Asia's major subregions: Northeast Asia, Southeast Asia, South Asia and Central Asia. Its increasingly confident and collaborative diplomacy is remarked upon across the region. In the context of the protracted North Korean nuclear crisis, its role is essentially important to the United States, as well. We, therefore, have an inherent interest in cultivating and realizing a stable, amicable relationship with China, for the simple reason that there is no realistic alternative. Perhaps later we can return to whether and how China and the United States can avoid a major crisis either over Taiwan or potentially over Korea, and also questions of how we might avoid rivalry that compel various states to choose sides. Suffice it to say that neither is a possibility we should seek or one that we should welcome.

Let me turn next to the future of America's regional alliances. Unlike in Europe, as we all know, the United States never had a multinational alliance structure in the Asia-Pacific region. The alliances that have endured in this region were bilateral; each configured to the specific security circumstances that mandated their creation. So the alliance bargains for the most part here were highly asymmetrical. The United States dominated and others followed, if not always eagerly. This dynamic has now changed irrevocably. I would characterize the pivotal internal changes that we witness as the three Ds: development, democratization, and demilitarization. Our regional partners, even those with deep commitments and close ties to the United States, have ideas and interests of their own. The challenge for them and for us is whether we can jointly recraft our mutual alliance bargains, thereby keeping these ties viable and of mutual benefit in the decades to come. Though the prospects vary from case to case, I would not want to be breezily optimistic about the prospects. Let me illustrate this by focusing on the U.S.-Korean alliance, where change has been especially marked. I will draw on some of the results from a recent conference I convened at the Naval War College on Korea's future. The conference included some of the Republic of Korea's leading younger scholars, as well as other very prominent analysts from across East Asia and the United States. It seemed incontestable to me, in the context of this conference, that the ground is truly shifting on the Korean Peninsula.

A few conclusions from our proceedings are especially relevant. First, the most important changes on the peninsula are those occurring in the Republic of Korea

[ROK], not those occurring in the Democratic People's Republic of Korea—North Korea, that is. There is an extraordinary internal political realignment underway in the south, manifested along generational lines. The differences in attitude are stark, with pronounced cleavages between those basically in their 30s, and those who came to prominence at an earlier point in Korea's history—those in their 50s and 60s. These changes are manifested on a wide range of issues of political identity, issues including policies and threat assessments towards North Korea, ROK defense policy, relations with China, and the future of the U.S.-ROK alliance. Though there is certainly widespread support for maintaining the alliance, support is much more pronounced and unconditional among older generations. Periodic outbursts of anti-American sentiment have generally occurred in response to specific incidents involving U.S. personnel, but they also highlight an intense, if frequently submerged, set of grievances against the United States. The alliance asymmetries are, thus, a potent and growing force in Korean domestic politics.

Looking ahead, the future prospects of the alliance are far from ensured. There is a compelling need for a credible strategic concept and rationale to shape future alliance ties. Deterrence and containment of North Korea, though still essential to alliance planning, is no longer enough, either for the United States or for South Korea. But ROK planners seem quite wary of a more regional concept of the alliance that the United States appears to favor. It is possible that the U.S. encouraging the ROK to pursue the long-term goal of a more self-reliant defense can bridge some of these looming differences. This would involve a reduced U.S. footprint on the Korean Peninsula and revised command arrangements as both sides test the feasibility of a redefined alliance bargain for the 21st century. But neither side will get there if we fail to be attentive to the expectations of a very different Korean society and political system, and if both sides shy away from a deeper strategic conversation on their mutual needs and expectations. In the absence of such a dialogue, the alliance would drift and decline, especially as the United States proceeds with its announced troop withdrawals from the peninsula, to which I will return momentarily. This could lead to an ever-diminishing U.S. pride of place in Korean eyes, something that we should not welcome for reasons that are only too obvious to enumerate.

Finally, let me turn to future American regional defense strategy. In June of this year, officials from the Department of Defense [DoD] visited South Korea and announced that the United States would withdraw approximately 12,500 troops stationed on the Korean Peninsula by the end of 2005. This is, in absolute terms, about one-third of the forces on the peninsula, but in terms of combat capabilities—ground in particular—I think it is a much larger share. These are the largest personnel reductions on the peninsula since 1992 and take place after a year of often-contentious negotiations between Washington and Seoul on U.S. plans to relocate U.S. ground force units from areas north of Seoul to areas well south of Seoul, mainly near Osan. It has also followed the decision announced in May of this year to reassign the Second Brigade of the Second Infantry Division to Iraq, a move that took place without elaborate fanfare last month. Thus, even amidst the protracted and still wholly unresolved North Korean nuclear weapons crisis, the Bush administration seems determined to move toward a very different mix of forces on the peninsula, which also presages, I believe, a larger realignment of U.S. regional defense strategy in the years to come. There is little doubt that the Iraqi insurgency was among the triggers necessitating these moves, but it is also linked to the global posture review that is underway within DoD. In my view, short of major hostilities on the peninsula, and perhaps not even then, it is virtually inconceivable that these forces will return to the Korean Peninsula.

The Defense Department deems the current configuration of U.S. forces a leftover of the Cold War that it believes is increasingly irrelevant to future regional security requirements and to potential contingencies on the peninsula. There is an indisputable logic to much of what DoD is conveying. In the department's view, the United States can ill afford open-ended static deployments in locales geographically remote from far more pressing concerns in service of a defense strategy that presumes a repeat of the Korean War of 1950 to 1953. DoD argues that North Korea can be deterred by the U.S. capability to bring overwhelming lethal force to bear in a crisis, primarily long-range air and naval power, Marine Corps brigades and presumably some ballistic missile defense assets. The United States has, thus, concluded that there is a different way to fight in Korea, if we have to fight, as well as elsewhere. In this alternative view, American forces must become much more agile and flexible, with the remaining U.S. forces in Korea presumably geared to a range of regional contingencies that are, as yet, unspecified. Defense officials argue that even at diminished numbers there will be no diminution of combat capability or commitment.

Now, to the Koreans, and also in a certain sense to the Japanese, both for whom history and symbolism matter very deeply, simple assurances may be less than wholly persuasive. Movement to a more hub concept in Korea and elsewhere redefines the basis of regional defense strategy. The major augmentation of U.S. long-range air power and increased submarine deployments planned for Guam are occurring simultaneously with these withdrawals, underscoring the shift away from a predominant strategic orientation toward Northeast Asia. If anything, a future rationalization of U.S. command relationships in the Pacific may find the United States moving more fully to a regional maritime strategy centered very much on Japan. Other emergent trends highlight this: notably, the 7th Fleet's increased responsibilities for missile defense in the Sea of Japan; the predominantly maritime thrust of the Proliferation Security Initiative, again presumably oriented heavily against North Korea; and proposals from the Pacific Command for a regional maritime security initiative geared heavily toward Southeast Asia, where there are obvious terrorist threats.

All these concepts, of course, are not fully fleshed out. They're barely fleshed out, I would argue. The membership roster on some of these initiatives seems quite narrow. For example, the Asia-Pacific region members of the Proliferation Security

Initiative total three—Australia, Japan and Singapore, the three states most closely identified with U.S. regional defense strategy. Should we expect these activities to supplant previous security arrangements? It's a question we need to consider carefully. Unless and until regional arrangements are more inclusive, their strategic utility may prove fleeting and constrained, though geared obviously to critical security requirements and contingencies.

Is there a place for regional partnerships, independent of specific roles and missions, advocated by the United States? How do Russia and China fit into these concepts, if at all? Will our military posture in the region be ever more contingency-driven? Is there a common concept of threats and interests? Indeed, where and how does this concern over Taiwan fit into these new strategies? Is there an implication with respect to North Korea that we now need to plan on the assumption that North Korean missiles, and even nuclear weapons, are now a given in the strategic landscape?

For now, these are questions that remain less than fully examined, but warrant our urgent attention. They are missing in major U.S. strategy documents, but they need that kind of elaboration, clarification and discussion with our regional partners if the changes in the U.S. strategy are to be viable and credible, not only to ourselves but to East Asia as a whole.

Thank you, very much.

JOHN H. SANDROCK: I, too, would like to thank General McCaffrey for his very kind remarks. He mentioned that I was going to bat cleanup. Actually, I feel a little bit more like a utility infielder.

Your program says that Dr. Krishnamurthy Santanam was supposed to be the speaker here to talk about South and Central Asia. I found out in an e-mail on Sunday morning—that's the day before yesterday—that he could not come. There were probably a couple of reasons for that. The most immediate was that he couldn't get a visa in time. Whether this can be attributed to our security concerns and the normal delay for travel, particularly for foreign visitors, is unclear. It also may be that he simply waited a bit too long to apply for one. So, in any case, I'm here really as a last-minute fill-in. The remarks that I'm going to make are mine. They're not his. He did not send me his notes, although perhaps I wish he would have. You will hear from me, and these are my thoughts and my impressions based on several years in the region and my experiences over the last 30-odd years.

Before I get started with my remarks, General McCaffrey noted that I spent five months in Baghdad last year. I'm an Air Force guy. I graduated from the Air Force in 1992. I was in for 26 years. I enjoyed my career greatly and I've enjoyed my life ever since. But I wanted to tell you—most of you who are representative of the Army—I have worked with the Army throughout my entire career, in one fashion or another. I have never seen a finer set of troops, both men and women, than I saw in Iraq during my five months there. I had the opportunity to travel throughout Iraq. I saw them in Mosul; I saw them in Kirkuk. I saw them in camps and, of course, I saw them in

Baghdad. They're magnificent people.
Kind of chokes me up.

Few events in our history have had
such a profound effect on United States
security and foreign policy as the attacks
on 9/11. Aside from within the United
States itself, nowhere has the impact of
9/11 been of greater significance than
in the region I'll discuss today. But to
understand where we are today and
to consider where our alliances and
friendships might be in five to 10 years,
I think it's worthwhile to take a moment
to reflect on the rich history of this
region. I think we're so caught up in the
day-to-day events and the bad news that
we forget that this has been a very active
area and very important historically.

The nomadic tribes that inhabited
much of central Asia were conquered
by Alexander's armies and suffered

John H. Sandrock

invasions by Genghis Kahn and Tamerlane. Long before the Soviet invasion in
1979 and our own military action in 2001, Afghanistan was known as a crossroad
of conquerors. Rudyard Kipling saw the region as the focus of the Great Game
between the Russian and British empires. Most in this audience will recognize the
name Kandahar [Afghanistan]. It's been in the news often. What some may not
know is that Alexander the Great built the original city and that its name is derived
from Iskandar, which is a Persian version of Alexander. The city of Balkh, just west
of the Afghan city of Mazar-e-Sharif, was the legendary birthplace of Zoroaster and
became a major stop on the Silk Road and major center of learning. It was called the
Mother of Cities. Kabul was the birthplace of India's Moghul Empire and the base
of one of the major Muslim invasions of the subcontinent led by somebody named
Babar the Great. Babar's tomb is in Kabul. He asked to be buried there after he died
in India. Babar was the great-grandson of Tamerlane and became the first Moghul
emperor. He extended Muslim dominance throughout much of the subcontinent
and it was there the Moghul Empire existed until the British took over and made
it the jewel in the crown of their empire. In more recent times the British fought
three—one must say unsuccessful—wars with the Afghans, with the last one in
1919 resulting in total Afghan independence. On the subcontinent, the British
finally relinquished their colonial hold in 1947, giving birth to India and Pakistan,
both of which figure very prominently in what we're doing today. It's important to
recognize, in that context, that neither India nor Pakistan existed as independent
political entities in their current form or dimension prior to 1947.

We also must be aware that the nations of Central Asia—Kazakhstan, Kyrgyzstan, Tajikistan, Turkmenistan and Uzbekistan—all of which I have had the opportunity to visit and spend some time in, have enjoyed their independence only since the demise of the Soviet Union in 1991. Prior to their incorporation in the Russian Empire and then the Soviet Union, which was not completed until the 1930s, none of these states existed as independent political entities. Thus, in a very real sense, their current political systems, their ideas of democracy, their conception of democracy and their world view have a brief history of only about a dozen years. I think we tend to forget that every once in a while.

From a U.S. perspective, we didn't just discover the region on 9/11, after 9/11 or, more precisely, after the U.S. decision to eliminate the base of terrorism in Afghanistan by defeating the Taliban. During the 1950s and 1960s, Pakistan had been a member of the Baghdad Pact, which later became known as the Central Treaty Organization, and it was also a member of the Southeast Asia Treaty Organization. Although these alliances were not particularly successful, they were a phenomenon of the Cold War. In addition, the United States had concluded bilateral security arrangements with Pakistan. I trust many of you remember the name Francis Gary Powers, but may have forgotten or perhaps not known that his famous 1960 U-2 flight over the Soviet Union, which brought considerable embarrassment to the Eisenhower administration, began in Peshawar, Pakistan. That was the launch point. We had a U.S. Air Force base in Peshawar until 1965. So, indeed, Pakistan was a key component of U.S. efforts to contain the Soviet Union throughout much of the Cold War.

India, on the other hand, with its policies of neutrality and self-reliance instituted by its two most important political leaders, Jawaharlal Nehru and Mohandas Gandhi, sought to maintain a strict policy of nonalignment. India was more or less successful in this policy, although it became heavily reliant on the Soviet Union for advanced military equipment and as a trading partner. For much of the history over the last 10, 15 years or so, or prior to the fall of the Soviet Union, we followed the policy of "if you're not our friend, you must not be [neutral]." We didn't understand neutrality. I think the real misconception about our relationship with India for many years during that period was that they were, somehow, against us. Their voting record in the U.N. didn't help that perception particularly, but, happily, that has changed, and I'll talk about that a little bit more in a couple of minutes. India was also, of course, one of the original cofounders of the nonaligned movement, as was Afghanistan.

So let me turn to Afghanistan for a couple of minutes because I think it's on everyone's mind. We're still very concerned about Afghanistan. The Afghan king, Zahir Shah, and his prime minister, Muhammad Daoud, first approached the United States with a request for military and economic assistance in the mid-1950s. Though we refused to provide the requested military aid, we did engage in large economic development programs. These included, among other projects, the construction of a series of dams in the Helmand Valley; the construction in the

Kandahar airport, which we're using considerably right now, and the construction of modern highways from Kabul to Kandahar and to the Afghan border with Pakistan. I think we just completed reconstructing part of those roads that were originally built in the 1950s and early 1960s. For military assistance, Afghanistan turned to a more willing Soviet Union, which in 1956 began equipping and training Afghan military forces. I could outline the rest of the history of the region from the early 1960s to today, but, in the interest of time, I'll close this portion of my presentation by saying that the situation in which we find ourselves today had its origins in the Cold War and the decisions we and others made in the 1950s and 1960s.

So, where are we today? The global war on terrorism was forced on the United States in New York City, Washington, D.C., and in a lonely field in central Pennsylvania. Our effort to prosecute the conflict began at home and in Afghanistan and continues in many other parts of world. Ambassador Hunter has already mentioned that NATO, our most important and longest-standing alliance, invoked Article 5 of the North Atlantic Treaty for the first time in its history immediately after the 9/11 attacks. This was in recognition of the basic NATO principle that an attack on one NATO member is an attack on all. In Afghanistan, NATO has taken responsibility for the International Security Assistance Force and has a full and active part in promoting peace and stability in this troubled nation that has been at war since the communist coup in April 1978. Most of us think of the war in Afghanistan starting with the Soviet invasion, which started Christmas Day 1979, but I had a front-row seat in April 1978. I was at the U.S. Embassy at that time and watched the attack on the presidential palace. I watched the MiG-21s [Soviet-built jet "Fishbed"] and the Su-7s [Soviet-built ground-attack aircraft "Fitter-A"] bombing the palace. My house had five bullet holes in it and three shattered windows. I'll never forget Ambassador Ted Eliot [former U.S. ambassador to Afghanistan]. He and I were standing next to each other at the top of the embassy, watching the air strikes coming in and he made a very impassioned remark. He said, "This poor Afghanistan. It's struggling so hard to get out of the 19th century and it's bombing itself back to the 15th century." That was absolutely an accurate assessment. We are in the process of trying to help it regain its proper role and hopefully a much brighter future.

All right. More specific to the region and the center of my presentation, we have also reinvigorated our alliance with Pakistan. We have forged new relations with several of the nations in Central Asia, especially with Uzbekistan, Kyrgyzstan, and Tajikistan, and we have received important assistance and cooperation from several others in the region including India, Georgia, and Azerbaijan. Beyond the recognition that these relationships were and are necessary to the immediate prosecution of the global war on terrorism, we have become increasingly conscious of the need to forge more lasting ties with all of the countries in the region.

So let me turn to a brief consideration of the future for our alliances and franchise on a country-by-country basis. I'll start with South Asia, and then consider the countries—briefly consider the countries—of Central Asia, and conclude with a few remarks about the south Caucuses region.

India, I already mentioned. Today relations with India have been and will continue to be good, although they can never be taken for granted. I think India has to figure into and take a much more prominent role in our considerations in the future. While perhaps not the most important nation in the war on terrorism at the moment, India is the most important country in the region. With more than 1.3 million men under arms, a demonstrated nuclear-weapons capability, and both short- and intermediate-range ballistic missiles already in or soon to be incorporated into their arsenal, India is one of the most capable military powers in a tier second only to the United States. Its citizens, who now number in excess of one billion, enjoy a growing economy and rapidly expanding international trade. On that, I just want to make a parenthetical comment. We hear about outsourcing. I think one of the biggest mistakes we could make is to stop outsourcing to countries like India. It's helping them tremendously and eventually that will help us as well.

As a result of its security concerns, India has important national interests that extend throughout the entire region. We can work with those interests, we can understand their interests, and we can work together in achieving both our interests and theirs, but it has to be in a systematic fashion, and in a friendly fashion open to dialogue. The major security challenge that India has is Pakistan, which, of course, is one of our most important and closest allies in the struggle against terrorism. The confrontation between India and Pakistan has continued since both nations won their independence from Great Britain in 1947. Three wars and numerous confrontations later, the fundamental issues of this confrontation continue to confound and defy resolution, although the just-concluded round of bilateral meetings at the foreign minister level made some progress, and both sides pledged to continue the dialogue.

I won't go into the issues that divide India and Pakistan, but they really are pretty basic. We, happily, have stayed out of the confrontation. In fact, a major success of the U.S. foreign policy has been the maintenance of good relations between India and Pakistan. Although it's sometimes been quite difficult, the United States has been largely successful in encouraging both sides that their confrontation over Kashmir and other issues is best settled peacefully by the contending parties. I think we've always been willing to play a helpful role, but our position has been absolutely correct that we should not mix into something unless we're invited to do so. The difficulties between India and Pakistan, particularly over Kashmir, need to be resolved by them. The challenge for the United States will be continuing to strengthen its friendship with India, while we also assist Pakistan in improving its military capability to deal with its troubled northwest frontier, which has become a major battleground in the war on terrorism. The potential complicating factor in U.S. relations with India may be the just-completed change in administrations there. To the surprise of most observers of Indian politics, and to India's two major political coalitions, one that is led by the Bharatiya Janata Party, or the BJP, and the other led by the Congress Party, the Congress Party prevailed and formed a new government under Prime Minister Manmohan Singh.

The short- and longer-term implications of this change in government, vis-a-vis the United States, are yet to be determined, although significant change of bilateral relationships is unlikely. What is likely is that India will continue to play a very important and constructive role in world affairs, and, while it may not always agree with U.S. policies, it is unlikely to oppose them in a manner that would be considered unacceptable to the United States. What is also likely is that India's voice in international organizations will become increasingly important, particularly in the United Nations. Close bilateral consultations between India and the United States on common actions in the war on terrorism and other matters that both consider important to their national security and economic interests will be key to ensuring a very positive and productive relationship. I'm very optimistic about our relations with India, not only because I like the Indians—I deliberately avoided putting this in my prepared remarks—but India claims, and justifiably, it's the largest democracy in the world. And it's true. I was always a little bit jaundiced about this, because I wasn't sure their democracy really worked the way it does here in the United States. But I think this last election really proved that democracy does work in India. The fact that the Congress Party won, as I mentioned, came as a surprise to everyone. I think this is a very positive development.

Let me turn to Pakistan for a couple of moments. As I already indicated, as we all well know, Pakistan plays a key role in the global war on terrorism. President Pervez Musharraf and his government have proved that Pakistan is a reliable and willing ally in dealing with some of the most difficult challenges encountered since the United States' decision to eliminate the Taliban regime in Afghanistan. Without going over the historical reasons, it must be understood that the border regions adjacent to Afghanistan have been largely autonomous and have never been under the full control of the government in Islamabad. The British were never able to control the northwest frontier area of Pakistan. The Pakistanis haven't been able to do it either. So, one should not be surprised that the Pakistani army has difficulty in projecting power any place along the Afghan-Pakistan border. It's an extremely rugged area. I have driven through parts of it, and it is just a very, very difficult area to operate in—militarily and otherwise. The political authority in this region has always been very tenuous from the central government's point of view.

Pakistan's efforts to root out and defeat the remaining support of al Qaeda and the Taliban at the frontier regions have been undertaken clearly with considerable political risk and certainly not without casualties. Pakistan's government faces substantial internal dissent, and much of the population appears to be opposed to the government's support of U.S. operations, not only in Afghanistan, but also in Iraq. Therefore, the United States must do all it can to support Pakistan and recognize the principled and very supportive stand it has taken. In other words, the longer-term relationship between the United States and Pakistan will depend greatly on U.S. actions and our ability to assist Afghanistan in becoming a stable government and society. As far as Pakistan is concerned, the United States must be a true friend and a steadfast friend—unfortunately, that has not always been the case in the past. I think we have to keep a consistent policy and remember where we are in Pakistan. Our interests are great there.

I only want to talk very briefly about one other aspect of Afghanistan. Ambassador Robert Oakley recently noted, "To appreciate Afghanistan's predicament, it is essential to understand that all Afghan politics are tribal. Thus, while Afghans share a genuine national identity, their immediate concern in any political process is to advance or preserve the welfare of their ethnic or extended family group." The important lesson here is that if you, a foreigner, will ask an Afghan who he is, he will tell you he is an Afghan. But to other Afghans he defines himself in much different terms, such as Pashtun, Tajik, Hazarah, Uzbek, Eimak and so forth. If you dig a bit more deeply, he may be a Gilzai, Durani, Mongol, or Jaji, or one of many other smaller layers in the ethnic strata of Afghan society. That's not to mention, also, the fundamental difference between the Shias and the Sunnis, which are also in the mix.

I'll conclude my remarks by just touching on Central Asia. Central Asia is a very important area for us as well. The relationship I want to mention in particular is with Uzbekistan. Uzbekistan has been very helpful. I'm optimistic with all the countries in the region—Uzbekistan, Tajikistan, and Kyrgyzstan—which have been very helpful. All have supported the war on terrorism. They are all members of the Partnership for Peace. I think we need to develop these relationships and strengthen them. The same goes for the South Caucuses region. Given our time, I would be happy to answer any questions that someone may have on either the Central Asia or the South Caucuses area.

With that, thank you very much.

McCAFFREY: Let me thank all three of the panelists, who provided very useful and informative comments. Perhaps we could open the floor now and have an opportunity for you to voice your own interests and pose questions. If you don't direct the question to a particular panel member, you're welcome just to make a comment, then we'll try and sort it out collectively up here.

HUNTER: If Admiral De Gaulle is here, he can make a statement, all right.

McCAFFREY: Here in the front, yes, sir.

AUDIENCE: Professor Pollack, here in the front row. Excuse me for not standing. I'm a civilian with the Department of the Army. You've teased us a little bit with China. I look at many of these general officers here and I say, well, over the next three, four or five years they'll turn over and go onto their next careers. But there are also officers here who may be captains and majors. I think, having participated in the Iraq process myself and having been over there, I'm fond of telling my children, "We dealt with the Middle East, but you guys will deal with China." I wonder if you could go a little deeper below the surface. What do we need to do to prepare? What types of conflicts do you think we'll face in the future, and how is the military going to play a role in that?

POLLACK: You have answered your own question. If the presumption is that we now better turn our attention precisely to those kinds of preparations, in whatever form they might take, you are presuming a predominantly adversarial relationship with China, which I don't see as impossible, but I don't see it as inevitable either.

It seems to me that the challenge with China is to be respectful of what I'll call Chinese patriotism or Chinese nationalism, recognizing it's not the kind of political system any of us would necessarily want to live under. This system is profoundly more open, profoundly more tolerant and flexible than it was not so many years ago. The other thing I would emphasize is that China's development of its military capabilities, in many respects, is long overdue. China is a country with significant capabilities as a land power, China is, of course, a growing maritime power. Given China's energy dependence and range of maritime interests, it shouldn't really surprise us that the Chinese want a voice and a vote in that process. So, it seems to me that we need to take China very seriously. That's obviously the case. I'm not arguing that we should necessarily assume that our relationship will be stable. But I would see the possibilities here, barring a major crisis over Taiwan, as really quite favorable.

The challenge, it seems to me, is very much how we address the question of Taiwan. One of the paradoxes of dealing with China is that here is a country with which we now, depending on how you measure it, run a trade relationship of about $175 billion a year. We have a major corporate presence there. The omnipresence of Chinese goods and so forth is here. Yet, at the same time, both sides do significant planning against the possibility that they may yet find themselves in a situation of significant confrontation and potentially overt crisis.

I think we ought to be able to do better at that, in the sense that, if we take China seriously and if they take us seriously, you've got ways that avoid the slippery slope heading you into a long-term rivalry. My emphasis today was very much on how the meaning of China has changed to the region. You can highlight the areas where there are clearly divergent American and Chinese interests, particularly over maritime issues. But Americans seem not to have an appreciation of the skill with which China has diversified its relationships with its neighbors and the degree to which they're economically enmeshed with all of its neighbors. So we need to be prudent with China. I wouldn't want to exaggerate its military reach, but I would highlight that Taiwan is still an enormously vexing issue in which neither they nor we have any possible, remote interest in seeing this situation spiral out of control. That's going to take, I think, considerable effort on our part—political planning and prudent military planning—clarifying as much as possible with the Chinese leadership what the stakes and the risks are, to see if we can avoid that kind of test of wills.

HUNTER: If I may add just one word to that, as kind of as a tease, here. I would argue that in the next 20 or 25 years, the most important geopolitical problem or concern that we will have is the future of China—the role it will play in the world and the nature of its relationship with us. We haven't even begun to work on that. Among other things, even today, we are taking responsibility for protecting the flow of oil to China. They're getting a free ride, in some ways, in the structuring of the outside world. In fact, if I were a Chinese planner, I would sit back in Beijing right now in a very smug way and say, "Here is the United States off doing our dirty work, among other things, because we have a terrorism problem, and we have an energy problem in the Middle East. We're able to sit here and run 8 percent or 10 percent in national growth and not have to spend so much money on chasing around the world. That sounds like a pretty good deal for us." So I think we're going to have to get on this sooner rather than later.

McCAFFREY: I think Dr. Pollack's remarks are right on the money. I spent several days wandering around China and listening to the government leadership in Beijing in 2001. The other question that struck me was who, if anybody, is in charge and who will be in charge 10 years from now? There is a good argument that the enormous outbursts and creativity in the economic realm in China is unguided by any human hand. The instruments of national power, one could argue, are no longer under firm centralized control, which is either an opportunity or problem, depending upon your perspective. It was a great question.

Next. Yes, sir. Up here.

AUDIENCE: I'm Bernard Brown from the National Committee on American Foreign Policy and a professor of political science at CUNY [City University of New York]. I have a question for Ambassador Hunter. The European Union is now trying to create a common foreign and security policy and an autonomous defense. General Meigs made the interesting comment this morning that the United States does not have a seat at the table in the European Union. Europeans have a seat at the table in NATO, but the Americans don't have a seat at the table in the European Union. What is your comment on that, and what is your own view of the relationship between the growing European Defense Force and NATO? What will be the consequences for NATO?

HUNTER: Well, thank you for your question. As the person who negotiated for the United States and at NATO, I never quite understood why anybody at NATO is worried about what's called the European Security and Defense Policy, or ESDP. We, the United States—we, NATO—continue to be the 800-pound gorilla and are going to continue to be in the future. We have the integrated command system. We have the place to which every ally looks in the first, second and third instance to be able to do the heavy lifting. ESDP and the common foreign security policy are about the overall creation of a unified European Union over time. The last thing these countries will ever see is the right of any large or super nation to decide whether their young men and women will put their lives at risk. Now, I look at it positively, provided that there's no European coalition at NATO that will decide if the E.U. says it will, and, frankly, we can crack that any time we want. People aren't going to do that if it means driving America away. As long as the planning is transparent and is integrated with NATO, which it is, I don't see a problem. Incidentally, the at least nominal commander of the forces under the so-called Rapid Reaction Force, the high-level task force that's being powered by the European Union, is the deputy supreme allied commander Europe. If that happens and leads to Europeans spending more on defense because they want to do it for E.U. reasons, and if it leads them to be willing to do what they're now doing in Bosnia—taking over for us at NATO, taking the first actions in Macedonia—that's all a gain for us. I've never quite understood why we worry about this. It's like when they were going to set up the planning staff in a barracks in a place called Ganshoren, which is a suburb of Brussels, and my line on that was very simple: If NATO is going to be threatened by 50 men and a dog, we might as well get out of the NATO business. That's nonsense.

McCAFFREY: All the way in the back. Yes, ma'am.

AUDIENCE: My question is for Dr. Pollack. There has been recent debate about whether or not a unified Korea is in America's interest or if a divided Korea serves as a rationale for a U.S. presence—either symbolically or physically—when it comes to national security and maintaining the U.S.-Korean alliance. I was wondering what you think about that.

POLLACK: You've asked a very good question. Clearly the division in Korea, for as long as we have seen it, has enabled us to create an alliance with Korea that has served both country's interests. The abnormality, of course, in Korea is quite marked. When I think about North Korea, this is the longest-running adversary the United States has in the world, bar none. Fidel Castro [leader of Cuba] looks like a late arrival by comparison. We've never had a normal relationship with North Korea, and I would argue that it might be far less a question of U.S. preferences. It's much more a function of the potential control or influence over the question of unification that both South Korea and China, in particular, would have. Now, the current argument is that neither China nor South Korea welcomes any kind of "instability" in the North. I should emphasize that North Korea has defied, time and again, all the predictions of its imminent demise. This is a very tough and resilient system that shows no inclination of going out of business, despite its incredibly dysfunctional political and economic system. So, in a way, regardless of whether or not we have unification, the question is how would this all transpire. If unification were to happen through some kind of cataclysmic, violent outcome, that's one process. The incentives that are there for the South Korean government, in particular—but in a different way for China and perhaps even for Japan, as well—are ones that find all of them, in different ways, seeking to engage with the North Koreans. Many people are cynical about this, of course. But, beyond anything else, our presence and our alliance ought to be dictated by our interests. I tried to emphasize in my remarks today that our judgment about those interests may be, to some significant extent, shifting. If we are pulling forces off the peninsula, it begs the issue of whether we expect to be there over the longer run and whether Korea is united or divided. The indisputable fact is that the center of economic gravity is compellingly in South Korea, not in the North. The North is in miserable shape in that regard, although, as I said, it endures and it persists. So American policy, though, really has never frontally addressed the question of—even as we aspire to the idea of a democratic, unified Korean Peninsula—how you move toward that goal and if you can move toward that goal. Indeed you could argue that our process of engagement now with the peninsula, particularly through the so-called Six-Party Talks in Beijing, in effect says to the Chinese, the South Koreans and the Japanese, this is much more your problem than it is our problem. There may have been a time when a divided Korea was seen as, if you will, substantiating, justifying and legitimating our security presence. In many ways, we're looking beyond that, but we really haven't asked ourselves fully, "What would a unified Korea look like? What would its identity be? What would its affiliations be?" That's a harder question to answer, and I don't think we've really asked it just yet. If there were unification, would there be a continuing security relationship between the United States and Korea? It's not self-evident, frankly.

McCAFFREY: That's a splendid response. There is only thing I might add to it, Jonathan, and I'm not sure what your views would be. I remember being in a room in, I think, 1994, when Dr. Bill Perry [then secretary of defense] called us all in worldwide, and at that time I thought we were 21 days from war with North Korea. We'd given them that an ultimatum: "Shut down Yongbyon [North Korean weapons facility] or we'll bomb it." They said, "If you do, it will be war." So we walked through the whole issue and it was clear to me—and still remains so—that we could dismantle the North Koreans with zero probability of any outcome but total success in less than six months. Of course the downside risk was so horrific: a million or so casualties—primarily civilian—and tens of millions of refugees. Notwithstanding my own view, and this might be a follow-on question to you, but I actually think the administration is doing a terrific job. [Secretary of State] Colin Powell and Six-Party Talks leave some doubt in their minds in South Korea whether we would say yes or no. But my own judgment is that the political system in the North is so opaque. It may be run by a sociopath; we're not sure. The probability of a miscalculation by the North in the coming 36 months, I would argue, is low, but there. There could be high-intensity war out of North Korea in the coming 10 years. How would you respond to that?

POLLACK: You know, it's an interesting question, because in many ways you can argue that deterrence on the peninsula is quite robust. And for the reasons that General McCaffrey just mentioned, we are deterred; they are deterred. Despite their fearsome rhetoric, the North Koreans can be very carefully calculating about where they direct their ire. I mean, one of the great ironies right now is that, even as the South has changed its attitude toward the North in ways that many Americans, frankly, find almost incomprehensible, when there are specific military incidents, as there continue to be in Korea, they always involve South Korean forces. They do not involve American forces. I think, in this respect, the North Koreans understand our power and, despite their rhetoric and despite their frequently brazen actions on a variety of fronts, they're not seeking a war with the United States. The question here would be, under the internal pressures that North Korea has, given the nature of their system, given the possibility for miscalculation and misperception, it may be a very good idea to pull U.S. forces back from where they are located. I think there is a lot to be said for that. But this will leave the question of how Koreans—north and south—sort out their own relations with one another. And, in that respect, we may not like all the answers we get from that. We may judge those to be adverse to our own interests. Again, as I am fond of saying, it is, after all, the Korean Peninsula, and this will be, frankly, a question that we're going to have to face up to in the future. As the South Koreans map out a course that is mindful of some of the risks, they may think they see ways of managing it. Others would doubt this. You could even argue that if you feed the north literally and figuratively, you are only guaranteeing that it remains an open-ended problem, because, at the end of the day, North Korea believes that only it is the legitimate embodiment of Korean nationalism, not the South. How you get from here to there—"there" presumably being, at a minimum, some kind of coexistence—is a very tough nut to crack.

HUNTER: I might add that this is an issue in the world of a very unique and special quality. This is the only serious communist country that has not gone through a process of transformation in a new direction. The Chinese, incidentally, have North Korea's respected leader come to Beijing every once in a while to try to tell him that North Korea could end up the way the Chinese have with a modern communist system. This, rather than what happened in the Soviet Union where [former Soviet president, Mikhail] Gorbachev tried to reform and ended up in the trash heap of history. My personal judgment is there will not be stability on the Korean Peninsula until we have a post-Stalinist regime in the North. The key thing is, can it end—and I borrow this from TS Eliot—with a whimper and not a bang. We were fortunate in what happened in the Soviet Union, the most heavily armed nuclear power in the communist world, ending in the way it did, between 1989 and 1991. That took a process of about 30 years of its opening up. You have this rigidly closed system, and, hence, highly fragile system. If, indeed, something began to happen there ... the process hasn't even begun, which is one argument for trying to do as much as one can as a major grand strategic objective—to get it to open up to radio, television, food, any kind of thing you can do. We must recognize it's an extremely risky process.

So, I think we need to have a long-term strategy, within which we see the short-term policy. But, in the short term, the acquisition of nuclear weapons by this country could up the ante in terms of the price if the situation does end with a bang and not a whimper. That's why, in many respects, this is the most consequential and most threatening situation in the world today.

McCAFFREY: Let me, if I may, go on here. I want to get some comments. Yes, sir.

AUDIENCE: General Hackett. This is for Ambassador Hunter, sir. We are talking about balancing essential requirements here. In your opinion, based on what you have seen and done in NATO, is the new reorganization that's underway right now trying to balance out command and control structure and rapid response forces? Has the United States—with its influence and with trying to balance all of our essential requirements—utilized NATO to its best extent in fighting this war on terrorism? If not, do you have any ideas where we could enhance that use of NATO and our alliances in the war on terrorism?

HUNTER: My personal judgment is that to the extent that fighting the war on terrorism is a military matter, what has evolved within NATO really has been exactly the direction you want it to go. This is with the qualification that, unless you get the Afghan piece right, you're going to end up with more terrorism rather than less. But in the war on terrorism, it's the overall relationship with the Europeans that I'm talking about. Whether it's intelligence, police work, border control, or getting at those things that are less NATO than the European Union and the strategic partnership—it's about dealing with those things that motivate people to turn a blind eye and a deaf ear to what the terrorists are doing. And that is in health, education and governance and all those things that also fit within the democratic process.

The real problem, I think, is more a classic geopolitical question—the structures of security in the Middle East, derived from Iraq, derived from what may or may not happen with Iran, derived from the Arab/Israeli peace process. The resolution of the peace process has become a strategic imperative, not a discretionary act, and I even hate to raise it. There is a great black hole of analysis and political understanding in the Middle East, that is, the future of Saudi Arabia. I must confess, at NATO after Bosnia, everybody whispered the word Kosovo, because they hoped it wouldn't arise, even though the United States, on Christmas Day in 1992, made an absolute commitment that Kosovo raised itself. We had to deal with it. We aren't doing that with Saudi Arabia. So, I would argue, the real issue at NATO, other than being successful in Afghanistan, is to succeed on working out new security structures for the Middle East. How we work together with the allies on it—and let me put it this way—we have no choice. The question is whether we collectively will do it well or badly, and the next president, no matter who it is, is going to have to do more or less the same thing. The choices are very narrow. American leadership is required. American commitment, allied participation—we have our task laid out for us. The scenarios can be written. We have to get on with it.

McCAFFREY: Question. Yes, sir, right up here.

AUDIENCE: Sir, Major Rick Bairett, from the United States Air Force. First, a comment. It seems that most of our alliances are based predominantly on the fact that we provide the preponderance of force and financial resources. Also, it seems our values are much different from those of Asia, and it seems there's a growing divide in the area of values with Europe as well as many other regions of world. Do we have a basis to build alliances on in the future other than the United States continuing to provide the preponderance of force and money?

McCAFFREY: Well, who wants to take that on?

HUNTER: I'll be happy to take that on. In terms of heavy lifting, if heavy lifting is required, like in Iraq, the United States is going to have to provide the preponderance of force. However, if you start talking about special forces, if you talk about nation building, peace keeping and other things in which we have been less engaged in the past—and in which a lot of the other nations have been more engaged and have the needed skills—that's a different story. It's one reason NATO today is emphasizing C4ISR—to be able and lift and get less-capable forces in terms of the high end of the strategic spectrum. But NATO also looks for these units to be able to do a lot of the other tasks that are absolutely required to be able to get them to the place where they are needed in order to act.

I also want to point out that, as we're talking about the overall strategic environment where we and the Europeans might be engaged, a lot of what has to be done is non-military. I'll leave it to my colleagues to talk about the Asian dimension, which may be dramatically different. For example, in the Balkans, most of the money that is going into reconstruction is not American money. In Central Europe, most of what's being done is European and not American. Much of what we're going to have to do in Iraq in future years is going to need to be done with things that are not in the U.S. military. So if we look at this as an overall strategic requirement, yes, we need allies to join with us in taking risks. Our society is not going to let you in the military be out there running the risks by yourselves if other people who benefit are not also running risks. When we talk about the overall perspective, there's an awful lot we need from allies that isn't at the high end of the strategic requirement. We need to understand that. If we do understand that, I think we will find a coalescence that's going to work very effectively for our interests and also for their interests and our common values, because, in the Western world, those values are very much in common.

McCAFFREY: I think we probably have time to squeeze in one more question. Yes, ma'am, right over here.

AUDIENCE: My question for the panel refers to Afghanistan and the fact that we have elections in less than three weeks there. I'm wondering what reasonably can be achieved by the U.S. military, by the U.S. government and by the international community in the next three weeks to ensure that the elections will be free and fair—if that, indeed, is a U.S. national interest. And it would be OK to define what "free and fair" means in this case, in Afghanistan.

McCAFFREY: John, you want to take that on?

SANDROCK: Let me see if I can address at least part of that. First of all, I think much of the groundwork has been laid. The number of individuals who have been registered to vote has been absolutely remarkable. I think there is a very real concern regarding security during the voting process. I am very confident that all the security forces, both the ISAF-U.S. and the Afghan forces that are available—those that are aligned with the national authorities, and also those that are maintaining control on the local level—will be dedicated to making this as safe and as fair as is reasonably possible. I think we should not expect perfect elections. It will not happen. In Bosnia, for instance—that's the parallel I draw from my OSCE days—we ran elections. The OSCE ran elections in successive years for five years before we finally were able to do it without international supervision. I think there will be problems in the election. I hope whatever security problems there may be will be at a minimum. But I think, to the extent possible, everyone and all the resources are going to be mobilized to try to make this as successful as possible. I think we should not expect an election that is going to be the model of a democratic process. In any case, I think it will be successful, and I think we'll have to have an election again in the next year and perhaps the year after that. Elections are not a one-time affair and one doesn't become a democratic country with only one set of elections. So, I'm very optimistic and I hope that optimism is well-founded.

McCAFFREY: Let me add to that. I just got back from Afghanistan a couple of weeks ago, after having poked around the country. To my astonishment, notwithstanding two giant problems looming out there—85,000 heavily armed warlord militias and this giant threat of $1.4 billion or more out of the drug industry—the short-run is really surprisingly positive. You have the creation of the Afghan National Army, the positive relationship between the Afghans and the coalition forces, and the leadership of Hamid Karzai. You have this unbelievable U.S. ambassador who came along at the right time and added enormously to our skills.

HUNTER: A RAND guy.

McCAFFREY: a RAND guy. So again, none of us wants to be overly optimistic, but Afghanistan has been really a surprise. None of us would have said that five years ago, thinking about military intervention in Afghanistan.

Let me, if I may, wrap up by thanking the panel for some incredibly useful insights. How do you summarize this? Number one, I'm sure that all of us on this panel, and probably a majority in the audience, believe the United States cannot act alone; we can only act in concert with alliances. Over the long run, neither the resources nor political legitimacy will be there if we don't construct cooperative partnerships. Secondly, and rather obviously, no kidding, the Cold War is over; 9/11 shattered the blueprint. The challenge to the colonels and brigadier generals and your colleagues in the interagency process is that you have 10 years or less to recreate a new system of alliances. It requires new thinking, and that will be the work of a decade. Finally, and again painfully, the new alliances won't necessarily be oriented around armored vehicles and artillery. They ought to deal with law enforcement, bioterrorism, drugs and weapons of mass destruction in the hands of non-state actors. This is going to be a very tricky world we're living in.

So, again, I think from all of us on the panel to those of you in the audience who are trying to craft sensible, cooperative strategies moving forward, we thank you for your service and admire you for who you are. Thanks very much.

LUNCHEON ADDRESS

SECURITY, GLOBALIZATION AND THE INTERNATIONAL CORPORATION

Harry C. Stonecipher, President and Chief Executive Officer, The Boeing
  Company

Introduction by: Brigadier General Jeffrey A. Sorenson, Deputy for
  Systems Management and Horizontal Technology Integration
  for the Assistant Secretary of the Army for Acquisition,
  Logistics and Technology

Summary

Harry C. Stonecipher

• Harry Stonecipher recalled the casualties, costs and sacrifices borne by Americans on Sept. 11 and since the terrorist attacks. He asserted that we are living in a period of "change and challenge." In such times, political leaders are severely tested. The nation's greatest leaders have been those who possess the judgment and the courage to make difficult decisions, whether or not those decisions are popular.

• Effective leaders ensure that everyone in their company knows his or her role, responsibility and authority; devote time and care to recruiting and mentoring their immediate subordinates; and develop a business strategy marked by efficiency and flexibility. In the corporate world, there are several, crucial ingredients for success:

1. Planning for success means succession planning; that is, developing mechanisms to identify and develop promising, second-tier leaders, which can "increase the velocity of decision making."

2. Leaders must be willing to admit error. Stonecipher used the case of a Boeing project—a passenger plane capable of sonic speeds—to highlight the importance of knowing when to quit. The engineers had the right product, but without the right market it was impossible to justify moving ahead.

3. Leaders must think globally. Globalization offers the contemporary corporation five benefits: access to markets, capital, technology, labor and intel-

lectual capital. For Boeing, thinking globally has meant opening a design bureau in Moscow to take advantage of the skills of Russian aviation engineers.

4. Management must make education a priority. To management, employee education should be seen as an end in itself. Subsidizing higher education makes sense, even in fields not directly related to the employee's current role. At the executive level, Boeing achieves its educational goals in its Leadership Center, whose sole charter is the creation of effective global leaders.

• Stonecipher condensed his own experiences as a leader into three lessons: leaders are paid for their judgment, a leader's most important asset is the will to lead, and people emulate their leaders.

Analysis

Harry Stonecipher's presentation focused on leadership, its conceptual basis and its development within an organization. He judged leaders by the difficulty and quality of the decisions they make. He emphasized the importance of restoring ethical and competent leadership within Boeing after the recent scandals that shook the company. He proposed familiar keys to successful leadership: the appointment of good people and delegation of responsibility and authority to them while retaining firm, direct supervision.

A second point he emphasized is the courage to admit error. Boeing's ability to do so is shown in its moving away from a focus on making platforms to integrating large-scale, complex systems. He noted that the reorientation is necessary in a globalized world where fierce competition for markets exists. Instilling a global perspective throughout the company is a necessary predicate to Boeing's new direction.

Stonecipher repeatedly stressed the importance of leadership selection and training programs as being essential for developing new leaders with an ethical compass and a global horizon. Globalization and the transformation of the world economy also force leaders into ever-faster modes of decision making. The velocity of decision making is increasing; thus, it is essential to build an organization that keeps pace with it. One way to reach this necessary velocity is for leaders to trust their judgment, because they were selected primarily for that quality and not for their technical abilities.

In that vein, he spoke of how Boeing seeks to identify future leaders early in young employees' careers and set them upon a pattern of professional development that provides them the best possible opportunities for future success. He did not address the difficulty of reliably identifying the best future leaders so early in their careers, the detrimental morale ramifications that could ensue from egalitarian concerns, or any valid measures for determining whether the early identification process is a successful one. To say that leaders should have confidence in their judgment because they were selected to be leaders is circular reasoning at best.

Stonecipher stated other truisms. Leaders also must possess a will to lead and a will to assume responsibility. Doing so sets the tone for the organization. Additionally, leadership entails respecting the ideas of everyone involved in decision making and supporting the development of the people for whom leaders are responsible. Moreover, once leaders discover dysfunctional trends, wrongdoing or negative trends within the company, they must personally correct, overcome or remove them.

Stonecipher consistently emphasized the need for a global company like Boeing to make extraordinary efforts to meet the human needs of its employees and establish strong leadership training programs so that talent can be recognized, encouraged and developed. Even if trained leaders move to other corporations, as he did through General Electric, the effectiveness of Boeing's executive and leadership recruitment and development programs is validated. Stonecipher made clear that such programs are essential and must inculcate a global perspective in order to move forward in a global environment.

As recounted by Stonecipher, these programs indicate that Boeing is on the right track. It is poised not just to be a major defense contractor, but to move forward with a new generation of products that are already available based on the principles of spiral development, sound engineering and fiscal management. His speech was not just an articulation of what has been done to improve the situation at Boeing and restore it to its previous competitive standing; rather, it represented a major effort at strategic communication. By accentuating the positive steps being taken at Boeing, he sought to give life to the steps that need to be taken by any large organization to maintain future competitiveness. Throughout the speech he attempted to sell Boeing to the U.S. Army as a positive supporter of Army efforts.

While much of what Stonecipher said was very familiar to military leaders, the U.S. Army can distill some useful points of reinforcement. Leadership, to be effective, must be ethical, constantly concerned with the promotion and development of future senior leaders, and responsive to the needs of the people led. Every leader must assume responsibility for the development and well-being of those they lead. Leaders will be evaluated on the quality of their judgment, their resolve to make the hard decisions, and willingness to assume responsibility.

Quality leadership and decision making mean having a global perspective and cross-cultural awareness that enable leaders to assess and predict the strategic consequences of decisions. Clearly, that could facilitate better decision making by Army leaders and enable them to understand the validity and context of alternative perspectives. America's Army is a force of global reach and influence. It requires visionary leaders who do not view national security only in domestic terms.

Likewise, the Army must not neglect strategic communications with its external environment. Stonecipher's speech was an example of how to weave a strategic communications message into a presentation. He clearly intended to restore confidence in Boeing after the recent scandals. Similarly, the Army constantly must deliver its messages, purposes and positive actions to audiences beyond the Army community. However, Army leaders must remain mindful of the different motivations between a large, for-profit corporation and the U.S. Army. A corporation's first loyalty is to its shareholders and its first objective is to maximize their gain over the long term.

As an organization whose activities span the globe, the Army must be able to communicate strategically with global populations to engage in dialogue that understands and respects their perspectives as well. Since U.S. Army personnel stationed abroad represent the United States, their conduct strongly shapes foreigners' perceptions of the United States. U.S. Army personnel, therefore, must be sensitive to foreign attitudes and values as they implement U.S. policies and conduct themselves appropriately. The Army communicates through actions as well as words.

Like General Electric and Boeing, the Army can select, promote, encourage and diversify the horizons of its future leaders so that they will be recognized—not just in the Army, but more widely—as strong, capable leaders who can lead their organizations into the future. The Army, by force, pays great attention to the human dimension of its organization, ensuring that Soldiers and civilian employees are treated with respect and given every opportunity to succeed. An integral part of leadership is the assumption of responsibility for the development and well-being of all subordinates. In considering Stonecipher's description of changes underway at Boeing, U.S. Army leaders will do

Transcript

ANNOUNCER: Once again, ladies and gentlemen, Brigadier General Kevin T. Ryan.

BRIGADIER GENERAL KEVIN T. RYAN: Well, I hope you enjoyed your lunch and the discussion from this morning. It is my privilege now to present Brigadier General Jeff Sorensen, who will introduce our luncheon speaker. General Sorenson is the deputy for acquisition and systems management in the Office of the Assistant Secretary of the Army for Acquisition, Logistics and Technology.

Please welcome Brigadier General Jeff Sorensen.

BRIGADIER GENERAL JEFFREY A. SORENSEN: Yes, this is the intro for the intro. But, clearly, General Schoomaker, distinguished guests, it is my privilege and honor today to introduce our lunchtime speaker, Mr. Harry Stonecipher. If all have looked at his bio, there's one resonant theme that comes through and that's his dedication and, if you will, mantra that he wants to make sure that all our war fighters have the most reliable products we have when engaging the enemy.

Mr. Stonecipher has been supporting our war fighters ever since he began his career at General Motors' Allison Division, where he started as a lab technician.

In 1960, he joined General Electric and progressed through the ranks in engineering and product development, to lead the division's commercial and military transport operations from 1984 to 1987. During his career at GE, he played a crucial role in the advancement of propulsion technology for passenger and military aircraft. In 1987, he became the corporate vice president for Sundstrand, two years later he was elected president and chief operating officer and then the chairman of the board in 1991. During his tenure at Sundstrand, he implemented quality improvement processes that made Sundstrand Aerospace products the most reliable systems in the world. In 1994 he was elected president and chief executive officer of McDonnell Douglas. Leveraging his prior experience, he once

Brigadier General Jeffrey Sorenson

again instituted high-performance work teams that focused on quality production. With the aerospace industry consolidation underway, Mr. Stonecipher received authorization in 1996 to engage in merger negotiations with Boeing. After a successful merger in 1997, he was elected president and chief operating officer, and this past December he became the president and chief executive officer of Boeing, the world's largest aerospace company. Among his many awards are the Wings Club Distinguished Achievement Award, the Navy League's Rear Admiral John J. Bergen Leadership Medal for Industry, the Air Force Association's John R. Allison Award, and, most importantly, our Army Association's John W. Dixon Award. Please give a warm welcome to an industrialist and provider of quality products to our war fighters, Mr. Harry Stonecipher.

HARRY C. STONECIPHER: Well, it got pretty quiet as I walked up here, but let's see if we can't talk about some things that you'll find of interest. I certainly found the panel and the presentations this morning very interesting. Thanks very much, General Sorenson and General Schoomaker. Is Susan Eisenhower still here? What a great tribute to have this going on in honor of your grandfather.

We're a nation at war, and today we heard some people say that it's a different kind of war. It is a different kind of war. As I've thought about it, sitting through the presentations, I think they've all been different. You know, everyone who goes into one of these conflicts, however big or however small, finds that they are all different. We are at war, and as a citizen and speaker today, I'd be remiss if I didn't acknowledge how pleased and proud I am of the armed forces that are standing in harm's way while we are here today. It's just great.

Last Saturday was the third anniversary of the 9/11 attack; many good people lost their lives in New York and the Pentagon and in Pennsylvania, including several Boeing employees who were on one of the flights. Tens of thousands of Boeing employees lost their jobs because of the economic downturn in the commercial airplane business after 9/11. It was dramatic. It was over 30,000 people. We're particularly grateful to those people who continue to work at Boeing who are on active duty today, or who have served in the last couple of years. We're particularly glad that we're able to support them because we consider it our duty and our privilege to support those people in the Reserves who go when called.

Harry C. Stonecipher

The war on terrorism and all current military operations remind us that this is a time of change and challenge. We are measured on how we adapt and respond, not in times of tranquility, but when consequences are the greatest. At some point there was a psychological profile test given by one of the states—I don't remember which one—that always asked, Who was your favorite president? As I thought about that, I came up with three. I've carried those three around and have mentioned them in many speeches that I've given. And it's because of the decisions they had to make. That's the way I judge leaders. I judge them by the difficulty—the trauma—involved in making the decisions. The first one was George Washington. I can't imagine the number of decisions and the decision process as you take over the leadership of a new, desperate, disparate nation. That must've been tough, and I haven't studied that as much as I have the next two. Abraham Lincoln—as president he had the opportunity to satisfy a lot of political enemies and friends by simply saying, "Hey, if they want slavery in the South, let them have it. We'll have our own way up here. So, let's just divide the place, everybody will be happy, cut the baby in half and then we can get on with it." What a decision to make that says, "No, we're not going to take the easy way out,"—the popular way, I would suggest to you it might have been. "We're going to be one nation." That was a great decision. The other president strikes those of us in the business a little closer. Harry Truman. The decision to use the first atomic bomb. How many years—God help us, that it never happens—how many years will it be before someone has to make a decision like that one? You can't really understand it, I don't think. It came home to me when I read a book recently called *Flags of Our Fathers*. I don't know how many of you have read it, but it's really about the battle of Iwo Jima, and it's written by the son of one of the people there. When you read that and think about the losses that were incurred there and then you think about the prospect of having to invade the mainland of Japan, it becomes understandable as to at least one parameter that you might use in making that decision. Those of you who study military history more than I do probably have several views of whether that decision was correct or incorrect, or whether it will ever be made again in today's times. I don't know.

Well, when I came back to work after being retired for 18 months our company was in trouble, not because of what the company did, but because of what some individuals did. As we think about corporations today and some of the things that have happened, as I'm quick to point out. Corporations don't do things, people do things. Individuals do things. In some cases it's greed and in some cases it's stupidity. Stupidity does not, in my terminology, have anything to do with intellectual capability. It has to do with knowing the right thing to do and doing the wrong thing. That's stupid. So, we got on the wrong side on a number of those things. I came back because it was the right thing to do. Unfortunately, I had been through this sort of thing twice before, at two other companies. Suspension, questionable practices, and I had more experience there than anyone deserves. I knew the company, I know the industry—I love the company and love the people and the industry—and I'm one of those people who likes working in Washington. I come here frequently. I know how the chief feels about it, and I heard him speak on that one night, but I happen to like it. I enjoy it. I find a lot of bright people here who are very dedicated.

Boeing does very important work. We describe it this way: "Connect and protect." "Connect" means we bring people together around the world, and we let commerce happen. "Protect" comes from providing all the different types of equipment that we make to our armed forces here and abroad. We have some 155,000-plus employees, and in leading those employees I ask, Do we have it right? Do we have the right strategy? Are we doing it right? Are we executing? Do our people understand their individual roles? That's leadership. I can tell you that I have 11 direct reports. All of the 155,000-plus people in The Boeing Company work for one of those 11 people. Each of those 11 people knows precisely what his or her job is, and they know their roles and responsibilities, and they know their authority. So my job gets really easy. We're going to talk about leadership here as we go forward. It's really easy if you select good people. If you select good people, the job is very easy. If you select mediocre people, it's impossible. So take time—make time—to be sure you are selecting the right people.

Strategy and being a leader. There are a lot of leaders who report to me. The 7E7 is a new airplane. It's a new airplane that we're just beginning to design and build. The first one will go into service in 2008. A few years ago, you heard us talk about a sonic cruiser. How do we get the speed of the airplane up to about Mach

'92, '93? I love that airplane; in fact, we made a decision that we were going to do that airplane. It never got launched because 9/11 interfered with the airlines' prospects. The prospect of going faster—it took us a long time to get something that we thought we could build at reasonable cost, and the reason was we were working on the wrong end of the equation. We kept trying to take a subsonic design and see how we could make it go faster, or take a supersonic design from some of our other products, and see if we could turn it into a commercial airplane. Someone finally said, "Wait a minute. Why don't we take the fast design and back into it from the top side?" Voila, an airplane, and I loved it. I retired. I came back.

We've got a new airplane. It's the 7E7 and it's subsonic. It's up to about Mach .85. Speed just doesn't seem to be in the cards; it's not about technology, it's about economics. Still today the fastest commercial airplane flying is really the 747. It went into service in 1969. People bought that airplane, not because of its size for passengers, but because of its range. That's where we're going with the 7E7—more efficient, environmentally friendly, and it's based on a point-to-point strategy.

As we were just discussing at this table, if you want to go to Syracuse, you don't want to come through O'Hare. What's this conversation about? It's about airplanes, but most of all it's about the courage to say we were wrong. You'll have to admire the folks who have put their blood and tears into this thing we were calling the sonic cruiser and then having to stand there and say we've got it wrong. This will be a failure. We have it right and we changed our mind and we're building that airplane.

Another big strategic decision we made was recognizing that it is not a platform game. We've built some great platforms. We've built some great ones for each of the services. But when we decided that this is really about systems, we described it as we want to be the integrator of large-scale, complex systems. That's what we are. Well, Future Combat Systems plays right to that tune. So, right away, we start thinking about network-centric warfare and within about 100 days, Jim Albaugh [president and chief executive office of Boeing's Integrated Defense Systems], sitting up here in this organization, built a Boeing Integration Center out on the West Coast. There you can bring in and integrate all of the aspects of all of the platforms and vehicles that exist in all the services. You can play any kind of game you want in that center. That was such a great idea for our customers and our employees who are working on these systems, that he built another one here on the East Coast so that people who want to go visit with them can visit with them back East. I hope that several of you have done that.

The proposition of where we're going with this is very important. And I'm going to stick in a little plug here for something that is as politically sensitive as anything you can imagine. Some of our people here who are from overseas probably already know what I'm talking about. It's ITAR [International Traffic in Arms Regulations]. If you're going to have interoperability, we are going to have to break down some of the ITAR situations that exist. We have to find a way to have some security agreements that we all feel good about with many of our allies, because you cannot have interoperability unless you can get over that hurdle. First thing, though, is we've got to have interoperability in and across our own services, and that's what all of this is about. If we go at the system and look at how we are going about some of our business, it's about globalization. It's ITAR, one piece.

It's globalization. And when we think about globalization, we think about why you want to go offshore or outsource. Everybody has great visions and it's really, once again, a policy issue—a sensitive policy issue about why you are moving jobs. I have an example where a couple of senators and congressmen showed up in my conference room in St. Louis, Mo., and were screaming at me that we were shipping jobs to China. And I was moving wiring harnesses from St. Charles, Mo., to Phoenix. But if you are in St. Charles it doesn't matter if you're moving from St. Charles to Phoenix or whether you're moving from St. Charles to China. The impact is still the same. Locally there were 30 jobs lost.

So what are we going to do?

Well, we look at globalization and say this is access to markets. That's important to us—access to technology. Not everything in the world was invented in the United States, and that will continue to be the case. There are some people who do some pretty great things elsewhere. It is important to have access to capital and access to labor and intellectual capital. Right now we have a big design bureau in Moscow, which designs modifications and special features for commercial airplanes. There are 13 time zones there, so we literally can design 24 hours a day. We're hiring the best and brightest we can. We walked through one of the nicest groups of Ph.D.s in applied science and engineering that you would want to talk about. That's a great thing for a number of reasons, and we've had this started up for over 10 years. The reason it's great is because it employs some people who have skills we need, who are very good at what they do, and they are working on products that are important to the world. If they weren't working on those, they might be working on things that we wouldn't like and selling them to people we wouldn't like. So, the whole concept is that we have to make this thing work internationally. The biggest reason we go global with our sourcing has to do with access to our markets. It also has to do with access to the best of industry. If you look at the 7E7 that we just sourced, you'll read lots of things in the newspaper about what we're doing in Japan—and we have been doing things in Japan ever since World War II ended. We have been doing things in Italy for over 40 years. They have been partners with us on nearly every airplane we have built. And they continue to be partners. Right now, in these economic times, you read a lot about it. But the 7E7 will be about 75 percent U.S. content, which is about what all of our airplanes are, and we sell about 70 percent of all of our Boeing commercial airplanes outside this country. So it seems like a fair deal. We collectively have to find a way to train our people to think globally. We're doing that through our leadership center. We have a leadership center that, quite frankly, is patterned after General Electric's Crotonville [N.Y.], which is where I learned an awful lot. I graduated from Tennessee Tech, but I got my education at GE.

We run all of our executives through this leadership center, and there's a select group that attends a global leadership program. This group, normally 28 to 30 people, spends about 30 days on an assignment with specific interviews set up with business leaders, government leaders and military leaders in other locations in the world. I can tell you that one of those people is headed to Russia in the next 18 days; we're a little concerned about what's happened over there, but hopefully everything will turn out OK. We'll be assessing that. Thus far, over five years, we have had people in Germany, China, the United Kingdom, India, Spain, Brazil, Japan, Italy, Australia, Korea, northern Europe and Turkey. And they come back with all kinds of great ideas. These are people who have very little international experience, and they come back really excited about what we could be doing in all these different countries. Out of that, they keep wanting us to start businesses there or do something there. I just want them to be smart about "there," wherever "there" is. We'll decide whether we buy a company there, whether we source there, whether we sell there, or what happens—but it's very important to us.

How do we develop leaders? Once again, I mention the leadership center. In putting our minds on different people and watching their growth, we have a place called the green room. It's interesting. It started as the green room a number of years ago. It's no longer green, but it started as the green room, like the beige book that's no longer beige. Every person in the top three levels of the company is on the wall in there, and it describes their experience, it describes how much money they make, what kind of bonuses they have gotten, their promotion track and all this stuff. The 11 who report directly to me and I go through that thing at least once a year, and we talk about successors for each spot in there.

Every October, I talk with the board of directors about successors for myself, at least three successors for each of my direct reports and at least three successors for each of theirs. In addition, we have 100 people to watch. That's about what it is, 100 this year. And those are people whom I have noticed in reviews or have come to the attention of one of our senior leaders, and he or she says, "We really ought to keep an eye on this person." Then we will start to move them around.

Those of you who are on the Army side—and that's most of you in here—any of you who have been to our Philadelphia operation, where we built the Chinook and a few slots for the B-22, may know Pat Shanahan. He runs Philadelphia, and has for the last few years. I hope a number of you know Pat. He has spent his whole career in commercial airplanes. He was a deputy vice president for the 747, the 767, then he had the whole 757 product line. We identified Pat, and said Pat needs to get some different experience. He's 38 years old. He could run this company some day. So we took Jerry Daniels, who was running all the military airplane business at that time, and said we want Shanahan to run Philadelphia. He said that he'd put him on the succession plan. And we said, no, like next month. That's the way you do things.

That brings me to a couple of things about leadership. There's a saying that's attributed to me. The first time I heard it, or read it, was in *Fortune* Magazine; it was a Jack Parker, vice chairman of GE a number of years ago, who first said it. He was talking about succession planning and hiring new MBAs into the company. He said, you know, we're doing succession planning on the basis of a calendar. These guys are looking at their watch. That's the way people describe my management style now. You know, Harry is looking at his watch and everybody else is looking at the calendar. There's some truth in that and that's a good thing. Think about one thing—velocity. If you say "velocity" to anyone in business, they'll give you asset turns, inventory turns, all kinds of velocity of turnover in capital. But do you know where we fail every day? We fail in the velocity of decision making. Everybody does. How do you get the velocity of decision making up? And so, as I described it many times, every day when we get up, we have a whole group of people wondering why we don't make up our minds where we're going and why we can't get on with it. So, encourage people to make decisions. I can tell you something, for those of you who are in the Army: When you're in combat, you make decisions really fast. How fast do you make them when you're sitting in the Pentagon? It's a different tempo. I know it is. But, you know something? You're just as good at making them under those conditions as you are in combat. So get them made and get moving. That is the thing that drives me crazy—not getting decisions made on time.

I started telling all of our leadership team—and, by the way, I personally go to our leadership center once a month, and I personally communicate in writing to every employee in this company once a month—as a managers you don't make anything. You're paid for your judgment. That's what leaders have. They have judgment. Use your judgment and get on with it. I have also learned that you can have people who are well-trained, well-educated, and have lots of savvy, but they really don't have the will to lead. There has to be a will to lead. There has to be a will to take responsibility. There has to be a will, not drive, to lead. That's one of the things I watch for. People emulate their leaders.

That comes back to the question of what kind of standard are you setting for the people you're leading. That's one of the things that we have gone through at Boeing, because of the ethics lapses that we had in some areas. We went through a situation that says we're going to rededicate ourselves to understanding what ethics is all about. We have a code of conduct. It's a great code of conduct. So in February we said everyone is going to read the code of conduct and going to sign it. This was not about questioning one's value system. It simply said, as a minimum, you will have a value system that matches the code of conduct of The Boeing Company or you can't work here. We got to the point where I said we're going to do this in 30 days, and everybody wanted to do it with a computer key strike. I said, no, I want people to read a piece of paper and at the end of the day I want to see their John Henry down there that says they read it, understand it, will comply with it and will continue to comply with it. Well, there was a little bit of an uproar, but for the most part, people got together and said, yes, let's do it. We had five people who refused to sign out of 156,000, or whatever the number is. That was all. After reflecting on it for about a week or so, two of them signed; following reflection after a little leave of absence, two more signed. The other one doesn't work for us anymore. This is not about being mean, but I said that furthermore, we're going to do it every year, just so we're all up on the step and we know what we're doing about this, bringing people together for a common cause. The Boeing Company is doing just great right now.

Many of you in here are honoring us with some contracts and letting us provide services to you. People ask me how did this happen so quickly. I explain that in the first place I made sure that people understood we have, and we speak openly about it, the Sears-Druyun incident [former Boeing Chief Financial Officer Michael Sears and former Air Force acquisition and management officer, Darleen Druyun], which is still wallowing around with the U.S. Attorney; we have the EELV [Evolved Expendable Launch Vehicle] suspension. We have the situation from that of some lawsuits going on over some documents we have of Lockheed Martin's. We did a lousy job of investigating it four years ago or whenever it was, and our reputation was slammed over it. So the first thing I did was say, look, we have a lot of outside lawyers and we have a great law department. They will take care of that. I want the other 155,000 people to run the business. That's what we have done. Everybody is engaged, and everybody knows what they're doing. They're having a good time, and there is nothing like a little success to make people feel good.

Execution, execution, execution. We're doing it. I would remind you of something: I used to work at GE for a guy named Gerhard Neumann. Actually I didn't work directly for him, but he thought I did. He treated everybody that way. He was involved. People call him Herman the German. He was a German Jew who got out of Germany just in time, ended up in Hong Kong, spending time as a mechanic for Claire Chenault and the Flying Tigers. Gerhard Neumann was the guy who put together the first captured Zero [World War II Japanese fighter aircraft] that was in bad shape when they flew it. He made his way to the United States after the war and ended up running all the aircraft engine groups for GE. He had in his office—this was how he wanted it—the poorest, cheapest desk you could find anywhere, and he wanted linoleum on the floor. On the wall behind his desk he had two plaques. One of them said "Feel Insecure." This was not about you personally. This was about your competitors; this was about the environment. Are you wise enough to understand what's happening to you? Are you wise enough to make the change? That's what we have been talking about all day. Are we wise enough to make the change? The other plaque was a little more pointed, and it did apply to you personally. It said, "No man is completely useless. He can always serve as a bad example." We don't want any bad examples. As I close, I want to say in the presence of all the Soldiers here, at any rank, that you have my thanks, the nation's appreciation for what you're doing and for the sacrifices that you're making, not only for us, but for your families. We ask that you make us strong, make us safe, and keep us free.

Thank you.

If you'll turn up the lights so I can see you, I'll take questions or leave—whichever you prefer. Not a single question, that's good. We have one. Yes, ma'am.

AUDIENCE: I'm Sheila Ronis, from the University Group. I would like to know if you think there's a chance that we'll have a BC–17X [Boeing air cargo prototype] to compete with the Antonov An–124 [heavy cargo plane].

STONECIPHER: I don't think so. We have tried to do that a number of times, and there was a great effort put into it. It really makes a great aircraft. I'm talking about a commercial C–17. I'm talking about your having to have an unimproved field as the C–17 has a lot of features on it that the Army loves and makes use of. But, quite frankly, when you start carrying cargo, it's not a very long-range airplane. It has to be refueled a lot, about every 3,600 miles. I don't think we're going to get there. We have really worked it hard as we have lots of people out there who want to buy one so they can fly it to places and bag sandbags. We have employees that can bag 1,000 sandbags every five minutes or so, and they said all we need is a C–17 to haul this equipment around. Again, it's economics, it's not technology. We are actually building a huge aircraft; it's an outsized 747 to haul the fuselages and components of the 7E7. So, once again, this is back to economics. There are so many great airplanes that make great freighters today and people are converting almost every airplane there is from 737s to 747s to freighters, so I don't think we're going to get there.

What else? Got a couple here. Whoever has the microphones can choose. Yes, sir.

AUDIENCE: Tim Coffin. You talked a little bit about investing in education and how you brought in people here in the United States into your education system, as well as harvested overseas some people that are promising there. As I look inside the Army at my areas of space and missile defense, we're trying to develop the expertise and the knowledge base within the Army. Is there a place for partnership there between business and industry where we work together to bring the educational level up within the country to ensure that our national security needs are met?

STONECIPHER: I think there probably is. As a company, and through our foundation, we probably put 40 or 50 percent of our money into education. We give away about a $100 million a year. In terms of education as a business and how we relate together, Boeing has a life-long learning program for all of its employees—all of the employees. They can study anything they want to. It doesn't have anything to do with their job, because we believe that the learning experience is an energizing experience. We pay for it. Right now we have 22,000 to 25,000 people enrolled in a college somewhere. When they earn an associate's degree, we give them 50 shares of stock. If they get a BS, MS, or Ph.D., we give them 100 shares of stock. They can study anything. I had a group of employees one day that was trying to make a different point and asked, Would you please tell me why we paid somebody to study mortuary science, because they're obviously going to leave the company? I said, we may be in worse trouble than you think we are, so just stick around. We had a couple of divinity degrees—same answer. So we're very engaged in education, and we'll be happy to engage with the Army or anybody else in any kind of a venture like that. We would embrace that.

AUDIENCE: Sir, Barbara Wilcox. This morning we talked a little bit about the battle of ideas and the fact that outsourcing in India was good and we really didn't want to see that go away. Winning hearts and minds. I am curious: With your outsourcing in various countries—particularly the countries where we ask why they hate us—have you been able to influence some of those countries through outsourcing or other methods? And what have you learned from that? Is it helping in the battle of ideas?

STONECIPHER: I think it's helping a great deal. There was a lot of the conversation this morning about China. I have a view that says we really want China as a friend; we don't want to fight China. We don't want to go to war with China. I think we'll get along just fine with China. There's one overarching issue that our colleagues on the panel touched on. It's Taiwan. I was in China the day that Newt Gingrich [former Georgia Republican congressman] said he thought that Taiwan ought to be independent. It was not a nice place to be. We have to have a consistent policy toward China. Think about our trade balance with China. It's horrible. But China as a country has a net negative trade balance; they don't have a positive trade balance. They're struggling with trade like we are. It's oil and it's raw materials. And as the trade minister pointed out when he traveled the country, 60 percent of every dollar that China is processing goes to a Western corporation, western Europe or the United States. It's our own corporations—Boeing included, by the way—that go through there, get something made and bring it back out. I was having dinner, seated next to [Samuel] Palmisano [IBM chairman and CEO], and I said, "How much business are you doing in China?" He said he thought they were doing $5 billion. We think we're doing $3 billion. And the reason is, its components really are from his company. They go in there and back out and into components back here to be shipped. So I think we're having an impact, which we work hard at. We certainly are having an impact, and we have one of the greatest guys as president of Russia for us. I think he was the youngest tenured professor ever in Russia. He's smart as a whip, and he's been working for Boeing for over 10 years. I guess by the end of this year or middle of next year, we'll have 1,000 engineers employed in the design bureau—it's in the McDonald's building over there. You get a visitor's badge. It's the golden arches on a chartreuse badge, going into the Boeing office. But we're getting the best and brightest out of there to help us design commercial airplane modifications. In India, we don't do as much as a lot of other countries

do, but we do some software there. Ratan Tata, a great personal friend—that's Tata Industries—I met him on a trip I made with Ron Brown back when Commerce Secretary Brown was making these trips around the world, trying to build friends. We have to become interdependent. When you become interdependent, then friendship breaks out all over. It really does. So I'm hopeful, and I think we're making a difference. We sell a lot of goods overseas, too.
What else? Yes.

AUDIENCE: Captain Taylor, Joint Staff. As the Department of Defense pushes forward with transformation, net-centric warfare and systems assistance have become some of the dominant concepts. You can't get a transformation briefing nowadays unless you've got net-centric or network in it somewhere . . . .

STONECIPHER: That's good—we like those words. "Future Combat System" is a good term, too.

AUDIENCE: As we pursue those concepts, there are a lot of technical hurdles and cultural hurdles we have to get over to bring those to fruition. I'd be interested in your thoughts on what some of the dominant issues are and how we solve those problems.

STONECIPHER: I think the dominant issues . . . . We have a group of people—one of them, Jim Albaugh, is seated right here—who can think in the most abstract terms. Jim Albaugh runs our integrated defense systems business. He really is a rocket scientist and he's a systems scientist. You can sit with him and and say, I have A, B, C, D, E, and F, and here is what I'm trying to do. He'll say, we'll come back and see you tomorrow and then do something for you. So we need to have those discussions. I would encourage you to go spend some time in our BIC, or Boeing Integration Center, because it really gives you a feel for what is possible. I tell you one of the biggest network-centric problems in the world today, it's air traffic management. We, Boeing, worked on that for about three years, and we are still working on the technology. But we're the bill payer. Sometimes a problem is just not big enough to solve. The final blow was in the last budget: the president actually cut the FAA's technology budget, and I said, wait a minute. So I went over to see [Secretary of Transportation Norman] Mineta and the FAA administrator and I said, we're here to go with you when you're ready, but you're obviously not ready. We're losing $50 million to $60 million a year on this thing. So we'll be there to go. Meanwhile, we put it back in the Phantom Works [Boeing's research and development unit] and we're developing the technologies. With what we know about space imaging and all the things you folks know, it will take time; but you really can control every aircraft in the world with a combination of space and ground. There's no reason in the world we can't do that, but it's going to take some time. So I would encourage you to get involved in the area as a group or individually. Get involved.

Yes. Got a hand but he doesn't have a microphone. You can have this one.

AUDIENCE: This is actually prompted by the previous question. Do you worry about our racing so far ahead in both applications of technology and particular issues of network-centric warfare? Even though we want to achieve that kind of interoperability with allies, we're so far ahead, so how do we bring them along in that process?

STONECIPHER: I don't worry about it. Only if we become "protectionist" in it. That's the only reason. In terms of technology racing ahead, the chief made a decision recently that said we're going into spiral development because we can't wait 14 years to get all this stuff ready. So we have some technologies that will become ready earlier; let's put those out there and get them going. Then we go into the next spiral. I think it's a masterful stroke, and we have to do that. I'll use an example right now with which I'm very familiar. I was just in the United Kingdom and a lot of people in government in the acquisition area over there beat up on me and said, point blank, if we can't get this problem solved, we're going to stop buying products from you. The issue is the joint strike fighter [JSF] airplane, which they put $10 billion of their own money into. But, they're a partner on this thing. They're not going to be able to get the source codes they need, and we're very sensitive about source codes. I know that. But they want to use some of their own equipment on their airplanes. In order to be able to maintain it and use it, they've got to have the data. I'll tell you something, and maybe I'm a little off, but I think you're a group that would appreciate this comment; if you don't, then we can argue about it. At the time of missile defense, when national defense came up and we had a problem with Russia, with Vladimir Putin [Russian president] and most of the rest of the world, Tony Blair [British prime minister] stood shoulder to shoulder with the president, which mitigated Putin's position. And so here we go. We're the guys who won that contract, and now it's changed or it wasn't just ground-based or boost-phase intercept. It's all together. When I retired, I thought, boy, we're going to get a national security agreement with the United Kingdom. When I came back, we were further away than ever. Here is a country—we fight together, we bleed together, and they stand beside us, through thick and thin. It seems to me, we have to find a way around that. I don't think it's that difficult if we get the right people working on it, but too many people can say no, and it just overwhelms the process. We have to get there if we're going to have interoperability. Otherwise, you're going, once again, to lay out all these big no-fly/no-fire zones, because we don't know where the Brits are, we don't know where the French are, where the Danes are, we don't know where anybody is. So we draw big circles on the map. But, we don't shoot anything in there because these other forces might be there, and we don't have any way to get in touch with them. Exaggerated to make the point, but it's almost that bad.

Yes.

AUDIENCE: When you read something unflattering toward your company on the front page of *The Washington Post*, what is your approach to resolve it? To what extent do you get personally involved in resolving this issue and changing it around so it has the least impact on the corporation as a whole?

STONECIPHER: Number one, I spend an awful lot of time with every newspaper, including *The Washington Post*. We give them access to me, we give them access to our leaders, and we say, look, if you want to talk about the facts, that's fine. I don't know how to deal with, and I won't live long enough to deal with, this "a source in the know." I don't know "a source in the know," "a senior official," and that sort of stuff. I don't know how to deal with that. What we do too is work through Todd Holland, head of communications for us, or here in Washington, Rudy deLeon, sitting right here at this table, who runs our Washington office. He has a great communications chief here in Washington, Maureen Cragin, and they can directly get a hold of Rudy. We would be happy to talk about it. I presume you're with *The Washington Post*.

AUDIENCE: No, sir, I'm with another company in the defense industry.

STONECIPHER: Having the same problem?

AUDIENCE: Thank God, no.

STONECIPHER: Are you one of those "sources in the know"? I think I just identified a competitor.

AUDIENCE: No, I work for a small 300-person company.

STONECIPHER: Good for you. Anyway, the only way to deal with it is to make yourself available and go after it. My goodness, if they're picking on you, things are really bad. I'm sorry.
Go ahead. You need a microphone.

AUDIENCE: Sir, the success of Boeing is no secret. Jacob Kulzer from Minnesota. Got a chance to meet 3M CEO Jim McNerney, the gentleman, whose name escapes me, who runs Home Depot [CEO Robert Nardelli]—you're all products of GE. What happened to GE? Or what do you attribute the success of that leadership development?

STONECIPHER: Management development. It happens at a place called Crotonville. It takes place in the succession planning process. I brought that system to McDonnell Douglas, and we started on that and merged with Boeing; we just expanded the process. It's a disciplined approach to management development. I can tell you that in 1982 I became an officer at GE, an elected officer by the board, in 1979. In 1982, Don Lester was head of personnel in the aircraft engine group, and at this time I was running all the large aircraft engines. I had a great business; I had about 25,000 people working for me. I'm thinking, I'm the hottest stuff there is. He comes around and says, OK, it's time for another learning experience. I said, I really don't have time for this. He said, you have time for it and here is the list of places. Now, why don't you pick from them?

I picked out of there the Dartmouth Institute and ended up after that serving 10 years on their board up there. This was a 30-day intensive program, and it was really liberal arts. As I describe it, this is the thing that made me a real person. There are not many people who know me that call me a real person, but it came closer. So, this thing took everything from the creation to Einstein on the basis that anyone could understand it. There were people there from the IRS [Internal Revenue Service], National Institutes of Health, and DoD [Department of Defense], as well as Texaco and IBM and GE, and a whole range of people.

Now, I'll give you an example. You have Dr. Ron Green, who is head of the religion department there, talking about the Bible, the Book of Genesis in particular. And you have Dr. Charles Drake, who is head of the earth sciences department and anthropology, talking about evolution and the Big Bang theory.

After you have gone through this for a week and you have other things mixed in—everything in the world—you have these breakout sessions. If you want to have a breakout session and talk about whether you believe that the creation of the earth and all that it beholds was according to the Book of Genesis or according to the Big Bang theory, you can have a hell of a discussion. You try never to put spouses—because your spouse goes with you—in the same room, because that's not good. If you take eight people—if you take the people at this table right here—and discuss what you believe about the creation, what do you think that does? Well, it can create an awful lot of angst. But after you have been through this for a while, you suddenly realize that this is not about which is right, this is about my having respect for your idea, your idea, and yours, and yours, and yours.

Even at that point in my career, I'm still worrying about how we're going to continue to develop this . . . . I'm pretty old now. I have been in business 49 years. He missed the first six years, but I don't like to talk about it anyway. I went from being a young high-potential to a senior counselor in what seems like overnight. So, it's been a rapid career. I have been very lucky that people were looking out for me. That's what I tell all of our people. We have 8,700 people in the finance organization in The Boeing Company. Their leadership team was having a meeting in California recently, and they were talking about how we develop people. Why doesn't the company do this and that? I was in the back of the room and they asked me to speak. I said, Let's get something very clear. I am responsible for James Bell. He's the CFO [chief financial officer]. I'm responsible for the people who report directly to him for their success. You folks are responsible for the people who are entrusted to you. It is your job to be sure that you identify the needs they have and be sure they get the leadership and training they need. So, we have carte blanche on training. Anybody who wants to go anywhere, study anything, we're right there. So that's the way I got there. Jim McNerney kind of followed me into the aircraft engine group, and Jim and I spent a lot of time together. Jim's on the Boeing board, by the way. He's a great guy. There are a lot of great leaders. The theory—our theory—was to develop more leaders than you need. When we built the leadership center, the first guy who ran it said, give us the metrics. What metrics do you want? I got so sick of hearing this. In fact, when I came to Boeing, we had some trouble in terms of measuring things, but I have never seen a place with so many metrics and so little performance. We measure everything. So I told him, I'll tell you two metrics. Number one, everybody who comes to this place, I want them to have the attitude they can't wait to come back. The second metric is, when people start stealing our executives, we'll know we have been successful. That's why you see GE executives everywhere, and that's why you see a number of others from other companies everywhere; that's the true test. When people are trying to steal your executives, you know you're building good ones.

Somebody raise a flag when you want me to shut up.

RYAN: Sir, I won't raise a flag . . .

STONECIPHER: Thank you, very much.

RYAN: Thank you, very much, Mr. Stonecipher, for your remarkable insights and comments.

Our next panel is sponsored by the International Institute for Strategic Studies—Balancing Nonproliferation Tools, Policies and Strategies—here in the Atrium Ballroom.

PANEL 2

BALANCING NONPROLIFERATION TOOLS, POLICIES AND STRATEGIES

Co-sponsor: International Institute for Strategic Studies

Introduction by: Scott D. Sagan, Ph.D., Co-Director, Center for
    International Security and Cooperation, Stanford
    University

Moderator: Gary Samore, Ph.D., Director of Studies, Senior Fellow for
    Nonproliferation, International Institute for Strategic Studies

Robert J. Einhorn, Senior Adviser, Center for Strategic and International
    Studies

Philippe Errera, Deputy Director of the Policy Planning Staff, French
    Foreign Ministry

His Excellency Nabil Fahmy, Ambassador of the Arab Republic of Egypt
    to the United States

His Excellency Rakesh Sood, Indian Deputy Chief of Mission to the
    United States

Panel Charter

In the wake of the Sept. 11 terrorist attacks, the threat posed by the nexus of proliferation and terrorism has dominated U.S. security concerns. However, there are different international views on the magnitude of this threat and on the most effective means to deal with it.

The international dispute over the war in Iraq triggered a larger debate on nonproliferation strategy. While the invasion decisively ended Baghdad's latent aspirations to acquire nuclear weapons, postwar assessments of Iraq's nuclear, chemical and biological weapons programs underscored the difficulties of using intelligence as a basis for pre-emptive military action. Moreover, the messy postwar occupation of Iraq has consumed American energy and resources, limiting options and leverage against other countries pursuing nuclear weapons and complicating the campaign against international terrorism.

Left to right: Gary Samore, Robert J. Einhorn, Philippe Errera,
Nabil Fahmy, and Rakesh Sood

Since the onset of the war in Iraq, the nonproliferation scorecard is mixed. On
the positive ledger, the disarmament agreement with Libya and the breakup of the
A.Q. Khan nuclear network were major successes. On the negative ledger, however,
neither Iran nor North Korea appears likely to follow the Libyan model. In both
cases, diplomatic efforts are underway, but their outcome is uncertain, and options
for increasing international pressure through sanctions or military actions are
difficult. Recent challenges to the nonproliferation regime has also spawned a host
of proposals to strengthen international efforts, including the Proliferation Security
Initiative, U.N. Security Council resolution 1540, and tighter Nuclear Suppliers
Group (NSG) guidelines. The upcoming Nuclear Nonproliferation Treaty Review
Conference in 2005 will provide a forum for debating these and other proposals
in the context of demands for advancing nuclear disarmament and allowing access
to peaceful nuclear technology.

The development of a comprehensive nonproliferation strategy rests on three
sets of interrelated issues. First, there are policies designed to deal with specific
countries pursuing nuclear weapons programs, such as Iran and North Korea, and
to respond to proliferation threats in specific regions where proliferation has already
occurred, like South Asia, or where additional proliferation may take place in the
near future, such as the Middle East and East Asia. A second set of issues concerns
the norms, treaties, supplier groups and international institutions that constitute
the international nonproliferation regime. The third set of issues concerns efforts
to prevent terrorist groups from acquiring nuclear materials or nuclear weapons.

The panel, comprised of current and former senior officials from the United States, France, Egypt and India, will address these issues from an international perspective.

Discussion Points

• What mix of inducements and threats are available to persuade countries such as Iran and North Korea to abandon their nuclear efforts, and, if diplomatic efforts fail, to what extent are international sanctions, military force and regime change viable options?

• What options are available for broader regional efforts to encourage arms control and confidence-building measures in regions such as the Middle East, South Asia and East Asia?

• Is it possible to limit the programs of the de facto nuclear weapons states, like India, Pakistan and Israel, and eventually integrate them into the nonproliferation regime?

• What steps can be taken to strengthen compliance and enforcement of existing treaties, like the NPT, and to negotiate new international instruments, such as a Fissile Material Cut-Off Treaty?

• What is the role of nuclear disarmament and arms control treaties, such as the Comprehensive Test Ban Treaty (CTBT), in advancing nonproliferation efforts?

• What measures should be taken by the NSG to tighten controls over exports of nuclear technologies, and can a new international mechanism be constructed to ban or limit the spread of sensitive nuclear fuel cycle capabilities?

• What can be done to strengthen the mandate and capabilities of the International Atomic Energy Agency (IAEA) and to enhance the role of the U.N. Security Council and other international institutions?

• What steps can be taken to ensure full implementation of U.N. Security Council resolution 1540, which requires states to criminalize proliferation activities and take effective measures to protect sensitive materials and technologies?

• What actions should be taken to strengthen security and accounting of nuclear materials, to accelerate Cooperative Threat Reduction programs, and to minimize the use and availability of weapons-usable nuclear materials in civilian nuclear programs?

Summary

Robert J. Einhorn

• There are clear differences between the two candidates, John Kerry and President George W. Bush, on approaches to nonproliferation. Neither has taken the military force option off the table. In recent months, the Bush administration has adopted pragmatic multilateralism. In addition, much will depend on the officials appointed to key posts by whomever is elected. Thus, although key differences exist, there is little reason to believe they would pursue fundamentally different policies.

• Regardless which candidate enters the White House in January, three proliferation challenges will top the agenda: how to get North Korea to dismantle its nuclear arsenal, how to head off Iran from acquiring one, and how to keep nuclear materials out of the hands of terrorists.

• With respect to North Korea, Bush would prefer a Libyan model, but is determined to apply pressure until Pyongyang capitulates to an immediate, comprehensive and verifiable dismantling of its nuclear weapons program. Kerry has the same goal, but appears to be willing to negotiate directly with North Korea through a step-by-step elimination process, and to encourage other countries to offer positive incentives to secure North Korea's cooperation.

• With respect to Iran, both Bush and Kerry favor a multilateral approach. Both insist that Iran adhere to the Additional Protocol of the Nonproliferation Treaty. Both retain the option of referral to the U.N. Security Council and possible imposition of sanctions. However, Kerry seems willing to engage Tehran on a bilateral basis to explore a wide range of issues, while the president appears more narrowly focused on the nuclear issue.

• Overall, whereas Kerry emphasizes strengthening the existing nonproliferation regime, Bush is inclined to ad hoc arrangements such as interdiction via the Proliferation Security Initiative.

• With respect to keeping nuclear materials out of the hands of terrorists, both support threat reduction programs, though Kerry appears to be the more aggressive of the two candidates on this front.

Philippe Errera

• With respect to nonproliferation, we face two main challenges: strengthening existing norms and dealing with proliferators.

• In terms of reinforcing the nuclear nonproliferation regime, the Nonproliferation Treaty is the core. Though a newcomer to the treaty, France recognizes that the NPT is the primary tool in the struggle to stop proliferation. The NPT should be bolstered in three ways: increase the political costs of withdrawal; penalize those who withdraw with losing, "freezing" or dismantling of nuclear technologies acquired under the NPT; and tighten export controls to nontreaty countries.

• What matters more than an institution is what the institution does. The cases of Iran and North Korea—both one-time NPT signatories—will test the usefulness and resolve of the NPT. Can the treaty be used to back them down? The United Nations' legal agreements and the European Union's economic power could both be leveraged as tools for enforcing the NPT.

     1. To strengthen the NPT and associated mechanisms, we must leverage existing institutions. In this respect, no institution is as important as the U.N. Security Council.

2. The economic power of the European Union can be, and should be, harnessed to nonproliferation objectives. The "conditionality clause" linking its economic relations to nonproliferation objectives is a step in the right direction.

3. With respect to violators, the challenge lies in how to prevent a state from using what it acquired as a party to the NPT when it is no longer a party. North Korea and Iran fall into this category since both countries embarked on their nuclear programs while still members of the NPT.

4. Military force might not be the answer to dealing with violators. Iraq is hardly a model in this respect. Since the war, Iran has been emboldened while North Korea remains intransigent and defiant.

• We must be mindful of several things: understanding the importance of the statements and actions of the United States in shaping perceptions, upholding commitments to collective security norms, supporting the importance of regional balances, and taking success anywhere and by any means.

• Was 2004 a turning point? The Iraq war has sucked the oxygen out of the nonproliferation discussion, emboldening North Korea and Iran. Stopping these countries from gaining nuclear weapons should be the world's greatest priority.

His Excellency Nabil Fahmy

• The NPT is the cornerstone of the nuclear nonproliferation regime and is regarded as such even by those who are not signatories. Yet, we should neither underestimate nor exaggerate the importance of the norms of behavior established because of the NPT and its associated activities.

1. In assessing the importance of the NPT, one should ask not just which countries joined but why they joined. In the cases of Japan, Brazil, and Egypt, the decisions to join the NPT were made primarily to address regional security concerns.

2. The nonproliferation debate today operates on an "incomplete premise." There is no evidence that NPT membership has given member countries greater access to civilian nuclear technology than they otherwise would have acquired or developed. Meanwhile, the members of the "nuclear club" have neglected to fulfill their part of the NPT nuclear bargain; they have not made a good faith effort to pursue nuclear disarmament.

3. The NPT must be regarded not as a static process aimed solely at containing proliferation activities, but as a comprehensive process that aims for nuclear disarmament and provides dividends for members by granting them access to civilian nuclear technology.

• With respect to the Middle East, the nuclear proliferation issue must be set within a broader regional security context. Our overarching objective must be to develop a framework whereby the security concerns of every state in the region are addressed. There are a number of steps that could be taken in that regard.

1. A Middle East regional security conference should be convened.

2. The U.N. Security Council should reaffirm the call for a nuclear-free zone in the Middle East embedded in paragraph 14 of the U.N. Security Council resolution 687.

3. IAEA officials and other experts should conduct a careful study of the experiences of other countries and regions, such as South Africa, with the aim of deriving lessons that could be applied in the Middle East.

His Excellency Rakesh Sood

• The NPT offered a good package of trade-offs for signatories. However, over the years, the objectives of the NPT bargain appear to have changed.

1. As originally conceived, the NPT provided that nuclear have-nots would voluntarily disarm or forego development of nuclear weapons, the nuclear powers would embark on a good faith effort to pursue disarmament, and NPT members would have access to civilian nuclear technology.

2. Over the years, nuclear powers found it politically unacceptable to pursue disarmament. Meanwhile, the distinction between permissible and proscribed research and development has grown fuzzy.

• Is "hedging" a structural problem in the NPT? How can we deal with countries that hold nuclear weapons technology "in reserve," ready to go nuclear in a matter of weeks? Does this situation jeopardize the NPT's future?

• A major goal of the NPT is now to restrict terrorists' access to nuclear weapons, and the NPT's "toolkit" must be updated to reflect that.

Analysis

In a discussion reminiscent of Cold War concerns, Panel II focused exclusively on the threat of nuclear proliferation—specifically, the question of how to strengthen the NPT, which comes up for its perennial five-year review in 2005. The panel thus set aside the growing threat posed by the proliferation of chemical and biological weapons, though some of the solutions offered for strengthening the NPT might also work to bolster the Chemical Weapons Convention (CWC) and Biological Weapons Convention (BWC). All panelists seemed to agree with Robert Einhorn that the main nuclear proliferation challenges facing the White House are getting North Korea to dismantle its nuclear arsenal, preventing Iran from developing nuclear arms, and keeping nuclear and radiological weapons from falling into the hands of terrorist groups. Despite the two weeks of unfruitful debate that plagued the NPT Preparatory Committee, chartered with establishing the key issues and agenda for the 2005 review, all panelists also agreed the NPT was a necessary, though insufficient instrument for meeting current proliferation challenges.

The panel's recommendations for strengthening the NPT fell into three broad categories. The first was increasing the legal force of the NPT by expanding the political and economic penalties that institutions like the U.N. Security Council can impose on violators or states that withdraw, as with Iran and North Korea. The second was modifying the NPT so that it is not just an instrument for "containing" proliferation, but one that also promotes disarmament. The third was addressing the regional security concerns of signatories. Even in this age of globalization, many states remain concerned over regional actors who may not have signed the NPT and may not admit to having nuclear weapons. Although they have admitted to possessing nuclear weapons, India and Pakistan also remain outside the treaty. Such circumstances put NPT signatories that are not nuclear-armed at risk. Indeed, Nabil Fahmy, Egypt's ambassador to the United States, implied as much when he pointed out that the NPT has not met the security concerns of many states in the Middle East.

Efforts to strengthen the NPT could well include measures from all three categories, as they are not mutually exclusive. In fact, if applied appropriately, they could also help strengthen the CWC and BWC. However, one senses that such measures will not amount to much unless more states which have not yet

Transcript

ANNOUNCER: Ladies and gentlemen, Dr. Scott Sagan, co-director, Center for International Security and Cooperation, Stanford University.

SCOTT D. SAGAN, Ph.D.: Good afternoon. Last year at this conference, I organized and chaired a panel on predicting proliferation in an unpredictable world. Well, what a difference a year makes. Who would have predicted that today we would be concerned that North Korea may be preparing for a nuclear test? That today we know that Libya has renounced nuclear weapons? That the PSI, Proliferation Security Initiative, intercepted a Chinese bomb design on its way to Tripoli wrapped inside an Islamabad laundry bag? Who would have predicted that Iran would be caught, if not with its hands in the nuclear cookie jar, then at least with a few crumbs of enriched uranium on its fingers?

I can't think of anyone better to organize and chair a panel on balancing nonproliferation tools, policies and strategy than the chair of this panel, Dr. Gary Samore, the director of studies of the International Institute of Strategic Studies [IISS] in London. I have been a friend and colleague of Dr. Samore's since we were in graduate school at Harvard together. His many achievements and appointments are outlined in your book: his scholarly and analytical positions at Livermore and RAND, his important positions in the State Department, and most importantly his high-ranking National Security Council job. I'm therefore not going to go over those.

I thought I could introduce him on a more personal note by stating the three things that I admire about Gary Samore's work. First, it has been his intellectual breadth and his published, valuable research that has provided insight on subjects as diverse as the nature of the royal family in Saudi Arabia and Chinese-American export control problems. He's produced major studies about Saddam's WMD [weapons of mass destruction] program and, most recently, North Korea's nuclear weapons efforts. Second, Dr. Samore's work inside and outside the government speaks truth to power. It's crucial, whether you are an academic, a government official or a military officer, to make sure that your difficult decisions are based on real facts on the ground and to avoid the tendency to see the world as you wish it were, rather than the way it really is. Dr. Samore's rigorous scholarship and his analytical skills have been a great effort to improve objectivity in both the scholarly and the government world. And third and lastly, Dr. Samore's work inside and outside the government has been fair and objective, in part because he listens and takes into account a variety

Scott D. Sagan

of views—other academics', other bureaucratic actors' and other countries' positions. And it's so important in the world today, whether or not we agree or disagree with other people's opinions on the question of proliferation, to engage with them in debate in efforts to find more effective solutions. So without further ado, I think you will see the debate and discussion and diversity of opinions in the panel today that Dr. Samore has put together. Let's welcome Gary Samore.

GARY SAMORE, Ph.D.: Hi, everybody. Scott, thank you very much for that extremely kind introduction. I would like to welcome all of you here to our panel discussion on balancing nonproliferation tools, policies and strategies. Scott did a good job of summarizing all of the dramatic nonproliferation events—some good, some bad—that have taken place in recent years. Those events have sparked a debate within the international community over how serious the threat posed by proliferation is—both by state and by non-state actors—on the kind of instruments that should be used to deal with those threats, including military force, political and diplomatic measures, economic sanctions and so forth. There has been debate on the balance among the different types of strategies. Some policies are focused on particular countries. Other strategies are focused on trying to achieve regional understandings and agreements. Finally there are the international treaties and organizations, which make up an important part of the international nonproliferation regime. I hope that our panel will provide a diverse international perspective on those issues.

Gary Samore

We have four very distinguished panelists, current and former officials, and I would like to invite them to please take their seats on the podium now.

Our first speaker is Robert Einhorn, who is currently a senior advisor at the Center for Strategic and International Studies [CSIS] here in Washington. Prior to joining CSIS, Bob was the iron-man of U.S. nonproliferation and arms-control policy, having served with the U.S. government for nearly 30 years in a number of key positions including, most recently, as assistant secretary of state for nonproliferation, both in the Clinton and the Bush administrations.

Bob will be followed by Philippe Errera, who is a rising star in the French diplomatic service. Philippe has served here in Washington in the French Embassy and currently he is the deputy director for the Policy Planning Staff in the French Foreign Ministry in Paris, with particular responsibility for long-range planning and developing innovative ideas for dealing with the proliferation threat.

Our third speaker is Ambassador Nabil Fahmy, one of Egypt's most distinguished diplomats and currently the Egyptian ambassador to the United States. During his long career, Ambassador Fahmy has held a number of key positions in Cairo, in New York and Geneva working on international and regional disarmament issues.

Finally, our last speaker, a cleanup batter in American parlance, is Rakesh Sood, who is the deputy chief of mission in the Indian Embassy here in Washington. Rakesh is famous as India's leading government expert on disarmament and nonproliferation issues, and he has served for many years in key positions in the Indian Ministry of External Affairs and also in the Indian Mission in Geneva. Bob and I have had the pleasure of dealing with all of these gentlemen in the course of our government careers and also outside of government.

I'll ask each of the speakers to talk for about 10 minutes, and then I'll open the floor for comments and questions. Bob, you're first.

ROBERT J. EINHORN: Gary, thank you very much. And especially, thank you for including me on a panel with three very good friends who happen to be three of the most capable diplomats I have worked with in the 30 years I was at the State Department. So, it's a pleasure to be here.

I'm going to talk a little bit about the future of U.S. policies in the area of nonproliferation. With the presidential election just about seven weeks away, and clearly real differences existing between the two presidential candidates on how to fight proliferation, it's hard to predict with any precision the kinds of policies that the United States will pursue in nonproliferation in, say, about six months time. Indeed, even if we knew today who is going to win the election, it would be difficult to predict U.S. policies. We can only speculate, for example, on whether a second Bush administration would continue with the relatively pragmatic multilateralist approach that the current Bush administration has taken in recent months, or whether it would revert to its earlier pre-Iraq emphasis on more

Robert J. Einhorn

muscular unilateralist policies. To some extent, this would depend on who would hold senior positions in the second Bush administration, and we don't know that either. Still, even with these uncertainties, it's possible to identify at least some policies the U.S. will pursue in the years ahead regardless of who will be president, as well as to describe some areas on which a Bush administration and a Kerry administration would probably differ.

Near the top of the agenda for any U.S. administration would be rolling back North Korea's nuclear program and heading off an Iranian nuclear weapons capability. But the Bush and Kerry approaches to these priorities would differ significantly. On North Korea, a second Bush administration would press the North Koreans to follow the so-called Libya model. That is, to get rid of North Korea's nuclear programs completely, verifiably and pretty quickly without the United States having to provide tangible rewards until disarmament by North Korea is essentially complete. If and when North Korea rejects this approach, a second Bush administration would seek to build multilateral support for pressuring the North Korean regime until it capitulates, it accepts disarmament on U.S. terms or until it simply collapses. A Kerry administration can be expected to insist on the same goal of completely and verifiably eliminating North Korea's nuclear capability. But it would probably be prepared to negotiate an agreement providing for a more prolonged, step-by-step elimination process, with the United States joining others in making rewards available to the North Koreans from the outset.

On Iran, both a Bush and Kerry administration can be expected to rely heavily on international pressures, including United Nations Security Council sanctions to persuade Iran to renounce, permanently, oil enrichment and other so-called fuel-cycled capabilities. But while a Bush administration would be reluctant to deal directly with the current regime in Teheran, a Kerry administration probably would be willing to engage bilaterally and explore prospects for resolving the wide range of issues that divide the two countries. Now in addition to focusing on the specific challenges posed by North Korea and Iran, both Bush and Kerry would pursue a range of multilateral measures. Among other things, they would seek to strengthen multilateral export control regimes. They would urge all countries to adhere to the International Atomic Energy Agency's [IAEA] Additional Protocol, which allows for much more intrusive inspections and more complete data declarations. And they would try to close a loophole in the NPT [Nuclear Nonproliferation Treaty] by trying to erect barriers to the spread of enrichment and reprocessing capabilities. But in approaching these multilateral measures there would clearly be differences of emphasis. A Bush administration would lean toward informal and ad hoc arrangements, for example, the Proliferation Security Initiative, which is a voluntary arrangement aimed at trying to interdict illicit WMD-related shipments. Tellingly, the Bush administration calls PSI an activity, not an organization. A Kerry administration would give greater weight to more formal and institutionalized arrangements and would be more supportive of existing multilateral agreements. The difference can be seen in the Kerry and Bush approach toward a fissile material cut-off treaty [FMCT]. Sen. Kerry has come out in favor of an FMCT as traditionally conceived, with fairly elaborate verification provisions. The Bush administration recently announced that it also supports a fissile material cut-off treaty. But what it has in mind is a very different thing, essentially a bare-bones, political commitment to stop producing fissile material for nuclear weapons without any verification provisions or compliance mechanism.

Now, in addition to dealing with the problem of proliferation in additional states, additional countries, we would expect both the Bush and Kerry administrations to give high priority, perhaps the highest priority, to preventing terrorists from getting their hands on weapons of mass destruction or ingredients to produce WMD. But in this area, too, there would be differences, with a Bush administration giving relatively greater emphasis to eliminating the terrorists themselves and a Kerry administration giving relatively greater emphasis to securing weapons and materials worldwide so that the terrorists couldn't get their hands on them. Therefore, while both administrations would support a continuation of the Nunn-Lugar-type cooperative threat reduction programs, a Kerry administration would be expected to pursue such programs more aggressively. These are only a handful of the issues on which we would expect differences to emerge between a Kerry and Bush administration; many other examples could be given. But it's important to recognize that on a wide range of proliferation issues, the differences between a Bush and Kerry administration may actually be a lot smaller than the differences between either of them and many key countries whose cooperation is essential in the fight against WMD proliferation.

Part of the explanation for this is the differing threat perceptions. The United States regards the WMD threat as greater and more imminent than do most other countries. This is especially true for the threat of WMD terrorism, especially nuclear terrorism. The United States sees the world through a 9/11 prism and believes that terrorist use of WMD is just a matter of time. Many other countries, including some that have been plagued by terrorism for many years, tend to focus on the threat with which they are familiar, and that is the conventional terrorist threat. Another difference between the United States and other countries is over methods of influencing the behavior of countries that are interested in pursuing weapons of mass destruction. Many in Europe and elsewhere prefer engagement over confrontation and incentives over penalties. In the United States, even the advocates of negotiation and engagement believe that a policy of all carrots and no sticks simply won't work. Americans are, therefore, more likely to include coercive measures, including economic sanctions in their antiproliferation tool kit. While there clearly are differences between Bush and Kerry on the use of military force to address proliferation threats, no U.S. administration will want to take the military option off the table all together. So the differences between the United States and its foreign partners will inevitably rise over the next several years, whoever is president. A key test for the next administration, whether led by Bush or Kerry, is whether it can narrow those differences and forge the common strategy that will be necessary to deal with today's WMD threats.

Thank you.

SAMORE: Thank you very much, Bob. Our second speaker is Philippe Errera.

PHILIPPE ERRERA: Thank you, Gary. With your permission, I'll speak sitting down. I would like to thank you, obviously, for those kind words. I would like to thank the IISS and the Eisenhower Conference for having me here. I'm thrilled, given the topic, which is one that I have worked on very much. I'm also somewhat awed, given the fact that four other people on this panel are individuals who have devoted all of their professional lives to the topic, or most of it, and who know far more about it than I do—and that's not just French humility that's speaking. It's true.

The fundamental questions that were asked today, I think, are how we strengthen the existing norms. I would like to run through a few ideas that Bob mentioned that are being discussed—French proposals on this. Diplomats, especially when they are diplomats with no responsibilities like myself—people on planning staffs—love to come up with new ideas and new institutions. But the question that somebody legitimately asked is, "Well, it's fine to strengthen and tighten and tweak, but what about upholding existing ones?" I think North Korea

and Iran are fundamental issues. So I
would like to go through these two sets
of issues with you.

In terms of reinforcing the nuclear
nonproliferation regime, the NPT is
at the core of this. Some may say that
France comes to the NPT with the zeal
of new converts; after all, they're only a
party since 1992. But it's fundamental
in our view to strengthening and to
upholding international security. The
NPT has kept the number of nuclear
states in the single digits, after all.
However, saying that it's essential doesn't
mean that it can't be perfected or that the
regime, which is at the core of the issue,
can't be tightened.

I would like to share three series
of ideas with you. First of all, the issue
of withdrawal. Now, it may seem like
an arcane legal issue, but when you

Philippe Errera

look at the North Korean crisis and perhaps others to come, it's at the core.
Like any treaty, the NPT has a withdrawal clause. But the particular danger with
withdrawal from this treaty is that what a state is entitled to while a party—that
is, nuclear cooperation—transfers know-how and materials, et cetera, is precisely
what is forbidden to nonparties, and for good reason. It's at the core of the nuclear
program.

Our objective is twofold in proposals that have been put before the G8
[Globalized Eight Nations] partners and more broadly within the NPT. First is
to increase the political cost of withdrawing, and second, to prevent a state quite
simply from having its cake and eating it, too. That is to say, to prevent a country
from using what it acquired as a party when it no longer is a party. Our proposal
is straightforward. First, a state that withdraws from the NPT should no longer
make use of all the nuclear materials, facilities, equipment or technologies that it
acquired before withdrawal. These should be returned to the supplying state, frozen
or dismantled under international verification. Second, the IAEA, or International
Atomic Energy Agency, should be able to implement safeguards or agreements for
a specified time after the withdrawal. This is not the case today.

A second series of ideas in strengthening the NPT has to do with tightening
the supply of some of the most sensitive and potentially proliferating technologies.
We need to keep in mind a very simple fact in a debate that looks complicated
technically and legally. In most cases, developing peaceful uses of nuclear energy
does not require sensitive and potentially proliferating technology, such as

enrichment reprocessing. You can have two approaches. You can either say, well, that was then and now is now, and we're going to forbid something that was authorized before—which is, by and large, President Bush's proposal. It may be, in the ideal, something that would solve the problem, but the issue is how you get from here to there. Among the difficulties that exist, there is the simple issue of feasibility. It's difficult to see how it would be implemented politically.

You can have another approach—a French approach with backing from other members of the European Union—which is to only envisage such exports if a certain number of criteria are met. That is to say, focus on the situation at hand in terms of the country that you're exporting it to and in terms of whether there is a real need in terms of economic rationality. This, I think, is one of the issues that, whether it be President Bush or Sen. Kerry, will be pushed forward under the next administration and that will reshape the regime, and luckily so.

A third proposal in terms of the NPT is to reverse the burden of proof, if you will, in terms of nuclear cooperation. The idea would be to suspend nuclear cooperation with states for which the IAEA cannot provide sufficient assurances that the nuclear program is devoted exclusively to peaceful purposes. Today the situation is the opposite, and as we see in the Iranian case and perhaps in others, it's much more difficult to prove a negative than to provide sufficient assurances that the program is exclusively for peaceful uses.

Now, this had to do with strengthening the NPT, which, by design, was an instrument devoted to nonproliferation. More importantly, or as importantly, I think we need to look at ways to leverage existing international institutions whose original purpose was either broader than or different from nonproliferation per se and leveraging institutions to fight proliferation. Obviously, at the core of this is the United Nations and the U.N. Security Council. We may defer across the Atlantic or within the United States regarding the issue of whether the United Nations is the foremost or the main source of legitimacy for the use of coercive measures and force. One thing that we can't differ about—because it's simply a fact—is that the United Nations Security Council is the only body that can adopt internationally binding legal rules. Resolution 1540, which did many things, including criminalizing domestic-level proliferation activities, is extremely important. It gives teeth to something that was important symbolically and rhetorically, which was the statement of the heads of state or government in January 1992, qualifying WMD proliferation as a threat to international peace and security.

The European Union is another institution that we tend not to think of in terms of the fight against proliferation. Some of you may be familiar with the E.U. security strategy that was adopted last December. It identifies, correctly in my mind, proliferation as one of the key strategic threats to the E.U.—to E.U. security and to E.U. interests more broadly, along with terrorism. Perhaps a more important development, which went largely unnoticed, was the adoption at that same summit of a so-called conditionality clause. Now, what this means, vis-à-vis proliferation, is that from now on, all trade agreements with third-world countries will contain a clause that includes respect for the nonproliferation commitment, considered a key element of the treaty. This means that any breech of these commitments will open a process leading ultimately to the suspension of the agreement if nothing is done to remedy this. Now, this is important because on top of the E.U.'s growing but still modest diplomatic weight, what we can do is leverage the economic and commercial power of the E.U. toward a nonproliferation objective. In jargon, this is called mainstreaming. Now, some of you, I'm sure, are familiar with the G8 and what we have done within the G8 in terms of strengthening nonproliferation, whether it be for global partnership and the countries of the former Soviet Union, and whether it be in terms of fighting the potential for NRBC [nuclear, radiological, biological, chemical] terrorism. So G8 is certainly important. I mentioned institutions. It's not to put institutions on the one hand and activities on the other. I think that's somewhat artificial. What matters more than institutions is what they do, and what matters more than activities per se is what is achieved. So I think the Proliferation Security Initiative is an extremely important development as well.

Now, back to the real world. It's time to strengthen norms, but what do you do about upholding existing ones when they're broken or challenged by proliferators? And here I would like to come to the real world cases we're dealing with today as analysts and as diplomats. I agree with the initial assessment made by Scott Sagan and Gary Samore in terms of the picture today. It's a mixed picture. But my sense is that what matters more than the snapshot is the dynamic for the years to come and how today's situation affects the future equation. People say every year that they're at a turning point of some form or other, but I would make the case that the choices made in the coming months and couple of years ahead will really shape the nonproliferation scene and future for the coming decades. Iran and North Korea do represent a turning point, for three reasons. First of all, vis-à-vis the nonproliferation regime, Iran and North Korea were members of the Nonproliferation Treaty when they embarked upon these activities. That is something that fundamentally changes the equation compared to the situation in India or Pakistan, and whether it works or whether it doesn't work.

Second, regarding regional balances: Just as in physics you can have a stable or unstable equilibrium, a situation where you have nine or 10 nuclear-capable states is an unstable equilibrium. In other words, the chances are that with a nuclear-armed Iran and with an nuclear-armed North Korea, you will not keep that number down because of the regional dynamics.

Thirdly, vis-à-vis our own security interests, I am speaking as a European. Whether it is the direct consequences of a nuclear-armed Iran—especially coupled with the ballistics programs—or the indirect consequences of what a nuclear-armed Iran would feel emboldened to do, that would be of strategic interest to us. So it's important. I guess we agreed on that much.

Now, how do we address it? The menu of options usually revolves around the use of force, diplomacy or some combination thereof. To come back to the use of military force: This is an issue that if we can't deal with in this room and with this audience, I don't know where we can. I would like to try to address it. It's sometimes an effective option in dealing with proliferation. Fortunately or unfortunately, depending on where you stand, it's far less often the case that military force is an effective tool—less often than we would like to think.

Now I would like to come to Iraq, which is the big elephant standing in the corner of the room, at least regarding this panel. The point isn't to debate the war and whether it was right or not, but how it affected our efforts in the field of nuclear nonproliferation and counterproliferation. Here, the paradox in my mind is that Iraq was supposed to be the first-ever international military intervention based on counterproliferation grounds. But on the whole, I'm afraid that it has hindered our efforts to combat proliferation more than it has helped. First of all, Iraq sucked up all the oxygen, if you will, out of the international diplomatic arena for a good part of 2002 and 2003. And the agenda in New York and elsewhere was entirely dominated by Iraq. The North Koreans tracked this situation very closely, and my guess is that when they came out in October 2002 defiantly, it wasn't a random choice. The continued defiance by North Korea of the international community—when they checked every one of the boxes in terms of kicking out inspectors, resuming reprocessing and announcing its withdrawal from the NPT—was not met by a firm response in the international community. For the United States, at the time, the United Nations Security Council agenda was to be left free in order to deal with Iraq, which was said quite explicitly. And for others, including China, it was quite a convenient situation. China didn't have to openly oppose U.N. Security Council action like it did in the first North Korean crisis.

As for Iran, my fear is that Iran has felt emboldened by the situation in Iraq. Here we have another interesting paradox. For some in this administration—by no means everybody, and I think by no means everybody in the Pentagon—the main purpose of the Iraq war was to demonstrate the extent of U.S. strength to the Arab world. I have heard it put this way in a number of instances. The problem in the paradox is that it did just that. It showed the neighbors of Iraq the limitations of the military tool for nonmilitary objectives, such as state building or fighting unconventional adversaries. No matter how dedicated, well-trained and well-equipped the occupying force is, it will always be at a structural disadvantage. The result is that Iran now feels far more emboldened now than in the past couple of years, and this is one of the reasons that firm, international pressure and the prospect of Security Council referral do not work today or may not work as effectively.

So what do we do about it? I think we use what we have; we leverage what we can. I would like to focus on Iran briefly because it's the issue of the day and because of the role that France played in this issue. Iran is not North Korea. Iran has always perceived its power and prestige as being incompatible with international isolation. So the focus has been on the short term when presented with a structured choice. Either go ahead with the nuclear weapons program and face the consequences—and here I would slightly differ with Bob, in that we're under no illusions that carrots alone can work—or give it up and explore ways in which it can improve its relationship with the outside world and work on the other issues, which are still problematic. This is what the three E.U. countries said to Iran last October when they were able to secure the pledge to suspend enrichment and reprocessing activities. The fact that we were able to get that pledge, however fragile, means that at the time, at least, the threat of Security Council referral was effective. Today we have the discussions in Vienna going on. I suspect that we'll obtain a consensus to set a date for a definitive determination, whether we call it a trigger or not. This matters less than the fact that it's a definitive determination, and between now and that date it's up to the Iranians to decide whether they really want to choose the path of confrontation. It's up to us to strengthen the consensus both within the Security Council—and here I think the role of the Chinese and the Russians is key—but more broadly in the international community.

No, proliferation isn't a rich country's problem. No, this isn't about Europeans and Americans ganging up on a Muslim country being unfairly discriminated against. This is about upholding some of the last collective security norms that we have left and making the world safer. In the longer term, the issue is shaping the perceptions that determine their choice. Ultimate success will be when Iranian leaders, either current ones or future, democratically elected ones—that doesn't make much of a difference—determine that they're better off without nuclear weapons than with them. Here I agree with Bob, that the U.S. has a key role to play in shaping this perception.

To briefly conclude—I've spoken for too long—two comments. First, we have a huge responsibility. Usually we can dissect proliferation cases after the fact. What signals did we miss? What actions did we not take that we should have? Here, we're in the midst of the crisis and, as I said in my introduction, we know that our actions, or lack thereof, will shape the world we live in for years to come. Second, in a relatively bleak environment, I think there are at least two causes for hope. One is the sense of unity of purpose of the international community that has resisted the divisions over Iraq regarding nonproliferation. This is something important, I believe. The other is a new, more pragmatic approach, on both sides of the Atlantic. On this side of the Atlantic you hear people who portray themselves, and are proud to portray themselves, as staunch unilateralists now lobbying the United Nations and the IAEA. You have people who equate engagement with appeasement gladly going along on the deal in Libya. So you know there is a greater readiness to take the successes where you find them. On a more Cartesian side of the Atlantic, where we like to make stark distinctions between unilateralism, multilateralism, ad hoc initiatives, institution initiatives, et cetera, that's not the issue anymore. A French diplomat, the joke goes, was supposed to have asked one day, "Well, it works in practice, but does it work in theory?"

Today, believe me, anything that works in practice is plenty fine with us.

SAMORE: Thank you, Ambassador Fahmy.

HIS EXCELLENCY NABIL FAHMY: Thank you, Gary. And if I can take Philippe's lead, I'll also speak from where we are. First, let me thank you for inviting me to come here and speak on the subject. Not only have you brought me back to old friends whom I have had the pleasure of working with for many, many years in the past, but frankly you've gotten me off the Middle East region as a crisis region into the area of disarmament. If one can say disarmament is easier in the Middle East, that doesn't say much of the Middle East.

Anyway, I'm happy to be here and I want to share with you my thoughts on the challenges that nonproliferation faces from a Middle Eastern perspective. And let me underline they are my own personal thoughts, they are not

Nabil Fahmy

necessarily the Egyptian government's thoughts. I have not attempted to navigate official positions here, but I want to make a contribution to the debate. If I'm too far off where our policy is, I'll hear about it, but I'll deal with that.

My point of departure is if we're talking about nuclear nonproliferation, for better or worse the cornerstone of the international regime is the NPT. That's what we've all taken as the cornerstone, even for those who have not adopted the NPT, who have not become parties of the treaty itself. Now, that's a dangerous road to follow by way of argument, because I believe on the one hand, one should not underestimate the importance of the norms that have been established because of the NPT. Also, I believe in the energy and efforts that have been made as a function of the NPT, even though they go beyond the NPT as a treaty per se. That said, one shouldn't exaggerate our achievements or the actual contribution that the NPT has had in getting us where we are in the nonproliferation arena, or for that matter where its contributions will be in the future, given the new challenges that we face.

Many like to argue that its success is in the treaty's wide-ranging membership. I argue that membership itself is not just numbers. I also argue also that not even who joins is an adequate criterion if we want to judge whether the NPT and this international proliferation regime have been successful or not. Again, I emphasize that one should not belittle the importance of the norms that have brought us so far, but should question why we haven't gone further and what have we done wrong.

In trying to understand the real value of the NPT, one should really look at why countries joined rather than who joined. One should look particularly in areas that were potential nonproliferation areas or countries that had the potential to pursue nuclear programs. If I look at the different situations over the years—even among significant countries like Japan, Brazil, Argentina or my own country, Egypt—have these countries decided to join the NPT because it fulfilled their nonproliferation security concerns? It was a decision made to create regional balance; a decision made for economic reasons; or a decision made because of the environment that exists in the world that led countries down that road. But for very few of these countries, was the decision purely a function of, "That's where our security concerns are being resolved. Admission to that treaty resolves our security concerns"? I can tell you, very frankly, that was not the reason behind Egypt joining the NPT.

The concern that many have in joining the treaty or not joining the treaty has been, "How do you respond to the security concerns?" The success of the NPT—the success of the operation or its failure at the end of the day—has to be evaluated on that basis more than on anything else. Many say today that the NPT, given the concerns raised that were mentioned by the previous speakers, has to be revisited. Many say that we need to look at it and see whether the basic trade-off that has served us in the past can serve us in the future. In particular, many question whether the commitment not to acquire nuclear weapons in exchange for peaceful access to nuclear technology remains a trade-off that we can continue to provide nations because of the challenges that we have seen over the years. I raise this issue because, frankly, I think it's the wrong question. I think it's the wrong question because I don't think that it was the basic trade-off of the NPT. I think it was one of the trade-offs in the NPT, but another important trade-off was the pursuit of nuclear disarmament. Look at the Article 6 provisions in the treaty; they actually go beyond nuclear disarmament. It calls directly for negotiations in good faith for a treaty on general and complete disarmament, with unrestricted and effective international control. This commitment was basically a trade-off for accepting the nuclear status of the five states that were nuclear at the time, for a period until this process could continue and move forward.

So my concern with the debate about the nonproliferation regime, generally, is that we're putting forward a premise that is factually incomplete and, therefore, missing the point behind the fundamental weakness of the regime and, in particular, the treaty. If one looks at these two trade-offs, the very least one will conclude is that the track record on both of them has not been particularly Olympian in terms of its results. There is no evidence that states that had peaceful nuclear programs in the past actually had more access to peaceful nuclear technology, by joining the NPT, than if they had decided not to become members of the NPT. And if I were to go to the second trade-off, we're coming close to the 40th anniversary of the NPT. If one argues that what we're witnessing today is a sincere effort to negotiate general and complete disarmament, frankly, that's a stretch even by Middle Eastern standards. The main concern I have about the NPT—and I use the term NPT loosely because it's the cornerstone of the nonproliferation regime, but it applies to many of the other measures that we have built into the system—we have become underachievers in the process. We've looked at the nonproliferation regime as a static process, trying to achieve nonproliferation by containment, rather than trying to achieve nonproliferation by ultimately pursuing a serious, concrete and aggressive disarmament process.

One should look at the problem areas of the world for the past few years— South Asia, the Korean Peninsula or the Middle East—and look at the situation in India, Pakistan and Israel, who decided not to join. And it is their right not to join the NPT. One should look at the situation in North Korea, which I'm not exactly sure what the legal status is, but it's basically deciding to opt out—or at one point decided it would opt out of the process. Look at Iraq, which violated the treaty, and the questions about Iran's nuclear posture. All of these states pursued their objectives, legitimately or illegitimately, because they had security concerns that they felt were not being addressed within the context of the treaty.

My country, Egypt, is a member of the NPT of long standing now. Nevertheless, we feel that the treaty and the international regime set up around the treaty have not fulfilled our security concerns in the region. Being a country in the Middle East with the issues that have been raised here today, it would be naive to argue that what's happening in our region with proliferation does not affect Egypt's security concerns.

But let me be very clear here. I'm not suggesting we tear down the temple and build a new one. That's simply too risky and unnecessary. What we need to do, once again, is use the nonproliferation regime as a tool to once again start a nuclear disarmament process, a process that provides dividends for parties who join the nonproliferation regime. The NPT parties, in particular, must be the force behind nuclear disarmament. The NPT and members of its international regime must provide more beneficial dividends to the parties than to those countries who decide not to join, be that in terms of security or developmental needs. Let me underline again, we have to find a way to provide more access to the peaceful use of nuclear energy and nuclear technology for members of the nonproliferation regime. I'm not suggesting sanctioning non-state parties. What I'm suggesting is providing a proactive reason for them to join the regime, by creating the environment in which international pressure is toward nuclear disarmament and providing dividends, security and development for membership to the treaties.

Let me simply state outright—be it in the Middle East or beyond—I don't think the status quo will stand. I say this with a word of caution. I say this, frankly, with tremendous concern. But I do not believe, given the last 25 years where every state of concern or concerned state has decided either to remain outside the NPT or to violate the NPT, that that situation can continue to go on without there being a reaction. What do I mean by a reaction? By a reaction, I'm talking most about non-nuclear weapon states. I think there are five possible options out there, and I will list them in reverse order of my preference. One, states may decide to pursue nuclear weapons. Again, these are in reverse order. Two, states will decide to raise the level of either their conventional or other weapons of mass destruction. Each of these will have a deterrent value, not necessarily relevant to the deceptive power of the weapon, but in terms of the possibility of being able to use them in different circumstances. Three, you'll have states that have joined treaties that will withdraw or freeze their membership in these treaties. Four, you will have states refrain from adhering to new arrangements or treaties. And five—my colleagues here around the table will not be surprised—my preference is actually to pursue, for the Middle East at least, a regional approach and try to achieve a nuclear-free zone in the Middle East.

Now, I'm pretty sure I wasn't asked to come up here and talk about North Korea or frankly about the Six-Party Talks, or the history of nuclear disarmament, so let me just say a few words on the Middle East. When I look at the Middle East and think about the issue of nuclear disarmament or nuclear nonproliferation, I look at the states that are players in this area today. Israel is the only non-NPT member in the region. Therefore, in the larger context of global nonproliferation, it is the most problematic situation. Because of its policy of nuclear weapons ambiguity, Iraq is in a traumatic state, a security paradigm today undefined. Iran is perceived to have chosen the posture of the non-nuclear weapon ambiguity. Iran and Israel's Arab neighbors are all members of the NPT. The reality is when India tested, Pakistan tested; when India declared, so did Pakistan. Countries react to the function their immediate regional concerns. They may be legitimate; they may not be legitimate. But the reality is, unless we attempt to pursue a drawing-down of the threat potential in the Middle East, there will be—if not a drawing-up—there will be a slowdown in adherence to any international efforts to pursue nonproliferation. That will be a problem not only for our region, but for the world at large.

It has often been argued that it doesn't seem logical to expect negotiations on a nuclear-free zone to start as long as the Arab-Israeli conflict is there, and, now, with the Iraq situation, that it is even more complicated in terms of getting the parties together. That may be true, but I would argue it's actually more illogical not to start, because if one looks at the nuclear programs in the region, they have actually increased in both their lack of ambiguity and their capacity as threat potentials have decreased in the region.

What has happened over the years is that people have become more ready to pursue a less ambiguous policy on proliferation in the Middle East as they felt the opportunity allowed. Now, the fact is, on the Iranian issue, as Philippe said, the IAEA is debating the issue this week. They have had their efforts with the Iranians and, of course, the United States is engaged in trying to deal with the Iranian situation. Whether one goes to the Security Council now or in November, whether there is a grand design, whether there is a grand compromise between light-water reactors and the determination not to pursue the fuel cycle, and so on and so forth, they are all issues that are out there. I think we will have to address those issues concretely as a step toward looking for a regional security arrangement that satisfies all the parties in the region. But again, let me say, I don't think that any of these steps will ultimately deal with the nonproliferation issues if they stand alone. The security concerns of Arab states—and of Israel, of Iran—have to be addressed if we are going to be able to put an end or at least significantly slow down nonproliferation threats in the Middle East.

And there are several suggestions that I would like to throw out to the audience. They can be looked at, not necessarily to be implemented immediately, but I think that they will, in time, have to be taken into account. First, it will be necessary to hold a regional security conference for the Middle East, where the security concerns of all the regions are addressed, be they nuclear, weapons of mass destruction or general security issues. I think the situation today is more and more in that direction.

Second, if we're talking about taking nonproliferation issues, particularly from the Middle East, to the Security Council, it's important that the council look back at its own resolution 687, paragraph 14, which calls for a zone free of all weapons of mass destruction in the Middle East, including nuclear weapons. I don't think that the council can on the one hand mention it, but on the other hand completely ignore it when it talks about proliferation issues, particularly in the Middle East.

Third, I think the United Nations itself and several expert groups in the past have actually gone through and put together studies that analyze the situation in the Middle East, the security elements in the Middle East and the experiences of other regions. One of these studies was adopted all the way back in 1998, and there was a very prominent American participant there—Ambassador [James] Leonard, if I'm not mistaken. It's also a good reference if one wants to look at what can be done taking into account the concerns of all.

My last two suggestions relate to the IAEA. The IAEA has announced that it intends to hold a seminar, I think, or an expert group to look at the experiences of different regions and how they could apply to the Middle East, taking into account all the different positions of different parties. I think that's a positive step, although it's not a major step forward.

Finally, I would suggest that the IAEA actually look at the South African experience, because if we're going to deal with nonproliferation in the region, we're going to have to deal with actual capacity. Unless one looks at the South African experience—not the Libyan experience, the South African experience—we will all continue to doubt what has been put to rest and what hasn't. There are four red lights up here already, so, while I have a couple of pages left, I'll put them into the question-and-answer period. Thank you very much.

SAMORE: Thank you, Nabil. Rakesh.

HIS EXCELLENCY RAKESH SOOD: Thank you, Gary, and thank you to the organizers of this conference. As the last speaker, I can probably sum up in less time. So let me start with—because everybody has talked about different perspectives—let me start by going back to the title, which is balancing nonproliferation tools, policies and strategies. I think, since I'm the last speaker, it's probably worth my while to step back and say, "Well, fair enough, we want to balance these tools and policies and strategies, but to what objective?" What is the objective we want to achieve with these strategies? You want to be able to talk about the nonproliferation regime and the NPT and a host of other things. Bob talked about possible differences and similarities between another Bush administration and a Kerry administration. But, then, where did this regime come from? After all, this regime that we are talking about today had, at some stage, its origin in trying to achieve

Rakesh Sood

certain objectives. So a host of tools and policies were generated in trying to achieve those objectives. I think it was Philippe who said that the NPT has been reasonably successful, it has kept the number of nuclear weapon states down into single digits. Well, if that was an objective, then to that extent, this package of tools, policies and strategies was a good package. If today we are worried, then are we worried because our objectives have changed and therefore we need some new tools, new strategies and new policies?

That's a useful question to look at because, in my view, I think immediately after nuclear weapons came into being and were used in Japan, a few more countries established themselves as nuclear weapon states, and gradually concerns about testing were generated. We're talking the late 1950s, the first hydrogen bomb test, things like that, which were all in the atmosphere at that point in time. Are people starting to get concerned about nuclear proliferation? But underlying the concern about nuclear proliferation was, presumably, a deeper, more existential concern. The use of nuclear weapons by states in war, because war was not something that was impossible at that point in time, and so it was of great concern. I think the deeper underlying objective was that, well, let's keep the numbers of countries that have nuclear weapons to a minimum because by doing that we will prevent the use of nuclear weapon by states.

So somewhere deep down that was the objective, and then a set of tools grew out of negotiations, in the case of the NPT, and Nabil talked about the trade-offs of the NPT. I think that, essentially, there were three basic trade-offs. The first trade-off was, as Nabil talked about, a commitment that countries that had nuclear weapons would get rid of their nuclear weapons. There was no timeframe, but it was a commitment in good faith. The second trade-off was that countries that did not have nuclear weapons and signed on to the treaty would refrain from anything to get these weapons. The third trade-off was that while the second category of countries would refrain from undertaking any nuclear-weapons related activity, they could not be deprived of peaceful applications of nuclear technology—whether it was in health, agriculture, electric power generation and so on.

Now, these trade-offs were already well-developed; they were negotiated, but eventually you found that these trade-offs started wearing thin. Now, just cast your mind back to that point in time and say, well, our objective is that countries should not use nuclear weapons as a hostile act. What's the best way to go about it? Somebody would say, well, the logical way is that each country should give up its nuclear weapons. Actually, some people did have those ideas, including the United States, that nuclear weapons ought to be given up by everybody. But politically it was not seen as a practical way of going about things. In other words, it was politically not acceptable.

And so, the new tool kit of policies and strategies that came up was one that was centered around the NPT. And so there is a trade-off in moving toward nuclear disarmament. For some time there was a certain momentum of arms control treaties moving in that direction. Things like negotiations, verification, something happening between the United States and the then-Soviet Union, other negotiations, like the CTBT [Comprehensive Test Ban Treaty] were happening, and now prospects of a fissile material cut-off treaty. There is actually a whole host of initiatives that have been put forward by large numbers of countries, including the United States, European countries, India, China, et cetera, about how to make that trade-off work. Somehow, it hasn't worked, which is why that particular trade-off is wearing thin.

The second trade-off was that countries that said they are non-nuclear weapons states and signed on as non-nuclear weapons states would not seek to acquire this technology; they are moving to the weapons direction. That's become a slightly tricky issue, because what is happening is that the definition of "not acquiring" has gotten fuzzy, because the nuclear technology is no longer as esoteric as it was 40 years ago. It has become much more matter-of-fact. Around that there is a whole host of more easily acquired engineering skills that give countries a certain capability. What is actually left in the definition is the fissile material part of it.

People can have highly sophisticated engineering skills, chemical skills, explosives skills, et cetera. These will take care of everything to go with a nuclear bomb as long as they don't have the precise nuclear material and the fissile material that would go and constitute that particular weapon. This means that there are a number of countries today that have moved along this spot, which in some parlance is called hedging. Tomorrow if they decide they wanted to step out of the treaty regime, they could quite easily, in a matter of weeks or just a couple of months, go nuclear. And that creates a lot of concerns because a lot of people feel that this was not the way it was originally. So what has happened is that new kinds of policies and strategies have been adopted—the expanded safeguards in the IAEA. People need to give advanced notice if they want to undertake any activity moving in these kinds of directions, or expand export controls on dual-use technologies. Countries are looking at special steels, special equipment, manufacturing, et cetera, and these may be dual-use equipment; but then people have become very careful about to whom and where these are exported.

But what has happened is that the second trade-off is also a little bit under strain. And the third trade-off was about the cooperation for peaceful purposes. And that, again, is now being questioned because now we're looking at the possibility that we need to establish more controls on fuel cycles, something that has gained a lot of currency in the last year or two years. And I think Philippe spoke about it. I think Gary or Bob also referred to it. In other words, because the earlier deal was if, say, Iran—since a lot of people here have talked about Iran—wanted to have uranium enrichment. It's a signed-up, fully paid-up member of the NPT, and it has accepted the full-scope safeguards that were in the original deal. Iran, by virtue of its legal obligation, is entitled to have an enrichment program as long as it is under safeguards. This would mean the international community is satisfied that the program is for peaceful purposes. But today when we talk of new initiatives of controlling fuel cycle, we say, well, is it really necessary? Because 20 countries are going to have enrichment programs and reprocessing programs for making plutonium, there are too many people around who might get their hands on it. Therefore, if we can make a promise to the Iranians that we'll supply uranium as fuel for its reactor, then that should be OK. And we give you a guarantee that we will supply you that stuff. That's the new kind of a thing. And now the Iranians are saying, well hang on, this was not the original bargain that we went into, because we are not prohibited from acquiring this technology or setting up an enrichment plant or whatever it is. So that was the third trade-off. And again, that is also showing signs of strain.

Which leads me to ask again—go back to my first question—what was the objective of the original tool kit? I think that if the original approach was that we needed to prevent use of nuclear weapons, then is it that today's concerns have changed in some fashion? I think they have. I don't think that in the '60s or '70s we thought about non-state actors—al Qaeda or other terrorists—getting their hands on weapons of mass destruction, or getting their hands on nuclear weapons or nuclear materials. That is something that has changed and that changed a couple of years ago, very dramatically. Since then we have actually seen pretty hard evidence of rogue states, rogue scientists, rogue elements, whatever. You know, nuclear Wal-Marts, that kind of stuff that has been written about a lot here. But there is a new set of concerns that have come out of the fact that we are now looking at the possibility of non-state actors using WMD or using nuclear weapons. And if that is so, then certainly we need to re-look at our tool kit. I think it's important to define that as an objective and then see how we balance our nonproliferation tools, policies and strategies if we have to address that particular requirement.

Now, once again, we can turn around and say, well, maybe all countries ought to get rid of their nuclear weapons, and I have seen some pieces written recently arguing for that approach. When I say get rid of them, I mean put them under international storage and cease to use them for military purposes. If countries get rid of their nuclear weapons and their stocks of fissile material, then clearly non-state actors are not going to be able to get their hands on them unless they set up clandestine facilities. The whole international community can get together and make sure that that doesn't happen, or if it happens, take action against it. But again, and everybody here I'm sure would say, that's not a practical way of going about it.

So we come back to what is a politically feasible, politically doable way of dealing with this particular objective and then seeing how we balance our tool kit. And on that, we heard a number of proposals. Bob spoke about some of the ideas. Philippe spoke about some more ideas—about initiatives that are being taken in that area. Nabil spoke about some of the ideas that are more region specific. I think all of these are great ideas. None of these are going to be ultimate ideas because the ultimate solution is one that is politically not feasible at this stage. So, these are not absolute ideas, but there's one thing in common with all the ideas that have been put forward—which is that we increase the cost of control. Now, as I said, this whole NPT trade-off is wearing thin, so now we were saying, well, if North Korea wants to withdraw, but the North Koreans actually acquired this capability while they were in the treaty, they shouldn't be allowed to withdraw that easily. But that's not the way the treaty has worked out. Or Iran did this and is still a member of the treaty. So maybe we should get the Security Council involved in it, which leads to a whole range of other complications. Other than the new initiative, called the Proliferation Security Initiative, which talks about interdiction on the high seas of equipment, materials related to weapons of mass destruction. This is not based on any treaty as such, but it's a grouping of a large number of countries who agreed to share intelligence and work together in order to undertake this kind of activity. More stringent export controls. But stringent means what? Stringent means that if they have to be effective, then more countries need to be able to work together in order to administer these export controls, and for that they need to have common definitions, common understandings, processes.

Criminalization of proliferation behavior: that every country says this is a criminal activity, so if somebody is caught doing this, then he or she shall be sentenced, or it will be treated as a criminal prosecution rather than a civil offense. Again, national measures . . . essentially it is national measures and international measures. And even if we are looking at national measures, then clearly we have to look at strong states, because strong states will ensure that laws are observed in their jurisdiction on their territory. If we are looking at international measures, then we have to look at measures that would require cooperation between countries. So, ultimately whichever way we look at it, in the absence of absolute solutions and redefining objectives, we come up with two things. One is that states have to take these steps. Second, they have to work together. This means they have to cooperate, and they have to negotiate. There has to be a process of give-and-take if they have to succeed in addressing the new, emerging threat objective that is preventing the use of nuclear weapons by non-state actors as distinct only from what it was earlier in enemy states. Thank you.

SAMORE: Thank you, Rakesh. Well, we have had four excellent presentations from some of the world's most experienced practitioners in the art of nonproliferation. We have about a half-hour now for questions and comments. So I would invite anyone in the audience who would like to speak. Yes, sir, over there.

AUDIENCE: Yes, Jonathan Pollack from the Naval War College. This question is directed to Bob Einhorn, but if anyone else wants to have a crack at it, by all means do so. Bob, you very nicely delineated ways in which you think the nonproliferation strategies of a second Bush administration or a Kerry administration might vary. Suppose, for the sake of argument, that on or about Jan. 20, 2005, North Korea decides to forego any residual ambiguity about its nuclear weapons potential and tests a nuclear weapon. In that event, putting aside the fact that then we are getting very uneasily close to that magic number of 10 [nuclear states], what would you see as differences—if there would be any significant differences— hypothetically speaking, in how an outgoing Bush administration or an incoming Kerry administration or a second Bush administration would deal with that phenomenon?

The parallel question is simply what would be the impact on this NPT regime as we know it? That's directed to the panel as a whole. I'm curious what any of your thoughts would be about this hypothetical situation.

EINHORN: Jonathan, I think at that point, the policies of a Kerry administration and a Bush administration would merge. I don't think there would be any difference. I don't think there would be any choice. It would not be to adjust and accommodate. The United States adjusted eventually to and accommodated nuclear testing in South Asia. It can't afford to adjust and accommodate in this case. India and Pakistan didn't violate any laws. We thought they were a threat primarily to themselves and not to the international community at large. A North Korean declaration that it's a nuclear weapons state and is testing would be a different kettle of fish all together. I think any U.S. administration would have to do its best—working with North Korea's neighbors, primarily our allies, South Korea and Japan, but also China and Russia—to contain this new threat to deter any use of these weapons or any intimidation by the North Koreans. Any administration would work for a long-term policy of roll-back. Roll-back probably means the eventual collapse of the regime. I don't know that you work for that directly and immediately, but I think over the long term, that's what you would have to be working for—the collapse of that regime and containing it until then.

SAMORE: I don't think any of the other panelists will want to talk about Bush versus Kerry policies, but perhaps you would like to talk about how you think the international community will respond if North Korea conducts a nuclear test. Philippe.

ERRERA: I would agree with Bob. And not only how the policies of Bush-two or Kerry would eventually merge. I think that in terms of the international community, you would find that the ambiguity or the space that some countries, such as China and some of the Asian allies, see as current, diplomatic space to try to get North Korea to walk back from where it is would immediately diminish. That would mean North Korea had crossed the threshold. So don't take it to mean more than it means. We would be in a situation where essentially the chips would be down and the only policy forward would be to contain and roll back. My hope is that that would also dispel any illusions about being able to engage the North Koreans in terms of getting them to roll this back.

SAMORE: Rakesh.

SOOD: Sure, it's always interesting to engage in hypothetical history. But, I think if North Korea were to test, I don't foresee any military action being taken against North Korea.
First, the Security Council would meet and pass a strong resolution. Second, I assume that there would be some kind of a task force that would be set up involving Russia and certainly China and Japan and South Korea, of course—things like that. And it would include, of course, the United States and France.

AUDIENCE: How about India?

SOOD: Probably not. I don't know. But, in any event, this emergency task force would have to engage the North Korean regime. Weeks, months—something like that—would pass. Then some kind of red lines would be drawn, I assume. Then we would have to see what the political environment is, meanwhile, in the region. It would also be changing, and I think that will then determine how the events would unfold from that time forward.

SAMORE: Thank you.

EINHORN: Could I just add one thing? I think it's very important, but neglected. One of the highest priorities at that point is to try to give South Korea and Japan confidence that they can afford to live without nuclear weapons. That means doing everything we can to bolster those alliances. The alliance with the ROK [Republic of Korea] has become frayed in the last couple of years. I think that alliance has to be reinforced if we're to reduce the ROK's incentives to go nuclear as well.

SAMORE: Yes, sir.

AUDIENCE: I have a question, beyond any legalities or a few surrounding the NPT concerning Iran. It's been told to me by folks who watched the process last year that the reason the E.U. Commission that met with the Iranians was successful is because, essentially, they used the American presence in Iraq at that time as a foil. Essentially, they said, "Look, you've got these crazy Americans over here with 130,000 troops, and we don't know if we'll keep them at bay. But if you guys settle up and make a deal, maybe we can hold them off. You know, we'll hold off those crazy Americans for you." I think that maybe the Iranians paid some heed to that since we were enough of a credible threat at the time. But now we're a bit bogged down in Iraq. They certainly see that we don't have the ability to turn any forces, practically, in that direction. And I think that has given them a little bit of wiggle room. So I have two questions to pose. Can the U.S. accept Iran going nuclear? Can Europe accept that? What will we do? And second, what would the implications be in the Middle East? How will other countries in that region respond?

SAMORE: Philippe, why don't you take the first crack at that?

ERRERA: In terms of holding off crazy Americans, believe me, we don't make promises to anybody. I mean, very seriously, that wasn't the way things happened, at least as far as the accounting and reporting I received from the meeting. In terms of the perceptions that the Iranians have of what was a potential threat on their borders, they did very, very well without us. The point we were making was quite the opposite. One of the main rationales they had always used for pursuing a nuclear weapons program and perhaps other WMD programs was the threat that Iraq posed, and the threat that an Iraq with Saddam Hussein at its head posed. This threat was no longer there. In terms of the acceptability of the nuclear-armed Iran, for Europe the answer is very simple: It's just not acceptable, which is the reason why we have committed this much, and we will see things through to the end in terms of preventing that from happening.

SAMORE: Perhaps I could ask Ambassador Fahmy, if Iran does acquire nuclear weapons, what kind of impact do you think that would have on other countries in the region, in terms of increasing pressure on them to pursue their own nuclear weapons programs?

FAHMY: Well, I think the main target in the past of the Iranian nuclear program—this started with the shah, by the way; it didn't start just recently—was the Arab states in the Persian Gulf and Iraq to counterbalance that issue in particular. The situation today, and during the shah's period, is that they weren't threatened or didn't feel threatened one way or the other, rightly or wrongly, by an American force or a Western force. Today, depending on what happens in Iraq, the motivation either may be there's an opportunity to do it and get it behind them or that they actually feel threatened by what they perceive to be the future security situation in Iraq. Or it may continue to be that they want dominance in the Arab Gulf area.

I would argue that emergence of any nuclear state in the Middle East, including Iran, would significantly shift the security paradigm for almost all the significant states in the region. That would not necessarily mean they would use force against Iran as a reaction; that would not necessarily mean that they would immediately go nuclear, but it would be a significant shift in the security balance, and people would react to it.

SAMORE: Bob?

EINHORN: It's interesting. Sen. Kerry and President Bush both have used the same words, "unacceptable for Iran to have nuclear weapons." [British] Prime Minister [Tony] Blair said the same thing. Philippe just mentioned that Europeans see it the same way. I don't know if anyone has really begun to act as if Iran's getting nuclear weapons is unacceptable. I think we have to do a lot more. For one thing, I think the Europeans have to get a lot tougher with Iran and make clear to Iran what the consequences would be of continuing down this path. So far, the sticks that the Europeans have used have been deferred carrots. In other words, if you don't get rid of your nuclear program, we won't talk to you about a future trade and cooperation agreement. I think Iranians have to believe that there are real consequences. I also think that the United States can help by readiness, at least to engage directly with Iran and talk about the full range of issues on which they have disagreements. I think Nabil is right. The impetus, certainly in the mid-1980s, for Iran to get nuclear weapons was the long bloody war with Iraq. But Iraq is not a military threat to Iran now. I think the main preoccupation Iran has, as far as security is concerned, is with the United States. And I think there has to be some engagement between the United States and Iran to deal with those concerns. But I would just like to ask one question of two of the panelists. I think everyone on the panel understands the very negative consequences of Iran getting nuclear weapons. All of the countries represented here on the panel are members of the IAEA board. But when we look at sending Iran to the Security Council or even adopting tough language in the IAEA board against Iran, it's the United States out here, then the "EU-3" [Great Britain, France and Germany] is next. But key friends of the United States who happen to be members of the nonaligned movement are not helping in these international bodies to explain to Iran that if it continues down this path, there's going to be real trouble. I think countries like Egypt and India have the standing within Iran to make that case very persuasively, but I don't see it being made.

SAMORE: Rakesh and then Nabil.

SOOD: On Iran, if there has to be a test, I think the North Koreans are probably much closer to it than the Iranians are today. They'll take some time before they get there. In the meanwhile, I think we've already said that Iran embarked on its program largely because of the long war with Iraq and so on. While it's true that Saddam Hussein was a threat for the Iranian regime, Iran had nuclear ambitions and started its nuclear program during the Shah of Iran's days. It was a whole different ballgame at that point. Of course, today, Iranian security concerns are much more U.S.-centered, and certainly during the shah's days they were not U.S.-centered.

Nonetheless, the only way the Iranians can be persuaded to provide the requisite degree of assurance to the international community that they have not embarked on a nuclear weapons program is if there is a process of engagement with the United States, which they perceive as their principal security concern. As long as the policy, vis-a-vis their primary security concern, namely the United States, is going to be a policy of containment, encirclement, pressure, coercion or diplomatic coercion, I don't think that the Iranians are going to be ready to provide assurances of any kind to the international community.

SAMORE: Go ahead. Yes. Ambassador Fahmy.

FAHMY: Well, to answer Bob's question, frankly, if there was a serious dialogue about the Middle East security concerns and how we move forward, you would find a much more proactive attempt to actually put pressure on nonproliferating states to do more. The question you're asking really is, "Why don't we support the present U.S. position on Iran?" We completely oppose Iran going nuclear and its proliferating. Do you go to the council now or do you try diplomacy a little bit more? If you go to the council, what are you going to do with it? We haven't had that strategic discussion amongst us. We have, for the last 25 years, argued that you can take some measures—interim measures—but unless you have an overriding attempt to achieve nuclear disarmament in the region, you will fail. And that hasn't started. Frankly, we're the ones that are frustrated about this. We have been arguing this case, all the way back to 1974. So engage with your friends in the region about the overall security concerns, and you will find many more of them agreeing with more of your positions. The problem is there isn't that serious engagement on what after.

SAMORE: Thank you. Scott Sagan.

SAGAN: Ben, I would like to take advantage of having the foreign diplomats here to ask them to comment on a debate that rages in the United States and will certainly be up in January. The twin debate in the United States concerns whether the United States should ratify the Comprehensive Test Ban Treaty [CTBT] and, if we don't, whether it will be appropriate for us to both design and ensure that they are reliable, test new nuclear weapons—so-called bunker busters for smaller tactical low-yield nuclear weapons. There are some in the U.S. labs and in the current administration who argue that if we go forward with this, it won't matter very much with respect to nonproliferation because other states react to their regional rivals, not to us. There are some in the U.S. military who say that would be great if we have that extra military capability. This is not a hypothetical history; it is a potential issue that may emerge post-January. If the United States tests nuclear weapons over the next three or four years, how will your governments and your region react?

SAMORE: I think I know the answer to that, Philippe.

ERRERA: Quickly, since I guess most people know the answer to that. First of all, we're realistic about the effect, unfortunately or fortunately, that foreign reactions would have on a U.S. debate, especially on an issue like this one. One of my first assignments at the embassy here in Washington when I arrived was dealing with CTBT and accompanying the ambassador on the Hill to make our case regarding why we thought it would be counterproductive for the Senate to reject the treaty. You know the effectiveness of that. Regarding bunker busters, it's an even more difficult issue. On the one hand, it's up to every nuclear weapons state to determine its force posture, its mix, et cetera. I do think, however, that if the United States felt that it needed to test, and if it unsigned the CTBT, in the same way that it explicitly unsigned the ICC [International Criminal Court], it would be something that would set us back many, many years.

SAMORE: Nabil.

FAHMY: First, disarmament, particularly in the international arena, has never succeeded if the United States wasn't leading the way. Every single time you hesitated, the process stopped. On the CWC [Conventional Weapons Convention], when you dragged your feet on verification for a while, we slowed down at the CD [Conference on Disarmament] in Geneva. When you shifted, it immediately gained ground. You need to look at yourself as the global power, not only a superpower. What you do today may be a function of the immediate security concern that you have on the battlefield, but it will also have an effect 10 years, 15 years, down the line on what other people acquire and what they do. That's where I see the missing link, and that's why, in my sort of general presentation, I wanted to emphasize trying to get back into a momentum to deal with the security issues of a global nature. You will remain the most powerful country in the world for many, many years to come. But the more you have nonfaith parties or states that are much smaller than you becoming your problems, the less important the major deterrence issues become. You have to look at your position globally. Consequently, my answer would be, if you move away from disarmament and more toward weapons testing, there will be ramifications, medium-term, at least internationally, that you will not be happy with.

SAMORE: Rakesh?

SOOD: Let me give a slightly more anecdotal answer. Gary, Bob and I were part of the discussions that India and the United States had—a very intense period of discussions that Strobe Talbott, who was then the deputy secretary [of state], had with Jaswant Singh, who was the Indian foreign minister, immediately after the tests in May of 1998. During the next, say, 18 months or so, we had eight or nine meetings. The only period of this kind of sustained high-level engagement was 1998 and 1999. At that point, one of the U.S. benchmarks in our dialogue—this is not that classified, since Strobe has just written a book on engaging India, which describes this engagement and dialogue—one of the U.S. benchmarks was getting India (and Pakistan at that point) to sign the CTBT. The Indian government had made certain commitments; this had been pointed out both privately to the U.S. authorities and also in speeches made by the prime minister of India to the Indian parliament. I don't think it comes as a surprise to anybody that when the U.S. Senate threw out the CTBT, that the moral authority with which Strobe Talbot and his colleagues—Bob and Gary and others—could try to convince the Indians to sign the CTBT was somewhat reduced, shall I say. And the other thing, which brings me to a slightly broader issue, I still remember Secretary [of State Madeleine] Albright at that point in time. She was doing the Hill in terms of trying to get the Senate to support the administration in its efforts to get the CTBT ratified. One of her key selling points to the U.S. Senate was that this was a great treaty for the United States because we, the United States, had an enormous lead having done the 1,100 or 1,200 tests. This would freeze everybody on the learning curve because nuclear weapons are not going to go away.

Now, in today's age of communications and things like that, it's not a good way to sell a treaty, because by definition any negotiated treaty has to be seen as a cooperative venture. It's no longer a plus/minus kind of issue. When countries do negotiate and come up with a treaty, they have to find virtue in it. It is not that one country by signing it is going to get something over another country, because these are win/win ventures, or have to be seen as win/win; it's a cooperative venture rather than an adversarial venture.

SAMORE: Thank you. I think we have time for two more quick questions.

AUDIENCE: Just a quick question for Mr. Sood. You mentioned the threat of non-states possessing nuclear weapons or getting access to this technology. Don't you think it's about time to look through this entire theory in light of what happened in Iraq and the fact that we didn't find any weapons of mass destruction there, let alone evidence to support that the regime there was planning to give anything to al Qaeda? How much validity is there in this theory anymore, in light of that experience? My second question, a quick one, to Mr. Einhorn relates to what Ambassador Fahmy mentioned about seeking the help of countries in the region with Iran. What about the United States showing more willingness to help with the issue of Israel, which is a major topic of concern to our part of the world? Thank you, very much.

SAMORE: Those are two good questions. Rakesh.

SOOD: It's true that no weapons of mass destruction and no nuclear weapons have been found in Iraq. But then I don't think that necessarily takes away from the thesis, because, at the same time, I think we have come across huge amounts of highly, highly worrisome information about the kind of nuclear and nuclear-related transfers that have taken place over years. You look at the North Korean program: where did the North Koreans get theirs? At the time, Bob and Gary were dealing with the North Koreans, and they dealt with every proliferation case. I'm quite sure that at that time they probably had no clue that there was a uranium enrichment program that was also going on. And that uranium enrichment program was courtesy of AQ Khan in Pakistan, which was part of the missile-nuclear trade-off. Because there was missile technology moving from North Korea to Pakistan, and then there was some nuclear technology that was moving in the other direction. Then you have another situation vis-a-vis Iran. Now, initially, you have a situation of proliferation in the case of centrifuge designs that we are looking at in Iran, designs that obviously have come from Pakistan. The same is true in the Libyan case. In Libya, we have seen that there is actually a bomb design—the design of a device—which came from Pakistan to Libya. The Pakistani government has said this is the work of AQ Kahn, who was acting on his own. But I have my views on that, and I'm sure others do. Even if you accept the fact that it is AQ Kahn acting on his own, who could actually pass off bomb designs, centrifuge designs, parts of centrifuges? Maybe there was a program going on where there was a transshipment point in Dubai, and there was somebody doing some stuff, and there were some companies in Europe that were giving chemicals, and there was some manufacturing unit in Malaysia that was producing some other components. They put it all together, and it was like a nuclear-dot-com on the Web. You could get around and pitch and make your bid for it. That much we are all aware of. We may not have found anything in Iraq, but the fact that something like this exists, has existed, may still exist, is there. And so, the prospects of the non-state actor or an organized group getting its hands on this is, I think, more likely than not.

SAMORE: Bob, Israel?

EINHORN: On Israel and the regional approach, the United States does support a regional approach to arms control and disarmament, in various regions, including the Middle East. But at the present time, the conditions just don't exist to move that goal to fruition. We know this because we have had lots of discussion with the Israelis on that point that they're not going to give up what they consider to be an essential deterrent unless and until there is a comprehensive peace in the region that they can count on. They're not going to move down that path. Nabil and I have had many discussions on the same point—the two of us with Israelis present, the same discussion. I see no practical prospect of genuine movement until there is a comprehensive and durable peace. So what do you do under those circumstances?

I think one thing you don't do is link the Iran question with the Israel question, because that simply is going to be a recipe for paralysis. I think what we need to do is work on the Iran problem—try to head off its capability—because if Iran succeeds in getting a nuclear capability, then I don't think there's any going back. I think moving to a zone free of all weapons of mass destruction becomes impossible for all time. You're beginning to move in the other direction as some of Iran's neighbors develop incentives to go down the same path. So I think what you have to do—and I know it's uncomfortable—is deal with the Iran problem. The asymmetry that Egypt has with its neighbor is an uncomfortable situation to be in politically, if not in security terms. Stop it if you can, and then work for conditions that will enable Israel, eventually, to consider giving up its deterrent weapons.

SAMORE: Nabil?

FAHMY: Bob said, correctly, that we talked about this a lot, and we did. We differed, also, frankly. Let me just simply say nobody is linking together that you can't talk to Iran unless you get Israel to sign off on the treaty. That's not realistic. What I was saying is simply that, while our position is the same, no country in the region should go nuclear. And they should all respect nonproliferation obligations. Those that have not joined the treaty should move in that direction. Ideally, all would pressure and work with neighboring states to create an environment that is also conducive to Iran becoming more proactive and more, if you want, helpful on this area. There is a reality in the region. Unless you deal with the security concerns in the region, the ability of states to go beyond a certain point of saying don't go nuclear will be limited. You haven't engaged them on that issue yet.

SAMORE: Okay, Philippe, last comment.

ERRERA: I just wanted to reinforce the point that, actually, Bob made, but I didn't know that at the time. If you think—and we do think—it's important to keep this perspective alive of a regional nuclear weapons-free zone, then what you need to do is to keep this perspective alive even though prospects are bleak today. One of the key things that would, as Bob said, get rid of that perspective—that would make this something that wouldn't even be political fiction 30 years down the road—would be an Iran acquiring nuclear weapons. So it's important to keep the perspective alive that we have to do everything we can to prevent, and for all the countries in the region and elsewhere to prevent, a nuclear-armed Iran.

SAMORE: Thank you, Philippe. I would like to ask you all to join me now in thanking our panelists. I think they have given us a good flavor of the kind of discussions that go on among the diplomatic community in dealing with these really tough issues. Thank you all very much.

KEYNOTE ADDRESS

WORLD SECURITY AND STABILITY IN THE BALANCE

Paul Wolfowitz, Deputy Secretary of Defense

Introduction by: General Peter J. Schoomaker, Chief of Staff, United States Army

Summary

Paul Wolfowitz

- Invoking former President Ronald Reagan, Paul Wolfowitz stated: "History doesn't just happen. History is made." He recalled General Dwight Eisenhower, then allied supreme commander, on the eve of the D–Day invasion, asserting that moral courage is as important as physical courage. Wolfowitz noted that we are fortunate to have a man in the White House who possesses moral courage.

- During the preparation for Operation Iraqi Freedom, Wolfowitz witnessed the signing of the orders authorizing the operation and learned firsthand that responsibility is the tremendous price of leadership.

- Twice in the 20th century, the United States faced and overcame a totalitarian adversary. Each time, America expected an era of peace as its reward. Today war has once again found us, and this time freedom itself is at stake.

- The Sept. 11 terrorist attacks shattered the hope for an "unbroken peace." That day "freedom was attacked," just as it had been by the totalitarian regimes of the 20th century.

- To be successful in this campaign to defend freedom, four strategic principles must guide U.S. strategy:

    1. The struggle will be long and arduous, with no dramatic event signaling our triumph.

    2. We must employ all of the instruments of power at our disposal, not solely or even primarily military force.

    3. We must wage the campaign against terrorism in multiple theaters, including the homeland, but carefully sequence our actions.

4. We must recognize that this is an ideological as well as a physical struggle.

• Wolfowitz stated that the threat the United States faces is not limited to the al Qaeda leadership and operatives, but encompasses state sponsors and supporters of terrorism, ungoverned territories that serve as incubators and bases for terrorist groups, and terrorist cells embedded in our very midst.

• Because of the complexity and gravity of this threat, we cannot accept living with terrorism as tolerable. Nor can we afford to treat terrorism as primarily a law enforcement problem. We must do all we can to prevent future attacks. We must aim to thoroughly discredit those ideologies that justify terrorism and aim to destroy global terrorist networks and regimes that sponsor them.

• It is perhaps a feature of American political culture that patience is in short supply. However, patience is desperately needed to wage this struggle. We must be prepared to stand firm for freedom, for "freedom is the glue of the world's strongest alliances and the solvent for dissolving tyrannical regimes."

• Our enemies are enemies of freedom. They have contempt for tolerance and diversity, and for human life itself. To defeat these enemies, we must go on the offensive and wage a struggle on many fronts. On two of these fronts, Afghanistan and Iraq, courageous citizens are waging a struggle for freedom along with us. The success of democracy in Iraq is the terrorists' greatest fear, for such success will marginalize extremists and substitute a more hopeful vision of the future throughout the region.

• The appeal of freedom is clear to the people of Iraq and Afghanistan; the forces of peace and reconstruction in both countries know what they are fighting for.

• In a crucial moment, America has once again recognized that "something had to be done." Armed with this knowledge and the moral resolve it gives, we are making our own history, moving forward to a more secure and peaceful future Ike would be proud of us.

Analysis

Any influential political appointee speaking at a public event held only two months before the national election would be expected to stay "on message" and avoid introducing new policy. Paul Wolfowitz fulfilled those expectations. His address, with the exception of introductory remarks about the Army chief of staff, was identical to his speech given two weeks earlier. At both events, his audience was sufficiently intellectually agile to understand the significance of timing on the content of such an address. In turn, Wolfowitz skillfully wove inspiring personal stories with support for policy, but avoided being overly heavy handed.

Wolfowitz reiterated the current administration's theme that the war in Iraq is a continuation of the 20th century U.S.-led historic struggles to defend freedom. He also reinforced the more recent theme of a long-term, greater-than-military struggle, with few discernible indications of victory. This theme is one that the administration has been accused of ignoring. He did not hide his conclusion that Operation IRAQI FREEDOM (OIF) is morally just, and the administration has done the right thing as effectively as possible. The implication of his statements was that the American public should support the continuation of this policy.

Rather than directly address the administration's critics, Wolfowitz chose to state counter arguments; his style avoided the appearance of being defensive and it did not credit adversaries with arguments worthy of rebuttal. He did not state that governments withholding international support for OIF have no sense of history or moral impartiles, but his historical and moral arguments for current policies seemed to imply as much. Nor did he say that Americans who are opposed to OIF are unappreciative of our troops, but his stories of service members' sacrifices and dedication when implementing those policies, by implication, seemed to debase those who challenge the nobility of the cause.

As expected in an election season, the address was a call for political support. It was archetypal political rhetoric—not without merit, but not a substantive addition to the body of collective knowledge either. The mix of stories about U.S. heroes, in front of an informed but sympathetic audience, linking policy to historic events and the international strategic environment resulted in a classic political speech.

Transcript

ANNOUNCER: Ladies and gentlemen, please welcome tonight's master of ceremonies, Brigadier General Kevin T. Ryan.

BRIGADIER GENERAL KEVIN T. RYAN: Well, I hope you all enjoyed your dinner and the discussions today. Before we go any further, I would like you to join me in thanking the Military District of Washington's Joint Color Guard, Sergeant Major Tony Nalker and the Army Blues Combo, and our singer of the National Anthem tonight, Staff Sergeant Lee Ann Hinton, who did a really great job. At this time, it is my privilege to introduce the chief of staff of the Army, General Peter J. Schoomaker.

GENERAL PETER J. SCHOOMAKER: Well, good evening, ladies and gentlemen. It is now my honor to introduce our keynote speaker, our deputy secretary of defense, the Honorable Paul Wolfowitz. Secretary Wolfowitz is now serving in his third tour of duty at the Pentagon, which I'm happy to say probably took up a couple of mine, which I appreciate. Formerly, from 1977 to 1980, he was the deputy assistant secretary of defense for regional programs. From 1989 to 1993, he was the undersecretary of defense for policy. He understands also how military might must go hand-in-hand with diplomatic skills because from 1982 to 1986, he was the assistant secretary of state for East Asian and Pacific affairs, followed in 1986 through 1989 as the ambassador to Indonesia, under President [Ronald] Reagan.

Secretary Wolfowitz is a scholar of global affairs and a widely published author on national security strategy and foreign policy. He was the dean and professor of international relations at the School of Advanced International Studies of the Johns Hopkins University for seven years prior to returning to the Pentagon in March 2001. He has a gift for looking at old problems in new ways, and I can attest to that. He is a man who tells it like it is. I know this audience will appreciate that. He is highly qualified to address the many challenges that confront our nation on the road ahead.

General Peter J. Schoomaker

Ladies and gentlemen, please join me in a warm welcome for tonight's keynote speaker, a true patriot, an outstanding leader, our deputy secretary of defense, the Honorable Paul Wolfowitz.

DEPUTY SECRETARY PAUL WOLFOWITZ: Thank you very much. I'd like to begin these remarks with a great big thank-you to the U.S. Army for outstanding leadership at all levels, from senior noncommissioned officers all the way up to chief of staff. [General] Dan McNeill [commanding general, U.S. Army Forces Command] is at the table that I was sitting at a few minutes ago. I had the privilege of working with Dan when he was leading our forces in Afghanistan—a truly magnificent job.

Two or three times a week—this morning being one of those—we were on a secure conference call with [the commander of Multi-National Force Iraq, General] George Casey, our commander in Baghdad, and [General] John Abizaid, our distinguished Central Command combatant commander.

The list is very long. I have a special debt of gratitude to three Army generals who served what are called tours of duty, but might better be called sentences. For some reason, every time I look for a new senior military assistant, it turns up Army. And I've had the privilege of having [Major General] John Batiste and then [Major General] Bill Caldwell and now [Brigadier General] Frank Helmick—outstanding gentlemen. [Army Vice Chief of Staff General] Dick Cody—I don't know, is Dick here tonight? He's a great, great general and somebody whom I know wakes up every day trying to figure out what he can do to support the troops in the field.

to save lives, and to reduce the horrible
wounds that are inflicted in war. And
last, but by no means least, Pete—thank
you for putting your uniform back on,
General Schoomaker.

As you probably know, General
Schoomaker was enjoying a very nice
life between his ranch in Wyoming and
his home in Florida, which I hope will
survive [Hurricane] Ivan. You do want
to go back there someday when your
sentence is served. But I really stand in
awe of this man. I'm in awe of his record
as a combat commander and hero. I'm
in awe of his leadership earlier in his
career at SOCOM [Special Operations
Command]. And most of all, I'm in
awe of his ability to lead this Army in
war effectively and, at the same time,
prepare it for the next battles. The Army
Transformation Plan—to increase the

Paul Wolfowitz

number of combat brigades by 50 percent with only a modest increase in personnel
— is really extraordinary to do at any time. To do it in the middle of wartime, Pete,
is a huge achievement, not just for you personally, but for the whole Army.

Some of you may know that your chief played football in his college days.
You may even know that in 1968 he helped his beloved Cowboys at University of
Wyoming make it to the Sugar Bowl. What you may not know is that back in those
days, they called Pete "the silent lineman." Well, that was then. General Schoomaker
is never silent these days, when it comes to speaking up for his Soldiers or his
Army, whether in public or in small meetings with the secretary of defense. He's
a powerful voice who commands respect here in Washington and throughout the
ranks of this great Army.

And, I would add, whatever may be true or not about his earlier taciturn
nature, I also admire Pete's way with words. I once heard him puncture a discussion
about some overdone piece of technology applied to some very simple task by
saying, "That's like putting a trailer hitch on a Porsche." Or how about these bits of
practical Schoomaker wisdom, most of which seem to be drawn from his cowboy
neighbors. One of them is, "Don't squat with your spurs on." Or, "The best way
to ride a bull is in the direction he's going." Or, "Never ask a barber if you need a
haircut." This one's good for all you fast burners: "If you're ahead of the herd, take
a look back every now and then to see if it's still there."

Those are all pretty good, I think. Pete, you must have been taking some
lessons from [Vice Chairman of the Joint Chiefs of Staff General] Pete Pace. General

Pace expresses his philosophy this way, "You should never let a promising career get in the way of a good joke." We like good jokes. We like people who are serious about their job. Pete, you're both, and we're mighty glad to have you back in the saddle leading the Army in the 21st century. Thank you.

Every time I come to this magnificent building, I think about Ronald Reagan, that apostle of small government, who once said, "The closest thing to eternal life we'll ever see on this earth is a government bureaucracy." And I wonder how he'd feel about having this building named after him. It's the largest building in the city of Washington, I think.

But, certainly, Ronald Reagan had to roll with the punches. He once referred to one wit's definition of history as "just one darned thing after another." But, he followed that up with an observation that was classic Reagan. He said, "History doesn't just happen, history is made."

This conference is named after a great general, a great president and a great leader who made history. I don't think I could begin my remarks without invoking his spirit.

For me, one of the most extraordinary items on display in the Eisenhower Corridor outside the [defense] secretary's office is a copy of a message that was, fortunately, never sent. It's a message General Eisenhower drafted the night before D–Day. He kept it in his pocket to be used in case the Normandy invasion failed. It shows us a man who sent Soldiers into battle and took upon himself the awful and awesome responsibility of command. It shows that Eisenhower was not only a man of great physical courage, but moral courage as well. "Our landings in the Cherbourg-Havre area," General Eisenhower wrote, "have failed to gain a satisfactory foothold and I have withdrawn the troops. My decision to attack at this time was based upon the best information available. The troops, the Air and the Navy, did all that bravery and devotion to duty could do. If any blame or fault attaches to the attempt," General Eisenhower was prepared to say, "it is mine alone."

I bring up this powerful lesson because I often think, as important as physical courage is, moral courage can be as important, and sometimes it seems to be even more rare.

America, once again, faces a time of great testing. It will need not only great physical courage from our troops, but moral courage from our leaders. We're fortunate, once again, to have a president who possesses that quality of moral courage.

I was in the Oval Office the day President Bush signed the Executive Order that authorized Operation IRAQI FREEDOM. He said at the time that it was the most difficult decision he'd ever made in his life. Two weeks ago, he gave all of us an insight into just how difficult. "I have returned the salute of wounded Soldiers," he said, "some with a very tough road ahead who say they were just doing their job. I've held the children of the fallen who were told their dad or mom is a hero, but would rather just have their mom or dad. I've met with the wives and husbands who have received a folded flag and said a final goodbye to a Soldier they loved. I am awed."

the president said, "that so many have used those meetings to say that I'm in their prayers and to offer encouragement to me." As the president said those words, the emotion in his voice made it clear that he understands the terrible cost of war.

Twice in the last century, the United States went to war against a totalitarian evil. First, in the bloody war against Nazism and fascism, and then later in that long twilight struggle, there was a confrontation with totalitarian communism. Each time when the war was over and the evil eliminated, we felt we could enjoy a long period of unbroken peace. Each time we suffered a rude awakening. This time, Sept. 11, 2001, was our wake-up call. With the cold-blooded murder of 3,000 Americans and citizens of many other countries, we are, once again, in the middle of a war we didn't look for—a war that found us. And, as in each past confrontation, the target is freedom itself.

President Reagan liked to tell the famous story about how British Prime Minister Harold Macmillan was delivering an address at the United Nations when Nikita Khrushchev took off his shoe and started banging it on the table. With that unflappability we associate with the British, Macmillan said, without missing a beat, "I'd like that translated, if I may."

Of course, no translation was required. Like the Nazis, the Soviets wanted to bury free societies. Today's terrorist fanatics are no different.

When freedom was attacked on Sept. 11, Americans fought back for the same reasons Americans have gone to war in the past. During a recent hearing before the Senate Armed Services Committee, Sen. Joseph Lieberman described it well, reminding us all that when America goes to war, "it's not for conquest, it's for security and for a principle that has driven American history from the beginning, which is freedom and democracy."

To be successful, once again, in defending our society and our freedom, four basic principles must guide our strategy in combating terrorist fanaticism.

First, we must recognize that the struggle will be long. We will win it, but victory will not be marked by anything as dramatic as a signing ceremony on the USS Missouri or the collapse of the Berlin Wall.

Second, we must use all the instruments of national power, including military force, but not solely, or even primarily, military force.

Third, we must wage this war in multiple theaters, including here in our own country. But we must sequence our efforts and focus our energies in the right places at the right times. We can't take on every problem all at once.

Fourth, and perhaps most important, we need to understand that this is an ideological as well as a physical struggle. We have to do more than simply kill and capture terrorists. As President Bush said in his very first State of the Union message a few months after Sept. 11, we must work to build "a just and peaceful world beyond the war on terror and particularly in the Muslim world."

From the beginning, the president recognized that this fight would be long and difficult. Just five days after the attacks on New York and the Pentagon, he said, "The American people must be patient. This will be a long campaign."

On Oct. 8, 2001, one day after the start of Operation ENDURING FREEDOM in Afghanistan, Secretary Rumsfeld told reporters that "these strikes in Afghanistan are part of a much larger effort, one that will be sustained for a period of years, not weeks or months. He continued, "This campaign will be much like the Cold War. We'll use every resource at our command. We will not stop until the terrorist networks are destroyed."

I remember at that time being struck by Don Rumsfeld's reference to the Cold War. It was a dramatic contrast to those who suggested that all we had to do was to eliminate al Qaeda in Afghanistan. As daunting as that task was, it was nothing compared to the task that Secretary Rumsfeld and the president laid out for us. Indeed, the problem does extend far beyond Afghanistan to other states that harbor terrorists and used terrorism as an instrument of national policy. It extends to ungoverned areas where terrorists can find safe harbor and even to our own country and many other free societies where terrorists can hide essentially in plain sight. And it extends far beyond al Qaeda, as dangerous as that organization is.

Perhaps the principal lesson of 9/11 is that we need to stop thinking about terrorism and state support for terrorism as something that we could continue living with as an evil, but inescapable, fact of international life, the way we have over the previous 20 or 30 years. We can't continue regarding a terrorist's capacity to inflict thousands of casualties in a single conventional attack, much less hundreds of thousands of casualties, if terrorists gain access to the most terrible weapons human beings have invented. We can't continue regarding that as primarily a law enforcement matter to be handled by catching and punishing perpetrators after they attack. We must do everything we can to prevent attacks.

We may not be able to eliminate every individual terrorist, but we can hope, over time, to eliminate global terrorist networks and to end state sponsorship of terrorism. We can hope to see the ideologies that justify terrorism discredited as thoroughly and made as disreputable as Nazism is today. We can hope to see the bombing of churches denounced by Muslim leaders as it was in Iraq last month or the slaughter of school children almost universally condemned as it was most recently after the horrendous attacks in Russia.

Americans have a reputation for impatience. That's not all bad. It's a strength, but it's also a weakness. In this struggle, as in the Cold War, we're right to be impatient for results. But looking at the stakes, we should also recognize that we're in this fight for the long haul.

It's striking, sometimes, in hindsight, to look back at how quickly we became impatient with the situation in Europe after V–E [Victory in Europe] Day. Just six months after Eisenhower's great victory in Europe, people were heard to say, "We've lost the peace." In 1946, The New York Times editorialized, "In every military headquarters, one meets alarmed officials doing their utmost to deal with the consequences of the occupation policy that they admit has failed." More amazingly, Life magazine was able to write also in 1946, "We have swept away Hitlerism, but a great many Europeans feel"—get this—"that the cure has been worse than the disease."

Sometimes it's hard to remember how long it took to begin to turn around the situation in Europe. It was a full two years after the end of the war when the situation looked so desperate that President Harry Truman courageously proposed the Marshall Plan. As late as the communist takeover of Czechoslovakia in 1948 a full three years later, people in the West were still debating whether there was even a new threat that we needed to confront. And the idea that we could eventually win that struggle after an effort that would extend over four decades was something that few besides George Kennan [former ambassador who developed the idea of containment and believed the grip of the Soviet Union would end] dared to predict.

Similarly, today, a problem that grew up over 20 or 30 years or longer is not going to disappear in two or three. So we must be resolved and patient. We know how Europe's story ends. We know that it can be done when leaders are determined to persevere, when the American people and their allies are resolved to stand firm for freedom.

Freedom has been the glue of the world's strongest alliances and it has been the solvent that has dissolved tyrannical rule. These are the same values that held the NATO allies together over the course of four decades of often-contentious debates. They are the values that have brought some 40 countries into the coalition effort in Afghanistan, more than 30 countries into Iraq, and some 80 or 90 countries into the larger coalition against global terror.

Our enemies know us by our love of liberty and democracy. We know them by their worship of death and their philosophy of despair. At the beginning of this year, we were given a window into that dark and barren world when we intercepted a letter from an al Qaeda associate in Iraq to his colleagues in Afghanistan. That letter from Abu Musab al Zarqawi, a major terrorist mastermind, gives us an idea of how he and his kind view the benefits of a free and open society emerging in the heart of the Middle East. "Democracy in Iraq," al Zarqawi wrote, "is coming." And that, he said, will mean "suffocation" for the terrorists.

He talks disparagingly about Iraqis who, in his words, "look ahead to a sunny tomorrow, a prosperous future, a carefree life, comfort and favor." Just imagine that. For al Zarqawi, prosperity and happiness are inconsistent with a terrorist's mission. That long letter, which I recommend to you, is readily available on the Internet, and is worth reading in detail. The contempt that al Zarqawi displays for whole groups of human beings, including Muslim Kurds and Muslim Shia, calls to mind the racism of the Nazis. His glorification of death and violence, like that of bin Laden and [Ayman al] Zawahiri [advisor to Osama bin Laden, founder of Egyptian Islmaic Jihad] and so many others, also calls to mind the tyrannical movements of the last century. While they claim the mantle of religion, their rhetoric recalls the death's head that Hitler's SS proudly displayed on its uniforms.

But the great majority of human beings, Muslims and non-Muslims alike, want to embrace life and freedom, if given a chance. A few months back, Hamid Karzai [Afghan leader] said that if they registered 6 million people to vote in Afghanistan, he'd consider it a great success. They've registered 10.5 million people who defied the Taliban philosophy and registered to vote in the forthcoming elections. Forty percent of those voters are women.

In Iraq, the early caucuses for the Iraqi National Conference were met with an almost overwhelming number of Iraqis eager to serve. In the city of Kut, more than 1,200 people competed for 22 seats. In Najaf, 920 candidates vied for those 20.

Like Nazism and communism before them, the terrorist brand of totalitarianism contains within it the seeds of its own defeat because it runs fundamentally counter to the love of life and the love of freedom that represent, I believe, the deepest longings of most human beings.

But they will not collapse simply of their own weight. To defeat them, we have to go on offense. That offensive means fighting on many and varied fronts and not just different geographical theaters, although there are many of those, and not even primarily military fronts. For this struggle is not just about killing and capturing terrorists, as important as that is. And we've had success here—important success. More than three-quarters of al Qaeda's leaders and facilitators, we estimate, have been killed or captured since Sept. 11. We'll never know how many Sept. 11s have been prevented by intercepting those facilitators and plotters in the last three years. Unfortunately, we can also be virtually certain that there are still people out there plotting major attacks against us. And even capturing or killing bin Laden himself will not eliminate al Qaeda, much less other terrorist groups.

While we cannot concentrate our efforts on only one front at a time, we also can't put equal effort into each one simultaneously. We need to sequence our efforts in a way that makes sense, recognizing also that what we do in one theater has impact on others. We cannot have an al Qaeda strategy by cutting aid to Pakistan, isolating a country like that, the way we did in the 1990s. At the same time, success in one theater can provide a platform for success in others. Success in Afghanistan has not only deprived al Qaeda of a sanctuary there and driven al Qaeda terrorists into Pakistan where we've been able to capture them, it has also supported President Pervez Musharraf's world position as a friend and ally of the United States.

The capture of terrorist operatives in Pakistan, in turn, has led to the arrests of key associates in places as far away as London and Chicago, Singapore and Morocco, and provided significant, new information about terrorist plans.

Saudi Arabia is another crucial theater. Terrorists once found Saudi Arabia a friendly place to find money. But since the suicide bombings in Riyadh on May 12 of last year, Saudi Arabia's own wake-up call, it's been a far less hospitable place for terrorists. The Saudis have been able to kill or capture more than 600 al Qaeda associates and their efforts have been facilitated by the fact, thanks to Operation Iraqi Freedom, that Saudi Arabia no longer has to be the pillar of a failing policy to contain Iraq.

Indonesia, where I was privileged to serve as a U.S. ambassador for three years, has the largest Muslim population of any country in the world and religious tolerance is a true hallmark of that country. For Indonesians, the attacks in Bali and Jakarta were their wake-up call, and they have taken serious steps to deal with our own terrorist problem. And they need our help.

The Palestinian-Israeli problem is another theater in this struggle. President Bush laid out the very clear solution to this problem—the establishment of two states living side-by-side in peace. As simple as it is to say it, getting to that solution is an enormous challenge. But getting there will bring enormous benefits for our other efforts in that struggle. An Israeli withdrawal from the Gaza Strip, though a limited step, is an important one in the right direction.

In other theaters, our diplomacy has been strengthened by our military success. It's been said, and I agree, that diplomacy without military capability is little more than prayer. In the process of performing their role so magnificently, brave American troops have also given our diplomats enormous credibility. As a result, not long ago Libya saw what was happening in the region and agreed to peacefully dismantle its weapons programs.

But for our military forces, of course, the two central fronts are Iraq and Afghanistan. Today, in those two countries, 50 million people have been freed from brutal tyranny. Afghanistan and Iraq are on the way to becoming America's newest allies in the fight for freedom.

There are those who debate whether Iraq was the right place to use military force. I agree strongly with Sen. John McCain [Republican senator from Ariz.] who recently said, "Our choice wasn't between the benign status quo and the bloodshed of war, it was between war and a greater threat." As the senator explained, "There was no status quo to be left alone. The years of keeping Saddam in a box were coming to a close. The international consensus," Sen. McCain went on, ". . . [that] Saddam [should] be kept isolated and unharmed had eroded to the point that many critics of military action had decided the time had come, once again, to do business with Saddam. [This] despite his nearly daily attacks on our pilots and his refusal, until his last day in power, to allow the unrestricted inspection of his arsenal."

The success of democracy in Iraq is a terrorist's greatest fear. "Suffocation," as I mentioned, is what Zarqawi calls it. For success in Iraq will have effects far beyond the borders of that country. When Iraqis possess freedom and lasting stability, that will be one more step in pushing this extremist ideology the terrorists espouse to the margins of civilized society and replacing it with a hopeful vision of freedom.

Winning in Iraq and Afghanistan is imperative, but it is only part of the larger war on terrorism. Winning in each of the geographical theaters I've mentioned is only part of the victory. Victory requires more than just killing and capturing terrorists, it requires planting the seeds of hope and expanding the appeal of freedom particularly in what we call the broader Middle East and the Muslim world.

As democracy grows in the Middle East, it becomes easier for peacemakers to succeed throughout the region. There are so many wonderful Muslims who are our best allies in fighting this ideological battle. If you'll indulge me, I'd like to tell you briefly about three whom I've been privileged to know personally.

One of them is Shaukat Aziz, the new prime minister of Pakistan. I first met him 10 years ago when he was a highly successful executive of Citicorp and I was a dean, out raising money for Johns Hopkins University. I was struck, even then, by his interest in substance. He's a man who has given up an incredible career in the American business world—some even talked of him as the next CEO of Citicorp—in order to go to Pakistan to help his country achieve a prosperity that he could have enjoyed personally without any effort. His reward for that has been one nearly successful assassination attempt just a few weeks ago. But that hasn't stopped him, and it hasn't stopped his brave president, Pervez Musharraf.

Another old friend of mine is Abdurrahman Wahid, the first democratically elected president of Indonesia. He is, perhaps, even more distinguished for his long leadership of an organization called Nahdlatul Ulama. With 40 million members, it's the largest Muslim organization in Indonesia and, indeed, it's larger than most countries in the world. Abdurrahman Wahid is a Muslim leader, but he is also a true apostle of tolerance.

One of his first acts as president—as the new president of that predominantly Muslim country—was to go to a Hindu temple in Bali to participate in Hindu prayers. While he was in Baghdad in the 1960s studying his own religion, he also studied Shia texts with an ayatollah now known to the world as Sistani. Tragically, he studied with a very distinguished Sunni cleric, al-Badri, who was taken away while Wahid was his student, tortured with hot irons and brutally murdered.

The third one, I'm happy to say, is a former deputy prime minister who was, thankfully, released just two weeks ago from six years of unjustified imprisonment in his own country, Malaysia. Anwar Ibrahim, again, is a devout Muslim. In fact, he started his career as a leader of the Muslim student movement in Malaysia.

I remember a conference I attended in Kuala Lumpur some eight years ago where Anwar was asked about his views of the relationship between Islam and politics. He said, "I have no use for countries that call themselves Islamic and then deny basic rights to half their population," clearly meaning their women.

These are three of the most wonderful human beings in public life anywhere. It's men and women like them who will lead change throughout the Muslim world.

Just as in the years after World War II, victory will require great risk and sacrifice and much hard work. The three Muslim leaders I've just mentioned have risked their reputations, their freedom and even their lives to stand up for freedom and democracy and religious tolerance.

Hamid Karzai in Afghanistan knows that his life is on the line every day. Thousands of Iraqis are joining the new army and the new national guard and the police force, even though they know they're risking their lives in doing so.

On my visit to Iraq this past June, I met a young Marine whose life had been saved by five members of the Iraqi National Guard. They had risked their own lives to pull him from the battlefield when he was wounded under fire. Afghans and Iraqis know what they're fighting for. They understand the risks. Nearly 700 Iraqi Soldiers, police and national guardsmen, by our official count and probably hundreds more, have already given their lives in this cause. But as one young woman we met in June up in Mosul, whose sister had recently been murdered, said to us, "My father said, 'You must never back down in the face of evil.'"

These people are not retreating in the face of evil, and they have the support of extraordinarily brave young Americans who are risking their lives so that other people can enjoy freedom and so that we, as Americans, can live in greater security.

We mourn each one of those Americans who have been lost for this cause. My friend, Joe Lieberman, put it eloquently when he called it "a noble cause as critical to American security as any we have fought over the centuries."

One of those American heroes who helped give them that opportunity is an extraordinary young man, Army Sergeant Adam Replogle of the 1st Armored Division. I met him at the hospital, at Walter Reed. He had been with his unit fighting Sadr's army in May near Karbala when an RPG [rocket-propelled grenade] slammed into him and he lost his left arm and sight in his left eye. Adam put that enormous sacrifice into perspective this way. He said, "We're fighting for everything we believe in. We've freed Iraqis from a dictator who was killing them by the millions."

And he described how he had personally changed so many lives in Iraq, how he'd helped destroy terrorist cells and get people back into their houses, how he and his fellow Soldiers helped multiply the number of schools in his sector from two to 40 in just a year. He'd even bought bikes for Iraqi girls and boys with his own money. "After all," he said, "they only cost five bucks and these kids didn't have anything."

Sergeant Replogle summed up the situation like this: "Saddam affected everything in that country. Something had to be done."

Just as Eisenhower not only defeated an evil enemy, but also helped us gain new allies in the fight for freedom, this generation of Americans is doing the same thing. Eisenhower would be proud of them—enormously proud.

Something had to be done. And once again, Americans are doing it, just as Americans have always stood up to evil.

There are others in the Muslim world who will one day join us as allies in this fight. That's because history has shown that, in their hearts, most people do not want to live under tyrants. Clearly, hope remains. As the president reminded us, "As freedom advances, heart by heart, nation by nation, America will be more secure and the world will be more peaceful."

With that, ladies and gentlemen, as the hour grows late, I think I'll close, once again, by invoking the immortal wisdom of our Army chief of staff who once wisely observed: "Never miss a chance to shut up." Thank you, very much.

MORNING ADDRESS

SAFEGUARDING OUR CITIES: HOMELAND SECURITY FROM THE LOCAL PERSPECTIVE

Ambassador Michael Sheehan, Deputy Commissioner of Counter-Terrorism, New York City Police Department

Introduction by Peter Verga, Principal Deputy Assistant Secretary of Defense for Homeland Defense

Summary

Ambassador Michael Sheehan

• Terrorism presents us with a clear and present danger. It is useful to look at the nature of global terrorism and the campaign against it through a historical lens. The scourge of terrorism did not begin Sept. 11, 2001. It began at least 10 years prior to these attacks and will continue for at least the next 10 years.

    1. During the 1980s, jihad in Egypt led to radicalization and growth of fundamentalist movements, which provided a breeding ground for terrorists.

    2. By the 1990s, the threat was present within the United States. In New York City, spiritual leader Sheikh Omar Abdel Rahman was preaching his message of hate. In November 1990, Rabbi Meir Kahane, the founder of the Jewish Defense League, was murdered. In fact, the 1993 World Trade Center bombing was originally intended to be the final attack in that string of assaults. Rahman and the Egyptian Islamic Jihad also planned bombing the Lincoln Tunnel with ammonium nitrate in 1993.

    3. The Sept. 11 attack itself actually grew out of a 1995 plan to crash commercial airliners.

• The current threat facing the United States is a complex combination of extremists' anger over perceived repression of their brethren, anger at U.S. foreign policy, and frustration with their own secular rulers.

• Afghanistan once formed the core of the terrorist threat led by al Qaeda. U.S. actions in Afghanistan have upset the leadership structure in the region, but jihadists still find sanctuary in other pockets of the world.

1. Insurgencies in Pakistan, the Philippines and Iraq also fuel jihadists. In fact, Mohammad Atta, the leader of the Sept. 11 attacks, originally wanted to go to Chechnya to aid that insurgency.

2. The new trend in terrorism ranges "from rhetoric to action" and flourishes without the aid of formal al Qaeda training.

• The challenge facing New York City is to identify terrorist cells within the city that may not be linked to al Qaeda and to act before they have the opportunity to attack. At this time, al Qaeda is increasingly looking for U.S. citizens to aid in its cause, as shown by those convicted of casing the Brooklyn Bridge. While there is no specific knowledge of an operational threat at this time, tracking of identified individuals is crucial.

1. Proper tracking of individuals requires developing an understanding of terrorist connections, while still building a case against that individual. Often this requires walking a fine line between knowing when to arrest a suspect before he strikes, and when to find his connection higher up on the terrorist ladder. However, when in doubt, the NYPD always errs on the side of prevention.

2. The problem that cannot be planned for is the fact that "You don't know what you don't know." Mohammad Atta, as well as those responsible for the Madrid bombings, specifically stayed away from "suspicious sites" such as mosques.

3. The NYPD has been alerted to hundreds of attacks over the last three years. Although most of these tips have not been credible, the NYPD must follow up on all leads. The problem is, credible reporting is not specific and specific reporting is not credible.

• The NYPD remains committed to four main tasks: detecting, deterring, investigating and arresting terrorist cells.

1. The main force responsible for fighting terrorism is the Joint Terrorism Task Force, which consists of 135 detectives working in collaboration with the FBI. They work alongside a highly visible police force to convince terrorists that landmarks are "too hot."

2. Increasing intelligence provides the proper force to combat terrorism.

3. Intelligence requires learning from terrorist attacks around the world, as in the adjusting of security in New York subways following the Madrid attacks.

4. Security must start with a commitment from the top and worrying about funding later. However, the NYPD must also fulfill its task of reducing crime, as it has by 15 percent over the past three years.

• The biggest nut to crack is improving intelligence collection capability through developing confidential informants, timely use of electronic eavesdropping, and more extensive and more effective undercover strategies. We must also improve the defense posture of cities, while at the same time ensuring and protecting free and open public use and enjoyment.

• People often ask why there have been no al Qaeda attacks since Sept. 11. There is no clear answer. Perhaps it is because they have been disrupted in their bases in Iraq or Afghanistan. Perhaps they are waiting. One thing is certain, we do know the terrorists are patient.

• The lessons from Dwight Eisenhower apply to the war on terrorism. In both cases, teamwork and alliances are important. Eisenhower built the NATO alliance, but he also knew when it was appropriate to "go it alone," as shown by his actions in the 1956 Suez Canal crisis. The campaign on terrorism needs Eisenhower's blend of realism and ideology.

• We must eliminate the conditions of despair that allow terrorism to fester. "We will win and terrorism will be thrown on the trash heap of 'isms' of the 20th century."

Analysis

Michael Sheehan's frank and provocative address brought a distinctive "local" flavor to a conference that emphasized international issues. Yet he managed to show that New York City's links to international economic and ethnic communities requires the NYPD to become involved internationally in a variety of ways. Such involvement adds a vertical twist to requirements for interagency cooperation.

The audience was well-informed about NYPD efforts to protect its citizens, but the address begged the question of whether New York is unique or can be used as a model, to some degree, for how other major cities could address their security issues. Few other cities have police departments that equal the U.S. Coast Guard in size, are at the center of the U.S. economy, and have such a high volume of international traffic. But some other cities will be similar to New York with respect to one or more of these characteristics.

Sheehan pointed to the difficulty and expense of addressing local security issues, but offered encouragement with news of successes. New York City has devoted more resources for a longer period of time than any other major city and is still faced with monumental difficulty of ensuring security for its citizens. New York's experience makes clear the challenges faced by other U.S. cities—many with far less resources and expertise. His comments offer support for current Department of Homeland Security policies that provide financial support for first responders and share national intelligence with potentially affected local authorities.

The address brought home that even international politics can be distinctly local. The New York City government has chosen to aggressively face its international security challenges and should, to the degree practical, inspire other local governments to do the same. Now is the right time for local government to take on the task, while unprecedented support and funding from the federal government are available to improve local capabilities for security and consequence management.

Transcript

ANNOUNCER: Ladies and gentlemen, please welcome today's master of ceremonies, Brigadier General Kevin T. Ryan.

BRIGADIER GENERAL KEVIN T. RYAN: Thanks and welcome back to our second day of the Eisenhower Conference. Thanks for coming back here. Now, I know a lot of you have been here since early this morning, eating our pastries and the fruit. You may have missed the news. Let me just bring you up to speed. A suicide bombing in Baghdad outside police headquarters Tuesday killed 47 people, mostly young men waiting to take jobs in the Iraq Security Services. On the good news side, the Turkish man held hostage in Iraq for over 50 days was released yesterday, and children in Beslan, Russia, returned to school this morning for the first time since their terrorist attack two weeks ago. On the national scene, Ivan is bearing down on the Alabama coast. It should hit sometime after midnight tonight, near Mobile [Ala.] or Biloxi [Miss.] It is a Category 4 storm with 140 mph sustained winds. And locally, former [Washington,] D.C. Mayor Marion Barry has won the Democratic primary to run again for council member for the city's Ward Eight.

Well, welcome back. I hope you had a chance last night to hear [Deputy Defense] Secretary [Paul] Wolfowitz's capstone speech at dinner. It ended a very productive first day.

We have another special day for you today. We start and end with two exceptional speakers. In just a moment you'll hear from Michael Sheehan, and we end the day with Lee H. Hamilton. In between, we have two dynamite panels that are sure to generate a lot of discussion. To introduce our first speaker today, it is my honor to present Mr. Peter Verga, who is a principal deputy assistant secretary of defense for homeland defense.

He is the principal adviser to the assistant secretary for homeland defense on all matters related to the overall supervision of homeland defense activities for Department of Defense. Mr. Verga is also a retired U.S. Army officer with over 26 years of service in various operational and managerial positions, including combat service in Vietnam.

Please join me in welcoming Mr. Peter Verga.

PETER VERGA: Well, thank you, General Ryan. I appreciate that kind introduction. It's really great to have an opportunity to introduce our speaker today. I've known Mike for quite a few years, and he's a wonderful speaker; you guys are going to get a lot out of him. You know, in September 2002, President Bush said, "The world changed on Sept. 11, 2001. We learned that a threat that gathers on the other side of the earth can strike our own cities and kill our own citizens. It's an important lesson and one that we can never forget. Oceans no longer protect America from the dangers of this world. We're protected by daily vigilance at home, and we will be protected by resolute and decisive action against threats abroad."

Peter Verga

It's also been said that there is no front line in the war or terrorism. There is no home game; there is no away game. There is only one battle space. Arguably, the cities of the United States are in the forefront of that worldwide battle space, especially in what some consider the world's premier city, New York. It's a city that starts off the year with the world's largest New Year's celebration. It hosts millions of visitors a year, major sporting events, the United States Navy Fleet Week every year, a major political convention this year, the U.S. Open Tennis Championship, the U.N. General Assembly, to name a few. Quite a challenge, as you might imagine.

Well, the man who's been chosen to be the deputy commissioner of the New York City Police Department for Counter-Terrorism, the Honorable Michael Sheehan, is the man for that job. He is a graduate of the United States Military Academy, has counterinsurgency combat experience, served on National Security Council staff for two presidents, and was a deputy assistant secretary of state, the ambassador-at-large for counterterrorism and assistant secretary general of the United Nations in the Department of Peacekeeping Operations. Since June 2003, he has been the deputy commissioner for counterterrorism of the some 40,000-person New York Police Department. They've done a magnificent job over the last couple of years, with all those events that I talked about, presenting terrific counterterrorism-type challenges. This morning we're very fortunate to hear from Michael, and he's going to tell us the view of homeland security from the local perspective, which is very important. So I'd ask you to join me in welcoming the Honorable Michael Sheehan, deputy commissioner for counterterrorism of the New York City Police Department.

AMBASSADOR MICHAEL SHEEHAN: Thank you very much, Pete, for that kind introduction. I appreciate it very much. It's good to see you again, and it's great to be back in Washington, which was my home for so many years. I've been in New York City now for about four years, and I now call "The Big Apple" my home. I walked around the streets of Washington last night. I definitely miss the relative quiet and peace of this city, compared to the hustle and bustle of Manhattan. I live in Manhattan across the street from a fire house that lost nine brave members of that small station on Sept. 11, 2001. I work in a department that lost 23 of the finest

police officers in the world during that
same attack, and I'm reminded almost
every day as I pass by the Trade Center
site—the huge, gaping construction site
at ground zero—that the terrorist threat
is a real and present danger.

This morning I would like to take
the opportunity to talk to you from the
field, from our perspective in New York
City, a truly global city, about where we
are three years after the 9/11 attacks. I'll
discuss three broad subjects: the nature
of the terrorist threat, what we are doing
about it at the NYPD [New York City
Police Department], and the key issues
that we face on the road ahead.

First, the threat. The scourge of
extremist Islamic terrorism in the United
States did not start on Sept. 11, 2001.
New York City had been targeted by
Islamic extremists or radical jihadists

Michael Sheehan

for at least 10 years before that date and will most likely be threatened for at least
another 10 years from today. These terrorists did not appear overnight, and they
will not be vanquished overnight, either. Let's take a quick look at the last 10 years,
for they provide invaluable insights to the nature of the threat we continue to face
today and for the foreseeable future.

The current brand of Islamic extremist terrorism grew out of a radical split
from the Muslim Brotherhood in Egypt in the 1980s—the creation of the Egyptian
Islamic Jihad [EIJ] and the Gamat al Islamaya, terrorist organizations with the goal
of overthrowing the secular Egyptian regime. The same trend of radicalization of the
Muslim Brotherhood that existed in Egypt showed up concurrently in parts of the
Diaspora community of Metropolitan New York. The EIJ's spiritual leader, Sheikh
Omar Abdul Rahman, expelled from Egypt, arrived in the United States in 1990,
and he began preaching his brand of extremist hatred here as soon as he got off the
plane. At the same time, a prominent mosque in Brooklyn was establishing ties to al
Qaeda through the NGO [nongovernmental organization] al-Kifah Refugee Center,
which originally was a support mechanism for the anti-Soviet mujahideen [Islamic
jihadists] but had increasing ties to Osama bin Laden and the nascent al Qaeda.

In November 1990, Rabbi Meir Kahane, the founder of the Jewish Defense
League, was murdered by El Sayyid Nosair. We now know that out of this murder
there are clear links to individuals involved in the February 1993 attack against the
World Trade Center [WTC]. This plot, originally designed against Jewish synagogues
in Brooklyn and the outer boroughs, was shifted to the more important strategic

economic target by its mastermind, Ramzi Yousef. Members of his crew were in direct contact with Nosair prior to the attack. After the attack on the World Trade Center, and later on in that year, there was another less well-known plot where another group linked to Rahman was planning to attack several landmarks in New York City, including the Lincoln and Holland Tunnels. This group of terrorists was caught on tape, preparing explosives in an apartment in Brooklyn, mixing a slurry of ammonium nitrate to use in an attack, when they were apprehended.

Although these were separate plots—the murder of Kahane, the World Trade Center and the aborted plot—there were linkages in many of them. Khalid Sheikh Mohammed [KSM] was the uncle of the 1993 World Trade Center mastermind, Yousef. KSM of course was the mastermind of the 9/11 plot, which evolved out of his plotting with Ramzi Yousef to sabotage U.S. airliners over the Pacific Ocean in January 1995.

From the pre-9/11 era, we get a very strong lesson: Terrorist trends abroad show up in New York very quickly and can turn into violent plots under our noses if we are not vigilant.

The current terrorist threat is not an isolated phenomenon; it grows out of the turmoil in the Islamic world that has been building for at least the past 20 to 30 years. It entails a complex set of issues, including their frustration with their secular regimes at home, the perceived oppression of their Muslim brothers at the hands of infidels in various parts of the world, and a particular resentment of U.S. foreign policy in the Middle East.

In the 1990s, Afghanistan had become a festering swamp of terrorist activity, operating with virtual impunity from the world. Jihadists flowed in and out of Afghanistan, primarily from Saudi Arabia, Yemen and Pakistan, but from all over the world including Europe and the United States. In Afghanistan they trained to fight for numerous jihads: the local Taliban war against the Northern Alliance [Afghan ethnic coalition formed to defeat the Taliban], against the Indians in Kashmir, the Serbs in the Balkans, the Russians in Chechnya and in many other local jihads around the world. Some became more closely affiliated with bin Laden and joined his organization. These so-called "Afghan alumni"—veterans of the training camps and war in Afghanistan—formed the core of an international network of terrorists, most notably, but not exclusively, led by al Qaeda.

After the 9/11 attacks and subsequent American response in Afghanistan, the Afghan sanctuary was significantly reduced and somewhat displaced to the Pakistan-Afghan border and the tribal areas of eastern Afghanistan.

Afghanistan no longer provides a sanctuary of impunity for global jihadists, but they continue to fight in various pockets of the world and take refuge in many more spots around the globe both in and out of their combat zones, to include remote parts of Afghanistan.

What is also clear is that the proliferation of jihadist movements and insurgencies around the world is extremely problematic. They include the terrible sectarian violence between Sunnis and Shias, such as in Pakistan, Afghanistan and other places, and a variety of active insurgencies, such as the Palestinians and in Chechnya, Kashmir, the southern islands of the Philippines and, of course, Iraq. Other movements seek to overthrow secular regimes in the Islamic world and establish local or pan-Islamic caliphate, such as in Algeria, Saudi Arabia and Indonesia.

All of these movements generate jihadists in troubling numbers, and some inevitably come to the United States sooner rather than later. That's our experience. These struggles also inspire and inflame some that are already in the United States, stoking resentments that have the potential to flare into real problems. We see this on a regular basis in New York City. The previous terrorists who either attacked or planned attacks in New York City come from this world of international jihad: Mohammed Attah, for instance, was on his way to jihad in Chechnya when he was diverted in Europe over to Afghanistan, where he joined al Qaeda and eventually led the 9/11 operation; Iyman Faris, the Brooklyn Bridge plotter, was an "Afghan alumni," a veteran of combat there; and recently arrested in the United Kingdom, Issa al Hindi, the man who cased the Citigroup building and other sites in New York City and Washington, D.C., was a veteran of the Kashmiri conflict. These three people, who had attacked or were planning to attack in New York City, were all veterans of jihads.

There is a new and even more troubling trend evolving that we saw both in the Madrid train attack on March 11 of this year and in Operation CREVICE, a broken up United Kingdom cell that had already procured the precursors for a massive truck bomb. In these cases, members of operational cells were not veterans of jihad, but had skipped straight from extremist rhetoric in coffee houses to operational terrorist activity, bypassing the normal progression of training and radicalization in Afghan or other jihad campaigns. This is a trend we have to follow very, very closely in New York City.

Our challenge in New York City today is to identify the al Qaeda operative or support cells that are operating within our city. It is also to identify those persons, although not directly connected to al Qaeda, who may be in a position to act if the operational support is made available, or if they are able to organize an attack with their own resources, apparently as they were able to do in London and Madrid.

We know al Qaeda has been in New York City in the recent past. I touched on these affiliations. In March 2003, Uzair Paracha was arrested and charged with providing material support to an al Qaeda associate. His family, actually, ran a shipping business from Pakistan into New York City through shipping containers, one of our major nightmares. Months later, Iyman Faris pleaded guilty to the charge of material support to terrorism. We know he had previously cased the Brooklyn Bridge only to report back to his contacts that the weather was "too hot"—that the security was too tight in New York City. We also now know Issa al Hindi conducted sophisticated reconnaissance on financial institutions in New York and New Jersey in 2001 and briefed his concept to al Qaeda leadership in early 2004. These are people we believe to be members of al Qaeda or closely associated with its leadership.

We also know that post-9/11, al Qaeda has had a much more difficult time moving internationally, but by no means has it been shut down. It increasingly is looking for local operatives or those with citizenship or passports who makes it easier to operate in the United States.

We know that al Qaeda and its associated groups have a presence in New York City, primarily involved in networking and fundraising, primarily for activities abroad. There are no specific operational plans that we are aware of at this time, and we have no knowledge that an operational cell exists in New York City.

We have already identified some people of interest. Many are involved in criminal activities, some are not. We keep track of these people with two intentions: to develop a better understanding of their connections, and to further develop criminal or terrorist cases against them for their eventual prosecution. It's a delicate balance that we always try to manage between tracking the suspect and finding more links to his other operational cells or potential cells, versus moving in and preempting, arresting and preventing an attack. If we have to go one way or the other, we always go toward preemption of an attack rather than stretching out the investigation. But it's a very tough balance. It is an art rather than a science.

There are other pockets of individuals we need to worry about. They discuss jihad, violence and training. Some raise money and send it abroad, but its final source is often difficult to pinpoint. They are often in extremist movements that in public are a bit coy about terrorism, but behind closed doors are much more explicit. Some have troublesome connections with organizations abroad. They often operate at the fringe of the law, both in criminal activity and in terms of terrorist support.

We are worried that these feeder groups, as we normally refer to them, are recruitment grounds for al Qaeda operatives. We also worry that members of these groups may skip the jihad recruitment phase and move from these feeder groups like al muhajiroun [Islamic extremists based in Great Britain] straight to an operational activity, as was done in Madrid and the United Kingdom. These groups, although not labeled terrorist organizations, are hubs of violent rhetoric. That is troublesome.

The potential for terrorist activity can be discerned from some of the recent sting operations conducted in and around New York. Although in each case, the sting determined no real operational capability, the intent of those arrested to conduct a terrorist attack was clear.

So, we know they have been here, before and after 9/11, and there are some traces of presence today. But as was so correctly stated by the secretary of defense, "You don't know what you don't know."

Is there a Mohammad Atta-like cell in our midst? Mohammed Atta was instructed, "Don't go near mosques, don't go near extremist groups, stay low, blend into the society." The Madrid group was very much the same. Is there a cell operating outside the box of known extremists, blending into our landscape, preparing to initiate an attack? Or are there others preparing to enter the United States with a set plan and operational capacity? Frankly, we don't know, but there are some indications from national intelligence sources that this is a possibility we cannot discount.

We receive specific but unreliable threats to the city of New York in a constant stream. We have been alerted to hundreds of attacks in the past two years alone, many with exact specifics of time and place. In the past two weeks we received dozens of very specific threats to target the city, many from anonymous e-mails, some from walk-ins with reports of wild plots against our city, and even one from an ancient biblical code told me that they were going to shoot a rocket at President Bush on the Sept. 2. It was in the Torah, and the guy had figured it out. I told him, "Well, I'll get the ambulance ready, because I can't work against the Bible." Fortunately, none have panned out to date. Our dilemma is that the credible reporting from our national intelligence sources is not very specific and the specific reporting is not very credible.

So how do we respond?

NYPD operates under the assumption that we are targeted for attack 24 hours a day, seven days a week, 365 days a year. That never changes. We do not have the luxury to make any other assumption.

Our mission is both clear and direct. We strive to detect terrorist cells, deter those thinking of a plot, mitigate the effects of an attack, investigate a terrorist act if it occurs and capture perpetrators.

NYPD Commissioner Ray Kelly has put into place a comprehensive counterterrorism strategy over the past three years. Let me briefly review some of the major components of our strategy.

The first is the Joint Terrorism Task Force (JTTF). The NYPD has dramatically expanded its participation in the FBI's Joint Terrorism Task Force. The NY JTTF is the largest and oldest JTTF, and prior to 9/11 housed the principal al Qaeda unit for the FBI. Under Commissioner Kelly's leadership, the number of NYPD detectives in the task force has grown from 17 to 135. These seasoned detectives, with years of experience in narcotics, organized crime, homicide and other crimes, work with their partners in the FBI in conducting terrorist investigations from leads generated by federal sources. They are increasingly active in developing their own information sources in the city.

The second is the NYPD's Intelligence Division, which was revamped and expanded by Commissioner Kelly and my partner, Deputy Commissioner David Cohen, a former director of operations for the CIA, and is now developing an extensive capability to detect any potential terrorist activity that may be brewing in the city. Working groups with the JTTF are improving their working relationship in synchronizing these key initiatives. All of these investigations are conducted under the strict guidelines of the law that has been promulgated since Sept. 11. NYPD is now able to investigate with reasonable suspicion rather than criminal predicate, which is crucial to Intel's operation.

The third is counterterrorism deployments. The department also deploys highly visible uniformed counterterrorism surge operations designed to deter terrorists through a show of force. This initiative is key, as we know from multiple sources that al Qaeda operatives assess our security measures and shy away from targets with high levels of police concentration. Also it increases public awareness and refocuses our police officers on counterterrorism—a mission they are asked to perform in addition to crime fighting and improving the quality of life of New Yorkers.

The fourth is security. NYPD is improving its security at key locations around the city and during special events. We have created and trained a specialized unit that works with public and private entities to raise the bar of security at places like the NYSE [New York Stock Exchange], the Empire State Building, Grand Central Station, theaters in Times Square and hotels around the city. We are also looking at a sectoral approach to security in such areas as the transportation and chemical industries.

The fifth is CBRNE. We are improving our chemical, biological, radiological, nuclear and explosive [CBRNE] detection and response capability, which was developing prior to 9/11, but has improved dramatically in the past two and a half years. All patrol officers in the NYPD have individual protective units and have received basic counterterrorism training. In addition, we have trained numerous specialized units in WMD [weapons of mass destruction] awareness and COBRA [chemical biological radiological attack] cohort training, which occurred prior to the RNC [Republican National Convention]. In addition to participation in federal and citywide exercises, Commissioner Kelly has chaired our own internal tabletop exercises to further develop our CBRNE capability.

The sixth is intelligence analysis. We are boosting our own strategic intelligence analysis by tracking the development of international terrorism and following the modus operandi of overseas attacks. Understanding phenomena, trends and the terrorist mindset will help us predict what our national intelligence collection and investigations fail to uncover. In addition to police detectives, we are hiring civilian analysts to give us additional capability for strategic analysis of the threat—the foundation for our CT policy and programs.

The seventh is training. NYPD has numerous additional specialized training programs in place for cops and specialists to improve their counterterrorism knowledge and tactics. Our lesson plans cover areas like WMD and critical infrastructure protection. Our joint regional training center with DHS [Department of Homeland Security] also builds our connectivity with other local law enforcement.

The eighth is public outreach. We are staying in touch with local precincts and groups in the city to enhance our public and private partnerships. At the same time, we are increasing our public awareness and working on more ways to disseminate information to the public about how to stay vigilant and be responsive.

The ninth is international outreach. We are enhancing our international partnerships through overseas deployments. JTTF-NYPD detectives were sent to interrogate suspects in Guantanamo Bay [Cuba] and Afghanistan. An NYPD team was deployed to assess the Madrid subway bombing within hours of the attack to look at ways to reinforce NYC's transportation infrastructure. We sent a team to evaluate Olympic security measures in Athens [Greece]. Detectives are also posted to Interpol headquarters in Lyon [France], Tel Aviv [Israel], Montreal, Singapore, Toronto and London. In the coming year, we plan to expand our contacts with other governments to include several key partners in the Middle East.

New York City has made an unprecedented commitment to counterterrorism—and it starts from the top. Mayor Michael Bloomberg has supported Police Commissioner Kelly on all of his initiatives, even as the city faced some fiscal constraint following the Sept. 11 attacks. They do what needs to be done first and figure out how to fund it later. Despite this, the department was able to continue crime reductions, which were broadly expected to rise, with a shrinking police force and expanded CT commitments for some of the department's best detectives.

Nevertheless, crime has dropped 15 percent during the past three years. I make this comment not to praise my bosses but to underscore the importance of local commitment to get it done. We in New York have not waited for federal funding to move forward. Instead, we do what we need to do, and hopefully we will get a little more federal assistance this year to help us cover the gap for new requirements.

Much of the Washington debate has focused on information sharing, intelligence bureaucratic structures and funding for the first responder. These are important, but I think much more time should be spent discussing intelligence collection: the development of confidential informants; undercover networks; the ability to use wire taps in a responsible, yet timely manner; and the training of a whole new generation of counterterrorist investigators and analysts who focus on identifying the cell prior to an attack, rather than cleaning up after it.

Going forward, our priorities include continuing to expand our intelligence operations in the JTTF and NYPD intelligence units. Expanding the number and quality of our current investigations to track terrorists embedded in our society is the key. We must detect terrorist activity before it can operationalize. We will continue to refine the art of surveillance, detection and the timing of our arrests and sting operations.

We will continue to improve the defense posture of the city by mitigating the risk to key sites and targets and boosting our post-attack preparations, especially in the case of a chemical, biological or radiological attack.

Our priority is also to continue improving our relationship with our federal partners. As the federal government augments its capabilities through the cooperation of the FBI, DHS, CIA and NORTHCOM [U.S. Northern Command], we in local law enforcement will look to foster tighter relationships and share information with them to fortify our defenses on the ground.

It is imperative to appropriately balance each operational area with other important principals. We need to protect our crucial buildings and special events without creating an armed camp in the city, choking off traffic and needlessly worrying people. We need to have aggressive intelligence programs and protect the privacy right of all Americans. And we need to build a partnership with the federal government but retain an NYPD capability that protects our city from the threat of terrorism.

There remain outstanding issues I want to briefly touch on—questions the security community still needs to address in the post-9/11 operating environment.

The first is the Iraq war. What about the Iraq war? Will it improve the situation or make it worse? In my view, it is too soon to say. But as I said in my earlier remarks, jihadist insurgencies generate more terrorist recruits and seasoned operatives, who often find their way back here, than they kill. It is very important that Iraq be stabilized for the long term. We must closely monitor jihadists there—who seem mostly local, but clearly some are international—to see if they make their way outside of Iraq and form the types of operational networks that were characteristic of the Afghan alumni of the 1990s. Will an international Iraqi alumnus begin to be seen outside of Iraq's borders? We have to stabilize Iraq and Afghanistan or they eventually will come to New York City.

The second is the al Qaeda attacks. Why hasn't al Qaeda attacked us since 9/11? We don't really know for sure. There could be multiple explanations. Perhaps it is a result of their disrupted operations, both here and abroad. Perhaps they can, but are holding back for a big attack, not wanting to burn their operatives on a small hit. Perhaps they are waiting for the right time, although based on their previous operations, they generally would not wait once an operation is ready. It would be too risky. They generally hit when they are ready. Yet, we know well that they are patient—very patient.

In any case, what we do know is that we cannot be lulled into a sense of complacency, nor can we unreasonably scare our citizens into unwarranted panic. We must find an appropriate level of public awareness, coupled with a steady intensity of effort in law enforcement and intelligence operations against these organizations.

The third is "the Lone Wolf." Why haven't we been hit by "lone wolf" suicide bombings like the Chechnyans or Palestinians have conducted abroad? Again, we don't know. Perhaps it is because we are not sitting on a homeland scenario in the United States, like the Palestinians or in Chechnya or Kashmir. But, it is something about which we must be vigilant.

The fourth is information sharing. What about information sharing? It is one of the key issues in the post-9/11 reviews of our nation's failure to prevent the attacks.

The sharing of threat information is generally good. We have been very aggressive in placing people within the system to ensure we have direct access to national intelligence sources. Threat information is shared very quickly. The problem with most threat information is that it has very little credibility. Thank God for that, or we would have been attacked hundreds of times in New York City alone in the past year.

Sharing of sensitive sources and specifics of case information is a more difficult issue. The more credible information is very closely protected and normally very vague. We in New York, who often have to deploy resources to respond to these threats, are intensely interested in the details of the report and the quality of the source. It helps us measure our response, for resources are limited.

Let me conclude my remarks by referring to the great American after whom this conference is named: Dwight David Eisenhower.

Eisenhower's greatest skill during World War II was his ability to build and sustain a winning coalition. He understood that teamwork among the Allies, particularly the British, was the key to victory. He was able to lead the great allied armies even though many of his subordinates—[British General Bernard] Montgomery, [General George S.] Patton and even [General Omar N.] Bradley— often griped about his decisions that did not fully favor their desired approach to a campaign, which generally meant more troops and supplies for their respective commands. During his presidency, he continued to build the NATO alliance, but also knew when our interests diverged with our most important allies. In July 1956, when [Egyptian Premier Gamal Abdel] Nasser nationalized the Suez Canal, the French, British and Israeli governments intervened without consulting the United States. Eisenhower was appalled and subsequently sponsored a U.N. resolution that led to the withdrawal of the French, British and Israeli forces and the establishment of a U.N. monitoring force to help manage the process.

The campaign to defeat terrorism will also require improved teamwork within the federal government and with state and local authorities. It will also require a blend of American hardheaded realism and its idealistic principles in forging effective coalitions when possible and going it alone when necessary.

Finally, let me put in a plug for local law enforcement in this conference of strategic choices. Local governments, from New York to Karachi, from Madrid to Jakarta, unlike any time in modern history, will be in the center of national security issues. They are on the real front lines of this struggle collecting intelligence, arresting suspects, protecting sensitive sites and events, and preparing to mitigate any disaster that may befall them. I hope that in the United States we will do more to support local efforts in the future to detect, deter and ultimately defeat the scourge of terrorism.

We will prevail in this struggle. Violent Islamic extremism will be added to the trash heap of history with the other "isms" of the 20th century: fascism, communism and totalitarianism. It will take time to win decisively—make no mistake about that—and victory will not be easily defined. But success can be measured to the extent we crush these organizations and eliminate the conditions of despair that exacerbate the problem and help mend the broken governments that enable these conditions to fester.

Thank you for the opportunity to speak here today and share with you my report from the field.

PANEL 3

INTEGRATING NATIONAL POWER
FOR THE 21ST CENTURY ENVIRONMENT

Co-sponsor: The Henry L. Stimson Center

Introduction by: Janne E. Nolan, Ph.D., Professor, Graduate School of Public and International Affairs, University of Pittsburgh

Moderator: Ellen Laipson, President and CEO, The Henry L. Stimson Center

Ambassador Chas. W. Freeman Jr., Former Ambassador to the Kingdom of Saudi Arabia and former Assistant Secretary of Defense for International Security Affairs

Ambassador James R. Lilley, Former Central Intelligence Agency Chief of Station and former Ambassador to the Republic of Korea and the People's Republic of China

General Peter Pace, U.S. Marine Corps, Vice Chairman of the Joint Chiefs of Staff

Panel Charter

The United States is confronted by an international security environment that has become increasingly complex and unpredictable over the last two decades. This will, in all probability, increase in coming decades due to globalization, the erosion of state sovereignty, the growth of transnational actors, and other international forces. Ambitious states and transnational actors will use these trends to advance their aggressive and even violent agendas. Further, the complexity of the 21st century international security environment will be manifested in the threat of asymmetric attacks, international terrorism, proliferation of weapons of mass destruction, regional security, peace enforcement operations as well as other security issues.

The 21st century international security environment requires the seamless integration of U.S. military, diplomatic and intelligence instruments. Interagency coordination and cooperation must occur when formulating policy in Washington and implementing policy in "the field." These interagency processes are essential

Left to right: *Ellen Laipson, Chas. W. Freeman Jr.,
James R. Lilley, and Peter Pace*

for the effective and efficient application of national power to achieve political objectives. However, national security policy processes have been found sorely lacking in such integration on many occasions. Most recently, this was a principal finding of the post-Sept. 11 commissions.

This panel will discuss the challenges that the 21st century international security environment presents to the U.S. government's interagency processes. The panel discussion will focus on three dimensions of interagency coordination: the interagency policy process in Washington, interagency collaboration in the field, and cultivation of interagency expertise among national security professionals.

Discussion Points

• When you were a rising professional, what training did you receive and how much awareness was there of being "part of a larger team"?

• What are your perceptions of being in the field and running a team?

• From a Department of Defense perspective, what will affect the exit strategy in Iraq?

• How do you communicate through a large, bureaucratic system?

• How well-suited is each department to the tasks assigned it?

• What is the current relationship of the United States with Europe, particularly with Great Britain?

• In this age of globalization, how great is the need for regional knowledge?

Summary

Ambassador Chas. W. Freeman Jr.

• Chas. Freeman joined the Foreign Service in 1965 when he received a post in India. At that point, he was fortunate enough to have a base chief who wanted to share information between the intelligence and military communities. In his opinion, the greatest difference between the diplomatic culture and the military was the sense of mentoring and experience in the diplomatic corps.

• While serving as ambassador to the Kingdom of Saudi Arabia during Operation DESERT STORM, Freeman felt his main responsibility was to be America's eyes and ears abroad. When it came to deployment of American troops through Saudi Arabia, Freeman interacted well with General Norman Schwarzkopf, although both employed different leadership styles. In his estimation, the greatest problem in DESERT STORM was a disconnect between the military and civilian spheres, which ultimately allowed Saddam Hussein to stay in power. In particular, the power structure lacked a civilian counterpart to Schwarzkopf, which further intensified the unanswered questions of the war. What were the United States' war aims? How does one end the war?

• Freeman insisted there are things that an interagency system "can and can't do." In an orderly system, such a mechanism can allow all perspectives and expertise to be utilized. The interagency process is a potentially valuable mechanism for planning and enforcing discipline across bureaucratic lines, but not for decision making.

• The notion that security and military are synonymous is incorrect, as the military specializes in the use of force, not necessarily prevention. For that reason, new structures need to be considered, such as an interagency national security service to parallel its civilian counterpart. In addition, more foreign service officers should be kept in reserve, to help in the complicated, yet crucial task of diplomacy.

• A further problem with the Foreign Service today is the manner in which diplomats are appointed. According to Freeman, the process in which individuals who make large monetary campaign donations are appointed to ambassadorships is archaic.

• A focus on cross-training between intelligence gatherers and military personnel would help the military to understand and appreciate when no intelligence is available.

• While the representation overseas of various U.S. government agencies and departments is important, the United States must be careful about "casting the net too wide."

• In Freeman's opinion, there is a need to re-examine the United State's role in the U.N. Security Council. The National Security Act of 1947 is not necessarily applicable to the United States in the 21st century. However, he was also distressed by the "arrogance of foreign policy" and the "alienation of allies." Overall, he urged a return to a "listening mode."

• While academics try to divide the world into broad terms, such as "proliferators and nonproliferators," individuals still act primarily in terms of national or cultural allegiances. Therefore, foreign policy should focus on specific intelligence and regional knowledge. The challenge facing the United States "has never been greater," and is a "different game" that requires greater regional language skills and drawing upon the one-fifth of the world's population that is Muslim.

Ambassador James R. Lilley

• As a case officer in the clandestine service in Southeast Asia, Lilley experienced first-hand the problems of miscommunication, when two operations used the same location as a safe house and were ultimately discovered. The result was the arrest of both U.S. and Chinese citizens, and ultimately the closure of the post.

• Lilley also discussed the diplomacy necessary in the redeployment of American troops prior to the 1988 Olympics in Seoul, South Korea. In an effort to remove a sizeable American presence from the middle of the city, Lilley had to work closely with military officials to move the troops from the center of the city, without depriving them of amenities from the city center.

• Cases in which coordination has broken down should be recorded, thoroughly examined and utilized in order to avoid repeating mistakes.

• In his experience, countries "rise through history" depending on how they act during covert operations, as shown in Laos, China, and Vietnam. The challenge facing the United States is the rebuilding of Afghanistan and the normalization process. Countries that ultimately seek self-control will not react well, therefore the United States should be aware of evolutionary issues that change with the times.

• Interaction with the academic community is crucial for the clandestine service. As shown in the former Soviet Union, only through infiltration can true success be achieved. Deception and manipulation are still the most important tools to be utilized to "protect the deal from contamination."

• Regional knowledge is still important, but the era of the big, 500-person station is over. At any one time, only about 20 percent of officers in an embassy carry their weight. A change in training must come from a bottom-up approach, not a top-down philosophy.

• In Lilley's opinion, nonproliferation is a high priority for the United States today. Information on the nuclear capabilities of other countries can only be achieved through infiltration of those at the highest levels, as in the case of a North Korean specialist ultimately brought to the United States.

General Peter Pace, U.S. Marine Corps

• Peter Pace's first realization of the need for integration came as a brigadier general in Somalia, when he had the responsibility of creating a coalition force without knowing what countries were participating, nor what troops and equipment they had. During his second tour in Somalia, the U.S. government assigned individuals to work for 30 or 60 days, causing a turnover problem. In Japan, Pace learned that the value of synergy is realized when one is lucky enough to have a leader with a true "ability to lead."

• In the field, the crucial ingredients for overcoming "stove pipe" tendencies are individual initiative and informal contact and communication. In Washington, the National Security Council serves well in preparing recommendations for the president. But policy tends to be stove-piped in implementation. There are a number of potentially useful ways to tackle this problem:

— revise the incentive structure to foster and reward interagency communication;

— move from an ad hoc to a systematic approach whereby cross-training is integrated into career development;

— ramp up cross-disciplinary education, perhaps by establishing an interagency academy;

— make more frequent and extensive use of military facilities for "working group" interactions;

— allow the State Department to take the lead in places like Afghanistan; and

— allow "multiple tours" for those currently rising through the ranks, rather than an entire career in the Department of Defense. This would enrich understanding of the duties of other branches of the service.

• While adopting some of these suggestions might require new legislation, many could be instituted merely by decision of the president. In any event, it is worth exploring these and other means of strengthening interagency processes at home and in the field. Meeting the security challenges of the 21st century requires that we capture the synergy from all aspects of national power.

Analysis

Panel III provided unique insights regarding systemic tensions in the interagency process. The panel discussion illuminated the oft-incongruous perspectives and activities among the U.S. Foreign Service, intelligence service and the military during conflicts or crises. Clearly, a degree of parochialism exists in each area as a result of differing educational systems, assignment histories and experiences. That the interagency process does not break down is a tribute to the professionalism and interpersonal skills of the various actors, who are brought together during a crisis. The question that the panel addressed, if somewhat obliquely, is whether these tensions can be mitigated.

The current system of appointing ambassadors based on political versus professional pedigree may undercut the officers of the Foreign Service, but a political appointee is not necessarily a recipe for incompetence. An ambassador relies substantially on the regional expertise of the embassy personnel, who come from these three communities. As ambassadors bring along different political qualities that fall outside the Foreign Service, a professional functionary may not bring the credentials needed to properly represent the United States. This subject is worthy of debate, but it is not clear-cut.

The panel emphasized throughout that the hallmark of the interagency process is the informal, personal interactions of the service personnel. Whether interacting on a daily basis or during a crisis, the ability of agency subordinates to form into informal working groups for the exchange of information and preliminary analysis certainly strengthens the interagency process. Naturally, the service educational systems should provide as many culturally and linguistically skilled personnel as possible, but the panelists placed such emphasis on interpersonal skills that these should become part of the curriculum as well a criterion for career progression.

Understanding that the interagency process is deliberative rather than executive is noteworthy. Decision makers rely on subordinates to present information in such a manner that it can be acted upon. Subordinates must sift through the plethora of intelligence, historical, background and other pertinent factors—cultural, political, economic and social—vet their conclusions with the other agencies, and then package the information for a decision. The panel's recommendation for formal interagency training is appropriate, but the school must focus on the decision-making process. In this manner, the executive can hear all agency viewpoints and caveats before making an informed decision. Finally, the curriculum must emphasize that the executive's decision is final, and to undermine that decision is the worst of all sins. Too often, national efforts are undermined by parochialism and partisanship.

Two final points that the panel discussed rather freely were not properly resolved. First, the idea that the United States has damaged diplomatic relations with Europe ignores the historic record. NATO scholars would view the recent disagreements as par for U.S.-European relations. Specifically, concerns that the alliance was crumbling as a result of a crisis have been the one constant since 1949. This can be seen over the years with issues and events such as the rearming of Germany, the Suez Canal crisis in 1956, FLEXIBLE RESPONSE, France's withdrawal from the integrated military structure, Vietnam, the neutron bomb, and introducing theater nuclear missiles into Germany, to name the most salient. In terms of tensions, Iraq is a rather tame affair. Understanding that liberal democracies disagree, often bitterly, is normal. Characterizing the latest dispute as a debacle is undiplomatic. Second, making an issue of no end state in Iraq and Afghanistan or any conflict may reflect partisan politics, but is at least ill-considered. The historical record offers few instances of definitive end states of conflicts, particularly with insurgencies. Perhaps a more constructive approach would have been to demonstrate how the interagency process could mitigate the problems associated with end state rather than lobbing rhetorical grenades.

In short, formalizing the inter-agency process is a worthy goal and promises to be the best approach to promoting a harmonized response to future crises and conflicts. In this regard, the panel offered noteworthy and constructive insights.

Transcript

ANNOUNCER: Ladies and gentlemen, Dr. Janne Nolan, professor, Graduate School of Public and International Affairs, University of Pittsburgh.

Janne E. Nolan

JANNE E. NOLAN, Ph.D.: Good morning. Thank you. Good morning to all of you. I'm very delighted to be here, to introduce the next panel moderator. Like others who have spoken before me, I want to extend my pride, thanks and congratulations to General Schoomaker and his remarkable people who have worked so hard to make this event the way it is. This is a third year of absolute excellence. I've told some of my Army colleagues that they should come with me sometime to an academic conference because some of them are talking about their loose ends and details that they haven't been able to get to. They have no idea what an extraordinarily organizational genius they have put forward. One day, if some of you want to come to an academic conference where people arrive 45 minutes late and there are dogs walking around the room, I will take you.

It's a time of such deep division in our country, a time of vicious polemic, a time of really horrible partisanship that has interfered in so many ways with our ability to come to a clear consensus for all of the very urgent needs of our country. This is such a welcome respite that the Army has this forum for reasoned discourse, and brings to this very difficult time its very, very best face. This is the Army. These are the voices of reason, which I look at as the three Ps of the Army: progressive, professional and problem solving. And in that spirit, let me introduce our next panel moderator, Ellen Laipson, who, as you can see from your programs, is the president and CEO of The Henry L. Stimson Center. She has a 25-year, very distinguished record of public service, including vice chair of the National Intelligence Council, the National Security Council and is a very well-recognized expert on the Middle East and other topics. She was a pioneer in recognizing the emergence of the

transnational nature of threats and
challenges, and she's an ideal person
both to lead this panel and to serve in
the capacity she does now. The Henry
L. Stimson Center's motto is "pragmatic
steps to ideal objectives," a quote from
Henry L. Stimson. So, please join me in
thanking her and welcoming her to the
panel. Thank you.

ELLEN LAIPSON: Well, good
morning everyone. It's really a pleasure
to be here, and I join with Janne
in thanking the Army for putting
together such a useful and constructive
conference that I hope will be of benefit
to all who attend and to those who will
learn about it through other media when
it's over.

Ellen Laipson

It is perhaps the case that the topic
in front of us, the interagency process,
will seem to some to be inside-the-beltway baseball. But I think since the 9-11
Commission report, we have all been sobered into a greater realization that our
complex bureaucracy over the past years has reached the point where not all parts
of the system know how to relate to each other. While each part of the national
security system has its own distinct mission, there are certain challenges—post-
Cold War challenges—that require some new thinking about better fusion, better
integration. I appreciate the thought that integration isn't necessarily the be all and
end all, and there are times when each of these disciplines in the national security
community must remain distinct. I hope we will hear about some of these ideas
from our panel.

We are tasked with trying to generate some new thinking and some new ideas
about ways to improve the interagency process and to prepare the next generation
of national security professionals for the continually evolving strategic environment
that our country and the international community faces. So it's with great pleasure
that I invite our panelists to come to their seats. We have Ambassador Chas
Freeman, a distinguished career diplomat who also served as assistant secretary of
defense. We have Ambassador James Lilley, who is a career operations officer in the
intelligence community and also served as U.S. ambassador to Korea and China.
And we are particularly honored to have General Peter Pace, who is currently the
vice chairman of the Joint Chiefs. Thank you, all.

To begin the discussion, what we are planning to do is conduct our conversation
in a talk-show format. So I will pose a series of questions to the panel, and, as

time permits, intermittently open it up to you, the audience, for some additional questions. The most logical way to proceed is to ask our three panelists to think back to when they were rising professionals in their distinct disciplines and to give us a sense of the kind of mission and training that they received that made them think, "I'm a diplomat," "I'm an intelligence officer" or "I'm a military officer." I hope they will share with us, perhaps, to what extent they were also inculcated with some values to think about being part of a larger team. How much awareness was there in their earlier careers of the way in which their particular piece of the national security puzzle fit into the other pieces? So, I've asked them to turn the clock back a bit and share with us any analytic thoughts or personal reflections and experiences that they might have from that period. Chas, I wonder if you'd like to go first.

AMBASSADOR CHAS. W. FREEMAN, JR.: Well, I joined the United States Foreign Service in December of 1965 from Harvard Law School. I had an intense interest in China as Jim Lilley had, but unlike him, I had no previous experience with it. So, I asked to be assigned somewhere on the rim of China—at that time we didn't have relations with China—but not to Taiwan, because I wanted to see whether I really wanted to make the commitment required to learn the language and master the area studies. I said anywhere on the rim of China except India, so, of course, they assigned me to Madras in India. The assignment process at the State Department at that time consisted of throwing a dart over your shoulder at a map, and so I drew India.

I think I very rapidly became aware of the distinction between the Foreign Service diplomatic culture and Jim's culture of the clandestine service. Our training in the Foreign Service is largely by apprenticeship. In fact, it's by mentoring, and it's by experience. I was very fortunate to have two very fine senior officers and the counsel general in Madras take me under their wings and begin to help me learn how to do reporting and analysis and how to be presentable in public. But I was also fortunate because the base chief, the CIA representative there, was a man of considerable experience who understood that we all have to work together. He wanted me to understand as much as I could be told without violating security about what he did and what his base was doing, and, in effect, he co-opted me to support his operations. So from the beginning I had a very close relationship with the intelligence community.

I received a draft notice while I was in Madras, but the draft board then decided that since I was already serving my country abroad, I would not have to go into the Army. But I did—then in Taiwan when I learned Chinese—find myself among military officers in yet another culture. I think probably I will stop by saying that five years later, when I went to CINCPAC/PACOM [commander in chief Pacific Command/Pacific Command], to talk to the political advisor to the CINC—I guess you would call him a combatant commander now—the thing he told me was that generally when State Department people speak to the military they sound as though they're spouting utter nonsense, which is incomprehensible and totally useless for purposes of military operations. And I must say, listening to the military, if you're not used to it, not only is it confusing—you probably all read the science fiction novel in which the Pentagon is torn down after it's discovered that acronyms cause cancer—but the whole way in which guidance commands are passed down the chain of command and the information goes back up, is radically different. And I think spending two years amongst you was enormously helpful to me later in dealing with a very complex interagency environment in some of the places where I subsequently served, including as ambassador in the Gulf War in Saudi Arabia.

Chas. W. Freeman Jr.

LAIPSON: Thanks, Chas. Ambassador Lilley.

AMBASSADOR JAMES R. LILLEY: As Ellen pointed out to you, I was a case officer for about 24 years in the clandestine service. I thought it would be worthwhile talking about one particular episode that I encountered in my career, which may be illustrative of some of the negative aspects of coordination. This happened in a small, Southeast Asian country, probably during the 1950s and 1960s. The CIA had an operation there running basically against China, and we were collecting against China fairly low-level stuff; but in terms of the Great Leap Forward that was decimating China and causing starvation, exoduses and dissatisfaction, you have to cover it. We were covering it because we had used the overseas Chinese communities to select these people, recruit them, train them and send them to specific targets to collect information on rations, government organization of the communes, changing organization, popular response, et cetera. It was considered very valuable by the government. We had very low standards then, actually. What happened was that one of the officers, an ethnic Chinese, was working one of our agents who did this sort of thing back and forth into China. He used a safe house, which was also used by a man who was handling a Vietnamese liaison from Saigon to penetrate the Viet Cong in Cambodia. Well, it turns out the South Vietnamese service was thoroughly penetrated by the Chinese and the Viet Cong, and they tipped off the Cambodian police that this safe house was an American intelligence thing. The guy who got caught was our case officer with his agent.

James R. Lilley

Now, this is a fundamental problem in tradecraft. You don't cross a unilateral operation with a liaison operation in the same place. We did that and it blew up. Our American case officer was arrested. The Chinese with whom he worked was arrested. The word went to the embassy, this man had his cover in USAID [U.S. Agency for International Development], and the leader of the country blew up in rage. The ambassador who just arrived was an old China hand, and was very, very upset. He said, "I am closing down all operations. You aren't going to do anything." Well, this puts you in a dilemma, because here you are collecting what you think is important stuff, with a lot of pressure from home to do this and do more of it. But the people at home were unwilling to take on the State Department or the NSC [National Security Council] to try to turn this decision around. What happened was that we decided, despite the imposition of this freeze on everything we did, we had to go out there and meet these agents to pay them and reassure them that we weren't pulling back from them. I was selected to do this . . . have you go out at night and then go to an ambassador's reception after that, after you've carried out your mission. Later, it turned out that the leader of China came to this country, and the country rounded up all the Chinese that were not favorable to the PRC [People's Republic of China], put them in a concentration camp and grabbed a couple of the people who worked with me and shipped them off to China. So I was exposed, as I said, I was outed three times. It's no big deal. So I had to leave the country prematurely, as I've done in other countries in the course of my career. But this was a case where there were no communications. We had to cheat to sustain our effort, and we did sustain the effort and eventually resumed operations in about six months. But by that time the American Embassy was kicked out of the country, and then we had to work it through a friendly country. Actually, it was an interesting case of stay-behind operation where we had gotten the friendly country embassy to pick up our contacts, and they worked them and actually our coverage went up.

Let me just make one more point. This is an incident where your coordination breaks down, and eventually is corrected. But I think it's extremely important for people who work in the clandestine service to have a very good appreciation of what the past is and of past mistakes. There are some enduring lessons and verities about the clandestine business. I would say first of all cover, tradecraft, authentication, access to intelligence. Realizing that you can only get 5 percent to 10 percent, which is actually the intelligence you should be going after. And I think that this has been contaminated through the years. I think most recently, perhaps in Iraq, where you take—my understanding is—shortcuts beyond the standard process, that you have to use in the clandestine service, and you get into trouble just as we did. I think it's very important that this legacy—the historic record of what we've done, what's failed and what's succeeded—be part of the current record for all case officers and so-called managers that work with the director of operations.

LAIPSON: Thank you, Ambassador. General Pace?

GENERAL PETER PACE: Thank you. I think my first realization of the need for interagency cooperation was as a lieutenant colonel as a member of the combined forces command staff in Korea. Ambassador Lilley was the U.S. ambassador there, and General James Lindsay was the commander in chief. On occasion they would both come to the staff meetings and hear the briefings together, and it was obvious to me that the two of them had a hand-in-glove relationship that was serving our country very well. I had just come from the National War College the preceding year, where Goldwater-Nichols was just being discussed and where "joint" was the topic of the day. I had had no formal education inside of our school system for how we might act interagency. So I spent my year with the opportunity to learn a little bit more about interagency—really focused in Korea on how it was, how we were going to be joint. If you remember 1986, 1987, 1988, we were just putting the training wheels on that particular operation.

My first opportunity then to see and start forming my own personal opinions about how a lack of interagency coordination can impact you was as a brigadier general. I had two tours in Somalia. The first was as a deputy commander of U.S. Marine forces. One of my responsibilities was to greet whichever of the 37 coalition countries was going to arrive that day at the airfield. I did not know at that time how many countries had joined the coalition, or what size force they were going to send, or what missions they were allowed to perform. I would literally greet them at the airfield, introduce myself and ask the commander basic questions: "Who are you? How many troops do you have? What kind of equipment do you have? What was the last thing your national command authority told you that you could do or could not do?" I'd work with them to determine what they could or could not do as part of the coalition. We ended up with 7,000 troops protecting the airfield in Mogadishu—a fairly well-protected airfield.

My second tour in Somalia was after *Black Hawk Down*. It was clear to me that the U.N. command and the combatant commanders—command chains of command—were confused. We did not have a good way to communicate, certainly from ourselves in Mogadishu, in a way that would be inside of a recognized decision-making framework. We also had the problem, from my perspective, of our own government assigning individuals there from the other agencies for 30, 45 or 60 days. About the time we got to know who this person was and understand what he could and couldn't do, it was time for him to leave. So my opinions as a brigadier general were formed more on the negative side of the house than on a positive side.

As a major general, I was deputy commander of U.S. forces in Japan. Everything I did in Japan as deputy commander was focused on the relationship between the two countries, and everything I did was totally embedded in the country-team process. Ambassador [Walter] Mondale's team was extremely well-run. That's where I learned that synergy can be had when all of us sit down around a common table, and we have a leader who is not only a

General Peter Pace

leader, but who has the authority to lead and is able to task people to do things. In Japan I learned a lot about the right way to do things. I came back to be the J–3 [director of the Operations Directorate] on the Joint Staff where I then started sitting in on National Security Council meetings and began forming my opinions about the strengths and weaknesses of our current system. Maybe we're going to get to that in another part of this discussion, so I'll wait to express my opinions on that. But after about 18 months of being able to sit in various meetings here in Washington, you can get a feel for what it was that resulted in what I thought I had learned in Somalia and in Japan.

Subsequently as the commander in chief of U.S. Southern Command, I would not ever think of going to a country without spending the first half-day, at least, with the ambassador and his or her country team. I just made myself a part of that team when I arrived in the country and then worked as part of it. We could do that because it was, for the most part, a peaceful mission down there. We did have the events in Columbia, which added a different flavor, but for the most part I learned what I thought was a proper way for a combatant commander to associate himself with the ambassador and that country team and work as part of the ambassador's team in that country. Of course, now as vice chairman for the last three years, I've been involved daily in the interagency process and again have added to my conviction about what is right about our National Security Council system and what it is that we might want to think about changing. I'll get to that in the next session.

LAIPSON: Thank you, General. I appreciate the chronology of the evolution of your own experiences, particularly the country team experience in Tokyo and as the deputy commander of the JTF [Joint Task Force] in Somalia. Perhaps we could get Ambassador Freeman and Ambassador Lilley also give some perceptions of their own experiences of running a country team. I know that Chas. had the unique experience of being Ambassador to Saudi Arabia while General [Norman] Schwarzkopf was building up for DESERT STORM. I think that would be a great episode to focus on.

FREEMAN: Let me say at the outset that, just to follow up on something that Ambassador Lilley said earlier, you have to live with the consequences of your own misunderstanding or lack of sympathy for what the other guys do. There are three distinct functions that we perform. Diplomats are the eyes and the ears and the open voice of the U.S. government abroad, and our friends in the CIA and in the intelligence services are responsible for the clandestine collection of information. They are also our hidden hand in accomplishing things through covert action. That blends in to special operations, of course. But, finally, the military are the mailed fists that you bring to bear when the foregoing options have failed. I don't want to name names, but if you don't understand that—and I'm sorry to say that a succession of CINCs [commanders in chief] at CENTCOM [Central Command] did not understand it—then you end up as we did in Iraq, when Iraq invaded Kuwait, with no significant human capability at all. That was really a result, in no small measure, of military commanders with no experience in intelligence or sympathy for the risks that have to be taken to collect it, blocking the positioning of agents who could be run by case officers. That's an aside.

In a sense, I think I had been preparing all my life for the role that I had in Saudi Arabia as ambassador. This was the first time that a military combatant commander had been co-located forward in theater with an ambassador. Vietnam, of course, was run out of CINCPAC [HQ, commander in chief, Pacific Command], and we had CENTCOM sitting there with me. Everybody who was assigned to Saudi Arabia was technically assigned to my embassy. So I had an embassy staff of 550,000, which is probably not going to be exceeded any time soon. We had some remarkable successes, beginning with General Order Number One, which was not much appreciated by those who received it initially, but which worked. It was cooked up by Schwarzkopf and me right after the meeting with the king, who produced the deployment. Now, of course, we have the norm of forward deployment into the theater. I think we would usefully spend some time doing what the State Department never does, but what the military does very well, which is looking at successes and failures in terms of relationships between embassies and combatant commanders. I'm very proud of the relationship that I had with General Schwarzkopf, notwithstanding our rather severe differences in leadership style.

There is a serious problem, however, and I will just allude to it. I think it's a continuing issue in the interagency. General Schwarzkopf, as a regional commander, really had no counterpart on the civilian side. There was nobody forward deployed who could, as he could, address the entire theater. This was a serious problem. I think the reason that war did not meet the criterion of General Sherman and produce a more perfect peace, and therefore was not a success—and in some sense has never ended—was because of a disconnect between the military and civilians, most notably in the field. There were two issues that absolutely had to be addressed but weren't. One was what our war aims were. Believe it or not, there was never a statement of war aims provided to CINCCENT [commander in chief, Central Command]. Never. In the end, four days before we counterattacked, I wrote what I considered to be the lowest common denominator set of war aims that I had intuited by listening to people and sent it to Washington and said, with Norm's approval, "Unless instructed otherwise, this is what Norm is going to do." And we never heard. Colin Powell said, "Sounds good to me," and that was the end of it. How can you fight a war with no war aims? Well, actually the United States has a long history of doing this, and it's a big mistake. We fought the Spanish-American War and then tried to figure out after the fact what it was all about. And very often we fight wars, and our objective is the total annihilation of the enemy so we don't think about the second issue, which is war termination. How do you end the war? How do you persuade the other side to agree to stop? General Schwarzkopf was beside himself trying to figure out what he was to do at the meeting in Safwan [airfield, southern Iraq], which concluded the truce, and wanted some instructions. I was the ambassador to Saudi Arabia, not the ambassador to Iraq, and I had been belaboring this issue of war termination to the point where no one wanted to hear from me again anyway. And so he didn't have any instructions at all. At the time, I thought the Iraqi generals who went into that tent were probably hard pressed not to do cartwheels out of it. They had to have expected that he would say Tariq Aziz or Saddam Hussein will report to location X, two days from now, to discuss the terms of your surrender. No. The discussion was about where the line of control was, how to handle POW [prisoner of war], MIA [missing in action] exchanges, overflight of the U.S.-occupied/coalition-occupied zone. And mine clearance. That was it.

So we didn't end the war. We didn't turn the military triumph into a political victory. We left Saddam Hussein in the position to say, look, they threw all this stuff at me and I'm still here. And then we compounded the error with some other stupid policies and the result was the war never really ended. And we're still in it. And guess what? This time we also didn't figure out how to end the war. And we still don't know how to do it.

Now, my contention—and these are big issues—is that one of the reasons that happened is we don't know how to integrate the political and military element in the field where the rubber hits the road. I could talk a lot more about this, but I'm going to stop.

LAIPSON: Thank you very much. Ambassador Lilley, any experiences from your tours in Seoul or Beijing that you think are relevant at this point?

LILLEY: Yes, I think that I faced a situation similar to Chas. I think that General Pace has already mentioned that there's a four-star general in Korea who has a number of hats—the Eighth Army, U.N. Command, Combined Forces Command, et cetera—and a large staff, perhaps as many as 37,000 people when I was there. There are two separate lines of communication to Washington. This general communicates directly to the chairman and to the secretary of defense into the White House, and I, of course, go through State. This can cause certain problems. Although General Pace is right, that we had working relationships with both General James Lindsay and General Louis Menetry, there were clearly tensions in the relationship. We approached things somewhat differently, and this, I think, manifested itself in two separate issues. One was the coming of democratization in Korea, which was handled largely out of the embassy and State. The CIA, as far as I know, didn't play a role in this. There was usually some sort of covert action, but there wasn't in this case. I had certain experiences in the past, in not being obvious in meetings and in what I said about them. And this perhaps protected our quiet role.

But the question came up: How much history have you been able to read, for instance, about Kwangju? The Kwangju Uprising in 1980, seven years before our problems in the summer of 1987, the American ambassador and the CINC worked fairly closely together. But there were differences. The State attempted, rather, to prevent bloodshed and massacring and to try to avoid a United States implication if this happened. State attempted to make sure that, working with our military, we protected the border with North Korea so the North Koreans couldn't take advantage of this and launch some sort of adventurous move. But what happened is, it wasn't closely coordinated, and the CINC made certain statements, which the press picked up, which reflected, let's say, more of an acceptance of what the results were of the put-down of this uprising in Kwangju, that were given in the embassy. In Korea, which is a very conspiratorial country, this was taken up and played up all over the place. It was in screaming headlines about what the Americans said about what happened. Well, when we came into a similar situation in 1987, we had several hundred thousand protesters in the streets. It was going into the middle class—it wasn't just the radicals—and they were violently attacking our consulate in Pusan and other areas. The president was a former four-star general. His tendency was to use force. He was the one who did the crackdown in Kwangju seven years earlier. And our intervention was to keep him from doing that. We had a letter from President [Ronald] Reagan, which I was to deliver to him directly and embellish this with certain creative thoughts of my own about the consequences of any kind of a military put-down of these demonstrations.

But before I went there, I had lunch with the CINC, and we talked. I told him I was going to see the president and we were going to talk about what was happening in the streets so that when I went into the president I said, "The CINC and I stand together on this. There is no light between us. If you take military action against these demonstrators there will be consequences." He didn't do it. He was just about ready to call in the military to crush a movement in Pusan in South Korea. It didn't happen. But I think our military was somewhat perturbed that I had gone further than I had told the CINC that I was going to go, and threw him into our own plans that we had for preventing this violence from happening.

The second area where we had some coordination differences was in the deployment of U.S. forces in Korea. There was a golf course in downtown Seoul, which looked like Central Park in New York City. It was the Eighth Army golf course, and we felt with the Olympics coming to Seoul in 1988 that this should be moved. The Koreans thought it was an eyesore, and they're very sensitive to this sort of obvious demonstration of American presence. Well, I proposed moving it to the suburbs, closing down, and turning most of the land back to the Koreans, but there wasn't agreement on this. There was not agreement on it. It affected, obviously, the military commander's handling of his own troops. This kind of a green area in the midst of Seoul—housing, clubs, golf and tennis, and this sort of thing—was important to sustain the morale of his troops. I could understand this, but in terms of measuring this against the political fallout of maintaining an obvious American presence in downtown Seoul, that took precedence. I remembered [former Ambassador Edwin] Reischauer's moving of the American military outside of Tokyo before the 1964 Olympics in Tokyo. And he was able to do a lot of this, to drop our presence. It's interesting that we finally did move the golf course out to Sung Nam outside the area, and we all agreed it was the right move. But it's interesting that even today Secretary [of Defense Donald] Rumsfeld, and his staff in ISA [International Security Affairs] and other places, are going through a major redeployment out of the major military base in downtown Seoul, Yongsan. He's going to move a huge headquarters to an air base in Osan and pull back the Second Infantry Division and put it in several brigades south of the Han River in a much more inconspicuous role, but with equal fire power and probably greater mobility. This is, again, causing different kinds of fallout in South Korea. You may have heard about the South Koreans demonstrating in the last election against two Americans who tragically and accidentally killed two Korean girls. It became a real issue in the election, and this president, in part, won the election on this. But now their insistence is that the American military presence cannot be seen as being diminished in the face of the recalcitrance in North Korea, because this severely affects the economy of South Korea and the stability and the confidence in the country. They now argue that we move very, very cautiously and not do anything to upset the stability and security of the South Korean government and economy, which is crucial to their prosperity and stability. So these things have a life of their own. It's a moving picture; it's not a still shot. It goes way back to Kwangju, up to the summer of 1987, into the movement of the golf course, into what Rumsfeld is trying to do today in different situations, but it isn't always tranquil.

LAIPSON: I think those are both very powerful examples. Decades later, Saudi Arabia and Korea, of course, remain very crucial arenas of U.S. national security interests.

This is the end of the round of field perspectives. We're going to switch to a focus on the interagency process in Washington. I think we have time for one or two questions from the floor at this juncture, if anybody would like to pose a question to any of the panelists. Is there a question?

AUDIENCE. As has been alluded to by the panel, the State Department, in coordination with the ambassadors, may have better success than the combatant commanders in theaters of operations. From a DoD perspective, what can we expect some of the changes that will take place to be that will further develop our exit strategy in those theaters?

FREEMAN: I'm not sure that I'd agree that the State Department necessarily does better than the combatant commanders on these issues. Rather, I think there is a natural division of labor. If you are fortunate enough at some point in your career to become a combatant commander, then you might bear in mind the difference in roles. Also bear in mind the fact that the ambassador can really be very helpful in whatever country you're stationed in, even if we don't fix this business of not having a regional envoy who can look at the whole region. I'll give you a concrete example, which I probably should have cited earlier, because it illustrates a difference in culture and the chain of command and how it works. It also illustrates how you can help each other. About three weeks after Saddam Hussein's occupation of Kuwait on Aug. 2, 1990, I received a telegram from the assistant secretary for Near East and South Asian affairs at State directing me to go see the king to arrange for bed-down of B–52s in Jeddah. Well, the only facility in Jeddah where this could be done is the Haj Terminal. Jeddah is the gateway to Mecca for the two-and-a-half to three million pilgrims who come every year to make Haj. So I sent a cable back saying, "Before I execute this instruction I would like to be assured that you have considered the impact on the Muslim world of the picture of a B–52 in the Haj terminal. And since our mission at present, pending further evolution, is to defend Saudi Arabia against Iraq and since the B–52 is not commonly thought of as a defensive weapon system, don't you think that we should reconsider this? Furthermore, if there really is a requirement to use B–52s, if there really is a war, they can, of course, recover in Jeddah, and no one will care if there's a war. We can move the equipment and the bombs and other things to support further missions from Jeddah in now, without the planes."

I sent this cable back after calling Norman Schwarzkopf and asking, "Did you ask for this?" Because I saw my role as ensuring that he got what he needed to do his job. And he gave me information that I needed to do my job. He said, "I never heard of this. I don't know where this came from." To be frank, it came from the then-chief of staff of the Air Force, who was looking for a way to demonstrate the budgetary importance of the B–52. So I got a cable back from the under secretary of state saying, "Please go do this," and I said, "Perhaps you didn't read my earlier message. You haven't addressed any of these questions." Then I got a message from the secretary of state and Brent Scowcroft, the national security advisor, and I sent back the same message essentially in different words saying, "There's no apparent requirement for this. We could prepare for the deployment by bringing in the support equipment and the bombs. Is it really necessary to have the aircraft there now? Have you considered what it would look like to have this on all the front pages of the world's press?" Then I got a message from the president telling me to do it. And I sent back the same message to the president. And I never heard anything until he came out at Thanksgiving and he said, "Thank God you didn't execute that instruction." Well, what happened was somebody had a pet rock they wanted to heave in the direction of the AOR [area of responsibility]. And the interagency process? Nobody thought it was worthwhile standing up and saying, "Hey, this doesn't make sense." Schwarzkopf was delighted. He didn't have to say anything. In your military chain of command there's nothing he could have done if he had gotten an instruction like that. I could. I did. I basically said, "Hey, I didn't ask to be out here anyway. You want to throw me out. Make my day."

That is an example of how the field and the interagency can relate, and maybe the field can, once in a while, help correct some of the deficiencies of the interagency.

PACE: Let me just add, if I could, that my experience is that every single American in uniform or in civilian clothes goes to work in the field to do the best they can that day. In some cases, the success we have is because of the processes. In most cases, the success we have interagency is because good folks, knowing what the mission is, are working together without any kind of official sanction or authority. They work through the problems that obviously don't have particular processes that allow coordination. What you have are stovepipes and different authorities. The first place in the current system where you actually have the ability to give direction across the interagency is here in Washington. So far, the question for us is not so much who's right and who's wrong in what particular war and in what particular instance. The question is what is it that we might do here today in this conference to talk about the things that we can and should do for the interagency. This, so when you, Captain, go out to your next assignment, you have better institutional support to do the things that you know are right. Right now we have got great Americans doing great things. I think we can talk through ways we can collectively make it more efficient and effective for our government, for the great Americans who are out there in harm's way, to do the right thing without having to either ignore or overcome bureaucratic problems.

LAIPSON: Thank you, General Pace. I think that's a great setup for the next section where we do want to talk about how the decision makers relate to each other here in Washington. General Pace participates, I know, in a lot of meetings at the NSC and both Ambassadors Lilley and Freeman have done so in their own earlier functions, particularly as an assistant secretary of defense for international security affairs.

I thought perhaps, again, we could do a little bit of history and a little bit of the current situation. Ambassador Lilley, I know we had chatted about what you thought worked well in the period of normalization of relations with China. Perhaps that might be one case we'd look at of how the Washington system can figure out smart ways to communicate across these large, bureaucratic structures. Then I think I'll turn to General Pace to tell us a little bit more about the current dynamics of the system.

LILLEY: I think that, until the normalization of China, Chas. was more involved in that than I was. But it was a case study, which I'll mention. But I will say in terms of the interagency process in Washington, I remember Secretary [of Defense Richard] Cheney saying to me when I joined ISA, he said if you have anything important, come directly to me. Don't get yourself bogged down in the "Rube Goldberg" [cartoonist] structure here. I did that about three times in the 15 months I was there. I didn't try to overuse it. But in terms of my own experiences being overseas and playing back into interagency process at work, I would say there were two times when this was most effective.

The first time was during the normalization. I was in Washington. but previous to that I had been in Beijing as the station chief. There were two things that happened. First, State kept the process very close-hold, but they were people who worked very closely together who knew each other very well and understood what was happening—and would make it happen. The names of these were people like Nick Platt, Mike Armacost and Morton Abramowitz. Mort was in ISA, Nick was in NSC and Armacost was at State. Basically, [Zbigniew] Brzezinski and [Michael] Oxenberg had taken the lead on this at the NSC. And they kept it very close-hold, because they were going on the pattern that [Secretary of State Henry] Kissinger used in 1971–1972 in the opening to China. Had you made this an open process for interagency discussion, it probably would never have happened. Had the word gotten out, you would have had the right wing and the left wing and the states raising hell. Your allies would be wringing their hands and looking for a sellout and the various problems in Taiwan that would obviously come. But this worked. This worked in the normalization process. It worked in part because they did keep it very close-hold.

We sensed it was coming, we, in fact, knew that it was coming by the traffic that was going back-channeled into the embassy in Beijing. [Ambassador Leonard] Woodcock was handling this for the United States. Basically, he was reporting directly from Brzezinski to the president.

I'll mention a second time that I found this most effective was when I served as head of mission in Taiwan and Korea. I go back to people. You had Gaston Sigur at the NSC, Paul Wolfowitz at State, Rich Armitage in Defense, who got along. You may have had Secretary [of State George] Schultz and Secretary [of Defense Casper] Weinberger not getting along all the time, to put it mildly. But these people did get along. They did have common views. They did have common views on bringing democracy to Asia. They did have common views about hitting the balance between our relationship with China and unofficial support for Taiwan. They did have common views about how we should manage the democratic transition in Korea and the Philippines and in Taiwan. This made my job much better for me. When I came back to the State Department briefly in 1985, 1986, I found that this process with these people working together really functioned well. In fact, they used to have meetings among the three principals, Gaston Sigur, Paul Wolfowitz and Rich Armitage, and they wouldn't put it on their schedule. They would meet very quietly in a room in the NSC to decide what they were going to do and how they were going to approach their superiors. They'd decide what sort of message they might send out to the ambassador or to the military on how to handle a particular situation.

I think Jim Mann in his book *The Rise of the Vulcans* talks about this period and how it worked in the younger time of these very bright, talented and experienced men. It's interesting to see that these men are still in even higher positions today. Gaston is dead, but Paul and Rich are in higher positions. You wonder sometimes about the successes that we achieved in Asia in the 1980s. Did this influence some of the actions that were taken in Iraq where the situation really was politically quite different? You can speculate on this, but the sweep in Asia clearly was working in our direction as these countries became democratic. Indonesia follows, Thailand follows, and you get a real ring of countries that are getting into the democratic process. Of course the results are not always what you want. If Korea goes democratic and has democratic elections you might get a populous president who is more to the left. Or if Taiwan has an elected president he might begin to flirt with the idea of independence, causing us all kinds of problems. But this is part of the process that we have created and that we have to live with.

Let me just make one more point. I think we evolved through history in terms of the way we manage ourselves in covert action. You remember that after World War II we imposed democracy militarily on Japan and Germany at a tremendous cost in World War II. We tried some of the same tactics that we used in the war in the early 1950s, when we had paramilitary activity against China, against North Vietnam, against Korea and even against Indonesia. The one common denominator is they did not work. They did not work. There were exceptions that came in a little bit later in Tibet and Laos, where in Tibet you had spectacular ambushes that you were able to get Chinese documents and get them out. But the movement was doomed to failure. The same was true of our effort in Laos, where we could save pilots, or we could carry out ambushes of Vietnamese using the trail. We could do these things, but it was doomed to failure. It could never win against Vietnam and China. It was the whole idea of your not being able to control the border areas, where infiltration was unstoppable. A huge base area in China, et cetera, that supported a continuing insurgency, introduction of direct Vietnamese main line forces. Then the fanatic urge for control and independence that you found both in China and in Vietnam. We were doomed. But we had successes.

This was then followed by our Afghan operation—covert action against the Soviet Union, which succeeded in the battle. The Soviets left and another government took over—the Taliban took over, and we're still living with the consequences of that. But covert action goes through a number of permutations, not the least of which were the coups that we pulled in the 1950s and 1960s in Guatemala, Iran, the Philippines—in a way, backing with "psy-psy." Iran, bringing down Mozambique, and of course in Guatemala. This was practiced in areas like Chile, but it's now been pulled back on the basis of experiences. So you do have a paramilitary experience, you do have an experience with democracy. But these are evolutionary issues that change with the times. Although there are certain constants in there, you've got to adjust always to the given situation that exists today.

LAIPSON: Thank you. Before I turn to General Pace, I think Chas. wants to come in on this particular topic.

FREEMAN: I want to make a couple of observations about what the interagency process can and can't do, based on some experiences with the issues that Jim just outlined. [Former Secretary of State Henry] Kissinger, in one sense, bypassed the interagency process, but in another he didn't. What he did was he commissioned a whole series of interagency activities, studies and the like. People laugh about this because they say, well, he was just doing it to keep everybody busy, but the fact is that what it did was enable him to synthesize a set of plans that rested on a very comprehensive examination of the issues. So I think the first thing I'd say is that the interagency process, if it's orderly, can be a wonderful way of ensuring that all the different perspectives and all the expertise that is resident in this government, which possesses great expertise, is assembled and considered. Second, the interagency process, like any committee process, can't make decisions. I've never been in a committee that ever made a decision. You know, when committees make decisions they turn horses into camels, and fish into shrimp and God knows what. Committees meet to ratify decisions that sensible people have already decided upon outside. So if you try to use the interagency process to manage things, which unfortunately, increasingly, we have tried to do, you're asking for trouble. It ought to be the mechanism for doing the planning. It shouldn't run the "ops," in your terms.

A final point is that interagency discipline is always a problem. If you're trying to make a big decision, like normalization with China, the ship of state is this vast creaky, leaky vessel with hundreds of crew aboard. If the captain gives an order to come up in with the wind 5 degrees, it takes a hell of a long time for them to run around and actually do that, and some of them will sit there and say they don't really want to do it. I remember in the case of China normalization, President Nixon issued an instruction that related to the use of dollars in trade with China. I was the desk officer for that at State and I had to implement it. So I had lunch with the head of the Foreign Assets Control Office at Treasury to see what he was going to do about this. And I had the president's statement there, and I gave it to him. He read it and he said, "Well, this may be the president's policy, but it isn't Treasury's." What he meant by that was until he got an order in writing, not some kind of, again, in your terms, "frag" order, he wasn't going to do anything. So you have three problems: First, you can use the interagency to make plans and to avoid overlooking things that otherwise will jump out of the bushes and bite you. If we'd done a little more planning in Iraq on an interagency basis, we'd all be better off. Second, you can't use it to make decisions. Don't try. And third, you have to use it to enforce discipline across bureaucratic lines. End of statement.

LAIPSON: Thank you very much, Chas. General Pace, the floor is yours. I wonder if you would try to grapple with Chas.'s thought of whether the interagency process is intended to or well-suited to these different functions: planning, decision making and implementing decisions once they're made. The floor is yours.

PACE: Thank you. I've been thinking about the interagency process since 1996, 1997, when I was the J-3. I've honed my thoughts on it in the last three years as vice chairman through the war in Afghanistan and Iraq and the other things we're doing in the global war on terrorism. I'd like to have the ability to share these with you—as thoughts, not conclusions—and to offer them to you as ideas for dialogue and discussion, because if I knew the answer, I'd be out and about trying to implement the answer. What I think I can highlight for you are some possibilities by using a military construct as the example.

First of all, my experience is that the national security council system we have, regardless of who is sitting in the White House, serves our country extremely well in teeing up for the president decisions that the one-star, two-star, three-star, four-star level, whether in uniform or civilian clothes, get a chance to talk about—problems that need to be fixed. It tees up recommendations for the president. The president then makes his decision. As far as that goes, we are very well served. What happens, though, once the decision is made, is that the execution goes back into the stovepipe, so that whatever the decision is, DoD takes its piece and takes it inside the department, State takes its piece and takes it inside the department, Treasury does likewise, et cetera. So, going up, it's very much an interagency discussion, then decision, then on execution it goes back into stovepipes.

Let me stop there for just a second and take you to 1980s U.S. military. You've got the world's best Army, the world's best Navy, the world's best Marine Corps, the world's best Air Force. The only problem was we weren't talking to each other. And when we went to battle, we at best deconflicted battle space, but we sure as heck weren't fighting joint and combined like we do today. We were forced into being joint by our Congress with the Goldwater-Nichols Act. Initially, the Joint Chiefs, who then were much more service chiefs than they were joint chiefs, were not enamored with the idea of giving up their prerogatives over their services. But, I would argue that in the last almost 20 years, and certainly as seen in the battlefields in Iraq and Afghanistan, what the service chiefs have given up in individual prerogatives of their service in the joint way of doing business, they have more than gotten back as joint chiefs sitting in the tank [closed-door briefing] as a body that advises the senior leadership of this country.

To execute our battles now, we have a joint task force commander, and that commander tells his Army, Navy, Air Force, Marines and Coast Guard what to do and when to do it. Ninety percent of the time, that works just great—even 95 percent and 99 percent. But inside of that system, if the Marine working for that joint task force commander feels that, for whatever reason, his advice is not being listened to or that damage is about to be done, then he has a right, authority, responsibility to go up the Marine Corps chain of command to the commandant of the Marine Corps with whatever the problem is and have the commandant take it into the tank as a member of the joint chiefs and have a discussion about it. So you have, day-to-day, the authority, responsibility of the joint task force commander, but you also have, day-to-day, an opportunity for those working the issues and executing to have a way to get back up to the top, so to speak, if there is a service-unique problem.

We might consider something at the national level that would allow the president of the United States to say, "This is what I want done in Afghanistan, and I want the State Department to be the lead agency on this. I want all the other departments of this government to work in support of the State Department in Afghanistan, and these are the goals and objectives." Day-to-day, here in Washington and also out in the field, I'll begin to talk about how you might do that. The State Department secretary, or his designated person, will be the one ensuring that the goals, as articulated by the president of the United States, are being met not only by the State Department, but in a tasking-authority way to the other agencies of our government. Hence, if someone in DoD is taking day-to-day tasking from the Department of State, and for whatever reason that person thinks that we're about to get off track a little bit, then he would come back up to the Secretary of Defense and the Secretary of Defense could take it back into the National Security Council for discussion just like we do on the military side.

There's a way to do that regionally, but as Ambassador Freeman pointed out before, we do not have a regional entity anything like the combatant commanders other than in the military. But you do have the combatant commander's facilities and communications equipment resident, and you do have, today, joint interagency coordination groups that meet in the CINC's facilities and discuss things. It is not too much of a leap to say that if State was in charge in Washington of this entity, then the State Department ambassador at the joint interagency task force using these combatant commander's facilities could be in charge. Then down inside whatever country it was, they'd also be in charge. That would call on our cabinet officials to give up some day-to-day prerogatives and authorities, but, I believe, they would get that back in spades as members of the National Security Council, where they would have 5 to 10 percent of the problems that needed to be discussed at the national level. How did we get the joint world's attention in the military? Congress made it very simple. They said to Lieutenant Colonel Pete Pace, because I was lieutenant colonel at the time, "If you want to get promoted you have got to be joint." I said, "I don't know what joint is, but I want some."

You could conceive of a system on the civilian side that would say—at whatever level, GS-12, GS-13, SES-1—that to get promoted to that level you must have a tour in another agency. So if you spent your whole life in DoD, you need to have a tour in the Department of State or in Treasury or in some other way so that we have an opportunity to get the same kind of education that we got in the military in developing a trust that we have to get in the military amongst our civilian counterparts.

Another problem that I mentioned before in Somalia, and it's still present today, is that there are very few departments in this government that have the authority to say, "You are going to Afghanistan for six months to do this government's work." So you end up with volunteers, and you end up with folks who are there 30 days or 60 days, and they don't get the experience they need. They're not there long enough to have impact. Again, I'm not talking about moving the cheese on people who have been in federal service for a long time. I'm talking about the future of where we want to go, so that for the next group of individuals who will come up for promotion to SES level, that we say to them, "First, you have to be interagency," meaning you must get a tour some place to continue to get promoted. Second, "If you accept this promotion, if you accept this responsibility, then you also accept the fact that your department is going to be able to send you someplace in the world for six months or a year, whatever is appropriate, as part of your agreement." I believe that there are many, many, very dedicated Americans who, if told what the rules are ahead of time, will volunteer for that just like you folks in the military have done.

In education, we went from Army, Navy, Marine, and Air Force war colleges that were totally focused on their services, to what we have today—schools that not only teach joint military-operations and have student populations that reflect the entire community, but have more and more civilians from our government in these schools. There are about 30 civilians from other than DoD agencies in this year's National War College class, as one example. Is the current military system of schools sufficient to educate the way we want in the interagency? Or maybe we need some kind of interagency schoolhouse that would allow us to grow the kinds of people that we need for the system that I'm talking about.

And, oh, by the way, in the military, Congress has allocated sufficient funds and resources to allow us to have enough people to run the day-to-day organization, and also have a portion in school. We don't have that opportunity on the civilian side of the house. If you want to take your key leaders who are growing up and give them a chance to go to school, you have to have some excess capacity in your personnel program to allow to you take a chunk of those folks and have them serving either in school or serving in the interagency.

There are many, many pros and cons to a lot of the things that I said, and the president of the United States has very specific prerogatives with how he sets up his National Security Council that I don't want to tread on at all. But I do believe there is an opportunity for us as a nation to discuss what efficiencies we are going to need as we look forward to the next decade or more of a war on terrorism, as just one example. Are our current mechanisms for making decisions flexible enough and efficient enough to stay ahead of the threats? I say that because the war on terrorism is not about security. Security is going to provide the environment inside of which economics, education and all the other elements of national power are going to win the battle for our nation. If that's true, then we need to look beyond being efficient in the security environment, which is critically important. But at the end of the day we're going to need to be efficient and effective in harnessing all elements of national power inside of a system that takes its leadership and guidance from the very top, but doesn't have to go back to the very top every time there's a disagreement between agencies.

I tried to give you the short version of what probably could be a two-hour presentation, and I've left out a lot. I would ask you not to take these as conclusions, but as things that I believe are worthy of discussion amongst those who have the experience in ways that might highlight for us things that are good ideas, things that are bad ideas, and things that we may want to recommend to our leadership as ways we can become more efficient. Thanks.

LAIPSON: Thank you very much, General Pace. I think there's now a rich menu of issues that cover the gamut from how people in policymaking positions relate to each other, as well as how to think about training and teaching a new way of doing business to a next generation of security professionals. I want to first ask the panel if they want to react, comment, agree or disagree with anything General Pace has said and, just as a three-minute warning to the audience, you'll have a chance to ask some questions at this point. Chas., would you like to go first?

FREEMAN: I like what General Pace is thinking, but I would respectfully disagree with him on one point. It's a semantic disagreement actually. Security and military affairs are not the same. I think we need a broader concept of security to deal with it and I think we probably agree on that.

PACE: Absolutely.

FREEMAN: I go back to my starting point, which is that statesmen, the NCA [National Command Authority], if you will, have a variety of tools, professions that support national security operations: intelligence collection, overt and covert; diplomacy; covert action; and the use of force in which you are specialists. These are the things that the NCA looks to. Question: Do we—we are all in the same business in this spectrum—do we adequately communicate with each other? Do we coordinate effectively? Are we aware of what you need to do your job? Are you aware of what I need to do my job? The answer is no. So I think we need to think about new structures.

When I was in the Pentagon, I tried, and of course failed, to do something that

I think still ought to be done, namely to create an interagency national security service to parallel the civil service. National security professionals who would serve in the NSC, at DoD, at State, at CIA. In other words, recognize that we are all doing the same job, and develop career ladders within which we specialize. I'd like to see foreign-service officers in the military reserve. I'd like to see more active-duty military seconded to brief tours in the Foreign Service. I think there are opportunities to do more cross-fertilization in the intelligence area as well, although I'll let Jim comment on that.

And I have to admit to a selfish motive here, as I did spend 30 years as a career diplomat—although now I'm in business. Diplomacy has not become a profession in the sense that the Army has. It's been a long time since units got to elect their officers. Of course, if Andy Jackson was qualified to lead an Army because he had a good gift of gab, you guys are professionals. In my former profession, we are pretty professional, too, up to a point, but what can you say about a profession where the top people very often are used-car salesmen who gave a lot of money to the president. The United States and the Philippines are the only two countries in the world that still staff ambassadorships in this manner, and here nothing changes. The 1837 *New York Herald Tribune* commenting on this American practice, which even then was seen as peculiar, said "Diplomacy is the sewer through which flows the scum and refuse of the political puddle. And a man not fit to keep at home is just the one to send abroad." Or a woman, I guess, these days. Anyway, I think we'd all do better if we focused on a common professionalism and some cross-fertilization and cross-training. I think we would have combatant commanders who are more sensitive to the requirements for intelligence collection, and therefore less unpleasantly surprised when there isn't any intelligence being provided. We'd have better diplomats, and I dare say we'd do better in murky situations, like the one in Iraq.

LAIPSON: Ambassador Lilley, I wonder if you think any of these ideas are applicable to the intelligence profession?

LILLEY: I've been out of that business for almost 20 years. Some people say you're never out of it. I am out of it.

FREEMAN: Really? You never can tell with these guys.

LILLEY: My ambassador in Laos was William Sullivan; I think the military referred to him as the field marshal. I was an FSR-4 [Foreign Service Reserve Officer] and was promoted to an FSR-3, which is all phony; it's my cover. And he said to me, as he gave me the promotion, he said, "Lilley, you phony." The next time I saw him, I was ambassador in Beijing and I said, "Bill, my cover has improved."

But I would say with the agency, you have to be very careful that you protect the deal from contamination. On the other hand, you have to be careful of outside forces seducing it into soft targets and trying to act like a Foreign Service officer, or do these various things, which is not his job. I think he should be largely preserved from the interagency community. I think they've gotten too much involved, it's gotten too heady and people are measured about their ability in interagency meetings rather than their ability to carry out operations overseas.

So I've got some ideas of what we should do to focus on hard targets and train our people to do it; but we talk about that later. The directorate of intelligence, which Ellen knows more about than I do, could use a good infusion from outside. They really need to have much closer contact with our academic community, particularly in the field that I've watched—the China field. I think the intellectual ability of the academic community far surpasses, in many ways, our ability in analysis, and sometimes your analysis tends to get into working with the latest information. I remember once arguing with the political-military [division] in State about whether the Russians were supporting the Chinese military programs. And the individual said, "Well, you know, we just don't have the intelligence to support that right now." I said, "Well, read some history, the Chinese haven't been involved with Russia since the 1950s." The whole military-industrial complex is built on the Russian model—the MiGs, the tanks, the AK-47. There's a very close connection between the two. They broke apart in the 1960s, and they almost fought a war in 1968. In fact they did have some shootouts. But they have come back together again and now, of course, Russia is a great supplier of the Chinese military. But the individual involved made his judgment on that day's intelligence, or the day before, or something like that. He came out and rejected this. Then Michael Gordon of *The New York Times* came out with a huge piece on this thing, outlining all of the things that are going on between the two sides.

So I think you need more exchanges between our intelligence analysts and the outside world, bringing people in, as they do in the INS [Immigration and Naturalization Service] structure, but not into DI [directorate of intelligence]. They really need them. I don't really see that the DI close connection with the DO [directorate of operations] is particularly healthy. I think it can work in certain exceptional instances, but by and large the DO officer has a job to do. It's to get his understanding of his targets, put his full focus on it, join an elite corps, be compensated for his successes based on our intelligence needs, be understood by people who can articulate them and give them to them—not requirements. You're telling a case officer how to crack a very tough project.

Put it this way: look at the difficulties we had in penetrating China early on. It was very, very difficult. We had failure after failure after failure. Eventually we began to get a hold of this thing, but the key in some areas was the use of ethnic American Chinese who breathed the culture and understood deception and manipulation, and who you could get to be primarily loyal to you and not to the motherland. That particular combination turned out the kind of case officer who could make a key recruitment that you really needed in the Chinese communist service. I think that this, again, reflected itself in our ability to crack the Soviet Union. One of the things that Aldrich Ames [spy within the CIA] did expose was the fact that it was a horrible thing that happened, but we really had that country penetrated. People say most of those were walk-ins. But the fact is you ran these people into place that went right into their missile rocket section, into the central committee of the party and the decision-making apparatus; we knew these things. This is what we did because we had trained a group of Soviet case officers who really got into the Soviet system and understood it. They had gone through all the quick fixes of fabricated networks, paramilitary airdrops, legal travelers who picked up superficial information, and the whole thrust to make you judge by the quantity of your reports, not the quality. But you were able to do this; it was an evolutionary process that took a number of years.

Now we face the great problem in the Islamic fanatic community, the penetration of terrorist organizations. We had a tough job in my time, but it wasn't anything like what these guys are facing. They really have a tough job. This goes to our next session: What kind of a guy do we need to really accomplish the intelligence job that faces us for, perhaps, the rest of the 21st century?

LAIPSON: Let me just make a comment about the cross-training that I think already does exist between analysts and policymakers. I think over the last decade and a half there has been some greater encouragement, slightly less rigid boundaries of people being able to rotate. I, myself, had the experience of rotating on to the NSC staff. I rotated from the Library of Congress to the policy planning staff at the State Department, so there is a lot of that cross-fertilization among people who are receptive and who are intellectually open to having those different experiences.

I think the rub comes with whether their receiving institution or their home institution knows what to do with them when they get back. Is that extra insight—that deeper understanding of the other guy's institutional perspective—rewarded? I know there are certainly cases in the DI of people going off and doing tours in embassies, filling in for foreign service officers, having some terrific experiences in the field. But, when they return, they sometimes feel that that experience is not valued or does not give them any extra advantage or status back in their organization. It's almost seen as dead time that would not even count toward promotion. So, I think General Pace's emphasis on the importance of incentive structures and that this has to be done systematically cannot be done. I think what we have today is some ad hoc experiences of creative managers who think it's a neat idea. It doesn't mean that when people come back to their service, it's necessary to integrate it into their own career development. Did you want to come in on that point?

FREEMAN: Well, exactly. But I wanted to agree with Jim about the distinction between the director of operations, which is the clandestine collection service, and the analytical arm of the intelligence community. I would not expect, if there were an exchange between foreign-service officers and military, you'd be likely to put the foreign service officer on point on a military reconnaissance operation, or in charge of an artillery battery, if they hadn't had adequate training in the Reserves to do that. Similarly, I don't think you want to put military or foreign-service people into the clandestine service, which is a highly specialized function.

That said, I do want to share one story with you, which I think illustrates an important point. Jim was talking about the Soviet Union. Ambassador Malcom Toon, a very distinguished ambassador to the Soviet Union, at one point was aboard an aircraft carrier of the 6th Fleet, and the admiral was giving him lunch, and after lunch the admiral leaned over and said, "What's it like being an ambassador?" He said, "I always thought I might try that after I retire." And Mac said, "You know, admiral, I was just about to ask you the same question. I was thinking of running a carrier battle group after I retire."

I think there needs to be a bit more understanding of what each of us do and don't do. We all have our expertise; we have our contributions. I do think the kind of exchanges that are going on are good. But they're not systematized and they're not "incentivized," as General Pace suggested they ought to be.

LAIPSON: What I'd like to do is open it up to the floor for two or three questions, depending on how many there are. Then we'll do one last quick round, staying focused on this question of training. I'd like just to give people a thought of where we would like to go for the final round, because as Jim Lilley said, the terrorist target is so illusive compared to a fixed geographic adversary of the past, how should we be thinking about training? Does regional knowledge matter as much? Should you be assigned a FAO [foreign area officer] in the military, or a regional specialist in diplomacy or intelligence? Are these things still relevant and appropriate for the transnational threat environment that we face? How should we think about some further ideas of training and of skills and of the qualities that we're going to need in our work force over the next decade or more?

But right now, I'll call on a few folks right in the middle there. Please, sir.

AUDIENCE: Lieutenant Colonel (retired) Robert Leonard. I'm from the Johns Hopkins University Applied Physics Lab. I'm very much in favor of this idea of legislating to improve interagency operations. I wonder if I could get the panel to comment on the idea of expanding that idea to include some of the agencies in the U.S. government other than the usual suspects of State, Defense, Intelligence and particularly with the view of modern stability and support operations. What would, in your view, be the utility of roping in Commerce, Energy, Health and Human Services, Housing, and bringing their expertise overseas in a big way as part of that kind of an interagency task force?

LAIPSON: Maybe this is the time for you to talk about your Bangkok experience.

FREEMAN: Actually, typically in a major regional embassy center like Bangkok, about 97 to 98 percent of the Americans do not work for State. They are representing other agencies. It is a managerial task of extraordinary complexity to make 30 to 35 different agencies work together that are present for varying reasons and that have different expectations of support and different operating styles. When I was running the embassy in Bangkok, I invented some new management mechanisms, sort of subsets of the country team that I think they are still using. So the first thing I'd say is actually these agencies by and large are, to some extent, overseas.

When I was ambassador in Saudi Arabia, I even had a visit from the Bureau of Indian Affairs to promote exports of Native American crafts to the Kingdom of Saudi Arabia. I don't think it was terribly successful, but it was a nice boondoggle for some of those guys. I think I would be very careful about casting the net too wide. I think there is a national security cluster that does go beyond the State, Defense, CIA nexus that includes some parts of the Department of Energy, includes the Treasury, and includes some parts of, obviously, Homeland Security and the Justice Department. It may or may not include very much of the Commerce Department. I've always felt the Commerce Department was a great ménagerie of a zoo without a theme. What can you say about a place that has NOAA [National Oceanic and Atmospheric Administration], the National Aquarium, the Bureau of Standards, now called NITS [National Institute of Training for Standardization] and trying to stop exports with one hand and promote them with the other. I'm very happy I never was asked to be Secretary of Commerce because I don't think anybody can run a place that's staffed with elephants and mice and giraffes and donkeys like that. I think your point is correct and what I'm suggesting is, in fact, an interagency mechanism. It should be run on an interagency basis independent of any particular agency, as OPM [Office of Personnel Management] runs the civil service. The question of who ought to be in and who ought to be out should be answered by careful study. I think there are things to be learned at the Department of Labor, no doubt, in the security area that I'm not aware of. So I'd take your point.

PACE: I don't know how much of this lends itself to legislation and how much of it is already capable of being enacted simply by the executive branch making decisions that this is the way they want to function. Certainly, as you get into the dialogue, you'll be able to determine what it is that the president could do right now, if he wanted to. Then there would be other things like expanding the size of the work force, mandating tour lengths overseas and promotion responsibilities and requirements. Those kinds of things we'll get into a little bit later. It might also lead you then to take a look at how we interact interagency with the Congress. The numbers of committees and various things impact the ability of those who are tasked to get something done—their ability to get the resources and to do that. So there are many ways to do that.

The other point I would make is that, in my mind, we are looking at task organizing, like we do on the military side. So when the president says, "I want to have this done in Afghanistan; Department of State, you've got it," the secretary of state then is designated leader and would do as you do on the military side. He would look at the problem at hand and ask for X number of Marines, Y number of sailors and that kind of thing, where you ask for the capability. So, I would see that that lead agency would ask for the capability from the other agencies so you would have different groups put together to take care of different tasks.

FREEMAN: And yet the Department of State, if asked today to do that, the Foreign Service Officer Corps is not qualified to do that. I have in mind the example of the debacle in the run-up to planning of the entry of U.S. troops into Haiti. Basically the people at State—I was at the DoD at the time—were sitting there saying, "We want to you have 503 troops of this kind to go into Port-au-Prince and "wheel" left and show how impressive they are and scare the hell out of the Haitians so they all run away." And what we were saying was, "No, don't tell us that. Tell us what you want to accomplish and we'll figure out whether we need 503 military engineers to do it or something else." So there is a problem of interagency coordination that gets back to culture and management training. This is another reason for having the exchanges between different jurisdictions.

LAIPSON: Another question over there, on the side, please.

AUDIENCE: I'm Mike Harwood from the Foreign Service Institute and my compliments on a great panel today. I think, Ellen, your panel has solved the interagency issue once and for all here. If I could just reiterate what I've heard today in a form of a five-point, very quick construct.

Number one, there is a need for political mandates supported by enlightened and empowered NSC leadership, either in the form of this mandating as an executive order, an NSPD [National Security Presidential Directive], and/or legislation that has some teeth to it.

Number two, there is a need for an agreed-upon and/or mandated coordination mechanism, such as a political-military plan, that includes executive oversight, like the EXCOM [executive committee], perhaps some kind of joint interagency doctrine, and, perhaps, as General Pace mentioned, the joint interagency coordination group, the JIACG [Joint Interagency Coordination Group] concept, which is currently not just a concept anymore since it's being implemented today.

Three, joint interagency training and education and exercise systems should be implemented and utilized.

Number four, interagency cultural immersion and cross-staffing supported by HR and rewarded, as was just mentioned by Ellen and others.

Fifth, and last, a viable lessons-learned collection and feedback loop that goes back not only to the operational side of ongoing operations, but also back to the schoolhouses.

So I would offer those five points as a construct of what I've heard today. Thank you.

LAIPSON: Thank you very much. That was very helpful. Down here in the second row. Yes.

AUDIENCE: Thank you. Carol Gould. I'm editor of *Current Viewpoint*, it's a British magazine. I'm in from London. First, before I ask my question regarding Ambassador Freeman's comments about U.S. ambassadors, it's generally believed in Britain that the special relationship is sustained because the U.S. ambassador to Britain breeds racehorses and Her Majesty, The Queen, and he adores race horses. Special relationship.

I know this may seem as coming out of left field, but big news in Britain is a play at the National Theater called *Stuff Happens* by Sir David Hare, directed by Nicholas Hytner. These are the greatest playwright and director in Britain alive today. The play is all about the National Security Council. It is two-and-a-half hours of the people that we see on television—on C-SPAN—everything General Pace deals with probably on a daily basis, screaming and shouting at each other. But what I find of concern about something like this—although it's just a play, the great British public is being exposed to this day-by-day—is the theme of the lack of consultation even with Britain, where there is supposed to be this special relationship. Is this of concern to you? There is a feeling over there in that universe that the consultation with Europe, and particularly with Britain, is becoming less and less apparent. I mean, in the play you get the feeling that there's a sort of contempt for Britain. I don't believe that at all. I wonder if this kind of media and this kind of propaganda in Europe is of concern to you, and if there needs to be some corrective action taken.

FREEMAN: On the first point, actually, the most interesting evolution in our diplomatic relationship at the technical level with Britain was when Ray Sykes, who had been deputy chief of mission, became ambassador. Because the tradition is the ambassador breeds horses and has fun and cuts ribbons and kisses babies, and the real work is done by the professional, who is number two in the embassy, the deputy chief of mission [DCM]. And, suddenly, the DCM became ambassador. So what were they to do? And to his credit, Ray continued recognizing that when he left, very likely the nonprofessional would come in, and continue to delegate an enormous amount of the work to the number two.

I think, since you've raised the issue of the National Security Council, it operates pursuant to [the National Security] Act of 1947 that was imposed on the White House from Congress, not initiated by Truman, although his administration ended up benefiting greatly from it. I believe it needs a relook. Nineteen forty-seven was a long time ago in a different world. In this connection, I commend to everyone's attention the report of the Hart-Rudman Commission, on which I served, which looked at that issue and, among other things, advocated the early establishment of some homeland security department or apparatus. Not exactly what we've ended up with, but something that would adjust the focus there.

On the third point, I think it's probably unfair to ask General Pace to respond to what is essentially a political question. I will say as a foreign service officer, retired, who spent 30 years trying to cultivate good relationships in cooperation with allies, partners and friends, and to manage relations with enemies abroad, that I am deeply distressed by the arrogance and incompetence of our current foreign policy and the extent to which we have succeeded in alienating allies, partners and friends. I think we have, essentially, emboldened and encouraged and assisted our enemies, particularly the terrorists, against us. So I hope for a return to what President Bush promised in the campaign in 2000, which is a more humble, more sensitive, more tactful return to a listening mode as opposed to a hectoring, lecturing or indifferent mode in relations with our principal foreign partners. But as I say, this is a highly political matter. Not everyone in the United States, by a long shot, would agree with me that there's even a problem.

PACE: I can't imagine a closer working relationship than the one between the United States and United Kingdom, starting with our president and your prime minister, working all the way down through our cabinet officials and certainly military-to-military. My counterpart is Air Chief Marshal Sir Tony Bagnall, he and I are on the phone multiple times a month, just talking to each other, as are each of our staffs. We have a U.K. officer who is embedded in our J–5 [Strategic Plans and Policy] on the Joint Staff. In this forum I can simply tell you that we have found ways within the last two or three years to be much more closely linked, not only intel-wise, but in the systems that we use to share the intelligence. From my perspective, and day-to-day working relationships, we clearly understand what great friends we have in the United Kingdom, and we value that, and we try to do all we can to ensure that we share what we know.

LILLEY: Ellen, can I just comment on the question you raised? Do we need regional knowledge? You bet we do, more than ever. Looking again at the director of operations, these people face organizational pressures to conform. This can influence the director of operations and make him go after soft targets for recruitment purposes. This deflects him. It also gets our friends from State ticked off because the CIA is paying the guy that State is getting information from. This always causes certain problems. It reminds me of the anecdote I heard about a European country where a new foreign-service officer comes in to call on someone in the foreign ministry. He walks in and the foreign ministry official says, "Well here's your package," and he gives it to him. The guy doesn't know what he's talking about and takes the package out, and inside are all sorts of top-secret foreign documents. Well, it turns out that this guy's case officer was supposed to just arrive and was going to call on him just after, but the agent got confused and gave it to the FSO. So this kind of thing can happen. If the case officer begins to think that he's working a political situation, he begins to step on people's toes, and it can cause friction. We want to get away from that.

The era of the big station, we hope, is over. We don't need a 400-, 500-man station. I can remember the chief of one of our big stations in Saigon in 1974, 400 people in it, calls in his reports officer and asks, "What did we produce last month?" The guy says 210 reports. The chief says, "Look, I want a report from every single officer in this station. I want it doubled. What are you going to do about this?" And the report officer says, "Why don't you cut your station in half?" This man is not upwardly mobile. He ran into problems.

In my own experiences in the DO, I found that probably around 20 percent of officers carried their weight in doing the actual work of the director of operations. I think this can be a contaminating element—I heard this about Iraq, and we ran into it in the Southeast Asia all the time. Three hundred case officers sent out for six months to carry out tasks. This doesn't make any sense whatsoever. But we still do it. You don't need DO officers to go to the National War College. I went there. It put me into a new frame of mind, where I got out of the DO business and went into the political aspect. I became contaminated.

I think you've got to make very sure that you're training. We've got a huge training camp down in Camp Perry [Ohio]. Is this relevant anymore to the kinds of DO operations you have to run in the 21st century? Isn't your training different? Isn't the kind of transference of experience, successes and failures in carrying out an operational job in the most difficult and dangerous of circumstances transmitted through, not so much formal tradecraft training, as the more senior officer transmitting to the more junior officer, and then putting him into the place where he can be effective?

So again, in answer to your question, Ellen, yes, absolutely, and look at it sometimes from the bottom up and not always from the top down, which we tend to do. I notice that [CIA Director] Porter Goss, by the way, in his testimony yesterday, really focused on this DO problem. He said that we need more than five years to straighten it out. Well, I hope he's right, but I hope in that process we'll have enough people inside who will be able to carry on the effective operations until we rejigger the system. Thanks.

LAIPSON: Thanks very much, Jim. Unfortunately we really are running out of time. I'm going to let the two other panelists, in sound-bite form, give us any last points or words of wisdom that they want to make, particularly on this issue of training and future skills that we'll need in the work force.

Chas.

FREEMAN: I think I agree with Jim. Regional expertise is absolutely essential and even more important than before, for two reasons. First, the world may be divided by academics into functional categories like proliferation, nonproliferation, disease and all this sort of thing, but people who are out there making decisions don't wake up one morning and say, "Hey, I'd like to be a proliferator." They have a reason for developing WMD, which relates to deterrence of other nasty people who live next to them, or deterrence of us. It isn't any use to think about them in functional terms. They think in Chinese, or Iranian, or Iraqi or North Korean terms or whatever cultural terms they think in.

Second, the challenge has never been greater. The principal field of our international operations—our principal enemies at the moment are a transnational movement headed by charismatic Saudis, managed by Egyptian Islamic fanatics, staffed by Yemeni foot soldiers. They operate across the span of the globe, and they can draw increasingly, unfortunately, on the one-fifth of the human race that is Muslim for support. To deal with these people in your business means recruiting case officers who are prepared to live under conditions of constant diarrhea and sleep with smelly men who kiss them with their beards. There are not a lot of Americans who particularly look forward to that kind of thing. This isn't James Bond. And it isn't Arnold Schwarzenegger at the casinos. It's a different game. It's a tough, tough game, and it requires a kind of dedication and a kind of regional and language knowledge that's greater than anything we've had to develop before.

LAIPSON: Thanks. General?

PACE: From a military standpoint I would say that we expect our young officers to learn a lot and to go to a lot of schools and to do a lot of training. Their lives are pretty well jammed right now, but we need to take a look at regional knowledge and language capability as two areas where we, as a military, would be very, very well served by having captains, majors and lieutenant colonels who can speak the languages and who can talk to the kind of histories that Ambassador Lilley was talking about. This, so when we're on the battlefield we're not dependent on interpreters and others to define for us the battle space in which we're operating.

We have a lot of great ethnic groups in this country. We might want to take a look at how we might have some affiliation with our armed forces Reserves for particular ethnic groups who might have a different relationship to our Reserves than do our current Reserves so that the population from that country who live here in the United States, if they wanted to, could be affiliated in some way with the government. This would allow us to quickly tap into their expertise, their language, their ethos.

Lastly, from an education standpoint, I absolutely agree with what's been said here about the opportunity to crossbreed and to understand each other. Imagine my surprise before Goldwater-Nichols, as a lieutenant colonel in the United States Marine Corps to find out that there were actually great Americans serving in the United States Army. For 16 years, my whole focus was the United States Marine Corps and I believe that my counterpart in the United States Army had the same focus on his institution—as well he should—and we still want to cultivate that inside of our young folks. We want these people to know that they are in the best Air Force in the world, and they are in the best Army in the world, and what they are doing inside that organization is the most important thing in the world. But our education system has allowed us in the military to develop trust.

For anything we have talked about here today to take root, we must have the same development of trust across the interagency.

LAIPSON: Sure. Very quickly.

LILLEY: Just one quickie. Case history. One of our greatest and most important targets is nuclear proliferation. There was a young ethnic Chinese American case officer who spotted a Chinese overseas in Taiwan who was a nuclear scientist, who was in the middle level. He cultivated this man through the art of Chinese opera, et cetera, and eventually recruited him with, you know, a nest egg in the United States. And about 15 years later this man became one of the 10 people probably in the island of Taiwan who knew about their nuclear weapons secret program. And he kept sending this stuff into us. We knew it was happening there, and we knew this would be very destabilizing in our relationships with China and Asia and all these things, if they really went ahead on this. We had to stop it. But you couldn't use this information because you would finger him. There were only a few people who knew what he knew. So what we had to do was to get him to go and get in the file, take out all the documents, bring them back and then "exfiltrate" him out of the country to the United States. He now lives in California under an assumed name somewhere. But we went in to the president of the country and laid it right on him with the documentation, "You're doing this and you said you wouldn't and you've got to stop it now. You put in jeopardy the whole relationship." It stopped. It stopped.

That is a classic kind of an operation and a very difficult target to work it over many years, using the kind of person you need who can carry out this kind of unique recruitment. You need this in North Korea today. You need it in other areas where we have to penetrate their top decision-making apparatus on strategic weapons through human penetration. And that's what the DO officer should try to do.

LAIPSON: Thank you. I think that last, rather dramatic example does remind us that some of the tasks ahead include traditional state-based threats. But we also have to be even more agile and creative in trying to penetrate some of the activities of non-state actors who may be U.S. adversaries. I want to thank, very happily, the wonderful panel and thank all of you for attending.

PANEL 4

COMBATING GLOBAL TERRORISM: SHARPENING DEFINITIONS, MISSIONS AND ROLES

Co-sponsor: Combating Terrorism Center, United States Military Academy

Introduction by: Brigadier General Robert L. Caslen Jr., Deputy Director for the War on Terrorism, Joint Staff Strategic Plans and Policy Directorate (J–5)

Moderator: Colonel Michael J. Meese, Deputy Department Head, Department of Social Sciences, United States Military Academy

Matthew Levitt, Senior Fellow, The Washington Institute for Near East Policy

Colonel Michael K. Nagata, Chief, Combatant Command Support Branch, Office of the Under Secretary of Defense for Intelligence

Steven Niegorski, Senior Intelligence Analyst

Panel Charter

This panel will present a cutting-edge look at the terrorist threat, highlighting the most current trends and assessing future developments. Operationally focused, the panel will outline what responses are required to meet today's challenges and prepare for those of tomorrow. The panel will propose a vision of how to move away from the ultimate challenge of counterterrorism policy-making and such reactive policy cycles. Participants will focus on the evolving terrorist threat and the challenges the changing threats present to the war on terrorism from a variety of perspectives.

Discussion Points

• How has the threat changed, what is the current threat and what can we expect tomorrow?

Left to right: *Michael J. Meese, Matthew Levitt,
Michael K. Nagata and Steven Niegórski (not pictured)*

• What are the roles of law enforcement, policy bodies, the public sector, the private sector, and traditional and nontraditional intelligence agencies in combating terrorism?

• Who are the key international partners for combating this changing threat?

• What are the roles of bilateral and multilateral mechanisms in sharing information and conducting joint counterterrorist investigations and operations?

SUMMARY

Matthew Levitt

• Who is the enemy? Defining terrorists by group is wrong; we must revise and refine our definition. The terrorist threat consists of a matrix of relationships. The time is past when we can look at terrorist groups as separate and distinct entities. It is misleading to compartmentalize. Even if there is no operational crossover between groups, there is likely to be some facilitation and connectivity. Individuals or groups can assist one another by indirect means—providing logistical or other kinds of support through personal relationships or front organizations.

• To combat the growing threat of networking jihadists, we need to "constrict the operating environment." This can be done through law enforcement and intelligence, as shown by the Patriot Act, which requires intelligence groups to look across group lines that are becoming increasingly blurred. The concept of blurring lines was exemplified during the bombings in Istanbul, Turkey, when one accused man stated that he was not a part of al Qaeda, although that group funded the bombings. The other accused contradicted by inciting that he was, in fact, al Qaeda. How can progress be made in defeating terrorism if the people acting are both part of and distinct from al Qaeda? Begin by applying the rule, "You can call yourself al Qaeda if you consider yourself al Qaeda."

• The Sept. 11 attacks proved that being a threat or a terrorist does not mean simply being the person who pulls the trigger. "The enemy is anyone facilitating this activity." Since so many larger terrorist networks are linked by individuals, tracking them may be the key to finding operational links and ending the terrorist threat.

Colonel Michael K. Nagata

• The principal challenge, from an intelligence perspective, is not finishing off the enemy but finding the enemy. The Department of Defense is wrestling with this challenge in large part because the institution is configured to fight wars against nation-states, rather than to conduct a global campaign inside states with which the United States is not at war.

• By law and tradition, the Defense Department provides intelligence to several audiences: combatant commanders, to satisfy tactical needs; the services, to inform decisions about how to plan to counter adversaries' capabilities; and the national security community.

• There are three myths about the Department of Defense that need to be dispelled:

1. Intelligence officers are the only people gathering intelligence. This, however, must be the job of all since the war on terrorism is an intelligence-based war.

2. Actionable intelligence, upon which an operation can be based, is the responsibility of intelligence officers, and operators must wait until intelligence is gathered. Instead, action must be taken first to make the terrorists operate in a way that information can be gathered.

3. The Defense Department only collects intelligence in declared combat zones and about opposing armies. This needs to end as well so that intelligence becomes the work not of isolated individuals or groups, but networks and effective relationships between them and among them.

Steven Niegorski

• Al Qaeda has evolved from a hierarchically organized group with a primary base in Afghanistan to a decentralized and more widely dispersed entity. Through military action in Afghanistan, as well as a slew of arrests and crackdowns around the world, we have disrupted their operations and gained a greater understanding of their conceptualization and planning. By degrading their ability, we have made it much more difficult for al Qaeda to pool the resources necessary to mount complex operations such as the Sept. 11 attacks. Working with coalition members behind the scenes, we have taken down or disrupted many plots and saved many lives in many places.

• Nevertheless, al Qaeda's new leaders are no less smart, fanatical or ruthless than those who have been killed or apprehended. The terrorist network is damaged, but not destroyed or docile. They have operatives in position and a continuing interest in strategic targets that we are most worried about. They have passed operational control to regional nodes and allies, and they have altered their tactics to employ simpler methods and technologies and shorter preparation timelines. At the same time, Osama bin Laden himself is still determined to launch strategic attacks and remains interested in acquiring chemical, biological, radiological or nuclear materials.

• Nicgorski offered five thoughts on how to interpret and address terrorism:

1. The United States must maintain its edge in the war and not forget why it is here because the enemy will not soon forget.

2. The war must have dimensions that go beyond taking down individual terrorists over time and prevent the rise of a generation poisoned by the ideal of murder achieving salvation.

3. Working with partners is essential, especially those at risk in the war--like Pakistan and Saudi Arabia. It is much easier to work with these states than without them.

4. The United States should apply a 1 percent standard, that is, take all threats seriously and follow all leads.

5. It is imperative that the United States not turn its back on Iraq. It must pay attention to Iraqis returning to their homeland with new ideas of jihad and an agenda of targeting the United States. It must not forget the turmoil that resulted in the Taliban takeover of Afghanistan.

Question-and-Answer Period

• When asked about links between al Qaeda and terrorist groups in Latin America, such as the FARC in Colombia, Levitt said there are connections between terrorist groups in each respective area, however the links are between Hamas and Hezbollah with groups in the area that encompasses Argentina, Paraguay and Bolivia. Prior to Sept. 11, Hamas leaders had set up terrorist organizations in South America. Yet after significant efforts by the United States to combat this, many of these people moved on to Africa where they are setting up new cells.

• Nagata added that there is a need to return some attention to the tri-state area without disrupting the delicate political balance in place there today.

• When asked about the role of the criminal network, Nicgorski said the criminal network is not new. Human smuggling networks are growing between terrorist organizations and becoming of particular interest. This interest should be followed, as there are links between the criminal enterprises of human smuggling and al Qaeda.

• Regarding links between al Qaeda and Iraq and the idea of the war as a possible distraction from the real war on terrorism, Levitt said that the links were weak between Iraq and al Qaeda, and Iran and Syria are actually of greater concern when it comes to state-sponsored terrorism. He continued that the main reason for the war was to combat the spread of weapons of mass destruction. Unfortunately, there are larger terror problems in the country today than before American intervention, and terrorist groups now have a better ability to recruit nationwide. The problem is that the United States is winning the war on the battlefield, but losing the war of ideas to the Islamic extremists.

• Levitt also responded when asked about possible links between the Irish Republican Army and Middle East terrorist groups and possible parallels in the situation in Northern Ireland and the Israeli-Palestinian issue. He said the war on terrorism is a war of intelligence, and it will be intelligence that tells if there are links between the IRA and the Middle East. Historically, there have been links between the IRA and Libya, but this is in the past and no longer of significance. He concluded that while there are parallels between the issues driving the IRA and Arab-Israeli crisis, they are not applicable.

• An audience member stated that success in the war on terrorism lies not in the number of terrorists killed, but in the number of people that are turned against jihad. He asked whether it was true that through U.S. actions in the Middle East, the United States is doing Osama bin Laden's work for him by creating the ground for cohesive ideology. Levitt responded that there are two angles by which we can look at the war on terrorism. The first is through root causes, which suggest that ideology is the main and first thing the United States needs to fight in the region. The second is an organizational perspective. It is organizations that radicalize into violent groups, even if the root causes do lie with ideology. The United States needs to figure out why there is a gun pointed at its head. However, first the United States must make the gun holder put the gun down; only then will the United States find out why it was pointed there.

1. Nagata agreed that there is a consequence to taking action, but there is still an intelligence struggle of whether this action is creating more terrorists. There is no way to measure the links between these two things, and there really is no definition as to what a link is.

2. Nicgorski, speaking in more general terms, said the intelligence community alone cannot win the war on terrorism. The United States government and the contributions of allies and partners will be necessary to win the war of ideas.

• The recent attack at a school in Beslan, Russia, was mentioned and the question was posed about a possible relationship between Chechen rebels and al Qaeda. Nagata asked if the attack was an extension of Chechen nationalism or al Qaeda terrorism. He asked if it is possible to measure which one was more of a factor in the attack. Without an answer, there is a problem with which opinion—al Qaeda or Chechen nationals being at fault—to use when making policy. There may he links between nationalistic terrorism in Chechnya and al Qaeda, but defining and understanding the meaning of these links is a very difficult challenge, he concluded.

• During follow-on discussions of Beslan and whether it really matters if there was a link between al Qaeda and the perpetrators of the attack, Levitt said that it depends on the nature of the activity involved. There may have been a link in the minds of the jihadists, however, seeing as two of the Sept. 11 hijackers wanted to go to Chechnya.

I. Nagata concluded by saying the war on terrorism is a global war, and thus all terror issues should be addressed. However, it is impossible for the United States to combat every terrorist activity across the globe at one time. It must instead decide on the correct sequence in which to fight various terrorist activities, gauging each activity's importance.

Analysis

During Panel IV, Matthew Levitt, Michael Nagata and Steven Nicgorski discredited many of the popular myths surrounding the current terrorist challenge, particularly the idea that a cohesive "terrorist international" is operating under centralized control, and with campaign-like deliberation, against the United States. Each argued that the extremist threat is increasingly virulent, persistent, complex and polycentric. All agreed that this necessitates adjustments in American strategy.

Levitt suggested that disparate Islamic terrorist groups interact so frequently on a number of different levels that treating them as distinct is imprudent. He proposed viewing the terrorist challenge as a complex whole, where terrorists and their supporters join in important but informal partnerships.

Nicgorski similarly argued that we are witnessing the rise of a loosely connected global movement unified not by common leadership but, rather, by common ideology. He acknowledged a distinct increase in extremist violence since Sept. 11. He attributed this increase not to a centrally controlled, deliberate counterattack but to the increasing decentralization and independence of transregional terrorist actors. He, like Levitt, suggested these actors cooperate when convenient, unified only by a common, general purpose that focuses on delimiting the influence of the United States.

Nagata identified a number of obstacles the Department of Defense faces in effectively countering the terrorist challenge. Principal among these, he argued, is not in the area of "finishing" the enemy, but rather in finding him. This task, he observed, may in fact be too big and complex for the formal intelligence system alone.

All predicted a complex and indeterminate course for the war on terrorism. All agreed that the United States will steadily improve its capacity to disrupt terrorist organizations. However, they did not enumerate specifically the myriad of factors that will likely limit the effectiveness of the U.S. response over the near term and midterm. For example, the atomization and decentralization of the challenge complicates the effective identification and targeting of threats. This comes at the very moment smaller threat packages are increasingly empowered. Additionally, the increase in terrorist violence worldwide portends greater difficulty in conveying a sense of security to at-risk populations and exposes our continuing vulnerability to less conventional security challenges. Finally, as the terrorist's center of gravity is ideological rather than physical, the challenge is less vulnerable to traditional American security institutions employed in classic combinations.

This all suggests that the war on terrorism will persist. The United States may actively pre-empt some of the most significant challenges, but the broader terrorist threat will persist as a costly reality for the foreseeable future.

Transcript

ANNOUNCER: Ladies and Gentlemen, Brigadier General Kevin Ryan.

BRIGADIER GENERAL KEVIN T. RYAN: Thank you. Our next panel is Combating Global Terrorism: Sharpening Definitions, Missions and Roles. And to introduce the moderator, I'd like to invite Brigadier General Robert L. Caslen Jr., the deputy director for the war on terrorism, Joint Staff Strategic Planning and Policy Directorate.

BRIGADIER GENERAL ROBERT L. CASLEN JR.: Thank you very much, General Ryan. Distinguished guests and ladies and gentlemen, it really is an honor for me to be able to introduce our moderator, who will subsequently introduce our panel.

I just want to say right up front that in the role that I have as the deputy director for the war on terrorism, we work issues for the chairman in his role of providing military advice for the president and the secretary of defense, which deal with the military strategy for the war on terrorism, and also the related policies. Therefore, to be asked to introduce this particular panel, Combating Global Terrorism: Sharpening Definitions, Missions and Roles, is really an honor. It's something that we in J-5 [Directorate for Strategic Plans and Policy] for the war on terrorism do all the time. We deal with these sorts of things. I remember years ago when I first went to the combat training centers, we had drilled into our minds there as commanders that intelligence drives operations. So as we in our government and we in our coalition of partners try to deal with the nature of the enemy and the nature of the conflict, it resonates back to my training center days, with the question, "Who is the enemy?" Because intelligence drives operations and as such as we define our enemy, we develop the strategies and the ways and means of that strategy to effectively deal with that particular enemy.

Heading up this panel is a very distinguished Army officer, Colonel Mike Meese from the Combating Terrorism Center at West Point, New York. I just want to take a second to talk about this distinguished center that West Point stood up just a couple of years ago. It is an outstanding initiative, because it stimulates discussion as we try to make sense of these terrorist threats, the ideology that drives these men and women to do what they do, and how to succeed in an increasingly complex and global environment. This West Point Combating Terrorism Center not only deals with the private sector, the academic sector and also the military sector, but, more importantly, it's taking these young future leaders

*Brigadier General
Robert L. Caslen Jr.*

who are coming out of the military academy, developing them and teaching them how to survive and how to be successful in this increasingly complex environment.

Colonel Mike Meese is currently a professor at the United States Military Academy and is the deputy head of the department of social sciences. In this capacity he teaches microeconomics and defense economics courses and leads the 62 military and civilian faculty members who teach in the social science department. His previous assignment was as the United States Military Academy Fellow at the National War College. During this particular year, this past year, he was asked by our Army to go to Iraq to serve with [then-Major General Dave] Petraeus in the 101st Airborne Division as an economic and political advisor to the work that he was doing up in Mosul. Very successful, as you know, the esteemed reputation that the 101st established for themselves in accomplishing the mission up there in Mosul. Mike also has experience as an executive officer to the assistant chief of staff in Bosnia conducting peacekeeping and counterterrorism operations there. Mike is a field artillery officer. He served an outstanding career pattern in the great Army divisions like the 7th Infantry Division, the 3rd Armored Division and the 1st Calvary Division. He is also a graduate of the National War College. He has two master's degrees and a doctorate from the Woodrow Wilson School of Public and International Affairs at Princeton University. Please join me in a warm welcome for Colonel Michael Meese.

COLONEL MICHAEL J. MEESE:
Thank you very much, General Caslen.
I think the only other time in your
military career where you're introduced
by your superior is at your court
marshal. So I hope that this is not a bad
omen. On behalf of the superintendent
at the United States Military Academy,
Lieutenant General Bill Lennox, I want to
thank the Eisenhower Series for putting
together such an outstanding conference
and for including the Combating
Terrorism Center at West Point as a
co-sponsor on this panel on combating
global terrorism.

This is a very appropriate week to
be discussing terrorism, almost exactly
three years after 9/11. Since that time,
the United States has been continuously
struggling to develop and execute a
cohesive picture of the threat and the

Colonel Michael J. Meese

requirements and responses needed to combat that threat. The success that the
United States has had on the global war on terror and that it will have in the future
is due to two great national assets. First, we have operational capabilities that are
the best in the world. On the other hand, we also have intellectual capacity that
is the best in the world. But given the challenges of today, it's no longer possible
for the operator to function entirely compartmentalized or for the intellectual to
deal with the aspects of terrorism at a safe theoretical distance undisturbed by
the facts of the day. The world's first historian, Thucydides, wrote that the nation
that makes a great distinction between its scholars and its warriors will have its
thinking done by cowards and its fighting done by fools. In the war on terrorism,
it is vital for us to link the scholars and the warriors, the intellectuals and the
operators. That's the purpose of the Combating Terrorism Center at West Point,
which leverages itself as both the United States Military Academy being a first-rate
university as well as being a military academy to capture the synergy of both aspects
of the institution to contribute to the fight against terror. That's also the purpose
of our panel today, and, I would say of the entire Eisenhower Series—to link the
exceptional operational capabilities with the exceptional intellectual capacity that
you see around the room today.

In other words, what we're doing at the Combating Terrorism Center at West
Point and what we've been doing for the last two days here, is to bring the operator
out from behind the green door and bring the intellectual down from the ivory
tower. The synergy that results between the linkage of the best operators in the

world and the best intellectuals of the world is truly awesome and is a vital part of our eventual victory on the global war on terror.

Our panel today is extremely well-qualified and is a great mix of both operators and intellectuals. And I would ask them to join me here on stage.

The format that we're going to take is that I'll introduce each panelist briefly. You see their extensive bios already in your packets. They'll each speak for 10 to 15 minutes, and then we'll leave plenty of time for questions at the end.

Defining the scope of the terrorist threat is extremely challenging and it's important to take a step back to look at the strategic nature of the threat—to understand the underlying trends that shape the overall threats so that we can begin to move ahead of the curve and determine the full extent of the real threat to our security. To address this part of the problem, we've asked Matt Levitt of the Washington Institute for Near East Policy to assess some of the key factors shaping the terrorist threat, including who the key players are, how they operate, and how this may change in the future. Mr. Levitt has not only served in the Washington Institute for Near East Policy, but has previously served as an analyst for the FBI and is one of the most well-noted commentators here in Washington. He holds a master's degree from Fletcher, soon to be a Ph.D. from Fletcher, and has a forthcoming book that will be done next year on Hamas.

Mr. Levitt.

MATTHEW LEVITT: Thank you very much. It's a tremendous pleasure to be here with such an auspicious audience on such an important topic, and as you said, at such a telling time. I looked at the calendar the other day and saw it was 9/11, and it was just a tremendous flashback. I led the analytical team for Flight 175, working the 9/11 threat. It's amazing to think that we're three years down the road and still have so far to go even as we have accomplished so much. And we have.

But I think that one of the questions that we still misunderstand is the key question that was posed at the beginning of our introductions here. Who is our enemy? Is it al Qaeda? Is it terrorism in general? Who are the actors? And so I would like to share with you some thoughts on a more strategic level about who we are trying to deal with? Who is this threat? Because there are some very, very important—not only strategic, but tactical—implications for how we understand our adversary. I think that if we look at the three main issues that we are facing today, in this area, the global war on terrorism, the war in Iraq, and the Israeli-Palestinian conflict—the latter two mainly manipulated very successfully by terrorists for recruitment purposes—we can see that this distinction is very telling.

The basic theme I want to share with you is that the time when we could look at terrorist groups individually, in pretty little square boxes, is long past. It's no longer sufficient to think about al Qaeda as distinct from Hamas or other groups, even though Hamas has nothing to do with al Qaeda. Hamas is not one of the al Qaeda affiliates. Hamas is not directly funded by al Qaeda. Yet thinking about them in entirely separate boxes is misleading, at the very least. The same goes for Hezbollah and other groups, and I'll tell you why. The bottom line is this. Even for those groups, among which there is no operational crossover, among which there is no direct financing of one another's operations, there is tremendous crossover at an individual level. Relationships between members of different groups cut across all of these different organizations. So if we still insist on using this diagram of the pretty square boxes, we at least need to have them overlap, which gets very complicated because the overlapping is significant. I think that this makes it important when we can think about this, this crossover, because the area where it's most dominant is in the logistical and financial support infrastructures. When you get out of the Middle East in particular, when you get into the

Matthew Levitt

Diaspora, when Middle Eastern terrorists are operating in Europe or the United States or South America, they are even more likely to work with one another. Jihadists, from whatever cause, will work with one another, for a variety of reasons. First, ideology; second, the old-boys' network that comes out of the al Qaeda and other training camps. You know, when I walk around Washington there are Fletcher graduates all over the place. I'm sure there are several in this room. And that's a similar kind of network, and even before the al Qaeda training camps in Afghanistan, there's the Muslim Brotherhood network. All of these facilitate interactions and connectivity, where someone in Madrid who's plotting an attack can reach out to an al Qaeda affiliate for assistance and be told that he won't get direct assistance, but talk to "this guy." And that happens a lot.

We saw this on Sept. 11. We saw this in Madrid. We have seen it many other times. I'm reminded back to the comment of a Palestinian general I interviewed for this dissertation that, Insha-Allah [God willing], will be done soon. Brigadier General Nizar Imar told me several years ago—I won't tell you how many—that the difference between the political and social and military wings of Hamas is a fiction. The people that we see and describe today as political leaders, tomorrow morning we find are involved in an attack. And far beyond the specific group of Hamas, we see this very, very frequently.

What we need to do is to constrict the operating environment. We need law enforcement. We need intelligence. We need military operations. What we need to do is make it more difficult for this network to be able to do what it needs to do at every level, from procuring bullets and explosives and false documents to traveling and connectivity and communications, because, all too often, we don't find the links between individuals until the day after. If you think about some of the more well-known examples of such links that we have uncovered in the course of the past few years, you'll see this over and over again. Consider, for example, the Bank al Taqwa network, which was designated as a terrorist front for its activities in support of al Qaeda, which we know also was used as the preferred means for transferring $60 million for Hamas in the mid-90s. It has been linked to other Palestinian groups—Algerian groups and others in North Africa—and is very closely affiliated with central figures in the Muslim Brotherhood.

Consider examples here in the United States. We don't need to look abroad. Consider the case of American Muslims in Portland [Ore.] associated with al Qaeda, who tried to enter Afghanistan to fight with the Taliban against U.S. forces. They were radicalized and recruited by two individuals here in the United States. One of them was a cofounder of the Global Relief Foundation, an al Qaeda front organization. The other is an individual who is jailed on fraud charges related to gun possession and other things, who had gone through Palestinian training camps in southern Lebanon and was closely identified with Hamas. There are many other examples like this. Does this mean that this individual is Hamas? Does it mean that he's al Qaeda? One can put an individual in the sphere of al Qaeda and still recognize the links that he or she has to other groups, and that's important.

The network of front organizations just five miles from here in Northern Virginia is perhaps the most prominent case where, to be honest—and I can say this as a former FBI person—I believe the reason we didn't crack this case earlier was, in large part, because of the way FBI units were organized. There were units that worked on Palestinian groups and units that worked on al Qaeda and other radical groups, and those units didn't necessarily hold regular meetings. So with one unit looking at this network in northern Virginia from a purely Palestinian angle, they wouldn't necessarily know about all the angles to al Qaeda. After the passage of the Patriot Act, when U.S. attorneys were not only given the authority, but were required to look across all these cases, they were the ones who drew these lines. When you put all this together and see that there are al Qaeda links and Palestinian Islamic Jihad links and Hamas links, in this one address, you're able to put together a case that you couldn't before.

There are many examples of this phenomenon in the war in Iraq; obviously the most prominent is Abu Musab al Zarqawi. I enjoyed giving that example before he was on everybody's plate. Now that he is, I don't enjoy giving him as an example so much because it's not so insightful. But just earlier this week in Turkey, the court system there identified on trial several individuals involved in Istanbul attacks. One guy got up there and said, "I'm not al Qaeda, although we were funded by al Qaeda." Then one of his associates got up the next day and with a long, drawn-out speech said, "We are al Qaeda. We are al Qaeda in Turkey, and we're here." How are we to understand this? And the answer is that it's the "pretty little box" theory.

You can call yourself al Qaeda if you think of yourself as al Qaeda. These are people who went through the camps. These are people who were directly funded by senior [Osama] bin Laden lieutenants. So whether you consider yourself al Qaeda by virtue of having sworn a pledge of allegiance to bin Laden, by virtue of having spent more time in the camps, it really doesn't make a difference.

If we think of it, therefore, as combating terrorism by group, we are going to have a problem. We've seen this many times before. In 2002, we sent a senior delegation to Europe, asking the Europeans to help us in combat terrorist financing. We sent officials to Europe with a lot of information about specific individuals and our financing of al Qaeda and Hamas. Because of the nature of information we were sharing with them, most of the information about financing al Qaeda could not be shared publicly. But because in the Middle East financing Hamas is not necessarily considered a bad thing, a lot of that was more open source—less sensitive—and that was information they could share with the public. Unfortunately, the answer they gave us at the time in 2002 was that, if all you can give us to use publicly is that these individuals are financing Hamas, we can't help you. And nothing happened. We found out later, for example, that the Tawheed network, associated with Zarqawi and others, was bringing people out of Afghanistan, out of the Middle East, and infiltrating them into Europe. Again, because they are seen only as a front—only as logistical supporters, not as operatives; they were not trigger-pullers; they were facilitators—nothing was done until the Germans got information that they were actually planning attacks in Germany. But by that time, we really didn't know how many al Qaeda operatives were infiltrated into Europe. So this has very operational consequences. It has consequences for the Israeli-Palestinian conflict, too. Next month, Oct. 15 will be the first anniversary of the attack on the convoy from our embassy in Gaza. Most Palestinian groups traditionally do not target the United States. But we are quite confident that, unfortunately, this was a very specific targeting of the U.S. Embassy convoy. In fact this was not the first time. About a month earlier, a group targeted a similar convoy and failed—the explosive just didn't happen to go off. Here, too, we're dealing with a group that has links to several entities, to Hamas, to Islamic Jihad, to some of the Palestinian intelligence services. Trying to pinpoint this group in one little box is very difficult.

Finally, sometimes there even are operational links—crossovers between disparate groups. There is a case of a Hamas operative, five actually, who went to Pakistan and were spotted and recruited to go into Afghan training camps, first to fight in Kashmir, and then into the mainstream al Qaeda camps. Some were then sent back home to Gaza to conduct operations there. One of them, Nabil Aqal, hosted Richard Reid, the now infamous shoe bomber, when he traveled through Israel, the West Bank and Gaza. Sheik [Ahmed] Yassin, the since-assassinated head of Hamas, spiritual leader of Hamas, gave this Hamas-al Qaeda crossover network, this small little cell, $10,000 to facilitate its operations, knowing full well that they had just come back from the training camps in Afghanistan. Is Nabil Aqal al Qaeda? Is he Hamas? It really doesn't make a difference. We need to understand the crossover. We need to understand that if we only look at al Qaeda, or we only look at other groups, we're going to miss a lot of activity.

So let's come back to our original question, "Who is the enemy?" The enemy is anybody who is facilitating this type of activity. If 9/11 taught us anything it should be that you don't have to be a trigger-puller, you don't have be the one detonating the bomb or crashing the airplane to be considered a terrorist. Ramzi bin al-Shib is a very bad man, and he didn't pull a trigger. We need to take this attitude and apply it across the war on terror. We need to understand that terrorism is a form of violence. Violence is a part of human nature in a sense that it will always be here, but we can constrict the environment. We can win this war and bring violence—including terrorism—down to tolerable levels where, based on intelligence, we are able to thwart the activities of those who are trying to do us harm. In order to do that we just need to have a broader understanding of the nature of the relationships, the matrix of relationships between terrorist groups—even terrorist groups that are disparate—that haven't trained together in that official capacity. The relationships between individuals are what are driving the terrorist threat today, specifically since we've cracked down so successfully since 9/11. It's no longer a headquarters-to-headquarters issue. It is a relationship-based issue between people who know each other or who are put in touch with each other. Thank you.

MEESE: Thank you very much, Matt, for that insightful and sobering view of the threat. It's clear that we face an asymmetric threat, and, arguably, a global insurgency that requires us to counter that threat in unconventional ways. One of the most important aspects of that is the integration of intelligence. To address this we have asked Colonel Mike Nagata of the Command Support Branch of the Office of the Under Secretary of Defense for Intelligence to comment on these operational and strategic issues.

I invite you to read Colonel Nagata's impressive bio in the conference packet, but I'll sum it up in the words of my boss, Colonel Russ Howard. When he commanded Mike Nagata, when he was the commander of First Group at Fort Lewis [Wash.], Colonel Howard told me that Mike was the best officer that ever worked for him, which is a rare and exceptional compliment indeed. Mike is a career special forces officer who truly understands the value of intelligence and operations. Colonel Nagata.

COLONEL MICHAEL K. NAGATA: Thank you. Colonel Howard doesn't have particularly high standards.

As you've already heard, I'm here from the Office of the Under Secretary of Defense for Intelligence [USDI], which, for those of you who don't know, is a fairly new organization. Dr. Steven Cambone, the under secretary, formed the staff of USDI only a little over a year ago. So we are in the mode where we are doing everything for the first time. I work specifically for Lieutenant General [William] Boykin, who is the deputy under secretary for war-fighting support. I run most of his war-on-

terrorism issues, which fundamentally
in our office boil down to intel policy,
resources and oversight issues.

I'm going to focus my initial
comments simply on DoD intelligence
issues that we are currently thinking
about and working on. I can certainly
entertain questions when we get to the
Q&A about broader topics, if you're
interested in that. The reform of the
national intelligence community has
been much in the news lately, as I'm sure
all of you know.

For the Department of Defense,
one of our principal challenges—and
it's not just the Department of Defense,
but it's also the broader intelligence
community—one of our principal
challenges is grappling with the fact,
and we believe it is a fact, that the
principal difficulty we have now

Colonel Michael K. Nagata

operationally is not so much in *finishing* this enemy, in either kinetic or nonkinetic
ways, but it is *finding* the enemy. I'm not trying to make light of the courage and
dedication and effort that is required to finish this foe, but the real challenge for
us has been in finding him. Because fundamentally, the Department of Defense
is still in a state where it is most optimally configured to take on a nation-state's
armed forces. And that is not what we are fighting today, as all of you know. We
are still wrestling with how to change the way the Department of Defense operates,
so that if required, we can still deal swiftly and decisively with a nation-state's
armed forces, but, in the meantime, successfully prosecute and win a global war
on terrorism.

At a very fundamental level, what that means mechanically for the Department
of Defense is we are trying to wage a global campaign, if you will, inside the
territory of nation-states with which we are not at war. But there are bad actors,
there are networks, there are capabilities within those nation-states that we have
decided—that the president has decided—we are at war against. That is a very,
very difficult challenge for the Department of Defense. It is really unlike anything
we've ever tried to wrestle with before.

Now, on the intelligence side, if you break the finding role of the Department
of Defense into its component pieces, they fundamentally all are intelligence
activities, or at least intelligence-related activities. And that leads me to where I'll
try to finish up, which is what our perspective is, what our view is in USDI about
the Department of Defense's role in doing intelligence, both traditionally and into

the future, which we think is going to look a lot different. We are certainly trying to change it.

By law, and by policy, the secretary of defense is responsible for providing intelligence support to three broad groups across the United States government. One obvious group is our combatant commanders, their tactical war-fighting needs, and I must say, and this is probably self-evident to all of you. For those of you who have been deployed, it is something you dealt with firsthand. DoD tactical intelligence requirements have gone up exponentially since 9/11. I mean, it is unprecedented the level of demand on the collection and analysis and production capabilities of the intel community at large, and the piece of the intel community that resides in DoD. Let me also add a footnote, for those of you who do not know: Depending on how you count assets, somewhere between 75 to 80 percent of all of the intelligence capability in the United States government today resides inside the Department of Defense.

Now, that is a subject of much debate in the larger national intel reform debate that is occurring across this country. But today, the vast majority of it is inside the Department of Defense and is under the authority, direction and control of the secretary.

The second group, which doesn't get a lot of attention, but is, by volume, an enormous demand on the intelligence community, is support to the services. A good example of that is a service working on a new weapons system or a new capability—knowing how fast a jet should be able to fly, knowing what kind or how thick or how good the armor on a vehicle needs to be. These are questions that can only be answered by the intelligence community, because it depends on what kind of capability we're going against, or we think we're going against. Someone has to gather that intelligence; someone has to analyze that intelligence; someone has to produce a product to support the people who are building a capability, writing doctrine, establishing training curricula in our various military school systems. These are all intelligence requirements that underpin the work they do. And for those of you who do not know, we put people in harm's way in order to gather information that is necessary to do what, at least on the face of it, sounds like very mundane tasks. But these are enormous intelligence requirements across the department.

Finally, and just as importantly, by law, the secretary of defense must provide intelligence support to the director of Central Intelligence and the rest of the national intelligence community. So whether it's the Department of State needing to know something about Haitian boat refugees or it's the Department of Justice needing to know something to support the FBI or the Department of Homeland Security, the secretary of defense, because he has the lion's share of the capability, must always provide intelligence support to all of those various partners.

Now having said all that, I'll close with just three things. There are things that color much of the work we do in USDI. I'm going to talk to them in terms of three kind-of myths we think we need to dispel inside the Department of Defense.

The first myth is that—and I'll say it in the first person: Since I'm not an intelligence officer, and I'm a special forces officer, in my case, I don't have a role. I have no responsibility for gathering intelligence. That's a myth, but there are many people in the Department of Defense, military and nonmilitary, who believe that. If you're not an intel guy or gal, you don't have a role. That is something we must dispel inside the Department of Defense. This is an intelligence-driven war. And if we don't have every single Soldier, sailor, airman and Marine gathering intelligence for a variety of purposes, we are likely to miss something critical. We have already seen examples of that.

Second myth: actionable intelligence—intelligence you can actually base an operation on, that a commander is confident in, to accept risk, put people in harm's way and conduct an operation. Actionable intelligence is the responsibility of the intelligence officer. It's his job and I, the operator, may have the best-trained force in the world, but I'm going to wait until the intel guy gives me my actionable intelligence, and I have no responsibility to take action until I get that actionable intelligence. We think that's a myth as well. We think the best way of getting actionable intelligence is to take action first. If left to his own devices, this enemy will not operate in ways that we can detect, identify, track and target. We have to force him out of his comfort zone. Make him operate in ways that we can actually detect. And you don't do that by sitting back and waiting for the intel guy or gal to deliver a magic box with actionable intelligence in it.

Final myth is that the Department of Defense only collects intelligence in a declared combat zone; it only collects intelligence against an army, or a navy or an air force. That's not what the law says, that's not what the definition of military intelligence is. The secretary of defense must, by law, gather intelligence, national intelligence, foreign intelligence and military intelligence to support those three categories that I talked about before to establish DoD policy, to build DoD capabilities and conduct DoD operations. It's not constrained to whether or not we have a declared combat zone, whether or not it's a nation-state army or not. Hopefully you understand, and I'll stop on this, that until we change this mindset inside the Department of Defense, it's going to be very difficult for us to get inside a clandestine, networked, highly agile and adaptive enemy, because they will always turn inside our decision loop until we dispel these myths. And with that I'll stop.

MEESE: Thank you very much, Colonel Nagata, for those insights on the operational and strategic issues of the intelligence system, focusing on defense. It's important for us to view this in a broader context, which is the perspective of the entire intelligence community. As Ambassador Mike Sheehan highlighted this morning, one of the most important outstanding issues is the overall intelligence management. That's why it's especially appropriate that we have with us one of the senior managers from the director of Central Intelligence's Counterterrorism Center. Steve Nicgorski is senior manager and has been with the CIA for over 15 years. Prior to his current assignment, he worked on the president's daily briefing staff; he holds a master's degree from USC [University of Southern California] and a bachelor of science degree in political science from Notre Dame. Steve.

STEVEN NICGORSKI: Thank you very much. I appreciate the opportunity to come and speak to this distinguished audience.

I would just say, to start off, I underscore what has been already said by our two previous panelists. I think they've hit the mark dead on. I think a lot of things we're talking about on a more global scale, we're trying to accomplish on a more micro scale within the CIA, within the Counterterrorism Center. I lead an analytical unit that focuses on al Qaeda. We focus on their plans, intentions and their leaders. We are co-located with the main operational arm of the CIA that targets those leaders. We have representatives in the same vault from DoD, FBI, Customs and Borders, DHS [Department of Homeland Security]. The synergy that is created by that kind of co-location, that kind of sharing of intelligence, is invaluable. I think it speaks to many of the successes we've had to this point.

With that, I think what I would like to do is give you a sense of where I think we've come from as a backdrop and then move on to where we're headed and what we still need to do. As I said, our focus—the way we interpret or look at this strategically—is try to break it down into phases. Phase one, for us, was a very clear mission. It was to destroy those who were most responsible for the attack on 11 September. Al Qaeda still exists, but it is no longer the same organization that attacked us on 11 September. Before that time, al Qaeda was a hierarchical organization that used the Taliban's protection to plot in safety, recruit and train new members, and run an international infrastructure. Bin Laden and his two deputies, [Ayman] al-Zawahiri, the late Abu Hamza, were intimately involved in the administration of the organization and directly managed multiple terrorist operations around the world.

Since then, al Qaeda has decentralized, not by choice, but because it was forced to do so. It has changed because of the loss of Afghanistan, the manhunt that has driven bin Laden and Zawahiri deep underground, and the arrest of many of al Qaeda's most capable leaders during crackdowns in Pakistan, Saudi Arabia, other places, even Iran. Some of these changes have been in our favor. The disruption operations of the past years, as well as our much greater understanding of how al Qaeda conceptualizes and executes attacks, have made it tougher for it to pool resources for complex operations like 9/11, though they still aim to match that attack. The lack of reliable safe havens means more attention has to be focused on day-to-day survival, rather than operations. We're better off with many of the group's highly capable planners like KSM [Khalid Sheikh Mohamed], the architect of 9/11, and others off the street. We have matched this disruption in al Qaeda's Afghan safe haven with a dogged campaign against the group's leaders abroad.

One of the advantages we've found through these three years of progress is that the new operators do not have the skills, leadership and experience of their predecessors. Detained terrorist planners, like KSM and others, are smart and, in some cases, extremely smart. They are driven and they are ruthless. Some of those who have replaced them lack their abilities and their authority. Now, one senior detainee talked of KSM's arrest as a melting of an iceberg, an indication of how he was revered in the organization. I would say if we had known the depth of the global terrorist infrastructure, which Matt so eloquently spoke of, which we faced when we started down this path, we would have been daunted. But those who say we are losing ground, that the time and effort we have invested is wasted, forget where we started and how far we have come.

Working with the worldwide coalition of partners and the global behind-the-scenes war of unprecedented proportions, we have taken down thousands of al Qaeda terrorists, their supporters and affiliates. These actions have delayed or disrupted plots that would have killed hundreds, maybe thousands, including second-wave aircraft attacks against the East and West Coast of the United States, attacks in the United Kingdom and more conventional truck vehicle bombs, attacks in places like Saudi Arabia, Pakistan and Jordan. In Saudi Arabia, in particular, since the 12 May 2003 bombing in Riyadh, Saudi authorities have detained or killed all six of the known al Qaeda cell leaders in the kingdom as well as over 200 foot soldiers. The Saudis also have captured thousands of pounds of explosives, much of it in the form of fully assembled bombs ready for use. The crackdown in Saudi Arabia also has reduced the financial resources that al Qaeda has at its disposal. The Saudis have arrested several al Qaeda financial figures and killed the organization's leading financial fundraiser and propagandist. Al Qaeda leaders in South Asia currently are suffering from shortages of funds because many of their lines of contact to operatives in Saudi Arabia have been cut. Many of the group's traditional donors are afraid to give money to al Qaeda, or are instead backing more vibrant groups now in Iraq, or elsewhere. But we should not dwell on these successes because our progress will mean nothing if we back off any aspect of this war, the offensive dimension that the colonel so eloquently talked about in a second. While damaged, the remnants of al Qaeda central leadership are not destroyed or docile. Even as we meet today, they are plotting to conduct another major operation inside the United States in the coming months. Moreover, an operational infrastructure has moved in to replace that, which was under KSM.

Now bin Laden faces an increasingly difficult choice: hide to survive at the price of seeing al Qaeda deprived of his guidance, or risk capture by making contact with even a handful of top aids to motivate the group into action. It appears to us that he has chosen the latter. Even so, his reach no longer extends as far as it once did. Our disruption operations have degraded al Qaeda's ability to mount the types of multiyear, carefully planned operations that could earlier be orchestrated from a safe haven such as the one they had in Afghanistan. Nonetheless, al Qaeda's new leaders, despite their relative lack of experience, are still looking at the spectacular foreign attacks as their highest goal. Though most of the attacks we've seen in places like Madrid have a local flavor, there are other plots that are still directly connected to and driven by al Qaeda central leadership. They talk about having operatives already in place for these plots. They talk about attacking the same strategic targets we have worried about for years. And most strikingly, they have talked about how they are evolving to stay ahead of us. For example, they know we have tightened visa and security procedures and are constantly looking at ways to circumvent them. By necessity, they also have passed much of the initiative to al Qaeda's regional nodes. I'm talking about networks in Saudi Arabia, East Africa and Turkey, like the one that conducted the attacks in Istanbul last fall. I'm also talking about ally organizations, such as Zarqawi's group in Iraq, Jamal Islamia in Southeast Asia. These groups are planning their own lethal operations with only limited guidance and assistance from al Qaeda's central leadership.

As we continue to work to break the back of al Qaeda's organization, we are witnessing the rise of a worldwide movement in Southeast Asia, Europe, the Middle East and elsewhere that may not respond to al Qaeda's direction in formal terms but is infected by bin Laden's ideology that only strikes against America can lead to the attainment of the network's broader goals.

Despite all of our successes in the past three years, we are still—and this is important—we are still witnessing a pace and intensity of extremist operations that exceeds what we saw before 11 September. Most of the significant attacks we have seen in the past few years—Madrid, Morocco, Turkey—have been carried out by people who were inspired by, and somehow connected to, al Qaeda, but these are not classic al Qaeda operations. This underscores the challenge ahead. There is no near-term end to this war, and the next stages, we believe, will be more demanding than what we have already faced. For example, the tactics we have seen, and we continue to see, are changing. The Madrid bombings illustrate the broader network's ability to conduct devastating attacks with even simpler methods, in this case by using relatively small amounts of explosives hooked up to inexpensive cell phones. The lack of planning, local nature and criminal connections of the Madrid attack all show us how rapidly our understanding of this terrorist phenomenon must change if we are to keep pace.

To highlight this point, let me emphasize just one aspect of the Madrid bombing; the preparation time line. Explosives were acquired three weeks before the attacks; cell phones were bought eight days before; the van was stolen two weeks prior. Anyone who says major attacks require a high level of sophistication, international networks, years of advanced work and senior operatives, is dead wrong. The fact that al Qaeda Central is not orchestrating every attack does not mean that fewer people will die in terrorist attacks. In the midst of this movement toward decentralization, however, we must not lose sight of the fact that strategic attacks against us remain bin Laden's top priority. And he is focusing his energy and remaining resources on such an attack. The discovery of specific case reports of U.S. targets on computers in Pakistan and the United Kingdom and the recent decision to raise the threat level in parts of the country to orange are stark reminders of that very fact.

We also must not lose sight, as we move forward, on how chemical, biological, radiological and nuclear [CBRN] weapons may play into this equation. We have consistently warned of continuing terrorist interest in CBRN weapons. This interest remains strong, and in bin Laden's eyes, it's a religious obligation. The risk remains high that al Qaeda or another group will succeed in acquiring and then using CBRN material in a future attack.

For example, we believe that fatwas, such as those issued last year by a radical Saudi cleric justifying the use of chemical, biological and nuclear weapons, reflect clear operational intent, not just propaganda. From a mass-casualty perspective, we judge al Qaeda's anthrax program as one of the most immediate terrorist CBRN threats we are likely to face. Information we have indicates al Qaeda obtained the equipment and expertise necessary to produce biological agents. We are alarmed by several things: what we know the al Qaeda leadership learned from its past experience with the anthrax program, its proven ability to recruit scientists and procure necessary equipment, and the group's ability to keep it hidden.

My sense is that this audience, no doubt, understands the scope and the urgency of the problem we face. Let me now offer five thoughts our former DCI [Director of Central Intelligence] George Tenant left us on how to interpret this threat and how to attack it. I think he was dead on.

First, we must remember to maintain our edge in this war. Never forget why we are here, because the adversary will not. One senior al Qaeda detainee recently said, after months and months of detection, that if he were ever let go he would return to his mission. This adversary will never go home. We will either take them down or they will kill us.

Second, we need to ensure, over time, that this war has dimensions that go well beyond taking down individual terrorists, effective as that may be. We have watched as the schools supporting Jamal Islamia in Indonesia have grown. We have listened as al Qaeda's propaganda is released almost daily in Saudi Arabia. To win this war, over the course of months and years, we need to help prevent the rise of a generation of people who are poisoned by an ideology that endorses the murder of innocents as a means to address grievances and achieve salvation.

Third, we are working with partners, such as Saudi Arabia and Pakistan, who are at risk in this war. The aim of this adversary, as you know, is not only to kill us, but also to oust the leaders who work with us. This will become more critical in the future as the enemy becomes more dispersed, more clandestine, and burrows more deeply into our own societies. It may also become more challenging as some may see our mounting victories as a reason to ease up. We need to keep in mind through all our ups and downs and working with these partners that working with them is far easier than working without them. We must help them succeed. Their failures are our failures.

Fourth, we need to evolve with the adversary. We are witnessing the democratization of the threat: poison recipes shared over the Internet, designs for chemical devices traded among terrorists, unanswered questions about how far al Qaeda succeeded in its goal to acquire anthrax. We need to apply a 1 percent standard for threats related to these types of weapons. If there's a 1 percent chance the threat is accurate, that's good enough. Living up to this standard is hard, however. We chase phantom threats every day, but that's the price; we cannot afford a WMD attack. But it will happen if we do not track down every lead we see.

Fifth, we cannot turn our backs on Iraq. The work we have remaining in Iraq is daunting, not just because we need to stabilize this country, but because we should be worried about what the foreign fighters there do after they return home. Remember what happened after the Afghan experience of the late 1980s and early 1990s. In those cases foreign fighters returned to places such as Algeria and Egypt, and challenged ruling governments. We now have a situation where Syrians, Saudis, Sudanese, Jordanians and others have gathered in Iraq and are cementing the kind of ties that we will have to break for years to come. As it stands now in Iraq, the jihad is developing into a new draw for recruiting and fund raising that is growing increasingly complex and whose leadership espouses the same global agenda of targeting us and restoring a pan-Islamic caliphate.

In closing, let me summarize. We are dismantling al Qaeda, but we are also proceeding to the next phase of this war: the dismantling of the groups that believe al Qaeda showed them the way. Our mission is to halt them; never forget, never lose that sense of urgency and never stop.

MEESE: Thank you very much, Steve. I want to thank all the panelists both for their insights as well as for sticking to their time limits. So we have plenty of time for some great questions from the audience. Sir, right here.

AUDIENCE: Luis Gutiérrez from Mexico, Latin American Circle for International Studies. To Mr. Levitt and Mr. Nicgorski, what do you know about the possible contacts or relations between al Qaeda and the terrorist groups in Latin America, South America, specifically Columbia, the FARC? And second, Mr. Nicgorski, you mentioned criminal contacts by al Qaeda or the groups acting there. What kinds of contacts do you think may have been used by al Qaeda for this purpose? Thank you.

LEVITT: The strongest link is not in Columbia, but farther south in the tri-border area, where Argentina, Paraguay and Brazil meet. There is a significant amount of activity there by a variety of groups, and it's another great example of where members of a variety of groups work together, particularly Hamas, Hezbollah—a very strong Hezbollah, a Lebanese Hezbollah-Shia stronghold in the tri-border area. But despite being Shia and Hamas and al Qaeda being Sunni there is significant crossover with Hamas activities and even with al Qaeda activists as well. There's been a significant U.S. effort, in cooperation with allies, to deal with that threat, which predates 9/11 but really picked up significantly post-9/11.

We've seen some benefits there to the extent that some senior Hezbollah members have moved on.

Interestingly, some of them have moved on to Africa, and we've now seen some of the Mafia-style shakedowns, which Hezbollah was known for in Latin America, happening in West Africa, in locations like Angola where we have seen some of these individuals go. It's another good example of how terrorists are not only *revolutionary*, but as you heard *evolutionary*, and how what we're dealing with is a global threat that will move across borders very quickly. As the colonel said, we will not be able to pick them up on the radar just by looking out the window.

MEESE: Mike, do you have anything to add to that on the Latin America?

NAGATA: No, I completely agree. There clearly are connections to a variety of groups down the tri-border area. From the department's point of view, it simply highlights the difficulty we are having in how do we conduct even DoD intelligence operations, let alone other kinds of military operations. Those are all nation-states. We're not at war with them. We've got diplomatic relations, economic relations, all kinds of relationships there, to include commercial interests. How do we get in there without upsetting the apple cart and still do the things that the president and the secretary of defense have charged us with doing?

MEESE: Steve, on the second question.

NICGORSKI: Sure. On the criminal networks, I think this phenomenon is not necessarily new. Al Qaeda and other terrorist groups have leveraged criminal networks in the past, to provide them documents and to provide them access to contraband that they may need for their operations. And a lot of those contacts remain established to this day. One of the criminal enterprises that—and this gets to the question of Latin America—that we are most interested in right now, in terms of investigating the linkages that might be there, is the human smuggling networks, in particular in terms of threats to the homeland and operatives that may use points south of our border to infiltrate into the United States. We have seen some of these linkages between those types of criminal enterprises and groups like al Qaeda.

MEESE: The question up front here. They want it on the microphone, sir. That way, you're saved for posterity in the Eisenhower archives.

AUDIENCE: I'm Bernard Brown from the National Committee on American Foreign Policy. I have a question for Mr. Levitt and perhaps the other two. One of the controversial questions about the war in Iraq is whether there were links between al Qaeda and the Iraqi regime. Some of the critics argue that the war on Iraq was a distraction from the real war on al Qaeda, and that it simply provoked Iraqi nationalism and recruits, helped recruit more terrorists. What's your take on this?

LEVITT: Well, I've written for the record and feel pretty strongly that the link to al Qaeda terrorism in Iraq was weak. Was weak. If we wanted to deal with state-sponsored terrorism, we have faced larger, more significant state-sponsored threats from Iran and Syria, which is not to say there were not links to Saddam. That was not the only, or I would argue even primary, reason for going into Iraq based on the information we had at the time. We were very concerned about WMD issues and, so, for the record, I also supported the war and I don't regret doing so. But I think that there have been political reasons why the terrorism link has continued to be propagated, and I think that's unfortunate. I think there is no denying—and, just from my counterterrorism colleagues, those of us who especially were in and now are out of government, there is consensus across partisan lines—the fact that we have a much larger terrorism problem in Iraq now than we did before. In fact, the ability for al Qaeda and related groups to radicalize and recruit worldwide has increased since 9/11, not decreased, and that's despite tremendous success. Some of my co-panelists have talked about the need for us to focus, and I completely concur, not only tactically but strategically. We are winning the war on the battlefield, and we are losing the war of ideas, which is a very, very serious problem.

MEESE: Any other comments? Question in the back there.

AUDIENCE: Hi I'm Mary Gillespie with American University. This is basically directed at Mr. Levitt, but either of you. It's about terrorists and the world. What about organizations, terrorists organizations, such as the IRA or any paramilitary group in the north of Ireland, that are really more or less dismantling at this point and are not really the strength that we were seeing in the early 1990s and late 1980s? Would you say that they still have links with the Middle East? And regarding Northern Ireland, do you see any similarities between, more specifically, the Israeli-Palestinian conflict in Northern Ireland? And is there any hope to maybe using political means similar to the way that they're trying to do things in Northern Ireland at this point in time?

LEVITT: There's been a theme on this panel—several really—but one of them is that this is a war driven by intelligence, and this is a good example. Intelligence will dictate the extent to which various militias and terrorist groups in Ireland or elsewhere are, in fact, still involved in terrorism or other forms of violence, or are not, and will verify the extent to which they are maintaining links with groups including groups in the Middle East. There have been, historically, of course, links between Libya and the IRA and other links—links to South America as well. But my impression is those are not the significant links we're looking at today. In terms of parallels to the Israeli-Palestinian peace process, yes, there are parallels. How useful they are nowadays, I think, is less a factor of the utility of a political science model being applicable across geographic boundaries and more one of the realities in the Middle East today, where, I would argue, you have a lack of leadership on both sides of the Israeli-Palestinian conflict, a much more serious one on the Palestinian side. There I see the only real hope for progress in the near term being a pullout—unilateral, if it has to be—from Gaza. I'd like to be more optimistic, but we can want peace there until we're blue in the face, and if the leaders in the region don't, for whatever reason, then we'll just get blue in the face.

MEESE: Next question, right up here.

AUDIENCE: Thank you. Philippe Errera from the planning staff of the French Foreign Ministry. I want to thank the members of the panel for superb presentations. I have a question more particularly for Matt Levitt—though any of the other members might like to comment. You all said that we had been successful, in part due to American capabilities, and in part due to a strong degree of international cooperation militarily in terms of law enforcement and so on in killing or capturing hundreds or thousands of al Qaeda operatives. My concern is that our success—rather, our success in making the world safer, which is perhaps a more honest way of saying it than our success in getting rid of terrorism—doesn't have to do with how many hundreds of thousands we have killed, but how many hundreds, thousands or hundreds of thousands will be out there in the years to come, who feel that jihadist ideology speaks for them. I think that figure is one that we don't know, and we don't know it, not because it's out there and our intelligence can't get it, but because most of the people who will either act for or support these jihadist groups two, three, five years down the road don't necessarily know it today. I would argue that our actions and the way we portray this fight and this war have some impact on this. My question is, "Aren't we doing, to some extent, bin Laden's bidding for him? Aren't we allowing him to have the cake and eat it too?" That is to say to have operational advantages, such as the resiliency you get from the decentralized network, while having the cohesiveness of a single ideology, by saying we're fighting a single enemy, or by saying that the operational links between different groups are tantamount to cohesiveness ideologically. In other words, by helping them think that al Qaeda is speaking for them when they ask themselves, "Who is the enemy?"

LEVITT: You're going to have to start asking my colleagues some questions. I'm sure that you guys have some input on this, and it's a very important question. I've said already we are not doing as good a job as we could be at winning the war of ideas. But I also think that you know significant study has demonstrated that you can look at this problem from two angles, both legitimate, but in this case I think we need to focus on one. You can look at the root causes—what drives an individual to adhere to jihadist ideology and, beyond that, to take action on that ideology and engage in violence. You also need to look at this kind of top-down from the organizational perspective. Really, many studies have shown that it is the organization that radicalizes to the point of violence. Yes, there are root causes, but if you look, for example, in the Israeli-Palestinian context, many studies have shown that without Palestinian extremist groups radicalizing society in the West Bank and Gaza and inciting them against Israel and against the United States at times, what you have are very angry and very poor individuals, who lack legitimate political outlets, and who are as angry or more angry at their own leaders as they are at anybody else. What pushes them to become violent? And so what's important is to focus, not only on the root causes—definitely—but also on the organization.

Look, I often put it to people like this: Someone has pointed a gun to our heads; we are fools if we don't get that gun pointed down. Tactically, we have to do that, and if that gives them some rhetorical advantage, that's a consequence. But after the gun is pointed down, we also need to figure out why that gun was pointed at us in the first place so it won't be pointed there again. The tactical answers to counterterrorism are important, but I would not say that we are giving bin Laden any kind of advantage. The rhetoric is as much out of desperation as anything else. Just because people are recruitable on being incited doesn't necessarily mean that they will, in fact, get to the point where they will conduct violence. There are opportunities in there and along that process to thwart that trend. So I think it's a little more complicated than just whether we are giving bin Laden his cake and letting him eat it, too. We have to fight the fight.

MEESE: Mike?

NAGATA: I once had a commander who told me, "Nagata, never lose the opportunity to keep your mouth shut." But I'm going to violate that rule here. To echo a particular point I think you tried to make, whether or not we are doing UBL's [Usama bin Laden] bidding or doing the bidding of the people that would do us harm, I guess I'll betray a little bit of a military bias. I think the people who are in Guantanamo today—the al Qaeda operatives who are in Guantanamo, the people whom we have taken on in a variety of ways, on battlefields, in a clandestine war that is being run by the CIA and many other people—would disagree with the notion they're doing their bidding. However, I take your point. There is a consequence, predictably a consequence, to taking action against those people who are an immediate threat to us.

Having said that, a thought that occurred to me through the last three questions is that much of the intellectual struggle we are having today is over "whether we are building more terrorists or not," or over "whether or not there are links between al Qaeda and the former Hussein regime," "whether or not non-Islamic, non-jihadist terrorist organizations or criminal organizations are part of this global network." One of the reasons we are really struggling with that is because we don't have a metric for measuring these things. There's no U.S. government publication that says, "If you meet these following criteria, this constitutes a link between a WMD capability and a nation-state or a terrorist group." There are lots of metrics, but there it depends on who you ask in this city or in the intelligence community. We have never had to do this before, I guess is the point I'm trying to make.

Before 9/11, our principal challenge was, how far will that ICBM [intercontinental ballistic missile] fly, and how much warning time do we have and must we build the capability for interdicting it, deterring it, what have you. Now, it is, as the previous gentleman asked, "Wasn't there a link between al Qaeda and the Hussein regime?" Well, what constitutes a link? Case in point, and this is not classified. Once we seized some documents at one point that were airline ticket stubs in Afghanistan, and they were airline tickets that showed a number of very interesting places on them, way outside of Iraq, arguably a pattern that an al Qaeda operative might be traveling on. But does that constitute a link? Well, he was a jihadist, he has some family or personal or operational relationships with people that are either in al Qaeda or know somebody that's in al Qaeda. So, hopefully, you catch what I'm saying here. Just the struggle of sorting out what constitutes an action that we take, that leads to someone adopting an anti-U.S. attitude is something that we don't have a metric for measuring. The city is full of opinions on that, but they're all different. Now, that sounds like an excuse for not answering your question, but it really is a struggle.

MEESE: Steve, would you like to comment on that?

NICGORSKI: I would say, you know, winning the war of ideas is really the main objective in the following phases of the war on terror, but the intelligence community can't win that war alone. I mean, to win the war of ideas, that's going to take much more than what the intelligence community can provide. That's going to take a total USG [U.S. government] effort, international effort, and a comprehensive strategy to win the war on ideas. Second is the idea that—and I think Matt put it very well in terms of a gun pointed to your head—the metrics often used are how many have we killed or captured. That is one of the metrics we have to gauge success. But it's not only in terms of the numbers we captured and killed; it's in terms of what they were doing at the time we captured and killed them. A lot of that doesn't make it into the press for obvious reasons. But hundreds of lives have been saved. We have to do that. So I just wanted to make that point. I think I'll leave it there.

MEESE: OK. Question way in the back there.

AUDIENCE: Bill Jones from Executive Intelligence Review. One of the most devastating recent attacks that has been made—a horrific attack—was in the city of Beslan [Russia] with the school children. Whoever would like to comment on this, what is the relationship to the situation in Chechnya? How does that play a role in terms of the al Qaeda networks? Do you see this as a part of what we have to deal with? If so, are the Russians doing the right thing? Is there the type of cooperation that this situation will be dealt with? Thank you.

NAGATA: I'll give you my brief view of that. In a way, I'm going to repeat what I just said. To what degree do we think there's a relationship? To what [degree] do we think there is a cause and effect? To what degree do we think—here is a question I've seen posed in newspapers since the story broke—this is simply an extension of the secular Chechen separatist movement, or is this an extension of a more insidious, proliferating jihadist campaign? And like I said, I'm repeating myself. Boy, how do you measure that? We don't have any direct interest in that particular activity; we have sucked up a lot of data about that, took a lot of imagery. We know certain things about what happened there and what didn't happen there. But how do you take that data—and this is an analyst's challenge; it's a challenge we're confronting DoD and IC [intelligence community] analysts with today—and ask, "OK, now, try to answer the question, is this an extension of the secular Chechnya independence movement, or is this something else?" And today, the reality is, we get a lot of different opinions. The policy problem for us is, "Which opinion do you use to make an executive decision?" This is something we are interested in, this is something we're not interested in. This is something we're willing to devote the capability against or we're not.

NICGORSKI: In general, we face a challenge as analysts—being the chief of a group of many analysts—when dealing with the terrorism problem (and having been a former analyst on the former Soviet Union). When you're analyzing a situation in a place like Russia, the problem is bounded by geography, it's bounded by history, and it's bounded by the economy. But we're dealing with the terrorist phenomenon. It's boundless. It's not bounded by geography; it's not bounded by a particular history; and it's not bounded by any kind of economy. That's what the challenge is when we try then to answer specific questions in terms of how the situation in Chechnya relates to the global jihadist movement. Certainly there are linkages. But defining exactly what those linkages are and what they mean, it's easier just to say they're there, we see them. To say exactly what they mean, and then try to rank-order them with respect to how they compare to al Qaeda's relationship with Jamal Islamia, or with Zarqawi's group, or something like that is a really difficult challenge.

MEESE: We have time for one more question. Let me go right to the back there. Good.

AUDIENCE: My name is Mark Lambert. I'm from the Army's Logistics Transformation Agency. And this has to deal with the question that you just answered. Does it matter, really, if there is a link between the jihadist terrorism and the secularist terrorism? I mean, this is the global war on terrorism, period, not the global war on jihadists.

MEESE: You just gave the answer that you almost gave on the last one.

LEVITT: Yes and no. The question I think was, "Is this international jihadist terrorism linked to a secular movement that is something other than terrorism?" A guerilla war that may be legal, may be not, but may be something other than terrorism. Hezbollah in Lebanon engages in terrorism, and it engages in guerilla warfare. Those are different and maybe neither is acceptable, but they need to be dealt with differently. I think part of the answer to both questions is what Steve said earlier: What is the nature of the activity that the individual or the group was involved in? When you mention the Chechen example, two things come to mind. I worked 9/11 at the FBI, and we now know from the 9-11 Commission Report that several of the hijackers originally wanted to go to Chechnya. So we know that there is, at least in the mind of jihadist, a link. That's more operational-intangible.

The Israelis just this week released, on the other hand, a CD of posters and incitement materials that they confiscated in the West Bank from Hamas student groups, which are all about linking in picture-format Hamas, al Qaeda and the Chechyan movement. Pictures of Yassin, bin Laden, and Katab, or others from the Chechen movement, maps of Greater Palestine with Afghanistan and Chechnya. How significant is that? It's not operational. It's showing a common ideology, an incitement. That's the type of thing that we need to work out more.

I was a terrorism analyst for the government. I'm now a terrorism analyst outside the government. I'm also a professor now, and so maybe I should really be the one calling for more measurement and more quantitative and qualitative analysis. But I really think that when it comes to the best counterterrorism analysis, unfortunately, it's about patterns and trends. And the whole ball game, like you heard, is about figuring out which pattern and which trend is really telling. To do that you need to develop expertise, not only in these groups, which is the thing everybody is doing today, but as Steve said, in the area, in the politics, and the economy. You actually need to understand what the Chechen issue is all about. You have to understand why it is that a good percentage of second-generation Muslims in Europe are extremely radicalized. These things aren't happening in a vacuum.

MEESE: Unless there are any final comments.

NAGATA: Just one quick comment. I think it does matter. I agree with you it is a global war on terrorism, as the president has defined it. However, we cannot do everything all the time. We can't do everything simultaneously. We've got to pick where we're going to fight kinetically, nonkinetically. We've got to figure out what the right sequence is in a campaign that is going to last, potentially, a generation in order to eventually solve this problem piece by piece, operation by operation, activity by activity. So it does matter. Whether or not idealistically we want to take on all of terrorism, we've got to disassemble it at a certain pace and in a certain way because we just can't do everything simultaneously.

MEESE: As we wrap up the panel, I want to thank them for three things. First, you can see the great amount of intellectual insight that each of them brings in their communities, in their groups, in their organizations, and that's great. Second, I thank them for actually taking the time to come over here. Each of you, I know for a fact, has had over 100 e-mails that have arrived at your desk while you've been sitting here talking with us. And third, the easy answer when we invited the real experts in their area to come in here would have been to take the relatively easier, less risky thing, and say, "Oh, no. I'm too busy. I'm going to be called in and won't be able to do it." But to come here and put the ideas on the table is the way that we get informed, the way the ideas get sharpened and the way that eventually being able to link the operations, the intelligence and the intellectuals will be successful in winning the global war on terrorism. So please join me in thanking the panel for their great comments today.

RYAN: And thank you very much, Mike, for the great moderating job you did here today.

CLOSING ADDRESS

TIME FOR A ROBUST DEBATE: KEY FOREIGN POLICY ISSUES FOR THE ELECTION

Lee H. Hamilton, President and Director, Woodrow Wilson Center for International Scholars

Introduction by Mark Chichester, Director, Institute for International Public Policy

Summary

Lee H. Hamilton

- America needs and deserves from its presidential candidates a "serious, civil, enlightened discussion" of national security issues.
- Regrettably, however, the presidential campaigns have emphasized, to an extraordinary degree and in general terms, the personal attributes of "strength" and "leadership." Rather than engage the public on the pressing matters of the future, President George W. Bush and Sen. John Kerry are wasting this opportunity by placing an extraordinary emphasis on the past.
- We must demand more of our candidates, that actual substance be injected into the debate: A functional democracy requires not only engaged, but also informed citizens.
- The American public wants to hear what will be done—not only the choices the candidates will make, but also the manner in which they will make them.
- The current political election atmosphere runs counter to the magic of the "dialogue of democracy." Television debates have evolved into simply making assertions and seeing if one can come up with catchy phrases and good sound bites. The facts have been lost. Lots of discussions produce heat, but not many produce light.
- Instead of these cheapened television debates, the candidates should videotape weekly addresses regarding a specific issue, and they should be shown to the public one after the other. That way, honest and intelligent discussions can be had.

• There are two enemies al Qaeda and radical Islam. The strategy to combat the former is more clearly defined: We need to play offense in order to win. However, the latter, an extremist ideological movement that is not tied down geographically, appears quite problematic. This long-term, ideological threat must be tackled using all of the tools of American power—military, economic and moral—and integrating them.

• Terrorism and Iraq are only part of the swelling turmoil around the world. There are difficult questions the candidates are not addressing. We have a responsibility to get these questions answered:

1. What do Bush and Kerry intend to do regarding North Korea and Iran?

2. How do they plan to use the unrivaled power, idealism and pragmatism of the United States to preserve the American way of life and achieve global stability?

3. What are the candidates' plans for Pakistan and Saudi Arabia? Pakistan is vital to the United States, but no progress is being made toward democracy, not to mention, it is still selling nuclear materials to our enemies. Meanwhile, the oil-for-security arrangement with Saudi Arabia is no longer satisfactory. We must demand pragmatic reform in this region.

4. We must win this war of ideas with the Islamic world; we cannot win this war on terrorism without their hearts and minds. They need hope. Yet, how do we have a genuine dialogue with Islamic world?

5. How will we deal with the proliferation of nuclear weapons? Iran's and North Korea's nuclear programs are matters that must be confronted, yet the candidates are still avoiding talking about this vital security issue.

6. What about competition for trade from China and from India? What is their solution for global poverty, which condemns half of the world's population, 3 billion of whom are under 25 years old, to live on less than $2 a day?

• How does one inject substance into the campaign? One approach might be to develop a campaign framework whereby each week for several weeks, the candidates focus on a specific policy issue, presenting—in depth—their positions and plans.

• More broadly, it is the responsibility of all Americans to hold candidates accountable. Dwight D. Eisenhower once stated, "The history of free men is never really written by chance, but by choice." The choice our leaders must make—and that we must demand of them—is a dialogue on the issues. Otherwise, we leave tomorrow's history to chance.

Analysis

The basic theme of Lee Hamilton's talk was "How can we inject more substance into this [presidential campaign] debate?" He reflected on the National Commission on Terrorist Attacks Upon the United States' research into the substance of the candidates' talks leading up to the election in 2000. In its examination of the 2000 campaign dialogue, the 9-11 Commission, as it is also known, found only one reference to terrorism, a topic that should have received much more attention considering the terrorist activities directed at the United States in the previous four years. While he suggested a pragmatic mechanism to structure the formal debate, the underlying message of the presentation was more subtle. To get the candidates to address the major national security issues of the day directly, Americans must gain a more informed appreciation of the issues. The American people must not accept assertions over facts in television advertisements, sound bites for substance in debates, and tough-sounding denunciations for clear diplomatic strategy on crucial issues. Only an informed electorate demanding democratic dialogue will persuade the candidates to engage in serious, civil and enlightened debate.

To set the stage for his later remarks, Hamilton offered a scathing review of recent election year attempts at democratic discourse. He lamented that for all our effort " . . . we can't seem to put together a substantive debate." Blending a combination of idealism and pragmatism, which he advocates, Hamilton offered a specific methodology for approaching a substantive debate in which the candidates would be forced to address, in depth, the momentous national issues of our day. Then he compromised, conceding that candidates need only offer a sense of the choices they are going to make and the way they will approach the tough issues that do not lend themselves to prescriptive solutions. The objective appeared to be less about understanding the candidates' specific policy positions and more about the discovery and refinement of alternative policy approaches and their potential consequences through informed dialogue.

Hamilton posed several rhetorical questions for the presidential candidates. Using this technique, he suggested crucial issues for campaign debate focus, summarized the key themes of the conference, and provided a context to offer some thoughts on how selected issues could be tackled. His first set of questions addressed the issue that clearly dominates the current discussions of national security policy: the war on terrorism. Accepting the strategy of decisive, offensive action as the generally agreed upon policy to address the threat posed by al Qaeda, Hamilton explored two subsequent challenges facing policy-makers. In order to map a way forward, policy-makers must clearly define the enemy. This task is not as easy as it might first appear. Drawing from the findings of the 9-11 Commission, Hamilton suggested future enemies will be radical Islamists. Defining an enemy in terms of an ideology, as opposed to the more traditional method of geographic or state affiliation, poses a unique challenge to policy-makers. The newly defined enemy will need to be defeated with equally unique and comprehensive strategies. To combat these new threats, policy-makers will be required to integrate and balance the application of all elements of national power. The nation will have to rely more heavily on soft-power instruments such as information, economics and diplomacy to be successful against this new enemy. Military power will still play a role, but it will not be as decisive as it was when facing a nation-state adversary.

Another category of questions related to the war on terrorism dealt with the larger issue of how can we deepen our understanding of and enhance our relationship with the Islamic world. Arguably, our nation can defeat any enemy it can identify. But to defeat Islamic terrorism we must understand and address the underlying causes of terrorism and the grievances many in the Arab and Islamic worlds attribute to us. Hamilton suggested that to succeed we must win the war of ideas, a war that must be fought on a new battleground. Public diplomacy to shape our future policy toward Saudi Arabia, Pakistan, Palestine and Indonesia must be accompanied by a more indirect pressure intended for the Islamic populace. This pressure would be characterized by activities that facilitate educational opportunities and exposure to Western and democratic thought. Examples offered included support to libraries, academic scholarships and military exchange programs. Over time, these activities would be expected to help shape Islamic opinion and create an environment in which diplomatic objectives could be reached. This notion is not without precedent. It has been employed successfully in Central and South America over the past 20 years and has fostered principally democratic governance throughout a region that was dominated by communist and socialist dictatorships in the 1980s.

The final category of questions posed by Hamilton addressed the challenges of nuclear proliferation, global poverty and the various economic policy decisions that dominate our relationships with other world powers including Russia, China, India and the European Union. Hamilton emphasized the importance of economic and trade policy because of its immediate impact on the American public and, therefore, domestic politics. He expressed amazement at the lack of debate on trade policy, noting that what dialogue does emerge is devoid of substance and plagued by generalities. Hamilton's observations on the state of pubic debate related to economic policy and nuclear proliferation were among the most provoking in his lecture. For those in the audience engaged in the debate from an academic or policy perspective, these are among the most thoroughly examined areas of study. In fact, every panel discussion during the conference touched on these policy issues in one way or another. Hamilton's observation that the public debate is anemic is particularly troubling on two counts. First, the use of these indirect approaches relying on soft power is vital to any effective strategy in this new war. Second, the price of a policy error in terms of the potential global and domestic impact is staggering.

The challenges the nation faces in this time of change are great, no matter who wins the election. Hamilton declared that one of the candidates ". . . is going to have to govern the politically divided country and deal with these challenges." How we face these challenges will affect both our physical security and our democratic institutions. The American people deserve leaders who will use the opportunity offered by the campaign season to educate and inform them on crucial national security issues. By engaging in informed, direct and civil dialogue instead of shallow, partisan, political rhetoric, the candidates could lead

America in a quest for deeper understanding and more informed action. As the candidates address these challenges, Hamilton asked perhaps the most crucial question of his soliloquy, "Are we going to have the leadership that will bring the American people along . . . " or will we " . . . leave tomorrow's history to chance, not to choice." The candidates could demonstrate leadership by facilitating the dialogue and preparing the American people for the challenges ahead.

Most importantly, Hamilton did not let the public off the hook. It is not enough to look to the candidates for leadership. He reminded us that as Americans, we have a responsibility in the democratic process. We must demand enlightened debate. We must be mentally disciplined to gain an appreciation for the complexity of the issues. Having gathered that knowledge, we must demand rigor and depth from the candidates in their policy debates. The national security challenges before us must be dealt with; they will not go away. Hamilton wisely invoked the magic of democratic dialogue as the surest method to arrive at an informed choice for action.

Transcript

ANNOUNCER: Once again, ladies and gentlemen, Brigadier General Kevin T. Ryan.

BRIGADIER GENERAL KEVIN T. RYAN: Ladies and gentlemen, for the capstone presentation of our conference, I have the pleasure of asking Mr. Mark Chichester to make the introduction of our final speaker. Mr. Chichester is the director at the International Institute for Public Policy at the United Negro College Fund Special Programs Corporation, a co-sponsor with the Army of the Eisenhower program. He and his institute put together an amazing program of speakers and panelists last May for a daylong seminar on cultural competence in our national security institutions. Mr. Chichester is also a member of the District of Columbia Human Rights Commission.

Ladies and gentlemen, Mr. Mark Chichester.

MARK CHICHESTER: Good afternoon. As a member of the 2004 Eisenhower National Security Series working group, it is a great honor and pleasure to introduce the conference's culminating speaker. I would be remiss if I didn't take just a second to recognize and commend the series and General Schoomaker on a year of stimulating and well-organized events, including the one that General Ryan just referenced, where we looked at cultural competence as a national security imperative. It is just one example of the success of the Eisenhower Series, that includes not only the traditional audiences stakeholders in the national security debate and discussion but reaches beyond that to an increasingly robust and diverse audience as well.

Our speaker is the Honorable Lee H. Hamilton. Mr. Hamilton has supported the important efforts of the Eisenhower Series since its inception three years ago, and his organization was, in fact, the first to co-sponsor an event with the series. He heads the Woodrow Wilson Center, the nation's official memorial to President Woodrow Wilson. This is a center that provides one of those rare spaces where scholars, policymakers and business leaders engage in nonpartisan dialogue on important policy issues, their relevance and their impact globally. I should note also that we have the pleasure of having two of our very own fellows from the institute working at the center.

Mark Chichester

Prior to heading up the Woodrow Wilson Center, Mr. Hamilton served for nearly two and a half decades as a United States congressman from Indiana, during which time he served as chairman and ranking member of the House Committee on Foreign Affairs, now known as the Committee on International Relations. He also chaired the subcommittee on Europe and the Middle East, the Permanent Select Committee on Intelligence and the Select Committee to Investigate Covert Arms Transactions with Iran. Mr. Hamilton has long been a leading voice on foreign affairs, with particular interests and involvement in promoting democracy and market reforms and in promoting peace and stability in the Middle East. He served on the influential Hart-Rudman Commission and co-chaired the Baker-Hamilton Commission to investigate security issues at Los Alamos. He serves now on the advisory council for the U.S. Department of Homeland Security and was appointed to serve as vice chairman of the 9-11 Commission, an independent bipartisan body created by congressional legislation and the signature of the president to prepare a full and complete account of the tragic circumstances around the terrorist attacks of Sept. 11, 2001.

Mr. Hamilton has received awards too many to list here, but I'll make mention of just a few that I think are noteworthy. He's a recipient of the Paul H. Nitze Award for Distinguished Authority on National Security Affairs. He has received medallions from both the CIA and the DIA [Defense Intelligence Agency]. This was some years ago, so there can be no accusation that folks were looking at the future and the debate that would take place about the role of these two agencies in our intelligence apparatus. And especially noteworthy, the Eisenhower National Security Series Award was bestowed on Mr. Hamilton. So we want to take a moment to recognize that one in particular. He is a graduate of DePauw University and Indiana University School of Law, and he studied for a time at Goethe University in Germany. Mr. Hamilton also holds honorary degrees from colleges and universities across this great nation—again, too many to list here. We're privileged to have with us, to frame the issues taken up over these past two days, a statesman truly of the highest order. Without further ado, I give you Mr. Hamilton.

THE HONORABLE LEE H. HAMILTON: Well, good afternoon to all of you. Mark, thank you for your gracious comments. You did your homework, and I appreciate that. I served in the Congress for 34 years. And the day I retired, I said that I had cast over 16,000 votes and that I was retiring. I did a little bragging, I guess, and it's always a mistake to brag. I went back to my office and had a call from a constituent, who said, "Lee, I understand you announced your retirement today." I said, "Yes." He said, "I understand you cast over 16,000 votes." I said, "Yes." He said, "I want you to know you finally made a decision I agree with."

Mark, that's why I like these nice introductions. I've had a few of the other kind. We had a speaker of the U.S. House some years ago; some of you may remember his name, John McCormick. He was a terrific debater. He'd get tired sitting up there on the chair, so he'd come down on the floor and invariably somebody on the other side of the isle would irritate him. He'd turn to that person and, you know how the elaborate courtesies are, he said, "I hold the gentleman from Iowa in minimum high regard." I want you to know that I hold each of you in maximum high regard, because of your extraordinary participation in this series of very serious efforts to understand some of the national security problems of this country.

I want to acknowledge, especially, General Schoomaker, who has had a marvelous, distinguished record in military service. He is one of our most decorated officers, held in the highest esteem in this country. He and his staff have put together this program and have had a successful and stimulating conference that you have participated in.

I heard the sigh of relief that went up from you when General Ryan said this is the final speaker. And then Mark said "the culminating speaker," and you almost broke out in applause, because you saw the finish line coming up. I've looked over that program, you've had a remarkable group of experts here. Anybody who went through all of this and didn't learn a lot would be pretty thick, I would think.

So you had an unusual opportunity. It's an extraordinary credit to the Army that they sponsor this kind of a conference and do it in such a highly professional and very competent way. I think this kind of dialogue I'm going to speak a little bit about that in a moment is just essential for the country.

The Wilson Center, where I work, has been very pleased with Rob Litwak's good direction—many of you know him—to partner with you in the development and sponsorship of this program. I couldn't help but think when I saw the image of General Eisenhower here, President Eisenhower, how very pleased he would be to know that the Army is making this kind of an effort.

I had a lot of fun while I was in the Congress. We're in election season now. I thought I might pass on to you my all-time favorite bumper sticker. We had in the Congress several years ago a Catholic priest. I don't think a Catholic priest can serve in the Congress anymore, but Father (Robert) Drinan was a priest. He was running for reelection in Boston, and he had an all-time great bumper sticker. It said, "Vote for Father Drinan or go to 'hell." I never had that kind of courage myself, but always admired it with Father Drinan.

Lee H. Hamilton

Well, I want to talk to you a bit about the presidential campaign and the dialogue of democracy. The stakes in this election are very high. Every time I pick up the paper I see another politician saying this is the most important election in the history of the country. I guess I've said that on at least 15 or 20 elections myself. But I understand that it is an important election. The next president will have momentous choices to make that will directly affect your life and mine and your families' lives and the lives of all Americans for years to come, and of course people across the globe. So I think, and I trust you think, that a robust debate on these great big national security issues is in order.

There are so many questions out there. I'm going to raise a few of them, in a minute, that need addressing. Several months ago, I was hopeful that we were going to have a unique election—unique because foreign policy questions appeared to be playing a central role. I thought, at least for a while, that they would be seriously addressed. And, of course, to some extent, they have been. The presidential candidates have focused a lot of remarks on the war on terrorism, or at least a part of it. But I'll tell you a familiar disappointment strikes me every four years.

Each presidential election, I hope for serious and civil and enlightened discussion of the great national security challenges. And each time, I have been disappointed. In foreign policy debates in the campaigns, we hear a lot of reference to the generalities: strength, leadership and security. And we should. And this campaign is no different. But there is a glaring lack of discussion about a plan in Iraq, or on the generational struggle against Islamic terrorism, or for securing the weapons of mass destruction around the world.

The words "Iran" and "North Korea" hardly ever come up. Indeed, they are mentioned about as frequently as the word "terrorism" was mentioned in the 2000 campaign. Mark mentioned I served on that 9-11 Commission, and we got interested in the question of how much the candidates talked about terrorism in the lead-up to the election in the year 2000. What we found was one reference—one—to terrorism. And that, after the World Trade Center bombing, the embassy bombings, the Millennium Plot, the bombing of the USS Cole in October of 2000, while in this campaign, at least from my perception, there has been an extraordinary emphasis on the past—events that happened 35 years ago. The candidates are spending too much time looking back, and not enough time looking forward. I believe the American voter cares more about the choices the candidates offer tomorrow, than the choices they made, as important as they are, decades ago.

And what bothers me, this year as in the past, is that we're missing a real opportunity in this country to address these global challenges and the U.S. role in the world. In a democracy, it is not only the choices that you make that are important; it is also the manner in which you make the choices. The 2004 election may be a precursor to extraordinary choices, but you'd never figure that out from the campaign, thus far.

So I come this afternoon, and I ask the question: How can we inject more substance into this debate? I believe that President George Bush and Sen. John Kerry are able and honorable men. I do not look upon them as enemies. You and I have enough enemies in this world and they do, too. But they are rivals. Surely, I say to myself, they must grow weary of pollsters and packagers and handlers and scripted appearances. I've been through 34 campaigns. I know a little bit about scripted appearances. Surely, they must say to themselves, "The American people deserve better. The American dialogue of democracy mandates better." And these tumultuous times cry out for Isaiah's plea, "Come, let us reason together." But for whatever reason, we can't seem to put together a substantive debate. The truth of the matter is that the dialogue of democracy does not always work. Many discussions produce a lot of heat, but not many of them produce light.

An adversary will be attacked, without an examination of the merits of their ideas. Somewhere, I have no doubt, the candidates have detailed policy papers, but I'm not sure anybody reads them. Maybe a Stanford professor reads them. I don't know. But they don't get out very much. Television advertisements are treated as news. More and more television news is made up of assertions, not facts. The debates become an opportunity to string together sound bites. I know how these candidates are prepped for the debates. I participated in that process, and the whole process is to see if you can come up with a good sound bite. So I'm not a great fan of presidential debates. The quality of discourse reminds me of talk radio, which is not exactly the pinnacle of rational discourse in this country.

Years ago, I suggested adding a new element to presidential campaigns. In each of, say, six weeks after Labor Day, the candidates would be required to address a single major issue. The topics would be obvious. This year topics would be Iraq, the war on terror, the economy, maybe healthcare. Each week the candidates would give a major statement, the same week, on the issue, and then submit themselves to a questioning by a panel of experts. Instead of the debate format, which puts too much emphasis on one-liners, the candidates would appear alone. Those appearances would take about an hour. They would be videotaped simultaneously to avoid giving one candidate the advantage of going second. The two presentations could then be broadcast to the American people, in juxtaposition to one another, to enable the American people to make a comparison on their positions.

Now, my proposal is not perfect by a long stretch, but I just think we've got to find a way in this country to induce our presidential candidates to debate the real issues. I understand that the responsibility for the campaign falls on the candidates. They are the nominees of their party. They are the leaders. They are entitled to set forth the agenda as they see it. But the rest of us have a responsibility as well—to find ways to put before the voter the best information possible about the choices that lie ahead. I believe, and I hope you believe, that for a democracy to work, you not only have to have engaged citizens, you have to have informed citizens. We've always understood that. Now, look, I don't expect presidential campaigns to be civic lessons. I understand, and I've participated in the pomp and the pageantry of American politics. There is something to all of that. But somewhere in all of that, we've got to find a way to make these candidates discuss substantive questions in depth to inform the voters, because without this scrutiny, the candidates and their country are less prepared to deal with the vital challenges that lie ahead.

Now, I'm going to suggest some of the questions I think they ought to address. I'll probably put in some of my own views along the way. You can forget those. They are not important. The important things are the questions. I understand, Iraq and terrorism are at the top of the list for the American people. And the war or terrorism is a great test for American foreign policy. But terrorism and Iraq are only parts of a swelling turmoil around the world. Conflict, violence, proliferation, repression, poverty, inequality, disease, environmental degradation . . . All you've got to do is travel around a little bit and you understand that these things are spiraling out of control. Great power politics and alliances and the global economy are all shifting.

So the point, I guess, is that we should not approach terrorism and Iraq in a vacuum. If you know anything about American foreign policy you know that everything's connected with everything else. And our efforts on these issues are tied to our efforts on a host of other challenges. The overarching question here for President Bush and Sen. Kerry to address is, "How do you intend to use the unrivalled power that we have—military, economic, cultural and lots of other ways? How do you blend the idealism and the pragmatism of the American people to preserve our American way of life, our freedom, our security, and achieve global stability? How do they define global stability? How do they plan to deal with these threats?" So, the American people have to ask, "How do you plan to wage the war on terror. How do you define the enemy?" That's not as simple a question as you might think in this world. In the 9-11 Commission report we said there are two enemies. One is al Qaeda. We're familiar with that. They hit us on 9/11. But the other, we said, was a radical ideological movement that goes from Morocco to Indonesia, across the Islamic world, inspired, in part, by al Qaeda, which has spawned more terrorist groups and violence. Well, we understand what President Bush and Sen. Kerry will say about the first enemy. They'll pledge—and they should pledge—to use every tool of American power to protect the American people. We need to play offense. You're not going to convert Osama bin Laden to the American way of life. You're not going to convert him to freedom. We're going to have to capture, we're going to have to kill. We're going to have to remove. No doubt about that. We're going to have to go after those sanctuaries. And, may I say, those of you associated with the United States Army can take a deep measure of satisfaction from the performance that the Army and the other services have had in some extraordinarily difficult conflicts. We honor your service, and we brace for the long work ahead.

I want to hear a little more about how they plan to tackle the second enemy, the long-term terrorist threat. There isn't any silver bullet here that can defeat Islamic terrorism. Indeed, if you think about counterterrorism policy, what strikes you is that in order to succeed you have to use all of the tools of American power. Military, certainly; covert action, certainly; diplomacy, law enforcement, economic policy, yes, foreign aid, homeland defense, all of these things. The trick in counterterrorism policy is to integrate and to balance all of those and use them effectively. If you look at the war on terrorism and you see it through the prism of military power, or you see it through the prism of draining the swamp, trying to dry up the money, or if you see it through the prism of just diplomacy or just covert actions, you don't understand the problem. It takes all of these aspects of American power to win.

How are you going to secure peace and stability in Afghanistan today? That's the incubator of al Qaeda. We pulled out of Afghanistan, if you remember, and look what happened. It became a sanctuary for Osama bin Laden. That nation today teeters on the brink, doesn't it? It has a chance. What are we going to do to create stability in Afghanistan? Are we going to have the leadership that will bring the American people along to understand how important it is in a country like Afghanistan or Iraq to create stability? How are you going to handle this relationship between the United States and Pakistan? Boy, if you want a foreign policy challenge, that's it. We have a long-term aid package to Pakistan. It's a very important country to us in the war on terror, but we can't possibly be satisfied with their proliferation activities. They were running a Wal-Mart, a Wal-Mart of nuclear materials. We didn't even know it for four years. We can't be satisfied with their progress toward democracy. President Pervez Musharraf, with all his attributes—and he has many—cannot be called a democrat.

How do you achieve a relationship with Saudi Arabia that goes beyond this old deal: you give us the oil for an affordable price, we'll provide security for the family? That's been the basis of our policy toward Saudi Arabia for as long as

I can remember. Decades. But it's not satisfactory today. How do you push that country toward a pragmatic reform, if you will? What are you going to do about managing this relationship, Mr. President, Sen. Kerry, with the Islamic world, which is becoming increasingly hostile to us? If you haven't gotten that figured out, you haven't been reading the paper.

How do you get a two-way, genuine dialogue going today with the Islamic world? How do we convey to that world that we are for those people? That we're on their side in their desire to want a better life? We want for them to have economic openness and development. We want for them to have better schools. We want for them to have political reform. We want for them to have tolerance and the rule of law. And somehow, we've got to figure out a way to give these young Muslim men you've heard about, with 30, 40, 50 percent unemployment in these countries, an avenue for expression and hope. How are you going to do that, if you're going to win the war on terrorism? It is not just a matter of knocking out al Qaeda. It's how you win this war of ideas with the great numbers of Islamists who probably admire Osama bin Laden and have a lot of grievances against us for whatever reasons—some right, some wrong. But don't think you can win the war on terror without winning that battle. And I want to know how they do it. I want to know how they're going to conduct public diplomacy.

We talk about, in the 9-11 Commission, the importance of exchange programs and scholarships and libraries. I've had some people say to me, "Oh, Hamilton, that's a lot of soft stuff." I don't buy it. I traveled all over Eastern Europe during the Cold War. I remember going to those libraries. I remember 10 o'clock at night, forcing the people out. They wanted to stay there all night to read more about America, about freedom, about liberty. I know the value of these scholarships and cultural exchanges. I'm up here in the Wilson Center, and we invite scholars from all over the world to come here. I know the value of those exchanges. Those of you in the military have all kinds of exchanges with foreign countries. It's a marvelous part of your program. These military leaders throughout the world who have been able to come here have had an exceptional opportunity to learn about this country through you. And may I say, I think it's one of the most important things you do.

I want to know how President Bush and Sen. Kerry are going to deal with the proliferation of nuclear weapons. That's at the top of my list. I don't know where you put it. You know, the worst-case scenario is a nuclear bomb in the hands of a terrorist. We've had the calculations put before us. If you detonate one of those weapons in Grand Central Station, the estimate is you kill 500,000 people. That's 500,000 people, one weapon. Trillion dollars in damages. OK, Mr. President, OK, Sen. Kerry, tell me what you're going to do about it. How are you going to secure those nuclear materials? How are you going to enforce nuclear safeguards? What are you going to do with the nonproliferation treaty? I want to hear what they have to say about that. I think the American people are entitled to hear it. I'm not suggesting they're easy questions to answer. I know they're not. But surely, our leaders have to address them. What are you going to do about Iran and North

Korea's nuclear programs? We should not let the candidates avoid talking in detail about North Korea and Iran. We shouldn't let them get away with it. Both of these countries are openly hostile to the United States. They either have or are very close to having nuclear weapons.

Four years from now, the administration that is elected will have faced one of the following: a military confrontation with one or both countries, the acceptance of one or both countries into the nuclear club, or a peaceful resolution of the differences with one or both countries that leads to their disarmament. We hope it is the third choice. Everybody hopes it's the third choice. How do you expect to get there? That's the question. North Korea is building nuclear weapons as we talk today. I'll tell you this, my friends, tough denunciations may resonate with the American people but they do not a policy make. I want to know what the diplomatic strategy is. I want to know what kind of a deal we're prepared to offer or to make. I want to know at what point we're going to use force or consider the use of force.

And really, there are the same kinds of questions with regard to Iran. What's our strategy for dealing with that nuclear program? Do we have to have direct dialogue with the Iranians? I've been perplexed for decades over our relationship with Iran. I've not been able to figure it out. Talk to the Iranians; they say we want to have the dialogue with the Americans. Talk to the Americans; they say we want to have a dialogue with the Iranians. But it never happens. Why not? I don't understand. I do not understand. How are you going to solve these problems without dialogue and discussion, or are we just going to go in there and demand a regime change? And if we're going to demand that, how are we going to accomplish it? You're going to think I'm as angry as [Georgia Sen.] Zell Miller, aren't you?

I'm not really all that angry. I know how tough these problems are. But I've been around longer than anybody in this room, and maybe my patience is wearing out. Maybe I think you and I have a responsibility. We just can't shift all of this off onto the candidates. You and I have a responsibility. We're Americans.

I'm going to give you a good quote in a minute from that gentleman right there, about the choices that we have. Well, you get the picture. Middle East: How are you going to resolve the Palestinian Israeli conflict? Look, I don't expect miracles here. But, by golly, that's been festering for decades. There's something not right with the system if a candidate can go into office and not have put before the American people a pretty clear idea of how he wants to deal with that problem. It's stumped us for decades. I don't think Sen. Kerry and I don't think President Bush can put before us a simple formula to deal with it. But I'd like to know how they're going to approach it. It's always been a complicated issue in American politics.

Well, I better finish up here pretty quickly. All these generals are getting nervous around here. I can see that. They have got things more important to do than listen to me, that's for sure. We have all these great power relationships. China and Russia: How do we engage those countries? You've been reading the newspaper in the recent days about [Russian] President [Vladimir] Putin, the steps he's taking to decrease democracy in Russia. Very worrisome. We want to engage Russia. We think it's important to bring it into the world community. We think there's a huge difference if Russia becomes dictatorial or if it becomes democratic. We think that we have a big interest there in that nation. We certainly think that about China and the European relationship. It goes on and on.

Trade. Isn't it amazing how little has been said about trade? Talk about generalities; I don't even like to listen to the television when they talk about trade. What are you going to do about competition from China in manufacturing? What are you going to do about it? What are you going to do about competition from India in services? I want to know. The American worker wants to know. It may not affect you all that much, and probably won't affect me. I'm very close to being unemployable. A lot of people would have made me that a long time ago. But the American worker has a lot at stake here. You can talk about free trade. You can talk about competition. You can talk about outsourcing. But I want to know how you're going to deal with it.

Then there is finally the question of global poverty. That doesn't excite too many people, but it ought to. Half of the people in the world live on less than $2 a day. Isn't that amazing? My wife and I went out to dinner the other night, and we got the bill, $50 or $60. By your standards, that's not much, but by my standards, it's a pretty good price. When I was coming out, one of my grandchildren said to me, "Grandfather, how can you justify spending that kind of money for dinner when you got all of these people living on $2 a day?" I was kind of proud of her, in a way. The sensitivity, the idealism, reflected in that question. It is a complicated question to answer. I'm sure I didn't answer it very well. Three billion of these people are under 25 years of age. Oh, what do you do? What do you do about this catastrophic situation in the world?

Well, my friends, those are some of the questions on my mind. We live in an age of great partisan division. I go up there and visit with my friends up on the Hill, and the constant calculation is, how do we win a few more seats in the House? How do we win a few more seats in the Senate? Every bill, every amendment and every debate is framed with that in the background. I believe in the magic of dialogue. I believe in the magic of dialogue in a democracy. But in order for that dialogue to work, candidates have to discuss the important issues before us. There are simply too many issues that are missing in action in this debate.

What happens in a presidential election matters an awful lot. I'm impressed with the fact that when this election is over, someone is going to have to govern the politically divided country and deal with these challenges I've been talking about. They're not going to be able to dodge them. You can't hide from these. They're going to be in there the day you walk in the Oval Office. We will be able to better face those challenges if we've explored the choices before us through a very robust and vigorous dialogue.

General Eisenhower said, and I quote, "The history of free men is never really written by chance, but by choice—their choice." It is now our choice, and our choices should be made through a strengthened dialogue democracy on American foreign policy, and the great challenges that lie ahead deserve an honest and a civil and a serious discussion of where we go from here. A great nation ought to be able to figure out some way to do that. Now, I know that it would be too much to ask the candidates to debate each and every issue I've discussed. I really don't expect that; but I do believe they will be doing far too little if they fail to give the American people a sense of the choices they are going to make.

You and I should expect . . . indeed, I would put it stronger. You and I should demand that candidates for president tell us how they're going to provide leadership in these extraordinary times, otherwise, picking up on General Eisenhower's comment, we leave tomorrow's history to chance, not to choice.

Thank you very much.

RYAN: Well, thank you so very much, Mr. Hamilton, for your insight and your thought-provoking remarks here. Let me close by thanking a few people. First let me thank the co-sponsors of this conference, without whose support the event would not have happened. They are The Atlantic Council of the United States, the International Institute for Strategic Studies, The Henry L. Stimson Center, and West Point's Combating Terrorism Center. Finally, I want to thank all of whom have participated in this conference for making it a success. I want to thank a short list of very special people: Mr. Bill Angerman and the MPRI team who conducted the operations; Ms. Sharon Baker and the SYColeman team who were in production; Special Agent Jack McKuhn and all the security people; Ms. Allegra Green and the Ronald Reagan Building staff who were so marvelous in their support; Sergeant Joyce and the Soldiers from Delta Company, Third Infantry Regiment; Specialist Patrick Malone, who has been our disembodied voice during the whole event, and a great voice it is; Grace Williams, the Army Protocol Office; Major Desiree Wineland and Public Affairs; Professor John Calabrese and all the students who came from American University who helped us and added so much; and finally Major Jim Craig, who really did the big shouldering of the work here.

Thank you all for coming.

BIOGRAPHIES

Brigadier General Robert L. Caslen Jr.

Brigadier General Robert (Bob) L. Caslen Jr., currently serves within the Joint Staff Strategic Plans and Policy Directorate (J–5) as the deputy director for the war on terrorism. In this position, he develops, coordinates, oversees and assesses U.S. military strategy for the war on terrorism and participates in the development of U.S. national security policies and strategies to control the proliferation of weapons of mass destruction. He began his current assignment July 6, 2004.

Caslen served in the 9th Infantry Division, Brigade S–4, as battalion executive officer during Operations Desert Shield/Desert Storm, and brigade operations officer in the 101st Airborne Division (Air Assault); on the faculty at the U.S. Military Academy, including Army football coach and company tactical officer; as an operations research officer at Picatinny Arsenal, N.J.; and as the senior brigade C–2 observer/controller at the Joint Readiness Training Center, Fort Polk, La. Caslen commanded the 1-14 Infantry Battalion in the 25th Infantry Division, and the 2d Brigade of the 101st Airborne Division; and served as the chief of staff for both the 101st Airborne Division (Air Assault) and the 10th Mountain Division.

Caslen served as the director, J–3, Joint Task Force Bravo in Honduras; as the executive officer to the commander of the multinational forces, and then to the commander of the U.S. Forces, United Nations Command during Operations Restore and Uphold Democracy; as the chief of staff of the Coalition Joint Task Force Mountain, 10th Mountain Division, in Baghran, Afghanistan; as the assistant deputy director for strategy and policy, J–5, on the Joint Staff; and most recently, as the assistant division commander for maneuver, 3d Infantry Division (Mechanized), which has units stationed at Fort Stewart, Hunter Army Airfield and Fort Benning, Ga.

His awards and decorations include the Defense Superior Service Medal, Legion of Merit, the Bronze Star, the Defense Meritorious Service Medal, the Meritorious Service Medal, the Joint Service Commendation Medal, the Army Commendation Medal, the Global War on Terrorism Expeditionary and Service Medals, the Armed Forces Expeditionary Medal, the Humanitarian Service Medal, the Joint Service Achievement Medal, the Army Achievement Medal, the Joint Meritorious Unit Award, the Meritorious Unit Commendation, the Ranger Tab, the Parachutist's Badge, the Air Assault Badge, and the Combat Infantryman's Badge.

Caslen was commissioned a lieutenant upon graduation from West Point and attended Infantry Officer Basic and Advanced Courses, U.S. Army Command and General Staff College, and the U.S. Army War College. He received a master's degree in business administration from Long Island University, and a master's degree from Kansas State University.

Mark Chichester

Mark Chichester is the director of the Institute for International Public Policy (IIPP) at the United Negro College Fund Special Programs Corporation, and also serves on the District of Columbia's Human Rights Commission.

At IIPP, he has overseen the awarding of several million dollars in capacity building grants to minority-serving institutions, and spearheaded the development of the institute's Web-based information and tracking system. He is often called upon to address international workforce development issues in a wide variety of fora—both foreign and domestic.

Before joining IIPP, Chichester was the interim constituent services director to District of Columbia at-large council member Linda Cropp, where he managed her constituent services staff office and served as liaison to the Washington business community. While in that position, Chichester also served on the mayor's international business task force.

Prior to that, Chichester was a Shapiro Fellow at Kyung Hee University in Seoul, Korea. He then served on the policy coordination staff of the director general of the Foreign Service at the Department of State.

Chichester has degrees in business and law from George Washington University. He is native of Washington, D.C.

Robert H. "Robin" Dorff, Ph.D.

Robert H. "Robin" Dorff is the executive director of the Institute of Political Leadership in Raleigh, N.C., a position he assumed on July 1, 2004. Prior to that, he was chairman of the Department of National Security and Strategy at the U.S. Army War College, where he previously served as professor of national security policy and strategy and holder of the General Maxwell D. Taylor Chair. Dorff is also senior adviser on democracy and governance for Creative Associates International Inc., working closely with its communities in transition division.

Dorff is the author or co-author of three books and numerous journal articles, many of which focus on U.S. national security strategy, democratization and failed states, and peace support operations. His most recent publication is *The Search for Security: A U.S. Grand Strategy for the Twenty-First Century* (co-editor) (Westport, Conn.: Praeger, 2003). His work on failed states includes *Responding to the Failed*

State: The Need for Strategy, Small Wars and Insurgencies, Vol. 10, No. 3 (Winter 1999); and *Democratization and Failed States: The Challenge of Ungovernability* in *Parameters,* Vol. 26, No. 2 (Summer 1996).

He lectures frequently on strategy, grand strategy and strategic leadership for corporate as well as national security audiences. He also lectures at institutions such as the Africa Center for Strategic Studies, the Near East-South Asia Center for Strategic Studies, the George C. Marshall Center and the National Defense University of Taiwan.

Dorff holds a bachelor's degree in political science from Colorado College, and a master's degree and a doctorate in political science from the University of North Carolina, Chapel Hill.

Robert J. Einhorn

Robert J. Einhorn is a senior adviser for the Center for Strategic and International Studies (CSIS) International Security Program, where he works on a broad range of nonproliferation, arms control and other national security issues.

Before joining CSIS, he served in the U.S. government for 29 years. From November 1999 to August 2001, he was assistant secretary for nonproliferation at the Department of State, where he was responsible for the nonproliferation of nuclear, chemical and biological weapons, missile delivery systems, and advanced conventional arms. In that capacity, he was the principal adviser to the secretary of state on nonproliferation matters, oversaw U.S. participation in the multilateral nonproliferation export-control regimes, and represented the United States in nonproliferation discussions and negotiations with a wide variety of countries in East Asia, South Asia, the Middle East and Europe.

Before becoming assistant secretary, Einhorn was deputy assistant secretary for nonproliferation in the State Department's Political-Military Bureau from 1992 to 1999 and a senior adviser in the State Department's Policy Planning Staff from 1986 to 1992. He served at the U.S. Arms Control and Disarmament Agency (ACDA) from 1972 to 1984, where he dealt with strategic arms issues, nuclear testing limits, chemical and biological weapons constraints, nonproliferation, and other security issues. From 1982 to 1986, he represented ACDA in the Strategic Arms Reduction Treaty talks.

He was presented the Secretary of State's Distinguished Service Award by Secretary Colin Powell in August 2001. Einhorn has authored several publications on strategic nuclear issues, arms control and nonproliferation. He is a member of the Council on Foreign Relations and the International Institute of Strategic Studies.

He received a bachelor's degree in government from Cornell University in 1969 and a master's degree in public affairs in international relations from the Woodrow Wilson School of Public and International Affairs, Princeton University, in 1971.

Susan Eisenhower

Susan Eisenhower is chairman of the board of directors for The Eisenhower Institute and is best known for her work in Russia and the former Soviet Union, during which she has testified before the Senate Armed Services and Senate Budget Committees on policy toward that region. She has also been appointed to the National Academy of Sciences' standing Committee on International Security and Arms Control where she is now serving a third term. In 2000, a year before the terrorist attacks of Sept. 11, she co-edited a book, *Islam and Central Asia*, which carried the prescient subtitle, *An Enduring Legacy or an Evolving Threat?*

In the spring of 2000, the secretary of energy appointed Eisenhower to a blue ribbon task force, the Baker-Cutler Commission, to evaluate U.S.-funded nuclear nonproliferation programs in Russia, and since that time she has served as an adviser on another Department of Energy study. In the fall of 2001, she was also appointed to serve on the International Space Station (ISS) Management and Cost Evaluation Task Force, which analyzed ISS management and cost overruns. She also serves as an academic fellow of the International Peace and Security program of Carnegie Corporation of New York, and is a director of the Carnegie Endowment for International Peace and the Nuclear Threat Initiative. She served two terms on the National Advisory Council of the National Aeronautics and Space Administration.

Eisenhower has spoken at myriad gatherings: universities, from Harvard to UCLA; World Affairs Councils; corporate gatherings; and to specialist audiences, such as the one assembled at the Army War College, where she gave the 1998 Commandant's Lecture. She has also given full speeches, by invitation, at other prominent locations such as the White House, the National Press Club, the Smithsonian Institution, the National Archives and the Hollywood Bowl.

Eisenhower's first professional experience was as a writer. In the 1970s, she lived overseas for six years, first while a student at the American University in Paris and then as a London resident and stringer for *The Saturday Evening Post*. Later she wrote a column for Wolfe Newspapers and went on to write for business. Within the last 10 years, she has authored three books, two of which, *Breaking Free* and *Mrs. Ike*, have appeared on best seller lists. She has also edited three collected volumes on regional security issues, and penned hundreds of op-eds and articles on foreign policy for publications such as *The Washington Post*, *The Los Angeles Times*, *USA Today*, the Naval Institute's *Proceedings*, *The London Spectator*, and Gannett newspapers. She has provided analysis for CNN International, MSNBC, *Nightline*, *World News Tonight* with Peter Jennings, *This Week* with David Brinkley, CBS News *Sunday Morning*, *Good Morning America*, *The News Hour* with Jim Lehrer, Fox News and *Hardball*, as well as National Public Radio and other nationwide television and radio programs.

Eisenhower has also consulted for major companies doing business overseas, such as IBM, American Express and Loral Space Systems. She currently serves on the advisory board of Stonebridge International, a Washington-based international consulting firm chaired by former National Security Advisor Samuel "Sandy" Berger.

Philippe Errera

Philippe Errera has been the deputy director of the Centre d'Analyse et de Prevision (Policy Planning Staff) at the Quai d'Orsay since April 2003.

Previously he served as counselor in charge of politico-military affairs at the French Embassy in Washington, D.C. (1999–2003), at the U.S. Department of State's Bureau of European Affairs (1998–1999) and at the French Ministry of Foreign Affairs (1996–1998), in the Office of the European Union Common Foreign and Security Policy.

Errera holds degrees from the Institut d'Études Politiques de Paris and the Ecole Nationale d'Administration in France.

His Excellency Nabil Fahmy

Ambassador Nabil Fahmy, ambassador of the Arab Republic of Egypt to the United States since October 1999, is a career diplomat who has played an active role in the numerous efforts to bring peace to the Middle East, as well as in international and regional disarmament affairs.

Fahmy has also served as Egypt's ambassador to Japan, and was the political adviser to the foreign minister. He has been a member of the Egyptian missions to the United Nations (disarmament and political affairs) in Geneva and New York, and has held numerous posts in the Egyptian government.

Fahmy headed the Egyptian delegation to the Middle East Peace Process Steering Committee in 1993 and the Egyptian delegation to the multilateral working group on regional security and arms control emanating from the Madrid Peace Conference in December 1991. He was elected vice chairman of the First Committee on Disarmament and International Security Affairs of the 44th Session of the U.N. General Assembly in 1986. He was a member of the U.N. secretary general's advisory board of disarmament matters until 2003, and its chairman during 2001.

Fahmy has written extensively on Middle East peacemaking and regional security and disarmament. He received his bachelor's degree in physics and mathematics and his master's degree in management, both from the American University in Cairo.

He was born in New York City and speaks English, French and Arabic.

Ambassador Chas. W. Freeman Jr.

Ambassador Chas. W. Freeman Jr. was assistant secretary of defense for international security affairs from 1993 to 1994, earning the highest public service awards of the Department of Defense. He served as U.S. ambassador to the Kingdom of Saudi Arabia during operations DESERT SHIELD and DESERT STORM, and was principal deputy assistant secretary of state for African affairs during the historic U.S. mediation of Namibian independence.

Freeman served as deputy chief of mission and charge d'affaires in the American embassies in Bangkok, Thailand (1984–1986) and Beijing (1981–1984), director for Chinese affairs at the Department of State (1979–1981), and the principal American interpreter during the late President Nixon's groundbreaking visit to China in 1972.

Freeman earned a certificate in Latin American studies from the National Autonomous University of Mexico, a bachelor's degree from Yale University, and a juris doctor degree from Harvard Law School. He was elected to the Academy of American Diplomacy in 1995. He is the author of *The Diplomat's Dictionary* (Revised Edition) and *Arts of Power*. Ambassador Freeman is chairman of the board of Projects International Inc. He also serves as co-chairman of the United States-China Policy Foundation and vice chairman of The Atlantic Council of the United States. He is a member of the boards of the Institute for Defense Analyses, the regional security centers of the Department of Defense and the Washington World Affairs Council.

Chaplain (Brigadier General) Jerome A. Haberek

Brigadier General Jerome A. Haberek, deputy chief of chaplains, received his commission in the Army Reserve as a chaplain candidate on Aug. 1, 1975. He served as a chaplain in the Rhode Island Army National Guard prior to entering active duty on Aug. 17, 1984. His assignments on active duty include deputy staff chaplain, 1st Corps Support Command, Fort Bragg, N.C.; group chaplain, 46th Support Group, Fort Bragg, N.C.; brigade chaplain, 2nd Brigade, 2d Infantry Division, Korea; assistant division chaplain, 101st Airborne Division (Air Assault), Fort Campbell, Ky.; brigade chaplain, 2nd Brigade, 101st Airborne Division (Air Assault), Fort Campbell, Ky.; staff chaplain, Supreme Headquarters Allied Powers Europe, Casteau, Belgium; command chaplain, XVIII Airborne Corps Artillery, Fort Bragg, N.C.; division chaplain, 82d Airborne Division, Fort Bragg, N.C.; chief, chaplain support manager, U.S. Army Special Operations Command, Fort Bragg, N.C.; the III Corps and Fort Hood chaplain, Fort Hood, Texas; the U.S. Army Europe/7th Army chaplain, Heidelberg, Germany; and the U.S. Army Special Operations Command chaplain.

Haberek graduated from Providence College in Providence, R.I., June 1973, and graduated from St. Meinrad School of Theology in St. Meinrad, Ind., May 1977. He was ordained for the Roman Catholic Diocese of Providence on Nov. 18, 1977. He served as an assistant pastor in St. Joseph's Church, North Scituate, R.I., St. Michael's Church, Smithfield, R.I., and St. Joseph's Church, Pascoag, R.I.

He is a graduate of the Chaplains Basic and Advanced Courses, Combined Arms Service Support School, Command and General Staff College, Defense Strategy

Course, Combat Life Savers Course, Cost Analysis Decision Management Course, and the U.S. Army War College.

Haberek's awards and decorations include the Defense Superior Service Medal, Legion of Merit, Meritorious Service Medal (seven Oak Leaf Clusters), Army Commendation Medal, Army Achievement Medal (three Oak Leaf Clusters), Army Reserve Commendation Medal, Army Reserve Achievement Medal, Army Service Ribbon, Army Superior Unit Award, Army Overseas Ribbon (one Oak Leaf Cluster), Air Assault Badge, Parachutist's Badge, and the Australian, German, and Canadian Parachutist's Badges.

Lee H. Hamilton

Lee H. Hamilton became director of the Woodrow Wilson International Center for Scholars in January 1999. Prior to becoming director of the Woodrow Wilson Center, Hamilton served for 34 years as a United States congressman from Indiana. During his tenure, he served as chairman and ranking member of the House Committee on Foreign Affairs (now the Committee on International Relations), and chaired the Subcommittee on Europe and the Middle East from the early 1970s until 1993. Hamilton also served as chairman of the Permanent Select Committee on Intelligence, and the Select Committee to Investigate Covert Arms Transactions with Iran. He established himself as a leading congressional voice on foreign affairs, with particular interests in promoting democracy and market reform in the former Soviet Union and Eastern Europe, promoting peace and stability in the Middle East, expanding U.S. markets and trade overseas, and overhauling U.S. export and foreign aid policies. His service enabled him to observe and participate in many significant historical events, including the fall of the Berlin Wall, the Arab/Israeli peace negotiations and the Gulf War.

Hamilton has also been a leading figure on economic policy and congressional organization. He served as chairman of the Joint Economic Committee, working to promote long-term economic growth and development, global market competition and a sound fiscal policy.

Hamilton remains active on matters of international relations and foreign affairs. He served as a commissioner on the influential United States Commission on National Security in the 21st Century (better known as the Hart-Rudman Commission) and was co-chairman with former Sen. Howard Baker of the Baker-Hamilton Commission to investigate certain security issues at Los Alamos. He is currently a member of the advisory council for the U.S. Department of Homeland Security, and in December 2002, he was appointed vice-chairman of the National Commission on Terrorist Attacks Upon the United States.

Hamilton has been honored with numerous awards in public service and human rights, including the Paul H. Nitze Award for Distinguished Authority on National Security Affairs in 1999, the Department of Defense Medal for Distinguished Public

Service in 1998, and the 2003 Eisenhower National Security Series Award. Other awards of distinction include the Central Intelligence Agency Medallion in 1988 and the Defense Intelligence Agency Medallion in 1987.

Hamilton has received several honorary degrees, including degrees from Detroit College of Law, University of Southern Indiana, American University, Indiana University and Indiana State University. Before his election to Congress, he practiced law in Chicago and Columbus, Ind.

He is a graduate of DePauw University and Indiana University law school, and studied for a year at Goethe University in Germany.

Ambassador Robert E. Hunter, Ph.D.

Ambassador Robert E. Hunter is a senior adviser at RAND Corporation in Washington, D.C. He is also president of the Atlantic Treaty Association, chairman of the Council for a Community of Democracies, a senior international consultant to Lockheed Martin Overseas Corporation, an associate at Harvard University's Belfer Center for Science and International Affairs, and a member of the Senior Advisory Group to the U.S. European Command.

From July 1993 to January 1998, he was U.S. ambassador to the North Atlantic Treaty Organization (NATO), and also represented the United States at the Western European Union. He was a principal architect of the "New NATO," created Partnership for Peace, negotiated nine "air strike" decisions for Bosnia and Implementation Force/Stabilization Force (IFOR/SFOR), and twice received the Pentagon's highest civilian award, the Department of Defense Medal for Distinguished Public Service. Previously, Ambassador Hunter was vice president at the Center for Strategic and International Studies. During the Carter administration, he was director of west European and then Middle East affairs at the National Security Council. Earlier, he was foreign policy adviser to Sen. Edward M. Kennedy, a senior fellow at the Overseas Development Council and research associate at the International Institute for Strategic Studies (IISS). He served on the White House staff during the Johnson administration and in the Navy's special projects office (Polaris).

Hunter has a bachelor's degree from Wesleyan University, and received his doctorate and taught at the London School of Economics, where he was a Fulbright Scholar and Noel Buxton Student. Hunter has been an author or editor of nearly 800 publications, including *Security in Europe*, *ESDP: NATO's Companion or Competitor?*, *Presidential Control of Foreign Policy*, *NATO: The Next Generation* (editor), *Grand Strategy for the West* (co-editor), *The Soviet Dilemma in the Middle East*, and *Organizing for National Security*. He has extensive media experience, traveled to more than 90 countries, lectured in more than 20 countries, played a senior national policy role in eight presidential campaigns, taught at five universities, and written speeches for U.S. presidents and other top officials for 40 years.

Ellen Laipson

Ellen Laipson joined The Henry L. Stimson Center after nearly 25 years of government service. Her last government positions included vice chairman of the National Intelligence Council (NIC) (1997–2002), and special assistant to the U.S. permanent representative to the United Nations (1995–1997). At the NIC, Laipson co-managed the interdisciplinary study, Global Trends 2015, and directed the NIC's outreach to think tanks and research organizations on a wide range of national security topics.

Her earlier government career focused on analysis and policy-making on Middle East and South Asian issues. She was the director for Near East and South Asian affairs for the National Security Council (1993–1995), national intelligence officer for Near and South Asia (1990–1993), a member of the Department of State's Policy Planning Staff (1986–1987), and a specialist in Middle East affairs for the Congressional Research Service.

Laipson is a frequent speaker on Middle East issues and on U.S. foreign policy and global trends. She is a member of the Council on Foreign Relations, the International Institute of Strategic Studies, the Middle East Institute, and the Middle East Studies Association. In 2003, she joined the boards of The Asia Foundation and the Education and Employment Foundation. Laipson has a master's degree from the School of Advanced International Studies, Johns Hopkins University, and a bachelor's degree from Cornell University.

Matthew Levitt

Matthew Levitt is a senior fellow at The Washington Institute for Near East Policy, specializing in terrorism and U.S. policy. Prior to joining the institute, Levitt served as a Federal Bureau of Investigation analyst providing tactical and strategic analysis in support of counterterrorism operations. His special focus has been on fundraising and logistical support networks for Middle East terrorist groups. In addition, he has participated as a team member in a number of crisis situations, including the terrorist threat surrounding the turn of the millennium and the Sept. 11 attacks.

Prior to joining the FBI, Levitt was a Soref fellow at The Washington Institute for Near East Policy, focusing on Arab-Israeli peace negotiations, Palestinian politics and society, and terrorism.

Levitt is a frequent guest on National Public Radio, CNN, BBC, ABC, CBS and NBC. He has served as an expert witness and consulted for the Department of Justice in several terrorism cases, lectured on international terrorism on behalf of the Department of State, and testified before both the U.S. Senate and House on matters relating to international terrorism. Levitt also serves on the Council on Foreign Relations task force on terrorist financing.

Levitt has written extensively about terrorism, the Middle East and Arab-Israeli peace negotiations, as well as a variety of classified articles published in FBI and U.S. intelligence community publications.

Levitt received a bachelor's degree in political science from Yeshiva University and a master's degree in law and diplomacy from Tufts University's Fletcher School of Law and Diplomacy, where he is currently completing his doctoral dissertation on the impact of terrorism on the process of Arab-Israeli peace negotiations. He was awarded several fellowships and grants in support of his graduate work, and served as a graduate research fellow at Harvard Law School's Program on Negotiation from 1997 to 1998, during which time he conducted extensive field research in Israel, the West Bank and the Gaza Strip.

Ambassador James R. Lilley

Ambassador James R. Lilley was the U.S. ambassador to the People's Republic of China from 1989 to 1991 and to the Republic of Korea from 1986 to 1989. He served as the director of the Institute for Global Chinese Affairs at the University of Maryland from 1996 to 1997 and senior adviser from 1998 to 1999. In 1995, he was the Philip M. McKenna visiting scholar at Claremont McKenna College. Prior to his time as a visiting scholar, he served as the assistant secretary of defense for international affairs from 1991 to 1993. In 1991 Lilley was a fellow at the Institute of Politics, Harvard University. In 1985, he was the deputy assistant secretary of state for East Asian affairs. From 1982 to 1984, Lilley was the director of the American Institute in Taiwan. He was a professor at Johns Hopkins School of Advanced International Studies from 1978 to 1980, and a national intelligence officer for China from 1975 to 1978.

Lilley earned a master's degree in international relations from The George Washington University and a bachelor's degree from Yale University. He is the author of *China Hands*, *China's Military Faces the Future*, *Crisis in the Taiwan Strait* and *Beyond MFN*.

General Barry R. McCaffrey (Ret.)

General Barry R. McCaffrey (Ret.) is the Bradley Distinguished Professor of International Security Studies at the U.S. Military Academy. He serves as a national security and terrorism analyst for NBC News, and is the author of a regular commentary on national security issues for Armed Forces Journal. McCaffrey is the chairman of the Fleishman-Hillard Homeland Security Practice, a member of its international advisory board, and a director of The Atlantic Council of the United States. From Feb. 29, 1996, to Jan. 7, 2001, McCaffrey served as the director of the White House Office of National Drug Control Policy. Prior to that, he was the commander of the U.S. Southern Command, coordinating national security operations in Latin America. He is also president of his consulting firm based in Alexandria, Va.

During his military career, he served overseas for 13 years, including four combat tours. He commanded the 24th Infantry Division (Mechanized) during the DESERT STORM 400-kilometer left-hook attack into Iraq. When he retired from service, he was the most highly decorated four-star general in the U.S. Army. He twice received the Distinguished Service Cross, the nation's second highest medal for valor; was awarded two Silver Stars; and received three Purple Heart medals for wounds sustained in combat. McCaffrey served as the assistant to General Colin Powell and supported the chairman as the Joint Chiefs of Staff adviser to the secretary of state and the U.S. ambassador to the United Nations.

McCaffrey graduated from Phillips Academy in Andover, Mass., and the United States Military Academy, West Point, N.Y.

He holds a master's degree in civil government from American University, and taught American government and comparative politics at West Point. He attended the Harvard University National Security Program and the Harvard Business School Executive Education Program.

He has received numerous awards from various U.S.-based governmental and nongovernmental organizations, along with decorations from France, Brazil, Argentina, Colombia, Peru, and Venezuela.

Colonel Michael J. Meese

Colonel Michael J. Meese is a professor and deputy head of the department of social sciences at the United States Military Academy. He teaches microeconomics and defense economics courses. From 2003 to 2004, he was assigned as the U.S. Military Academy fellow at the National War College where he taught national strategy, military policy, and bureaucratic politics courses. In 2003, he deployed as special adviser on political, economic, and military issues for the 101st Airborne Division (Air Assault), in Mosul, Iraq. From January to July 2002, he served as executive officer to the assistant chief of staff (operations) in Bosnia-Herzegovina conducting peacekeeping and counterterrorism operations.

His dissertation is entitled, "Defense Decision Making under Budget Stringency: Examining Downsizing in the United States Army." His research examines budget decisions during previous military reductions with implications for improving defense effectiveness today. In 2001, he assisted the Army Science Board Team, which examined alternative approaches to Headquarters, Department of the Army organization. He served as the executive director of the professional staff of the Department of Defense Panel on Commercialization and Globalization (the Dawkins Panel), which examined the opportunities and risks associated with current changes in the defense and business sectors. He has been a visiting lecturer on the U.S. Army's transition to the all-volunteer force at the Center for Hemispheric Defense

Studies. In May 1998, he was part of a two-person team that traveled to South Africa to assess and assist the transformation and integration of the South African National Defense Force. He has participated in four Marshall Center "Partnership for Peace" conferences as rapporteur and co-author of the final conference proceedings on the subjects of defense economics, extremism, transformation, and crime and corruption. In June 2004, he co-chaired West Point's Senior Conference on "Defense Transformation and the Army Profession."

He is a field artillery officer with previous assignments with the 7th Infantry Division (Light), as a Battery Commander in the 3rd Armored Division in Germany, and as a Battalion Operations Officer and Deputy Division Operations Officer in the 1st Cavalry Division at Fort Hood, Texas. He is a graduate of the National War College, an honor graduate of the Command and General Staff College, a distinguished graduate from West Point, and holds two master's degrees and a doctorate from the Woodrow Wilson School of Public and International Affairs at Princeton University.

He has written several papers and articles concerning economics and national security and is the author and editor of the *Armed Forces Guide to Personal Financial Planning: Strategies for Managing Your Budget, Savings, Insurance, Taxes, and Investments* (Stackpole Books, 1998). He is a member of the American Economics Association, the Western Economics Association and the International Studies Association.

General Montgomery C. Meigs (Ret.)

General Montgomery C. Meigs (Ret.) became the Louis A. Bantle Chair in Business and Government Policy at the Maxwell School of Syracuse University during August 2004. Meigs served on active duty for more than 35 years, most recently as commander of U.S. Army forces in Europe from 1998 to 2002, and as commander of the North Atlantic Treaty Organization's peacekeeping force in Bosnia from 1998 to 1999. He was a multinational division commander in Bosnia, a brigade commander during DESERT STORM, and a senior planner with the Joint Chiefs of Staff in Washington, D.C.

Meigs earned his bachelor's degree from the United States Military Academy at West Point, and his master's degree and doctorate in history from the University of Wisconsin at Madison. He has published a variety of articles on military policy and leadership, as well as a book entitled, *Slide Rules and Submarines* (National Defense University Press, 1990). Since 2003, Meigs has been the Tom Slick Visiting Professor of World Peace at the Lyndon B. Johnson School of Public Affairs, University of Texas at Austin. From 1997 to 1998, he was commandant of the U.S. Army Command and General Staff College at Fort Leavenworth, Kan., and before that an assistant professor of history at West Point. Meigs has lectured at the Royal Uniformed Services Institute, the U.S. Army War College and National War College, the Russian Army's Combined Arms Academy, and the Imperial Defense and Joint Staff Colleges in the United Kingdom.

Colonel Michael K. Nagata

Colonel Michael K. Nagata is chief of the combatant command support branch, office of the deputy under secretary of defense for intelligence (intelligence and warfighting support).

He was born in Hawaii. After graduating from college and practicing as a licensed physical therapist for several years, he enlisted into the Army in 1981 as an infantryman. His battalion commander, learning of his college degree, convinced Nagata to apply for Officer Candidate School, from which he graduated in 1982. After attending the Infantry Officer's Basic Course and Ranger School he was assigned to the 1st Battalion, 9th Infantry (Manchu), at Camp Greaves, South Korea, where he served as a mortar platoon leader and battalion motor officer.

In 1984, Nagata joined the U.S. Army Special Forces after graduating from the Special Forces Qualification Course in April of that year. He was assigned to the newly reactivated 2d Battalion, 1st Special Forces Group (Airborne), where he served as the scuba detachment commander in Alpha Company for 36 months. In 1987, he attended the Infantry Officers Advanced Course, and was subsequently assigned to 1st Battalion, 1st Special Forces Group (Airborne), in Okinawa, Japan, first as the Charlie company executive officer, and then as the battalion S–3. From 1990 to 1994, Nagata served as a troop commander in a special mission unit.

In 1995, Nagata returned to the 1st Special Forces Group (Airborne) in Fort Lewis, Wash., where he served initially as the executive officer for the 3d Battalion, and subsequently as the group operations officer until 1997. He served as a brigade-level staff officer in a special mission unit from 1997 to 1999, as the commander, 1st Battalion, 1st Special Warfare Training Group (Airborne), from 1999 to 2000, where he was responsible for both the Special Forces Assessment and Selection Course and Special Forces Qualification Course; and as a squadron commander in a special mission unit from 1999 to 2000.

From 1995 to 1996, he attended the Marine Corps Command and Staff College where he received a master's degree in military studies. Nagata has a bachelor's degree from Georgia State University, and graduated from the National War College at Fort McNair, Washington, D.C., in 2003.

His awards and decorations include the Combat Infantryman's Badge, Special Forces and Ranger Tabs, Master Parachutist and Free-Fall Parachutist Wings, SCUBA Badge, Legion of Merit, Bronze Star, Armed Forces Expeditionary Medal and Defense Meritorious Service Medals.

Janne E. Nolan, Ph.D.

Janne E. Nolan was recently appointed a professor at the Graduate School of Public and International Affairs at the University of Pittsburgh, and has served on the faculty of the International Security Program at Georgetown University since

1994. She is currently the project director for the study of Lessons of Strategic Surprise and Intelligence Failures sponsored by Georgetown's Institute for the Study of Diplomacy and the John D. and Catherine T. MacArthur Foundation. She is writing a book about dissent and national security under contract to the Century Foundation of New York.

Nolan has held numerous senior positions in the private sector, including foreign policy director at the Century Foundation, senior fellow in foreign policy at the Brookings Institution, and senior international security consultant at Science Applications International. Her public service includes positions as a foreign affairs officer in the Department of State, senior representative to the Senate Armed Services Committee for Sen. Gary Hart, and a member of the National Defense Panel, the secretary of defense's policy board, and several other congressionally appointed blue ribbon commissions. She has served as a policy adviser to several presidential and Senate campaigns.

Nolan is the author of six books, including *Guardians of the Arsenal: The Politics of Nuclear Strategy*, *Trappings of Power: Ballistic Missiles in the Third World*, and *Elusive Consensus*, and is the editor of *Ultimate Security: Combating Weapons of Mass Destruction*. She has published many articles on international security and foreign policy in publications such as *Foreign Affairs*, *Foreign Policy*, *The New York Times*, *The Washington Post*, *Science*, *Scientific American*, and *The New Republic*.

She received her doctorate from the Fletcher School of Law and Diplomacy at Tufts University.

General Peter Pace, U.S. Marine Corps

General Peter Pace is the vice chairman of the Joint Chiefs of Staff, where he serves as the chairman of the Joint Requirements Oversight Council, vice chairman of the Defense Acquisition Board, and a member of the National Security Council Deputies Committee and the Nuclear Weapons Council. In addition, he acts for the chairman in all aspects of the Planning, Programming and Budgeting System to include participating in meetings of the Defense Resources Board.

In 1968, he was assigned to the 2d Battalion, 5th Marines, 1st Marine Division in the Republic of Vietnam. In March 1969, he served as head, infantry writer unit, Marine Corps Institute; platoon leader, Guard Company; security detachment commander, Camp David; White House social aide; and platoon leader, Special Ceremonial Platoon. In October 1972, after attending the Infantry Officers' Advanced Course, Fort Benning, Ga., he was assigned to the security element, Marine Aircraft Group 15, 1st Marine Aircraft Wing, Nam Phong, Thailand.

In October 1973, he was assigned to Headquarters Marine Corps, Washington, D.C., as the assistant majors' monitor. During October 1976, he served as operations officer, 2d Battalion, 5th Marines; executive officer, 3d Battalion, 5th Marines; and division staff secretary at the 1st Marine Division, Camp Pendleton, Calif.

In August 1979, he attended the Marine Corps Command and Staff College, and upon completion in June 1980, was assigned duty as commanding officer, Marine Corps Recruiting Station, Buffalo, N.Y. Reassigned to the 1st Marine Division, Camp Pendleton, General Pace served from June 1983 until June 1985 as commanding officer, 2d Battalion, 1st Marines. In June 1985, he attended the National War College, Washington, D.C., after which he was assigned to the Combined/Joint Staff in Seoul, Korea. He served as chief, ground forces branch until April 1987, when he became executive officer to the assistant chief of staff, C/J/G–3, United Nations Command/Combined Forces Command/United States Forces Korea/Eighth United States Army.

In August 1988, he became commanding officer, Marine Barracks, Washington, D.C. In August 1991, he was assigned duty as chief of staff, 2d Marine Division, Camp Lejeune, N.C. During February 1992, he served as assistant division commander. On July 13, 1992, he became president of the Marine Corps University and commanding general, Marine Corps Schools, Quantico, Va. While serving in this capacity, he also was deputy commander, Marine Forces, Somalia, from December 1992 to February 1993, and deputy commander, Joint Task Force–Somalia, later that year. During June 1994, he was assigned as the deputy commander/chief of staff, U.S. Forces, Japan; and on Aug. 5, 1996, he was assigned as the director for operations (J–3), Joint Staff, Washington, D.C.

General Pace served as the commander, U.S. Marine Corps Forces, Atlantic/Europe/South from Nov. 23, 1997 to Sept. 8, 2000. From Sept. 8, 2000 to Sept. 30, 2001, he assumed duties as the commander, United States Southern Command.

Pace has been awarded the Defense Distinguished Service Medal, first oak leaf cluster; Defense Superior Service Medal; the Legion of Merit; Bronze Star Medal with Combat V; the Defense Meritorious Service Medal; Meritorious Service Medal with gold star; Navy Commendation Medal with Combat V; Navy Achievement Medal with gold star; and the Combat Action Ribbon.

Pace received his commission in June 1967 from the United States Naval Academy. He holds a master's degree in business administration from The George Washington University and attended Harvard University's Senior Executives in National and International Security program.

Jonathan D. Pollack, Ph.D.

Jonathan D. Pollack is professor of Asian and Pacific Studies, chairman of the Strategic Research Department and chairman of the Asia-Pacific Studies Group at the Naval War College. Before joining the war college faculty in October 2000, Pollack was affiliated with the RAND Corporation in a wide range of research and management capacities. He has taught at Brandeis University, UCLA, the RAND Graduate School of Policy Studies and the Naval War College.

Pollack has been published widely on China's political and strategic roles, the international politics of Northeast Asia, U.S. policy in Asia and the Pacific, and Chinese technological and military development. His recent publications include *Strategic Surprise? U.S.-China Relations in the Early 21st Century* (editor and contributor, 2004); articles in *Asia-Pacific Review*, Korea National Defense University Review, Naval War College Review, *Strategic Comments*, *Orbis*, and *Asian Survey*; chapters in *The China Threat-Perceptions, Myths, and Realities* (2002); *George W. Bush and Asia: A Midterm Assessment* (2003); *U.S. Strategy in the Asia-Pacific Region* (2004); and in *The Nuclear Tipping Point: Why States Reconsider Their Nuclear Choices* (2004).

His current research includes the role of short-range ballistic missiles in Chinese political-military strategies toward Taiwan, a re-assessment of future U.S. defense strategy in East Asia, the implications of China's national security strategy for the Asian security order, and the long-term dynamics of the Korean Peninsula.

He holds master's and doctoral degrees from the University of Michigan and was a postdoctoral research fellow at Harvard University.

Brigadier General Kevin T. Ryan

Brigadier General Kevin T. Ryan currently serves in the operations directorate of Army Staff as deputy director of policy, plans and strategy, where he is responsible for long-range war planning, strategic policy and international cooperation. Prior to this assignment, Ryan served in a variety of command and staff positions in Germany, Korea and the United States.

Commissioned from the United States Military Academy in 1976 as a second lieutenant in air defense artillery, Ryan has commanded air defense units from platoon to brigade.

His secondary specialty is as a Russian and European/Asian foreign area officer, and since 1982, he has served in several jobs in that specialty. Ryan taught Russian at West Point (1983–1986), served as a liaison officer to the Russian Western Group of Forces in East Germany (1989–1991), headed the U.S. Prisoner of War/Missing in Action Office in Moscow (1995–1996) and most recently worked as the U.S. defense attaché in Moscow (2001–2003). Following Operation DESERT STORM, Ryan served as a liaison officer in Northern Iraq during the Kurdish relief effort PROVIDE COMFORT. He also served as the chief of staff of the U.S. Army Space and Missile Defense Command and as regional director for Slavic States in the Office of the Secretary of Defense.

Ryan's medals and decorations include the Defense Superior Service Medal (with two Oak Leaf Clusters), Legion of Merit (with Oak Leaf Cluster), Defense Meritorious Service Medal, Meritorious Service Medal (with four Oak Leaf Clusters), Joint Service Commendation Medal, Army Commendation Medal, Army Achievement Medal (with Oak Leaf Cluster), and Parachutist Badge.

Ryan received a master's degree in Russian language and literature from Syracuse University, and a master's degree in National Security and Strategic Studies from the National Defense University. He also attended the United States Army's Command and General Staff College, the National War College, and the Air Defense Artillery Officer Basic and Advanced Courses.

Scott D. Sagan, Ph.D.

Scott D. Sagan is professor of political science and co-director of Stanford's Center for International Security and Cooperation (CISAC). Before joining the Stanford faculty, Sagan was a lecturer in the department of government at Harvard University and served as a special assistant to the director of the organization of the Joint Chiefs of Staff in the Pentagon. He has also served as a consultant to the Office of the Secretary of Defense and at the Los Alamos National Laboratory.

Sagan is the author of *Moving Targets: Nuclear Strategy and National Security* (Princeton University Press, 1989), *The Limits of Safety: Organizations, Accidents, and Nuclear Weapons* (Princeton University Press, 1993); and co-author with Kenneth N. Waltz of *The Spread of Nuclear Weapons: A Debate Renewed*, 2nd ed. (W.W. Norton, 2002). He is the co-editor with Peter R. Lavoy and James L. Wirtz of *Planning the Unthinkable: How New Powers Will Use Nuclear, Biological, and Chemical Weapons* (Cornell University Press, 2000). Sagan received Stanford University's 1996 Hoagland Prize for Undergraduate Teaching and the 1998 Dean's Award for Distinguished Teaching. As part of CISAC's mission of training the next generation of security specialists, he founded Stanford's Interschool Honors Program in International Security Studies in 2000.

Sagan's most recent articles are "The Madman Nuclear Alert: Secrecy, Signaling, and Safety in the October 1969 Crisis," co-authored with Jeremi Suri, (*International Security*, Spring 2003) and "The Problem of Redundancy Problem: Why More Nuclear Security Forces May Produce Less Nuclear Security" (*Risk Analysis*, Spring 2003). Sagan's redundancy article is also the 2003 winner of Columbia University's Institute of War and Peace Studies paper competition on political violence.

Currently, his main research interests are nuclear proliferation in South Asia, ethics and international relations, and accidents in complex organizations. He recently organized three CISAC-sponsored workshops on "Preventing Nuclear War in South Asia in India, Pakistan and Thailand." As part of this ongoing effort, he has lectured on the dangers of nuclear weapons theft and accidents at Pakistan's National Defense College and India's Institute for Defense and Strategic Analysis in New Delhi. Sagan will continue to collaborate with Indian and Pakistani officials and military officers on that project. He has been a and a member of the boards of trustees of the Gerald R. Ford Foundation, the Hoover Institution at Stanford University and the National Park Foundation, as well as chairman of the Eisenhower Exchange Fellowships Inc.

Gary Samore, Ph.D.

Gary Samore is the director of studies and a senior fellow for nonproliferation at the International Institute of Strategic Studies (IISS) in London. As director of studies, he is responsible for overall direction of the institute's research program, including fund raising for research projects, management of IISS research staff, and supervision of the IISS Adelphi Paper series. He also directs the institute's nonproliferation program, which seeks to strengthen trans-Atlantic cooperation and support international efforts to deal with proliferation threats in East Asia, the Middle East and South Asia. As director of the IISS Non-Proliferation Programme, he has organized numerous international conferences and workshops and produced a variety of IISS publications on proliferation issues. He is the editor of the IISS Strategic Dossier on Iraq's Weapons of Mass Destruction: A Net Assessment, published in September 2002, and North Korea's Weapons Programmes: A Net Assessment, published in January 2004.

Prior to joining the IISS in September 2001, Samore worked on proliferation issues for the U.S. government, focusing primarily on nonproliferation policy. From 1996 to 2000, he served as special assistant to President Clinton and senior director for nonproliferation and export controls at the National Security Council. From 1987 to 1995, he held various positions at the Department of State. As deputy to the ambassador-at-large for Korean affairs, he was one of the U.S. negotiators of the 1994 U.S.-Democratic People's Republic of Korea Agreed Framework. He also worked in the Department of State as director of the Office of Regional Nonproliferation Affairs in the Bureau of Political Military Affairs and as special assistant to the ambassador-at-large for nonproliferation and nuclear energy policy. He has also held positions at the Lawrence Livermore National Laboratory, the RAND Corporation and Harvard University, where he received a doctorate in government in 1984.

John H. Sandrock

John H. Sandrock is the director of the international security program at The Atlantic Council of the United States. He has more than 30 years' experience with international security affairs, including Europe, the Middle East and Central and South Asia.

Prior to joining The Atlantic Council in April 2004, he was a project and program manager with Science Applications International Corporation working on projects in direct support to the Coalition Provisional Authority in Iraq that included five months in Baghdad. Previously, he was an international civil servant with the Secretariat of the Organization for Security and Co-operation in Europe (OSCE) in Vienna, Austria, where he was the deputy director for mission support and chief of operations. He opened new OSCE missions and led senior diplomatic delegations in Eastern Europe, Central Asia, the South Caucasus and the Balkans. Prior to taking the position with the OSCE in Vienna, he was the acting head of mission and deputy head of the OSCE mission in Dushanbe, Tajikistan.

As a colonel with the United States Air Force, Sandrock served as the U.S. air attache in India and Afghanistan. His military career also included tours of duty with the Office of the Joint Chiefs of Staff, the Air Staff and NATO. He was a command pilot and served in Vietnam.

Sandrock speaks German, Dari/Tajik, and some French. He has a master's degree from Georgetown University and a bachelor's degree from the University of Montana.

General Peter J. Schoomaker

General Peter J. Schoomaker became the 35th chief of staff of the United States Army Aug. 1, 2003.

Prior to his current assignment, General Schoomaker spent 31 years in a variety of command and staff assignments with both conventional and special operations forces. He participated in numerous deployment operations, including DESERT ONE in Iran, URGENT FURY in Grenada, JUST CAUSE in Panama, DESERT SHIELD/DESERT STORM in Southwest Asia, and UPHOLD DEMOCRACY in Haiti, and supported various worldwide joint contingency operations, including those in the Balkans.

Early in his career, Schoomaker was a reconnaissance platoon leader and rifle company commander with the 2nd Battalion, 4th Infantry; a cavalry troop commander with the 2d Armored Cavalry Regiment in Germany; and in Korea as the S–3 operations officer of 1st Battalion, 73rd Armor, 2d Infantry Division. From 1978 to 1981, he commanded a squadron in the 1st Special Forces Operational Detachment - D. Next, Schoomaker served as the squadron executive officer, 2d Squadron, 2d Armored Cavalry Regiment in Germany. In 1983, he served as special operations officer, J–3, Joint Special Operations Command. From 1985 to 1988, Schoomaker commanded another squadron in the 1st Special Forces Operational Detachment - D. He returned as the commander, 1st Special Forces Operational Detachment - D from 1989 to 1992. Subsequently, Schoomaker served as the assistant division commander of the 1st Cavalry Division, Fort Hood, Texas, followed by a tour in the Headquarters, Department of the Army Staff as the deputy director for operations, readiness and mobilization.

General Schoomaker served as the commanding general of the Joint Special Operations Command from 1994 to 1996, followed by command of the United States Army Special Operations Command at Fort Bragg, N.C., through October 1997. His most recent assignment was as commander, United States Special Operations Command, at MacDill Air Force Base, Fla., from November 1997 to November 2000.

Schoomaker's awards and decorations include the Defense Distinguished Service Medal, two Army Distinguished Service Medals, four Defense Superior Service Medals, three Legions of Merit, two Bronze Star Medals, two Defense Meritorious Service Medals, three Meritorious Service Medals, Joint Service Commendation Medal, Joint Service Achievement Medal, Combat Infantryman Badge, Master Parachutist Badge and HALO Wings, the Special Forces Tab, and the Ranger Tab.

Schoomaker received a bachelor's degree from the University of Wyoming in 1969. He also holds a master's degree in management from Central Michigan University and an Honorary Doctorate of Laws from Hampden-Sydney College. His military education includes the Marine Corps Amphibious Warfare School, the U.S. Army Command and General Staff College, the National War College, and the John F. Kennedy School of Government Program for Senior Executives in National and International Security Management.

Ambassador Michael Sheehan

Ambassador Michael Sheehan graduated from the United States Military Academy at West Point in 1977 and was commissioned a second lieutenant in the infantry. In addition to field training that included airborne, ranger and special forces qualifications, he completed two master's degrees, one from the Georgetown University School of Foreign Service and one from the U.S. Army Command and General Staff College.

During the first phase of his career in the Army, Sheehan performed numerous overseas assignments, including Panama as a special forces detachment commander for the assault team of a counterterrorism unit, Korea as a mechanized rifle company commander on the Demilitarized Zone and El Salvador as a counterinsurgency adviser for which he was awarded the Combat Infantry Badge.

During the second phase of his Army career, Sheehan served at the White House for three different national security advisors and two presidents (George H. W. Bush and William J. Clinton), primarily in the areas of counternarcotics and peacekeeping. During this period, he deployed to Somalia and Haiti during the U.S.-led interventions there.

In 1997, Sheehan retired from the Army as a lieutenant colonel and was appointed a deputy assistant secretary of state in the Bureau of International Organizations, where he gained extensive experience in international policing issues in Bosnia and Kosovo.

In 1998, following the attacks against the American embassies in East Africa, Sheehan was appointed Department of State ambassador at-large for counterterrorism. A strong advocate for counterterrorism awareness, Sheehan extended counterterrorism partnerships around the world, not only with our traditional partners, the United Kingdom, Israel and Canada, but also many others including India and Russia.

In January 2001, U.N. Secretary General Kofi Annan appointed Sheehan as an assistant secretary general in the Department of Peacekeeping Operations. This office managed support to 15 peacekeeping operations with over 35,000 military and police deployed around the world.

In June 2003, Sheehan was appointed the deputy commissioner of counter-terrorism for the New York City Police Department (NYPD). In this role, he is responsible for counterterrorism operations in the department, including terrorism investigations in partnership with the Federal Bureau of Investigation's Joint Terrorist Task Force, training and exercises for NYPD personnel, and risk assessment and critical infrastructure protection of key sites within New York City.

His Excellency Rakesh Sood

Ambassador Rakesh Sood is the Indian deputy chief of mission to the United States. He is a member of the U.N. Secretary-General's Advisory Board on Disarmament Matters.

Sood served as ambassador and permanent representative of India to the Conference on Disarmament, Geneva, from September 2000 to December 2003.

In 2002, Sood was chairperson of the U.N. Secretary-General's group of government experts to identify and trace, in a timely and reliable manner, illicit small arms and light weapons, in all its aspects. From 2001 to 2003, Sood was an alternate representative of the Department of Atomic Energy of the government of India at the council of the Center for European Nuclear Research. From 1992 to 2000, he was director and joint secretary for disarmament and international security affairs in the Ministry of External Affairs in New Delhi. From 1992 to 1997, he engaged with the United States at bilateral level discussions relating to disarmament, nonproliferation, and export controls and, from 1999 to 2000, as part of the Strobe Talbott-Jaswant Singh dialogue.

Sood has participated in negotiations on the Chemical Weapons Convention and Nuclear Test-Ban Treaty (CTBT) at the Conference on Disarmament. He has represented India in U.N. Disarmament Commission meetings, First Committee of the U.N. General Assembly, CTBT negotiations, biological weapons convention and inhumane weapons convention review conferences, Third Special Session of the U.N. General Assembly devoted to disarmament, non-aligned movement conferences and summits, Association of Southeast Asian Nations Regional Forum meetings, Middle-East Arms Control and Regional Security Working Group, India-Pakistan talks, bilateral talks with United States, United Kingdom, France, Russia, Japan, Germany and China on disarmament, nonproliferation, international security and export-control issues. Sood is a member of U.N. Secretary-General's expert groups on conventional arms and on verification, and has presented papers at numerous United Nations and other international conferences such as Wilton Park, Oxford Research Group, International Institute for Strategic Studies,

Pugwash, and Geneva Forum on a range of disarmament, nonproliferation, and security-related issues.

He joined the Ministry of External Affairs, Government of India, in 1976 and has served in Indian missions in Brussels, Belgium; Dakar, Senegal; Geneva; and Islamabad, Pakistan.

Sood has post-graduate degrees in physics, economics and defense studies.

Brigadier General Jeffrey A. Sorenson

Brigadier General Jeffrey A. Sorenson is the program executive officer for tactical missiles, and is a certified U.S. Army materiel acquisition manager with 14 years of acquisition experience.

Prior to his current assignment, he was the assistant deputy for systems management and horizontal technology integration for the assistant secretary of the Army (acquisition, logistics and technology).

Upon graduating from the United States Military Academy at West Point, N.Y., Sorenson was commissioned as a second lieutenant in field artillery serving in tactical units at III Corps Artillery and in Germany. Following his transfer into the Military Intelligence Corps, he served as the division artillery intelligence officer and completed several division staff intelligence and tactical signal intelligence operational assignments.

His acquisition assignments include: director, program control (Joint Tactical Fusion Program Office); course director for the Executive Program Managers Course (Defense Systems Management College); director, science and technology integration (Office of the Assistant Secretary of the Army for Research and Development); product manager for Ground-Based Common Sensor–Light (GBCS–L)/TEAMMATE/TRACKWOLF programs; project manager for Night Vision/Reconnaissance, Surveillance and Target Acquisition; director, acquisition directorate (Office of the Director of Information Systems for Command, Control, Communications, and Computers); senior military assistant for the under secretary of defense for acquisition, technology and logistics.

In addition to a bachelor's degree from West Point, Sorenson earned a master of business administration from Northwestern University, majoring in finance, accounting and decision sciences. He is a graduate of the program manager and executive program managers courses at the Defense System Management College, the Armed Forces Staff College and the Army War College. Sorenson is a registered certified public accountant in Illinois.

His awards include the Army's Project Manager of the Year for 1998, the Defense Distinguished Service Medal, the Legion of Merit with two oak leaf clusters, the Defense Meritorious Service Medal, the Army Meritorious Service Medal with two oak leaf clusters, the Parachutist Badge and the Ranger Tab.

Harry C. Stonecipher

Harry C. Stonecipher became president and chief executive officer of The Boeing Company in December 2003. As the largest manufacturer of satellites, commercial jetliners and military aircraft, Boeing employs more than 150,000 people and serves customers in 145 countries. It is also a global market leader in missile defense, human space flight and launch services; and is the largest exporter in the United States, with revenues of more than $54 billion in 2002. Stonecipher was elected vice chairman of Boeing in May 2001 and retired on June 1, 2002. He has served on its board of directors since 1997.

Stonecipher's career began at General Motors' Allison Division. In 1960, he joined General Electric's (GE) Evendale Aircraft Engine Product Operations, where GE produces large jet engines. He became vice president and general manager of the division's commercial and military transport operations in 1979, headed the division from 1984 to 1987, and served on the board of directors of GE Financial Services. During his career at GE, Stonecipher participated in the development, support, sale and introduction of a number of engines for civilian and military application. Most significantly, Stonecipher played a vital role in GE's providing propulsion for passenger and military aircraft.

In 1987, Stonecipher became corporate executive vice president of Sundstrand, a worldwide market leader in the design and manufacture of technology-based products for aerospace and industrial markets. Shortly after joining Sundstrand, Stonecipher was elected president and chief operating officer and a member of the company's board of directors. He became president and chief executive officer in 1989 and assumed the additional office of chairman in 1991. During his 7 1/2 years at Sundstrand, Stonecipher repaired the company's seriously damaged customer relationship with the Department of Defense, instituted self-directed work teams and developed outstanding relations with the union work force. The company's financial position greatly improved, and the quality-improvement processes implemented by his team helped the company's aerospace products become some of the most reliable systems in the world.

In September 1994, Stonecipher was elected president and chief executive officer of McDonnell Douglas. He is credited with enhancing the company's relationships with all McDonnell Douglas stakeholders. McDonnell Douglas' financial performance soared under Stonecipher, with the stock increasing from $18.48 just prior to his arrival to more than $70 just before the company merged with Boeing in August 1997. In late 1996, with aerospace-industry consolidation well under way, Stonecipher requested and received authorization from the McDonnell Douglas board to negotiate a merger with Boeing. After the merger in August 1997, Stonecipher was elected president and chief operating officer and a member of Boeing's board of directors.

Stonecipher's awards include the Wings Club Distinguished Achievement Award for 2001; America-Israel Chamber of Commerce and Industry tribute in

March 2002; the U.S. Army Association's John W. Dixon Award in February 2002;
Rear Admiral John J. Bergen Leadership Medal for Industry from the Navy League
in November 1996; and two Air Force Association awards in 1996. He received
an honorary doctorate of science from Washington University in St. Louis, Mo.,
and in March 1998, he was named a fellow in The Royal Aeronautical Society.
Stonecipher serves on the board of directors of The Boeing Company, PACCAR
Inc., the U.S.-China Business Council, and the board and executive committee of
the U.S.-Saudi Arabian Business Council.

Peter Verga

Peter Verga is the principal assistant and adviser to the assistant secretary
of defense for homeland defense on matters related to the overall supervision
of the homeland defense activities of the Department of Defense. In addition,
he is responsible for the day-to-day management of Department of Defense
participation in interagency activities concerning homeland security, as well as
relations with the Department of Homeland Security. Prior to his current assignment,
Verga served as the special assistant for homeland security and director of the
Department of Defense Homeland Security Task Force.

Verga is a retired Army officer with over 26 years of service in a variety of
operations and management positions, including combat service in Vietnam from
September 1969 to November 1971. He has served as deputy under secretary of
defense for policy integration, deputy under secretary of defense for policy support,
and deputy director for emergency planning in the Office of the Secretary of Defense,
where he was responsible for interagency matters regarding emergency preparedness
and wartime continuity of government policy. Prior to that, he served on the White
House staff as special assistant to the assistant to the president for management and
administration, advising on a variety of matters including issues associated with
continuity of the office of the presidency and continuity of government; as deputy
director of the office of emergency operations of the White House Military Office
with responsibility for development and implementation of classified, sensitive
emergency plans and programs in direct support of the president; and in the
operations directorate of the Joint Chiefs of Staff.

Verga has been awarded the Defense Distinguished Civilian Service Award and
the Defense Meritorious Civilian Service Award. His military service awards include
the Combat Infantryman's Badge, the Defense Superior Service Medal, the Legion
of Merit, four Bronze Stars, the Purple Heart, three Defense Meritorious Service
Medals, 21 Air Medals and the Presidential Service Badge.

Born in Winston-Salem, N.C., Verga holds a bachelor's degree in public
administration from the University of La Verne, La Verne, Calif., and a master's
degree in public administration from Troy State University, Troy, Ala. He is a graduate
of the U.S. Army Command and General Staff College.

Paul Wolfowitz, Ph.D.

On Feb. 5, 2001, President Bush announced his intention to nominate Paul Wolfowitz to be deputy secretary of defense. He was unanimously confirmed by the Senate on Feb. 28 and sworn in on March 2, 2001. This is Wolfowitz's third tour of duty in the Pentagon.

For the last seven years, he has served as dean and professor of international relations at the Paul H. Nitze School of Advanced International Studies of Johns Hopkins University. He led a successful campaign that raised more than $75 million and doubled the school's endowment.

From 1989 to 1993, Wolfowitz served as under secretary of defense for policy in charge of the 700-person defense policy team responsible for matters concerning strategy, plans and policy. He and his staff had major responsibilities for reshaping strategy and force posture at the end of the Cold War. Other key initiatives included development of the Regional Defense Strategy, the Base Force and two presidential nuclear initiatives that led to the elimination of tens of thousands of U.S. and Soviet nuclear weapons.

During the Reagan administration, Wolfowitz served three years as U.S. ambassador to Indonesia. Before that, he served more than three years as assistant secretary of state for East Asian and Pacific affairs, where he was in charge of U.S. relations with more than 20 countries. In addition to contributing to substantial improvements in U.S. relations with Japan and China, he played a central role in coordinating U.S. policy toward the Philippines.

His previous government service included two years as head of the State Department's policy planning staff (1981–1982), a Pentagon tour as deputy assistant secretary of defense for regional programs (1977–1980), where he helped create the force that later became the United States Central Command; and four years (1973–1977) in the Arms Control and Disarmament Agency, working on the Strategic Arms Limitation Talks and a number of nuclear nonproliferation issues. Among his many awards are the Presidential Citizen's Medal, the Department of Defense's Distinguished Public Service and Distinguished Civilian Service Medals, the Department of State's Distinguished Honor Award, and the Arms Control and Disarmament Agency's Distinguished Honor Award.

Wolfowitz has taught at Yale and Johns Hopkins University. In 1993, he was the George F. Kennan Professor of National Security Strategy at the National War College. He has written widely on national strategy and foreign policy subjects and was a member of the advisory boards of the journals, *Foreign Affairs* and *National Interest*.

He received a bachelor's degree in mathematics from Cornell University and holds a doctorate in political science from the University of Chicago.

GLOSSARY

9-11 Commission	Commission that studied Sept. 11, 2001, terrorist attacks
AH–64	U.S. Army Blackhawk helicopter
AOR	area of responsibility
ATO	air tasking order
BATF	Bureau of Alcohol, Tobacco and Firearms
BCTP	Battle Command Training Program
BFT	Blue Force Tracker
BJP	Bharatiya Janata Party (India)
C4ISR	command, control, communications, computers, information, surveillance, reconnaissance
Caribinieri	Italy's national police force
CBO	Congressional Budget Office
CBRNE	chemical, biological, radiological, nuclear and explosive
CD	Conference on Disarmament
CENTCOM	Central Command
CEO	chief executive officer
CFO	chief financial officer
CG	commanding general
CIA	Central Intelligence Agency
CINC	commander in chief
CINCCENT	commander in chief, Central Command
CINCPAC	commander in chief, Pacific Command
COBRA	chemical, biological, radiological attack
CONOPS	concept of operations
Crusader	now-canceled, Army 155mm self-propelled Howitzer
CSIS	Center for Strategic and International Studies
CT	counterterrorism
CTC	combat training center
CTBT	Comprehensive Test Ban Treaty
CUNY	City University of New York

CWC	Conventional Weapons Convention
DCI	director of Central Intelligence
DCM	deputy chief of mission
DEA	Drug Enforcement Agency
DHS	Department of Homeland Security
DI	directorate of intelligence
DIA	Defense Intelligence Agency
DO	directorate of operations
DoD	Department of Defense
EIJ	Egyptian Islamic Jihad
E.U.	European Union
EU-3	Great Britain, France and Germany
EXCOM	executive committee
FAO	foreign area officer
FBI	Federal Bureau of Investigation
FCS	Future Combat Systems
FMCT	fissile material cut-off treaty
FORSCOM	Forces Command
FSR	Foreign Service Reserve Officer
G8	Globalized Eight Nations
GDP	gross domestic product
Gamat al Islamaya	terrorist organizations with the goal of overthrowing the secular Egyptian regime
GS	Government Service
HHS	Health and Human Services
IAEA	International Atomic Energy Agencies
IC	intelligence community
ICBM	intercontinental ballistic missile
ICC	International Criminal Court
IFOR/SFOR	implementation force/stabilization force
I MEF	1st Marine Expeditionary Force
INS	Immigration and Naturalization Service
ISA	International Security Affairs
ISAF	International Security Assistance Force
ITAR	International Traffic in Arms Regulations
JIACG	Joint Interagency Coordination Group
JTF	joint task force
JTTF	Joint Terrorism Task Force
KSM	Khalid Sheikh Mohammed
MIA	missing in action
MiG 21	Soviet-built jet "Fishbed"
Mujahideen	Islamic jihadists
NATO	North Atlantic Treaty Organization

NCA	National Command Authority
NCO	noncommissioned officer
NGO	nongovernmental organization
NITS	National Institute of training for Standardization
NOAA	National Oceanic and Atmospheric Administration
NORTHCOM	U.S. Northern Command
Northern Alliance	Afghan ethnic coalition formed to defeat the Taliban
NPT	Nuclear Nonproliferation Treaty
NRBC	nuclear, radiological, biological, chemical
NSC	National Security Council
NSPD	National Security Presidential Directive
NYPD	New York City Police Department
NYSE	New York Stock Exchange
OAS	Organization of American States
OMB	Office of Management and Budget
OPM	Office of Personnel Management
OSCE	Organization for Security and Co-operation in Europe
OSD	Office of the Secretary of Defense
PACOM	Pacific Command
PCS	permanent change of station
PIFWC	persons indicted for war crimes operations
POM	preparation for overseas movement of units
POW	prisoner of war
PPBES	Planning, Programming, Budgeting, Executing, System
PRC	People's Republic of China
PSI	Proliferation Security Initiative
RNC	Republican National Convention
ROE	rules of engagement
ROK	Republic of Korea
RPG	rocket-propelled grenade
SAIC	Science Applications International Corporation
SES	Senior Executive Service
SETAF	Southern European Task Force
SFOR	stabilization force
SOCOM	Special Operations Command
Stryker	Army's armored personnel carrier
Su-7	Soviet-built ground-attack aircraft "Fitter-A"
TDY	temporary duty
USAID	U.S. Agency for International Development

USAREUR   U.S. Army Europe
USDI   Under Secretary of Defense for Intelligence
WMD   weapons of mass destruction
Yongbyon   North Korean weapons facility

CO-SPONSORS

THE ATLANTIC COUNCIL OF THE UNITED STATES

The Atlantic Council of the United States promotes constructive U.S. leadership and engagement in international affairs based on the central role of the Atlantic community in meeting the international challenges of the 21st century.

The council embodies a nonpartisan network of leaders who aim to bring ideas to power and to give power to ideas by:

- stimulating dialogue and discussion about crucial international issues with a view to enriching public debate and promoting consensus on appropriate responses in the administration, Congress, the corporate and nonprofit sectors, and the media in the United States and among leaders in Europe, Asia and the Americas; and
- conducting educational and exchange programs for successor generations of U.S. leaders so that they will come to value U.S. international engagement and have the knowledge and understanding necessary to develop effective policies.

Through its diverse networks, the council builds broad constituencies to support constructive U.S. international leadership and policies. Examples of important contributions by the council are:

- identifying major issues facing the future of the Atlantic Alliance and trans-Atlantic economic relations;
- examining issues of integration into European structures of the countries of central and eastern Europe, including Russia;
- building consensus on U.S. policy towards Russia, China, Japan, Korea and Taiwan;
- balancing growing energy needs and environmental protection in Asia; and
- drafting road maps for U.S. policy towards the Balkans, Cuba, Iran and Panama.

http://www.acus.org/

INTERNATIONAL INSTITUTE FOR STRATEGIC STUDIES

The International Institute for Strategic Studies is the world's leading authority on political-military conflict. Based in London, it is both a limited company in U.K. law and a registered charity. It has offices in the United States and in Singapore with charitable status in each jurisdiction.

The IISS was founded in 1958 in the United Kingdom by individuals interested in how to maintain civilized international relations in the nuclear age. Much of the institute's early work focused on nuclear deterrence and arms control and was hugely influential in setting the intellectual structures for managing the Cold War.

The IISS grew dramatically during the 1980s and 1990s, expanding both because of the nature of its work and its geographical scope. Its mandate became to look into problems of conflict, however caused, that might have an important military context. This gave fresh impetus to the IISS as it began to cover more comprehensively political and military issues on all continents. As this mandate developed, the IISS worked hard to provide the best information and analysis on strategic trends and to facilitate contacts between government leaders, business people and analysts that would lead to the development of better public policy in the fields of international relations and international security.

The IISS is the primary source of accurate, objective information on international strategic issues for politicians, diplomats, foreign affairs analysts, international business, economists, the military, defense commentators, journalists, academics and the public. It owes no allegiance to any government or to any political or other organization. Its conference activities are considered to be at the forefront of public policy development, especially given that its convening power is such that it can often bring together government officials and others in formats and circumstances that they could not easily manage for themselves.

The institute's staff and governing boards are international and its network of some 3,000 individual members and 500 corporate and institutional members is drawn from more than 100 countries.

http://www.iiss.org/

THE HENRY L. STIMSON CENTER

The Henry L. Stimson Center is a nonprofit, nonpartisan institution devoted to enhancing international peace and security through a unique combination of rigorous analysis and outreach.

The center is committed to making the world a better place through its work. The center's vision is of "a world in which instruments of security cooperation and peace overtake historic tendencies toward conflict and war." It pursues this vision through work that is intensely practical, nonpartisan and oriented toward real-world policy-makers.

Guided by its motto of "taking pragmatic steps toward the ideal objectives of international peace and security," the center pursues its mission in several ways:

- combining analysis with carefully designed outreach, dialogue, networks and partnerships to achieve greater impact;
- conducting analysis that is independent, creative, anticipatory and integrative;
- producing works of excellence and influence to lead their field;
- building a culture of collaboration that infuses its work with a unique team spirit, intellectual energy and honesty;
- providing each employee an opportunity to grow professionally and personally, and in the process, nurturing future leaders;
- viewing a nonpartisan, nonideological approach to issues as one of its greatest strengths; and
- conducting a constant, rigorous self-assessment of its work, both as an institution and as individuals.

http://www.stimson.org/

Combating Terrorism Center

Recognizing the immediate need for a first-rate undergraduate education in intelligence and counterterrorism studies, the United States Military Academy at West Point opened the Combating Terrorism Center in February 2003. The events of Sept. 11 highlighted the changing and dangerous nature of the international security environment. Given these events and the ensuing war on terrorism, it is imperative that current and future leaders of our country be armed with the tools to make sense of new terrorist threats, lead our nation, and succeed in a very complex and increasingly hostile world.

The CTC endeavors to develop an internationally recognized center for terrorism studies to understand better the foreign and domestic terrorist threats to security, educate future leaders who will have responsibilities to counter terrorism, and provide policy analysis and assistance to leaders dealing with current and future terrorist threats.

The CTC develops strategically integrated and balanced perspectives on national and international security issues. It combines academic, public policy and military expertise to create a dynamic, intellectual and practical research approach to terrorism, counterterrorism, weapons of mass destruction and homeland security issues. Each area of research is crucial for understanding the national security environment and provides the underpinnings necessary for critical policy analysis.

Since its inception, the CTC has been actively involved in supporting the global war on terrorism through education, outreach and policy analysis. The center has engaged in outreach opportunities to numerous U.S. government agencies, such as the Department of Defense, Department of Homeland Security, Central Intelligence Agency and Federal Bureau of Investigation, and state governments of Florida, Ohio, Kentucky, Connecticut and Rhode Island. The CTC has also conducted work with the foreign governments of Taiwan, Romania, the United Kingdom, Canada and Ireland; and hosted a conference for the Partnership for Peace's Defense Consortium. The CTC has coordinated multiple West Point department efforts to provide support to the Department of Homeland Security, New York Fire Department, New York-New Jersey Port Authority, J-5 Staff, Picatinny Arsenal and Defense Threat Reduction Agency.

http://www.dean.usma.edu/sosh/CTC/

CONTRIBUTORS

STRATEGIC STUDIES INSTITUTE

The Strategic Studies Institute at Carlisle Barracks, Penn., is the U.S. Army's premier institute for global and national strategic security research and analysis. It is the Army's think tank for the analysis of national security policy and military strategy.

Its primary function is to provide direct analysis for Army and Department of Defense leadership and serve as a bridge to the wider strategic community. SSI is also the focal point for research at the Army War College, providing research and expertise for curriculum development and assisting other members of the faculty in research projects.

SSI is a unique organization that links the Army to the U.S. and international strategic communities. It is the only research organization in the United States that focuses on the strategic role of land power.

SSI collects the wisdom of the wider strategic community for Army senior leaders and explains the role of the Army and land power to both the strategic community and national decision makers. SSI does this through rigorous, independent analysis by its professional staff. Analysis of these conference presentations is but one example of the depth and breath of study done at the Strategic Studies Institute.

AMERICAN UNIVERSITY'S WASHINGTON SEMESTER PROGRAM

American University's Washington Semester Program was established in 1947. The aim of the program is to provide students with first-hand exposure to the policy process and to help them plan and acquire skills for professional careers in public service. The program has three components: an eight-credit seminar that incorporates meetings with public officials and other practitioners, an internship and a research project. On average, nearly 500 third- and fourth-year undergraduates from universities around the United States and abroad participate in this program. They live, dine and study together on the AU Tenley Circle campus, Washington, D.C. The 30 students who contributed to the Eisenhower National Security Series Conference are members of the U.S. Foreign Policy Unit for the fall 2004 Washington Semester Program.

PARTICIPANTS

Leeza Arkhangelskaya
Washington College

Benjamin Brubaker
Xavier University, Ohio

Michael Buxton
Saint Michael's College

Jörg Drechsler
Nuremberg, Germany

Monika Eder
Catholic University of
Eichstaett, Germany

Ross Fishbein
Brandeis University

Stephanie Gilbert
University of Southern
California

Mary Gillespie
University of Vermont

Anna Hansen
Copenhagen Business School,
Denmark

Patricia Heatherington
University of Redlands

Courtney Jonas
Saint Lawrence University

Daniel Kekalainen
Karlstads University, Sweden

Brian Kelly
Amherst College

Jeffrey Marsh
Miami University, Ohio

Ashley Marro
University of Portland

Matthew McGinn
Boston College

Emma Mcmahon
Lesley University

Rachel Navarre
Knox College

Anna Nazarenko
Lake Forest College

Jordan Parkhurst
Occidental College

Joshua Reil
McGill University

Emily Sahm
Vassar College

Laura Sartori
Bowdoin College

Ajata Shah
Tufts University

Aliyah Shahid
Tufts University

Elizabeth Steiner
College of Wooster

David Stern
University of Texas,
Austin

Lene Stevnhoved
Aalborg University,
Denmark

Asheley Tetteh
Beloit College

Christopher Tringale
Boston College

www.ingramcontent.com/pod-product-compliance
Lightning Source LLC
Chambersburg PA
CBHW051954280526
45793CB00005B/720